FRIDAYS OF RAGE

FRIDAYS OF RAGE

Al Jazeera, the Arab Spring,
and Political Islam

Sam Cherribi

OXFORD
UNIVERSITY PRESS

Oxford University Press is a department of the University of Oxford. It furthers the University's objective of excellence in research, scholarship, and education by publishing worldwide. Oxford is a registered trade mark of Oxford University Press in the UK and certain other countries.

Published in the United States of America by Oxford University Press
198 Madison Avenue, New York, NY 10016, United States of America.

Library of Congress Cataloging-in-Publication Data
Names: Cherribi, Sam, 1959– author.
Title: Fridays of rage : Al Jazeera, the Arab Spring, and political Islam /
Sam Cherribi.
Description: New York, NY : Oxford University Press, 2017. | Includes
bibliographical references and index.
Identifiers: LCCN 2016024417 (print) | LCCN 2016040498 (ebook) |
ISBN 9780199337385 (hardcover : alk. paper) | ISBN 9780199337408 (Updf) |
ISBN 9780199337415 (Epub)
Subjects: LCSH: Al Jazeera (Television network) | Arab Spring, 2010– | Islam
and politics. | Television broadcasting of news—Arab countries. | Mass
media—Political aspects—Arab countries. | Mass media—Religious
aspects—Islam.
Classification: LCC PN1992.92.A39 C48 2017 (print) | LCC PN1992.92.A39
(ebook) | DDC 384.5506/55363—dc23
LC record available at https://lccn.loc.gov/2016024417

9 8 7 6 5 4 3 2

Printed by Sheridan Books, Inc., United States of America

À la mémoire de Pierre Bourdieu et Mohammed Arkoun, qui nous ont appris à nous libérer de toutes formes de domination visible et invisible (dans les médias, en religion et en société).

In memory of Pierre Bourdieu and Mohammed Arkoun, who taught us how to liberate ourselves from all forms of visible and invisible domination in society.

CONTENTS

List of Figures   ix

Preface: Arab Revolutions on Demand   xi

Acknowledgments   xix

PART I *Al Jazeera Unites*

1. Al Jazeera by the Numbers   3

2. The Symbolic World of Al Jazeera   43

3. A Tinderbox for the Revolution: Subjectivity and Resistance   75

4. Gaza: A Perennial Arab Spring   104

5. Secret Mission: Shining a Spotlight on Tahrir Square   125

PART II *Al Jazeera: Global Fissures and Ruptures to Come*

6. Exile on Paradise Square   157

7. Bullets of Truth and Media Martyrdom   191

8. Islam Near and Far   211

9. The Emancipation of Political Islam?   243

   Postscript: Out of Order—Arab Media and Democracy in Distress   268

Notes   279

References   285

Index   295

LIST OF FIGURES

1   Secular versus Religious Friday Protest Slogans,
    2011–2013   26
2   Number of Religious Protests in Egypt and Syria,
    2011–2013   26
3   Google Hits of Al–Jazeera Contributors, January 2011   27
4   Veil (Women) and Headgear (Men) by Anchor on
    Al Jazeera   28
5   *Talk of the Revolution* Episodes Focusing on Arab
    Spring, 2011 and 2012   29
6   Revolution as a Topic per Country on Al–Jazeera,
    1997–2012   29
7   Number of Arab Spring Topics on Four Popular
    Shows, 2010–2012   30
8   Number of Episodes Dealing with Political Islam
    by Show, 2011–2012   30
9   Number of Episodes Dealing with Political Conflict
    by Show, 2011–2012   31
10 Number of *Talk of the Revolution* Episodes Focusing
    on Arab Spring, 2011–2012   31
11 Episodes on Islam in the West versus Islamic Banking,
    2006–2012   32
12 Focus of *Sharia and Life* Shows on Islamic Banking
    versus Democracy, 1998–2010   33
13 *Sharia and Life* per Topic, 1998–2012   33
14 *Opposite Direction* Topics Compared, 1997–2013   34
15 *Opposite Direction* Topics Compared, 1998–2012   34
16 Weight of the Mashreq as a Topic on Al Jazeera
    Shows, 1999–2007   35

17   Number of Shows about Palestine on Al Jazeera,
     1997–2013   35
18   Percentage of Gaza on Popular Shows, 2006–2013   36
19   Gulf Cities under the Radar of Political News,
     1997–2013   38
     Map of *Sharia and Life* Global Network   51

PREFACE: ARAB REVOLUTIONS ON DEMAND

The first olive tree on the way south marks the beginning of the Mediterranean
region and the first palm grove the end.

—Fernand Braudel (1995)

In short, in seeking to improve everything, they ended up creating turmoil everywhere.

—Alexis de Tocqueville, *The Ancient Regime and the French Revolution*

On Friday, all honorable Egyptians must come out to give me a mandate to end terrorism
and violence.

—General Abdul-Fattah el-Sisi (Al Jazeera, July 24, 2013)

You Say You Want a Revolution?

"*Athawra! Athawra!*" (Revolution! Revolution!), a professor shouted at Bab
L'had, a bustling Rabat square where students and visitors from neighboring cities arrive in Morocco's capital by bus and taxi. The professor hoped to stir public outrage that might lead to a spontaneous revolution. This was in 1982, my
last year as a student at Rabat's University Mohamed V. It was a period of mass
student protests and workers' strikes. The memory of the incendiary professor
rushed back to me when I arrived in Rabat from Atlanta, just days after the ousting of the Tunisian president Ben Ali, to find Morocco's streets filled with tension.
Thirty years had passed since the professor's demonstration, which ended, by my
recollection, with his arrest. Nobody understood his actions. Was he motivated
by despair or tremendous belief in the power of crowds to ignite an uprising?
I firmly believe he was lucid; driven by a desire to put lie to commonly accepted
notions about the inability of Arab peoples to shape their own destinies, without
the heavy-handed guidance of either domestic or imported autocrats. The act of
speaking out was, in itself, a powerful statement.

This was an era when anybody who spoke of revolution wound up in jail, was
suddenly unemployed, or simply disappeared. The 1980s were the peak of what was

termed in Morocco *les années de plomb* (years of lead). This represented the brutality of the minister of interior, Ahmed Basri. The city of Kenitra, where the professor who shouted "*Athawra!*" came from, was famous for its dissidents and multiple unsuccessful coup d'états. Originating from a former US military base, the city had one of the largest and harshest prisons in Africa, built by the French colonial rulers.

The late 1970s and the 1980s were an era of two converging processes, political repression and a piecemeal Arabization that remains incomplete today. The latter process included the dismantling of the institution of French liberal education. Throughout public life, French language was replaced with Arabic. These two processes may have created the conditions for the emergence of political Islam. The repressive tactics and crackdown on leftist activists slowed down secular progress and removed any viable alternative to counter political Islam as an emerging antiestablishment configuration. In eviscerating liberal institutions it saw as a threat, the Moroccan government left in its place a scorched earth where the seeds of political Islam would grow.

The word *athawra,* "revolution," had been appropriated previously by the Arab regimes that followed postwar independence. There was *thawra-t-al uruba* (revolution of pan-Arabism) in Egypt; *thawra-al-khadra* (green revolution) in Libya; *a-thwra-t-al malik wa-sha'ab* (revolution of king and people) in Morocco; and *athawra hata nasr* (revolution until victory) in Palestine.[1] The word "revolution," in the Arab world, has had a number of meanings over the years. In order to analyze the revolutionary landscape in the Arab world of the early 2010s—its genesis and its metaphorical, hidden, and overt expressions—we should connect meanings to events as framed by the media and manipulated by political and social actors. There is no one-size-fits-all explanation for the failure of democracy to bear fruit in the Arab world, since not all Arab countries are the same. However, if democratic change continues to founder following the eruption of the Arab Spring, the discontentment and disenchantment will settle into an unstable, potentially explosive situation.

Since my departure from Morocco, where I was a student in the 1980s, the country has changed a lot. I left to study in Europe and eventually settled in the Netherlands. In 1994, I became a member of Dutch Parliament, where I served two consecutive terms, representing the Netherlands at the Council of Europe, the Assembly of the Western European Union, and the North-South Centre at Lisbon. In 2003, I moved with my family to the United States to teach political sociology at Emory University in Atlanta, the city of the dream and the dreamer. I now work closely with the Martin Luther King Center and the Jimmy Carter Center. These institutions serve as a source of inspiration and motivation for my passion for the civil rights movement and democratic movements in developing nations. Despite my travels, I have never entirely left the Arab world.

I teach courses on political Islam, media and social movements, and the Arab diaspora. I host frequent guests from Algeria, Saudi Arabia, UAE, Qatar, Jordan, Israel, Egypt, Tunisia, Sudan, and Mauritania via Skype. In addition to returning frequently to Morocco, I visit countries across the Maghreb, Mashreq, and Khaleej. In 2007, I conducted the World Values Survey with Juan Díez Nicolàs of Universidad Complutense de Madrid.?

During my most recent stay in Morocco, two phenomena struck me dramatically. First was the visible Islamization, in terms of clothing and appearance (veils, headscarves, bearded men) and the ubiquitous religious CD/DVD vendors standing behind small aluminum carts, equipped with boom boxes blasting the same Saudi recitation of the Quran. The second striking change in the landscape was the overwhelming number of West African immigrants. Just as northern Mexico serves as the major terminal for traffic between Latin America and the United States, Morocco has become a hub for transferring goods and people between Africa and Europe, with a similarly attendant parallel economy, dominated by narco-culture, *passeurs* (commonly called "coyotes" in North America), and *harraga* (undocumented migrants who wish to enter Europe). The two enclaves of Spanish sovereignty on the Moroccan mainland, Ceuta and Melilla, are physically fenced off in order to deter entry by undocumented immigrants. These two phenomena are framed systematically in European and Arabic media outlets in a way that stresses the Islamic and African identities of Morocco. But the politics and society of Morocco stem from multiple histories and identities: Berber (Amzigh), Arab, Islamic, Jewish, African, Mediterranean, and European.

This book is, of course, not an examination of Moroccan culture; it is a journey through the revolutionary landscapes of the Arab world by means of a deconstruction and decoding of Al Jazeera Arabic's coverage of pivotal regional events. During the revolutions of the Arab Spring, Al Jazeera Arabic provided an instrumental link between the emerging social media activism and multinational satellite television broadcasts. Al Jazeera framed and promoted the term "revolution" as synonymous with Islamic virtue during the early phases of the Arab Spring. Its cameras continued to roll as revolutions turned to democratic disenchantment, malaise, and willing acceptance of any kind of authority.

Looking back, one is left to wonder how things might be different today if Al Jazeera Arabic had been around to cover the Moroccan professor's shouts of "*Athawra! Athawra!*" back in the early 1980s. Would the network's coverage of such demonstrations have applied the sort of pressure felt most recently by regimes in Tunisia and Egypt? Al Jazeera has been successfully exerting such pressure since its inception in 1996. What would the Arab world look like now? Would the world have witnessed an earlier Arab Spring? The answer is probably no, since Al Jazeera Arabic itself was a revolution in the Arab media landscape.

However, Al Jazeera might have engendered the sorts of feelings of empowerment and self-worth now felt by Arab publics in relation to their rulers. The tangible effect of Al Jazeera's coverage over the past two decades has been a sense of unity among Arab publics and an altered media landscape within the Arab world where static media configurations and silent audiences have given way to dynamic and vocal publics. There has been an undeniable emergence of spin-offs of Al Jazeera. An explosion of media initiatives has crowded the Arab space, with hundreds of new TV outlets attempting to emulate Al Jazeera. Abubakr Jamai, an engaged Moroccan journalist struggling for freedom of the press, argues that the novelty of Al Jazeera is its ability to make public debate a normal feature of Arab societies.[2] No single Arab news outlet can count on the loyalty of Arab publics or viewers without producing credible news, rejecting taboos, and being pluralist (Lamloum 2004, 105). However, according to Ahmed Ben Chemsi, a journalist and human rights activist, Al Jazeera did little to change Morocco during the Arab Spring, with its weak coverage of the February 20 movement, in spite of the fact that its coverage before then had outraged Moroccan authorities.[3]

And the rest of the Arab countries? Could an act of self-immolation à la Bouazizi, the ambulant fruit vendor in Tunisia who ignited the fire of the Arab Spring, have happened during those years? In order to answer this question, we have to consider two points. Al Jazeera contributed to a revolution of the behaviors of Arab publics and an erosion of fatalism in Arab polity. This process did not happen overnight, nor did it occur in a vacuum. It took years alongside contributing trends like globalization, individualization, Islamization, the "youth bulge," and the relative democratization processes of the late 1990s. Let's paint a triptych using the Maghreb, Mashreq, and Khaleej, the three main geographic regions of the Arab world, in order to compare and contrast the different policies toward society that have evolved since the tumultuous 1980s. During those years two important phenomena were observable: authoritarianism and the rise of political Islam. Many riots and acts of resistance took place in and across many countries, but none led to a popular uprising on the scale of the Jasmine Revolution in Tunisia or the revolution in Egypt. Political Islam became a major force of contestation. It emerged on Egyptian university campuses. From Egypt it spread to Tunisia and Algeria and Morocco.

It was a confusing period in the Arab world. In the Maghreb, Qaddafi's ongoing Green Book Revolution was promulgated throughout the Arab world by his propaganda machine. Algeria and Morocco waged radio wars of insults against each other over the western Sahara conflict. Meanwhile, in the Mashreq, Saddam Hussein's newspapers and books were given away for free to students at Iraqi embassies. Lebanon's civil war raged, drawing Syria into the conflict. Jordan cracked down on Palestinian groups. Egypt sunk into decline and isolation. Sudan was in the midst of its own complicated Islamic experience. In the Khaleej, the 1973 oil crisis spurred Gulf countries to amplify their funding of Arab extraparliamentary opposition in European capitals, mainly Paris and London. Islamist opposition efforts with the poor and attempts to influence the networks of the mosques built by North African guest workers in Europe were also beneficiaries of this funding. The cassettes of the Egyptian blind preacher, Mohamed Kichk, which Gilles Kepel immortalized in his seminal book *The Prophet and the Pharaoh*, were sold everywhere. The human rights records of Arab countries became more deplorable than ever.

The people of the Arab world were in need of freedom. Poverty, birth rates, and illiteracy were high everywhere, with the exception of the oil-rich countries. Youth in the 1980s were torn between political Islam and a vanishing Marxist-Leninist alternative. The only other choice for the youth of North Africa (Maghreb) was migration to Europe, and that for the youth of the Middle East (Mashreq) was migration to the wealthy Gulf countries (Khaleej). Migration was a path to survival. Emigration to Europe meant political freedom, while emigration to the Gulf meant the "unfreedom" and strict norms of Salafi Islam.

The long-term effects of emigration were devastating. By the 2010s, émigrés returning home after long sojourns found their home countries unrecognizable, as the secular institutions that had characterized their youths had been largely Islamized. These changes were brilliantly captured by Amin Maalouf in *Origines*, a novel about an émigré, Adam, who returns to Lebanon after the civil war and no longer recognizes what once was the "Switzerland of the Middle East." Adam is disillusioned by the disappearance of Levantine culture. He feels that the Lebanese people who have stayed in the country have changed, having abandoned their cosmopolitan ideals in favor of narrow and exclusive identities that perpetuate hatred and violence between communities. Living under a brutal Syrian occupation had forced the Lebanese people into a "rotten compromise" (Maalouf 2012). Similar accounts of Algeria, Iraq, Syria, and the Sudan were written in this period. The shift from secularization to Islamization stupefied one Egyptian, who was shocked to see his country move from the vanguard of Arab modernity, which ranged from movies to music, to the rulership of Morsi and the veil.

The Arab world's university campuses have seen a gradual process of Islamization, which began around the mid-1980s and reached a peak in the 2000s. In January 2011, during Tunisia's Jasmine Revolution, I was invited by Bayt al-Hikma (House of Wisdom) as a keynote speaker for a memorial in Rabat on the anniversary of the death of the Algerian thinker Mohammed Arkoun. I had the chance to visit a number of university campuses during my stay. Islamist student organizations were the dominant social force. An acquaintance at the well-known engineers' institute of Casablanca complained to me that many of his colleagues are *khwanjiyya* (bearded Islamists).

However, it is a sociological reality that Islam is becoming more pronounced as an identity than at any time in the recent past. The Tunisian psychoanalyst Fethi Benslama remembers that when he was young in Tunisia, there was a kind of silent religiosity without pronounced expressions in the public space (France Culture, June 15, 2012). At that time, one's being Muslim spoke for itself and there was no need to make overt displays of one's Islamic identity. The gradual Islamization that has taken place over the past decades helped plant the seeds that would eventually bloom into an Islamist victory during the first democratic elections following the Arab Spring.

The term "Arab Spring," coined first by the European media and thereafter adopted by Al Jazeera, is a reference to the European revolutions of 1848 and 1968. The Arab Spring was a turning point in the valuation of the previously suppressed voices of the "Arab street" and "common people." The Arab Spring marked a significant change in the dialogue between Arab governments and their peoples. The Arab street became, overnight, a potential ally and source of legitimacy for anyone hoping to gain or maintain power. Arab leaders sought to gain and legitimize power through a cycle of popular mobilization and countermobilization, revolution on demand. For example, after deposing President Morsi of Egypt, General Abdul-Fattah el-Sisi called for mass protests throughout the country in order to obtain a public mandate to "squash terrorism." The Muslim Brotherhood, in turn, called for a million-person-march and organized sit-ins to break up the "military coup." The Al Jazeera superstar preacher, Yusuf al-Qaradawi, used his pulpit on Al Jazeera to call for protests against Arab regimes in Egypt and Syria. The Moroccan king, Mohammed VI, mobilized the masses to support his referendum. Whether working in a top-down or bottom-up direction, the Arab street became the path to change. Social movements and counter-movements in the Arab world—such as April 6, Tamarod, Tajarud, and Third Square in Egypt; Egleb (meaning change) in Tunisia; the February 20 movement and March 9 in Morocco—are examples of mass mobilization.

This emergence of popular movements at the center of political discourse would have been impossible without the presence of Al Jazeera. The international satellite TV network served as a unifying force for the disparate elements of the unprecedented "youth bulge," societal Islamization, and the rise of social media in the Arab world that, once combined, would erupt in the harmonious cries for revolution now called the Arab Spring. By bringing these pieces together, Al Jazeera helped to create a mental predisposition toward revolution in Arab countries. As democratizing movements emerged, including those aligned with political Islam, the network amplified their voices. Al Jazeera pundits, like the Global Mufti, al-Qaradawi, legitimized popular challenges to the status quo with his impromptu call for the destabilization of Arab regimes.

Prickly Pears and *Molinos de Viento*

The dramatic outcomes of the Arab Spring in Libya, Egypt, and Syria have stoked doubts about the ability of Arab countries to adopt democracy, especially among those who hoped the revolutions signaled a move toward Western democracy in the Middle East. For disappointed observers in the West, it is appropriate to note that the challenges faced by Arab peoples are ones that have not been faced in the United States and most of Europe for generations. In the United States and Europe, the political landscape has been lush with democracy for so long that few residents can remember what it is to hunger for the opportunity to have even the slightest influence on their leadership. But, as recent attempts by the West to export popular rule have shown, the seeds of democracy come in many varieties, none of which will flourish uniformly in all soils and climates. We should no more expect a carbon copy of the Netherlands' parliamentary system to produce effective rule in Egypt than we would expect an olive crop to flourish in Amsterdam.

In Morocco, a complete lack of progress is referred to as *chih wa-rih* (a dry plant in the wind). For any democratic movement to succeed in the Arab world, it must be suited to the unique and challenging political climate of the region. Throughout the Arab Mediterranean, sturdy, prickly *hendi* bushes, also called the figs of Barbary or prickly pears, flourish in areas where most plants would whither.[4] They survive arid weather and the pounding Middle Eastern sun. They are nearly as resistant to harvest as they are to the elements. Picking the fruit on a windy day can result in prickles piercing the skin or even the eyes. It takes a special bamboo stick to harvest the fruit, piece by piece. Then the prickles have to be washed from the skin of the fruit before they can be handled . Even then, ingesting the hard seeds can lead to constipation.

The Arab revolutions, which seemed at first to nourish political and social progress, contained, like figs of Barbary, hardened, stubborn elements that have obstructed the mechanisms for digesting democratic ideas. Remnants of old regimes incite counterrevolutions, while forces of political Islam, having won power, obstruct the mechanisms of continued democracy. These are the hard seeds preventing Arab societies from absorbing the nourishing aspects of their revolutions and discarding the waste of political discord and remnant glut of the previous establishment.

Another Moroccan phrase, *sir t'nabag*, is used as a sort of subtle curse. Loosely translated, it refers to a dried fruit that is all pit, masked beneath a sweet skin, incapable of satisfying hunger.

It is understandable why the remnants of the old regimes would be resistant to being removed from their positions of power. But the Islamist leaders poised to take their places seemed equally slow in adapting to their new role. The Muslim

Brothers, despite decades of political organization, were loath to develop the sort of infrastructure that might form the foundations of a self-perpetuating system of governance in Egypt. Instead, the Morsi government administered acts of government, like the short-lived expansion of freedoms and a new constitution, in the same way it might have dispensed figs or dates at the end of Friday prayers. They were small acts of charity, expected to engender devotion. Like a preacher delivering a Friday congregational sermon, the Morsi government seemed content to preach to those Egyptians who supported it, with seemingly little concern for those who did not buy into the new Islamist rule.

The return of military rule to Egypt, the continuing bloody war in Syria, and the outflow of refugees fleeing the counterrevolution seem to sadly confirm the Arab proverb "One cannot exchange one friend for a better one." The saying itself betrays a kind of fatalism that is common in Arab societies. Yet people across the Arab world have stood up again and again in the past five years to demand a change in the status quo. It remains to be seen how these struggles will ultimately play out. But it is clear that voices from the streets and squares of the Maghreb, Mashreq, and Khaleej have become far more difficult to silence than that of the professor I saw in Bab L'had all those years ago. One reason for that is the tremendous reach and popularity of Al Jazeera, which served as a mirror to an audience that saw in its reflection a powerful and determined force. Given its power to shape the self-image of an entire region, it is appropriate that we closely examine the motivations, values, and underlying assumptions that go into constructing the portrayal of the Arab world Al Jazeera presents to its largely Arab audience. That is precisely what I have done in this book. My overall intention is to warn against revolutions that are carried out in the absence of shared political and intellectual agendas, and are propagated without charismatic and popular figures, not as Don Quixote did with the windmills.

ACKNOWLEDGMENTS

I dedicate this book to the memory of Pierre Bourdieu and Mohammed Arkoun for their reflexive and liberating approaches to research methodology and their continuous epistemological scrutiny in the pursuit of a better understanding of the changing nature of societies affected by Islam as a social, cultural, and religious phenomenon. Their generosity surpassed all of my expectations as a student and as a friend. Arkoun and Bourdieu were unable to witness the full unfolding of the Arab Spring and the eruption of youth revolutions. However, Bourdieu wrote about youth extensively, once noting that "youth is just a word." Arkoun saw the future of the Arab and Muslim world, revolutionizing the repetitive tradition of reciting the Quran and the Hadith without reflexive knowledge and breaking from the circular and dogmatic production of knowledge in order to contribute to the present and future of human civilization. They both loved Algeria, the country where great intellectuals such as Jacques Derrida, Albert Camus, Kateb Yassine, Mouloud Memri, Frantz Fanon, Leila Sabbar, Asia Djebar, and Hélène Cixous helped to empower and advance the cause of global emancipation.

I want to thank my very dear friend, the poet Khedija Gadhoum (University of Georgia), for her support and continuous feedback on my research on the Tunisian revolution. I want also to thank her family for their generous hospitality in Tunis, putting me in contact with people like Basma and Nabil Kanzari, Adil Hajji of Dar al-kitab, and bloggers such as Lina Mheni. I want to thank my friend and mentor Mohammed Boudoudou (University of Mohammed V) for providing relevant information and insights from the Maghreb and for discussing key issues related to the Arab world with me. I thank Juan Díez, with whom I conducted the 2007 World Values Survey in Morocco, and Ron Engelhard and Pippa Norris, who invited me to present the results in 2008 at the Swedish Cultural Center in Alexandria and at Bahshishir University in Istanbul. I benefited greatly from my discussions with Fares Braizat of Jordan. I would like to thank Mrs. Touria Yacoubi-Arkoun, the widow of Mohammed Arkoun, who died at the height of the Egyptian revolution in January 2011, as well as the human rights activist, Morocco MP, and president *bayt al hikma*, Khadija Rouissi. Yacoubi-Arkoun and Rouissi honored me with an invitation to speak in Rabat at the commemoration of the first anniversary of Mohammed Arkoun's death. The occasion gave me the opportunity to serve on the same panel with my former professor, the great sociologist Rahma Bourkia, along with Mohamed Tozy, to whom I am also grateful.

My colleague and friend, Roberto Franzosi, ignited my curiosity with his excellent ideas and enthusiasm, methodological insights, and innovative technical advice. His book, *From Words to Numbers*, was extremely helpful and inspiring. The frequent conversations with my friends Tyrone Forman, Abdul Janmohamed, Michel Laguerre, Rachid Benzine, Stephan Sanders, Claude Heurtaux, Mohamed Sekkat, and Awatif and Zine El Abidine were a great source of inspiration and intellectual exchange. I want to extend my warmest thanks to James Cook and the Oxford University Press reviewers for their feedback on early drafts of this work. I appreciate their enthusiasm, insight, and constructive criticism.

I am indebted to Jack Murray for his phenomenal skill and tireless help in solving all my laptop-related problems, as there have been many over the past ten years. I want to thank Jessica Perlove, Lori Jahnke, Leonie Duyvis, Rob O'Reilly, and Michael C. Page of the Woodruff Library and the Center for Digital Scholarship at Emory University, who helped with the process of data collection and data visualization. Page redrew the network map of Islamic scholars connected by satellite from different studios around the world to Yusuf al-Qaradawi. I would like to give O'Reilly a special thank you for assisting in the revision of figures. I want to extend my warmest thanks to Ouail Mahir, who was instrumental in the data analytics, Nick Nasr for making revisions to the graphs, Stephanie Ramage, Rebecca Liebskind, Rebecca Rozen, Ashley Easton, and Nico Fournier, who, along with Gabrielle Corrigan and Kevin Kinder. were involved in the early process of editing many of the transcripts of Al Jazeera shows. The very talented Chuck Stanley was superb in scrutinizing every comma, clause, note, and citation. He brought a meticulous approach to the task of editing this manuscript.

I want to thank Gadi Wolfsfeld, who commented many times on my Al Jazeera papers at multiple American Political Science Association meetings. I am indebted to Holli Semetko, Doris Graber, Robert Entman, Paolo Mancini, Steve Livingston, Thomas Patterson, Gianpietro Mazzoleni, and Lance Bennett for their inspiring contributions to the field of media framing theory. Thanks to John Esposito, Johan Goudsblom, Aldelkader, Ben Ali, Eve Livet, Jonathan Gitlen, Chef Rafih BenJelloun, and Samir Mahir. My students, Kadiata Mamadou Sy, Jordan Stein, Thanh Thuy Phan, and Melissa Brovarly, greatly aided my research for this book. Special thanks to Fethi Benslama (*Soudain la Révolution!*), and

Mohammed Ben Madani (*Maghreb Review*) for their great contribution in enriching the intellectual and political debate in the Arab world. I'm indebted to a number of journalists, intellectuals, and bloggers who participated in and contributed to my classroom discussions on the Arab Spring via Skype: Sara Khorshid in Egypt; Aboubakr Jamai, Ahmed Benchemsi, Nadir Bouhmouch, Omar Alaoui, and Omar Radi in Morroco; Lina Benmeni in Tunisia; and James Dorsey in Turkey and Asia. I would like to extend my appreciation to Debra and Nic Vidali for including me in their project, Youth and Democracy.

The support of Emory University's provost, Claire Sterk, has been invaluable to me over the course of this project. I want to thank Deans Robert Paul and Michael Elliott for ensuring the conditions necessary to write this book. I also want to thank Lynette Lee at the office of the Dean of Arts and Sciences; the chair of MESAS, Vincent J. Cornell; and the chair of the Economics Department, Hashem Dezhbakhsh. Thanks to Esfandiar Maasoumi, Gordon and Wendy Newby, Devin Stewart, Beny Harry, Roxani Margariti, Scott Kugle, Ruby Lal, Juana McGhee, Tarje Lacy, and the Moroccan poet Allal Al Hajam. R'kia Cornell's excellent dissertation on Rabaa al-Adawiyya was also extremely helpful to me. Thanks to my colleagues at Emory University and the Carter Center, John Boli, Robert Agnew, Rick Rubinson, Peter Little, Abdullahi Anaim, Houda Abadi, and Balian Hrair. I also want to thank my friends Fouad Laroui, Gayatri Spivak, Kay Lawson, Klaus Schoenbach, John Hope Bryant, Iman Partoredjo, Wafa Chafic, Rachid and Zoubida Lyazidi, and Ambassador Andrew Young for their incredible hospitality.

I want to thank my current and former students, including Sam Cammer, who wrote his honors thesis on the role of Twitter in the Egyptian revolution, along with Lara Townzen, who wrote a paper using her original collected data investigating "the effects of social media usage, regional activity, and regime response on subsequent protest activity." Many other papers addressing this topic were written over many semesters during which I taught upper-level classes on the Arab Spring. We invited cyber activists to speak with us via Skype, invited filmmakers from the Arab world like Sonia Chamkhi to speak to the class, and also participated in the dialogue series on the Arab world organized by CNN and Emory University. My students also participated in a series of talks given by the Washington, DC, Al Jazeera bureau chief, Abederrahim Foukara, who spoke extensively about the role of social media in Al Jazeera's reporting, which created a wider positive spin-off for more social protests. I am thankful for everybody who made these projects and events possible.

I want to thank the cartoonists Jean Plantu of *Le Monde*, Algerian Ali Dilem, Israeli Michel Kichka, Palestinian Baha Boukhari, Turkey's Piyale Madra, and the *Atlanta Journal-Constitution*'s Mike Luckovich, who spent time at Emory University during "Cartooning for Peace" (2007 and 2012).

During the Algerian civil war Pierre Bourdieu, Abram de Swaan, Jacques Derrida, Salman Rushdie, and Adriaan van Dis contributed to the Villes Refuges and the University of Amsterdam Exile Fund created by Abram de Swaan and hosted in Amsterdam, where I was on the board, to help the many Algerian journalists, writers, and social scientists who were targets of extreme violence in Algeria. I had the honor of having the late Khaled Ouadah (in early 1990) for a year as a scholar in residence at the University of Amsterdam, invited by Abram de Swaan after a recommendation by Pierre Bourdieu. Ouadah, a psychoanalyst, introduced me to the many Algerians living in France who had experienced the difficulties of life under violent radical political Islam. Also, the late Fatema Mernissi and the late Abdelwahab Medeb, who hosted and produced the show "Cultures d'Islam" on France Culture, was very helpful.

I want to thank my sister Leila Cherribi (University of Amsterdam), who was crucial in helping me understand the interplay between news coverage and revolution in Egypt. Lastly, I want to thank my friends and family for their unconditional love and support, especially Marijke Jansen for helping me with Excel sheets, infinite transcriptions, and making the painting for the cover page based on a picture I took in Tunis. Thank you, Miriam, Sophia, Tya Kyara, Jasmine, Yasin, Omar, Mehdi, Driss, Fatiha, Rania, Abdellatif, Adil, and my dad, Simohamed.

FRIDAYS OF RAGE

AL JAZEERA UNITES

1 AL JAZEERA BY THE NUMBERS

In January 2011, the world watched as Tunisia's despotic regime was shockingly and decisively overthrown. The global audience held its breath as the so-called Arab Spring spread to Egypt, Libya, Yemen, Syria, and Bahrain, toppling decades-old governments in a matter of weeks. Rather than ushering in a wave of democracy, as many in the West believed would occur, the Arab Spring demonstrated what Al Jazeera termed a "forced failure" of political Islam—something the young protestors had hardly anticipated. These popular uprisings, deposing some of the most oppressive dictators in the Arab world, cleared the way for a wave of political Islamist groups ranging from political parties like the Muslim Brotherhood, the Ennahda party (Tunisia), and the Justice and Development Party (PJD, Morocco) to radically violent and brutal militant groups such as ISIS. The success of Islamist parties in co-opting this burgeoning energy for their own purposes is a central plotline in this book's analysis of Al Jazeera.

In just fifteen years since its founding in 1996, Al Jazeera—the flagship media network of the Arab world—has ascended to the zenith of the global media market, now reaching 270 million viewers around the world. Its audience is currently larger than that of CNN and the BBC combined. Al Jazeera Arabic, from its origins as a state-sponsored channel, has expanded to become a central pillar of an international media empire. In 2006, the Al Jazeera channel became Al Jazeera Network, after being heralded as one of the world's most popular commercial brands (Seib 2012; Sakr 2007; Lamloum 2004). This expansion included a tremendous effort to reach out to new regions and cultures not only in Arabic and English, but also in Turkish, Swahili, Balkan, and other languages (Qadiri-Issa 2008, 77).

Al Jazeera earned unprecedented popularity in the Arab world for its courage in challenging the Arab establishment and its role as a forum for free speech in a landscape defined by dictatorial propaganda (el-Oifi 2011; Lamloum 2006; Lynch 2006; Talon 2011). As a result, wildly disparate camps—radicals, conservatives, and liberals alike—saw their interests represented in the network's programming. French sociologist Pierre Bourdieu calls this kind of identification with and recognition of the medium (Al Jazeera) the "domestication of domination" (Bourdieu 2013, 564). Al Jazeera succeeded in domesticating or taming widely varied political, revolutionary, and religious expressions and then fitting them into the format of televised debates. The network gave Islamist leaders and dissidents of various Arab regimes broader access to transnational Arab publics than they could have ever before dreamed of reaching. By providing a competitive forum with obvious appeal to a diverse group of stakeholders, Al Jazeera attained a widespread buy-in to a habitus of Islamized pan-Arab ontology. This method of pushing a political agenda through ostensibly benevolent action is far from a new phenomenon. However, Al Jazeera's creation of an interactive transnational Arabic space was unprecedented in the Arab world and earned it significant leverage in the cultural interchange that it was itself facilitating.

There is a significant body of literature devoted to Al Jazeera's origins and impact on the Arab world. Despite a general agreement in the social sciences literature on the impact of Al Jazeera on the Arab media landscape, the broader cultural influence of the network's efforts remains a subject of debate. On this front, three dominant perspectives can be distinguished. In the first, Al Jazeera is seen as a modernizing force in Arab culture. Marc Lynch, Mohammed el-Nawawy, and Adil Iskandar and Hugh Miles have all written in support of this perspective. In the second, Al Jazeera is described as radicalizing its audience. Mamoun Fandy has argued for this perspective. In the third, the network's message is regarded as ambiguous and its motives and methods as lacking transparency. Olfa Lamloum and Mohammed el-Oifi fall in this camp. Al Jazeera is, of course, an evolving entity. As such, interpretations and opinions are subject to change. The present chapter will provide a brief overview of the data collection on and subsequent analysis of Al Jazeera Arabic, as well as an overview of what the data tell us about the network. It also includes important historical information about the network's founding and rise to prominence. Furthermore, it outlines the research on media theory that forms the theoretical framework for this analysis of Al Jazeera.[1]

Modernization

Authors like Seib (2012), Noueihed and Warren (2012), Talon (2011), and Braizat and Berger (2012)) have acknowledged that Al Jazeera played a role in the Arab Spring and has had an influence on Arab countries. The sudden domino effect of Arab regimes, triggered by a single dramatic act of self-immolation by a Tunisian fruit vendor, must be contextualized in a long-term perspective. It can actually be seen as the result of a trickle-down effect of a number of challenges affecting the Arab world, including globalization and the rise of transnational media, in addition to economic crises and the "youth bulge."[2] Most significantly, Al Jazeera was the nursery for the Arab world's democratic revolutions, promoting Friday as the "day of rage" to express popular protest on the Arab street. By deconstructing the effect that Al Jazeera has on its intended audience, this book provides Western readers with an unusual glimpse into Al Jazeera Arabic. The analysis presented here explores how the network has strategically cast its reporters and camera operators as martyrs in the struggle for Arab freedom while promoting itself as the mouthpiece and advocate of the Arab publics. But rather than assuming that Al Jazeera is a monolithic force for positive transformation in Arab society, *Fridays of Rage* examines the potentially dark underbelly of Al Jazeera's radical reconceptualization of media as a strategic tool and as a weapon, and its global implications moving forward.

Al Jazeera's blueprint for "Muslim democracy" is part of a vision that the network has advocated since the airing of its first programs (both secular and religious) in 1998. Al Jazeera embarked upon a mission to reconstruct the Arab mindset and psyche, a massive makeover that relied on changing the perceptions of audiences. It introduced a variety of exiled Islamist leaders to Arab publics and gave Muslim feminists a space to express their views. The inclusion and consideration of Westerners, Israelis, Hamas members, secularists, and others with diverse viewpoints earned the network a reputation for pluralism. Al Jazeera presented a mirror to an Arab world that had previously been reticent to examine itself and its democratic deficiencies (el-Oifi 2011; Lamloum 2006; Talon 2011). Paraphrasing the French sociologist Pierre Bourdieu, Al Jazeera invested enough in the game of mediating between radical opponents like secularists, Islamists, feminists, and conservatives that each group believed there was something to gain from joining in. Al Jazeera has played both hero and villain to Western observers. Against the backdrop of the Iraq and Afghanistan wars, critics, pundits, and government officials in the United States portrayed the network as a terrorist mouthpiece due to its airing of Al Qaeda video and audiotapes. However, a growing body of research on the network has revealed the complexity of its impact on the Arab religious, cultural, and political order and the Arab diaspora in the West (Lynch 2006; el-Oifi 2011; Lamloun 2004; Kepel 2013; Cherribi 2006). Observers in the West began to recognize that the network was using its first-mover advantage in the Arab satellite media field to change the character of news production and consumption in the Arab world. Phillip Seib (2011) described the "Al Jazeera effect" as a transformative force for regional reform. With the sudden emergence of pro-democracy movements across the Arab Mediterranean, collectively referred to as the Arab Spring, Al Jazeera acquired a reputation as a force for democracy. The network was recognized for its reporting on revolutionary movements, as well as its role in advancing a climate of debate and dissent in the years leading up to the first protests against the Ben Ali regime in Tunisia. However, there remains a debate over the motives behind Al Jazeera's reporting, stemming largely from the network's ties to the Qatari government and apparent bias toward Islamist political parties. The network's coverage of the recent Arab Spring events can be used to build on the work of Marc Lynch and Marwan Kraidy, who emphasized the democratizing effect of Al Jazeera and the creation of a new Arab landscape that led to the transformation of the Arab public configuration (Lynch 2006, 2; Kraidy 2008).

A common theme of the literature on Al Jazeera is the success it has achieved through the encouragement of free thought, creativity, and personal initiative among its employees combined with a BBC-like precision and CNN-like speed. Al Jazeera is also described as the "channel of Arab disenchantment" that "shares and stages the sorrows of the Arabs" (Zayani and Sahraoui 2007, 61–62; Kraidy 2008, 24–25; Lamloum 2004; el-Nawawy and Iskandar 2003; Powers and Youmans 2012; Lynch 2006; Seib 2011). In addition, el-Oifi (2015) argues that Al Jazeera's major contribution to the media landscape lies in its reinvention of an Arab journalistic field that transcends the borders of Middle Eastern nation-states. In this sense, Al Jazeera has seized for itself a level of power and influence that rivals that of Arab governments (el-Oifi 2015).

Radicalization

Al Jazeera has created a transnational cultural platform that serves as a threat to the cultural and political status quo. The network functions as an arena for debate between radicals, conservatives, and moderates in front of international audiences. Consequently, Arab governments—with the exception of the network's home country, Qatar—consider Al Jazeera a troublemaker and destabilizing force. Most studies of the network emphasize Al Jazeera's instrumental role in facilitating the transition from an Arab TV culture based on monologue to a new culture of dialogue and debate. By this measure, Al Jazeera has allowed Arab publics to at least mentally escape censorship and the hold of Arab governments on the media field.

The perceived scope of Al Jazeera's ability to disrupt the status quo is evidenced by the confusion articulated by researchers, writing in the years prior to the Arab Spring, regarding the lack of political change realized during the network's ascendant years. The tone of resignation to the region's political stagnancy that characterizes this research also illustrates how truly blindsided the international community was by the sudden upheavals of the Arab Spring. In *Voices of the New Arab Public*, Marc Lynch describes an Arab cultural landscape where

Arabic satellite television has challenged the state's monopoly on information throughout the region. Yet, writing in 2006, Lynch explores the failure of the new discourse to translate into a transition toward political openness. He describes Arab publics as disjointed, leaderless, and vulnerable to foreign forces that would exploit their divisions. Voice of the Arabs, the radio station created by Nasser as a vehicle to promote pan-Arabism, serves as a past example of media attempts to unite Arab publics into a mobilized force through "emotional, angry rhetoric aimed at energizing dangerous mobs" (Lynch 2006, 36). However, these efforts failed to bring about political change.

El-Mustpha Lahlali cited the Arab Spring revolutions as a refutation of Lynch's argument, writing, "The Egyptian and Tunisian revolutions, along with uprisings and protests across the Arab world, have shown—contrary to what Lynch has referred to—that the Arab publics are capable of making drastic changes, even in the absence of leadership" (2011, 69). However, Lynch was not incorrect in describing the weak position of the Arab publics. It took many years for the Arab street protests to rise up in such a manner as to bring about political change. Lynch argued that Arabs were unable to achieve lasting change, but he also wrote hopefully about the possibility of the long-term democratizing effects of Al Jazeera—a theme that will be revisited in this book. This issue of agency for the Arab publics is also ripe for examination in light of Bourdieu's description of different types of accumulated capital—including religious, political, and symbolic—all of which can have transformative effects on society.

Kai Hafez, also writing in the years prior to the first Arab Spring demonstrations, argued that hope for a political revolution spurred by changes in the Arab media had been met with a revolution confined to the entertainment field. Using data indices from Freedom House, Hafez noted that Arab political systems had not substantially improved during the "Al Jazeera Era" (2008, 4). According to Hafez, Arab governments are able to slow down the processes of globalization by stifling any movement toward substantive political change. He acknowledges a movement toward more freedom of discourse in transnational Arab media (2008, 5). However, he posits that censorship remains the rule, even in the Arab world's most liberal, "democratic" states (2008, 4). Sadly, the changing seasons since the outbreak of the Arab Spring have seen the status quo Hafez describes return throughout the region, with the notable exception of Tunisia.

Media scholars have also previously addressed Al Jazeera's status as a relatively religious or secular media outlet. In *Arab Media: Globalization and Emerging Media Industries*, Noha Mellor, Khalil Rinnawi, Nabil Dajani, and Muhammad I. Ayish stress the importance of religious programs on Arab local broadcast stations, including Quran recitations and live coverage of prayers and religious events like the Hajj (Mellor et al. 2011, 80). By contrast, on Arab satellite TV channels, religious programs make up only 10 percent of programming. The authors see Al Jazeera's programing of secular topics in a market defined by religious programing as a democratizing force in the Middle East (Mellor et al. 2011, 91).

Khaled Al Hroub states, in accordance with the conclusion of Marwan Kraidy (2009), that votes cast for competitors on the popular Arab talent competition shows *Star Academy* and *Super Star* exceeded the number of votes cast in any Jordanian parliamentary elections, a phenomenon with deep social and cultural implications (Al Hroub 2006,109). Al Hroub speaks of a social modernist–religious rift caused by the two attractive forces of entertainment and news. However, within this tension "there is a dissemination of certain aspects of an extremist, exclusive culture to which satellite news media has contributed" (Al Hroub 200, 109). Al Hroub retraces these aspects to 9/11, the rise of Al Qaeda, and the war in Iraq. This phenomenon reached its highest point between 2002 and 2004. Al Hroub explains that the label of "jihad" attached to the broadcasting of Bin Laden's tapes helped establish and normalize a culture of religious violence (2006, 110). Al Hroub describes how allowing media share competition to be the driving force behind Al Jazeera's programming strategy put the network at risk of playing into the hands of extremists. In this push for shares, the "Mujahidin videos" were instrumental, placing the network in the awkward position of relying on its function as a platform for terrorist propaganda videos in order to bolster its notoriety (Al Hroub 2006,110).

However, Al Hroub adds that this openness to extreme opinions was part of a strategy that placed the network at the intersection of competing views of the Arab world. The network enhanced its popularity by promoting strongly opinionated commentators, experts, and pundits (Al Hroub 2006, 112). Al Hroub asserts that the display of particularism was a way to monopolize the truth and, by extension, prop up the network as the guardian of the truth (2006,113). In other words, taking the logic that the truth in any argument lies somewhere between diverging viewpoints, Al Jazeera claimed as its own the middle ground where all viewpoints meet and compete. What's more, the network reserves for itself the ability to steer and frame the argument.

Observers of Al Jazeera also note that Arab satellite media have contributed to a divide between the developed West and the developing Arab world that cuts across political and geographic boundaries. Al Hroub points out that members of the Arab diaspora who remain unassimilated in Western societies are particularly vulnerable to the discourse of satellite media, which creates a negative image of their host societies. Al Hroub refers to a ghettolike isolationism that results from this situation (2006, 114–115). Musa Shteiwi wrote that "the transnational Arab satellite channels helped to foster a pan-Arab identity" (2006,132). Ali Darwish goes even further, explaining that "the divide is widening between the haves and have-nots along the fault line between western-oriented and fortunate and privileged few, and a largely disadvantaged pan-Arab broad base that is teetering between pan-Arabism and Islamism" (2010, 233).

Ambiguity

Al Jazeera has become a major media empire, and it plays a complex role in the developing Arab world: it is thus impossible to sum up Al Jazeera's impact with a succinct label like "McArabism" (Rinnawi 2006) or "Islamized pan-Arabism" (Cherribi 2006). This complexity has been analyzed by scholars who have mapped the Al Jazeera effect in the Arab media, political order, social movements, and democratization efforts.

However, Al Jazeera journalist Khaled Al Hroub argues the contrary. In a chapter of *Arab Media in the Information Age* entitled "Satellite Media and Social Change in the Arab world" he writes, "Satellite news media, either directly or indirectly, enhances the Islamic faction at the expense of the modernist faction for several reasons—including regional tension, foreign interventions that breed radical reactions, the power of Islamic factions among the Arab public, and the national and Islamic orientation of the most important Arab news channel, Al Jazeera" (Al Hroub 2006, 94).

Al Jazeera unpacked the disparities between the global North and global South by serving as a powerful voice for and of the South. As Mahjoob Zweiri and Emma Murphy write, "[Al Jazeera] has re-mapped problems of the south, and has itself literally become a victim of the aggressions of the north. It has brought new levels of professionalism (both in format and in journalistic conduct) to the Arab media, and been condemned by the same for its subordination to a hybridized form of westernization. Yet wherever one stands on these issues, one can't deny that Al Jazeera has had a tremendous impact on public consciousness and political dialogue in the Arab world. Notably, it has spawned a whole new generation of privately owned sister channels, competing to broadcast news and other formats in Arabic to the Arab world" (2011, xvi). In the West, mainly in Europe and North America, Al Jazeera English has become a significant alternative to domestic media outlets. According to Zweiri and Murphy, "Al Jazeera continues to play a major role today in Middle Eastern and international politics as it is increasingly recognized by international audiences as a reliable source of news expressing the pan-Arab orientation" (2011, x).

Observers of Al Jazeera have relied on a variety of theoretical frameworks through which to view the network and its role in the Arab world. Kai Hafez was inspired by the political contest model of Gadi Wolfsfeld (1997) in which authorities and their challengers compete to have their story come out first in the media. Obtaining control of the political field through media influence tends to involve demonstrations, sit-ins, and violent events (Hafez 2008, 4–6). Hafez urged the application of Wolfsfeld's theoretical model to Al Jazeera's role in the Arab world, writing, "It is perhaps symptomatic that even years after 9/11 hardly any content analyses on Al Jazeera exist that combine quantitative state-of-the-art-methodology with qualitative analysis of content. Channels like Al Jazeera are much debated but they are still under-researched" (2008, 9).

Marc Lynch believes that opportunity structures are the mechanism now generating political and social adherence, as the vanishing media monopoly of Arab states has left a new political context up for grabs. The global context is also more present than ever, in this view, as the scramble to fill the vacuum left by state domination of the media is also a contest to act as the face of the Arab world abroad. Building on Lynch's research, Zweiri and Murphy argue that "Al Jazeera provides a global platform to contest a hegemonic world view of American satellite television" and that "jihadist websites take center stage in the western security consciousness and Facebook becomes the frontline of popular mobilization" (2011, xv).

In sum, the literature shows that the three aforementioned effects of Al Jazeera—modernization (including democratization), radicalization (antiestablishment), and ambiguity—are not contradictory processes in the worldview of Al Jazeera. These effects are iterations of soft power transforming the political, religious, and media fields, and they apply to Al Jazeera and Qatar themselves. Amid the turmoil of regional change, Al Jazeera remains a regional and global superpower in the Arab media configuration in spite of a recent decline in viewership.

Taking Bourdieu into the Field

Watching and analyzing the Arab Spring unfold on Al Jazeera evokes the role of "specific effects of sociology" in interpreting social reality, giving meaning to events, and putting the researcher "in situations of auto-analysis" (Bourdieu and Chartier 2010, 20).[3] One concern of this book is to avoid painting a glowing image of Al Jazeera, and instead to provide a balanced analysis of the news agency. Use of biased language in the text, including phrases like "watchdog of democracy" and "the nursery for the Arab world's democratic revolutions," is not meant to be a reflection of the author's own opinion. Rather, these phrases offer examples of how Al Jazeera is often portrayed by various entities, including the network itself. This volume's original contribution, and its departure from existing work, lie in its attempt to reconcile Al Jazeera's divisive effects on international Muslim communities with the findings of previous work that emphasized the "democratizing effects" of Al Jazeera (Abdelmoula 2015; Seib 2011; Lynch 2006). This reflexive approach is essential to all the stages of the author's research.

The theoretical framework for this book is inspired largely by the work of Pierre Bourdieu, as well as the work of Robert Entman and Mohammed Arkoun, Fethi Benslama, Gilles Kepel, Olivier Roy, John Esposito, Roberto Fransozi, Marc Lynch, Lance Bennett, Doris Graber, and Gadi Wolfsfeld. Bourdieu's concept of fields is well suited to an analysis of Al Jazeera. Bourdieu describes a field as a structured space characterized by a hierarchy of positions and a relative independence. Specific interests define the field. Actors within the field with specific forms of economic and cultural capital struggle for dominant positions. The media field conforms to Bourdieu's description of a field "structured around the opposition between a heteronymous pole representing forces external to the field of primary economics and the autonomous field representing the specific capital unique to the field" (Benson 2006, 190). Within the media field, "economic capital is expressed via circulation or advertising revenues or audience ratings. Cultural capital takes the form of intelligent commentary, in-depth reporting and journalistic practices that are outstanding" (Benson 2006, 190). The pan-Arab media field is also a field of power structured around a new logic that involves many external players—the United States, Russia, France, the United Kingdom, Iran, Turkey, and Israel, to name a few—in addition to the Arab countries, which include Saudi Arabia as a dominant player. Al Jazeera represents a unique actor in the media field. The network is not particularly devoted to increasing its economic capital, which comes mainly from advertising revenue. It is, however, very driven to achieve a dominant position in cultural and social configurations. However, even if Al Jazeera dominates the religious, cultural, and economic fields, it still belongs to a weak autonomous field and a weak media field when it comes to its critical relationship with Qatar. Bourdieu's definition helps us to understand the pan-Arab media field in which Al Jazeera operates. In this media field there are anchors, preachers, camera operators, journalists, and pundits. But states that use their financial and political might to serve as benefactors or manipulators of these media outlets are also important players within the field (Bourdieu 1984).

The concept of fields is particularly useful for an analysis of Al Jazeera because of the network's ability to operate concurrently in multiple, interrelated fields. Al Jazeera produces media goods outside the national media fields of individual Arab countries. It operates in a transnational pan-Arab field that has the ability to affect and transform the media fields of individual Arab countries, which in their turn functioned as subfields for a number of years. Al Jazeera has created a dominant discourse with a particular symbolic shape, characterized by a set of media practices that articulate its dominant frames. These dominant frames compete directly with the frames of official media outlets for control of a hegemonic message. Al Jazeera as a player engages daily in strategies, as do its competing Arab media outlets, to win the hearts and minds of Arab publics.

Al Jazeera's repertoire of frames influences, directly or indirectly, consciously or unconsciously, a massive captive audience that sees these frames as a counternarrative to the dominant hegemonic discourse of nation-states and their communication apparatuses. In other words, these frames affect the habitus of these publics. The habitus is the "regulating mechanism" or "the strategy generating principle." It is "a system of lasting, transposable dispositions which—integrating past experiences—functions at every moment as a matrix of perceptions, appreciations and actions and makes possible the achievements of infinitely diversified tasks, thanks to the analogical transfer of schemes permitting the solution of the similarly shaped problems" (Bourdieu 1977, 83). The daily drumbeat of the same dominant frames can produce predispositions toward acceptance of Al Jazeera's interpretation of social or political problems.

Al Jazeera's frames are constructed according to a binary scheme of distinction between negative and positive stances regarding states, groups, individuals, and ideas. These distinctions form the core of the Al Jazeera's dominant frames. When these frames are internalized by members of publics, they could create the conditions for a group habitus similar to a class habitus. Given Al Jazeera's consistent use of the frames of oppression and resistance, this could be described as the habitus of the "dominated." There is no presumption of automatic inculcation of frames in a given habitus. Individuals who are aware of the frames affecting their habitus are empowered to free themselves from or modify their reaction to those frames. However, a number of indicators in the empirical data, such as the widespread adoption of named Fridays and other mobilizations of particular social groups, can be seen as evidence of Al Jazeera's success in this realm. Bourdieu argues that it is the habitus plus the social trajectory of a person that determines that person's position in a certain social field. Thus the term "habitus" is based on probability.

In order to capture the work of Al Jazeera, especially at the level of the social imagination of the publics, this work offers detailed accounts of specific shows. This is important, because Al Jazeera outlines and guides political struggles in different countries and situations in a systematic way, reflected in similar themes that run throughout various programs. For example, the available data show that Al Jazeera paid enormous attention to Tunisia, Egypt, and Gaza throughout the fifteen years of its existence prior to the Arab Spring. Without giving Al Jazeera more credit than it deserves regarding the mobilization of Arab publics, it is important to understand that bloggers and social media activists looked to Al Jazeera as a vehicle for their revolutionary cause, especially in the early stages of the Tunisian revolution. Tunisian blogger Lina ben Mhenni praised Al Jazeera for its role in spreading the message of her country's social media rebels. A simple word count for specific terms demonstrates the relationship between some Al Jazeera frames and antiestablishment movements in the Arab world and the diaspora in Europe.

If the habitus gives logic and structure to interpretation, analysis, and action, it is the author's argument that the presence of dominant media frames can crowd out some of this collective analytical search for solutions. The conditions under which publics consume these media frames may seem objective, according to their subjective experience. The publics that make up the majority of Al Jazeera's audience have a common characteristic: they are politically, economically, and culturally dominated by their ruling regimes. For dominated people who wish to escape the trap of oppression and un-freedom, the alternative frames provided by Al Jazeera may serve as a refuge from oppressive regimes. Hence the antiestablishment frame and the identification frame presented by Al Jazeera appear to be natural choices. Al Jazeera's frames emphasize the value of freedom, autonomy, and dignity but also advocate a "blessed" unity called for by the network's religious voice. Religion is by definition a place of unity and legitimate mobilization against injustice. It gives meaning and structure to life under autocratic rule, promising a "decent" life under god.

As Bourdieu explains, we cannot reduce the field of pan-Arab media to a single player. Al Jazeera competes in this field with many other players, and the configuration of the playing field is transforming rapidly. If Al Jazeera once thrived as the source of foreign reporting on the network's exclusive access to Bin Laden tapes or facets of the Arab world that were sealed off to Western journalists, it bears noting that Al Jazeera now often acts as the establishment news outlet relying on footage delivered by others. Meanwhile, pressure from regional actors has caused Al Jazeera to stop airing its flagship religious program. The dismantling of the powerful platform previously enjoyed by Yusuf al-Qaradawi may be evidence that the post–Arab Spring international climate places new limitations on the network's freedom to antagonize the Global Mufti's enemies in Saudi Arabia and Egypt. In silencing al-Qaradawi, the network has lost an important aspect of its ability to wield power by legitimizing or delegitimizing various groups and actors in the Arab world. In particular, the absence of al-Qaradawi's show *Sharia and Life* from the network's lineup erodes Al Jazeera's maneuverability in the face of the emergence of ISIS's Abu Bakr al-Baghdadi as the new voice of religious extremism in the region. In years past, the network could enjoy the notoriety inherent in airing tapes from Al Qaeda leaders while simultaneously distancing itself from the group through condemnations and other commentary voiced by al-Qaradawi. It is possible that, in silencing al-Qaradawi, Al Jazeera has lost a key aspect of its ability to shape the fields in which it operates.

Media Framing and the Illusion of Objectivity

As the previously described audience data demonstrates, Al Jazeera has seen a relative decline in viewership and credibility since the early stages of the Arab Spring. Two of Bourdieu's concepts can help us to understand the decline of Al Jazeera's popularity. The first is the idea of the life cycle of a cultural or a media phenomenon. The second is the idea that audiences grow immune to the influence of images and words as they begin to understand how they are manipulated for a specific effect (Bourdieu 1998, 36). Referencing Wittgenstein, Bourdieu explains that language used by the media can act, at times, in place of our own cognitive reasoning. This notion forms a major part of framing theory, as advanced by Robert Entman, Gadi Wolfsfeld, Lance Bennett and Doris Graber, among others.

As will be further described in the coming chapters, Al Jazeera relies on a number of ready-made frames through which it presents its reporting. A focus on violence and blood is one example of a frame that uses real events to advance the interests of the network. Al Jazeera does not create catastrophes, destroy houses, or bomb buildings. However, its focus on these events and its signature graphic video accounts of them draw viewers in while advancing a narrative in which the world is a symbolic battlefield.

Luc Boltanski argues that even in video and photography there is no objectivity. Rather, the captured image serves only to systematize the media outlet's message according to preestablished frames. Rather than an objective documentation of events, video footage is an expression of the physical presence of the journalist or the camera operator. In this view, showing and commenting on video footage of an event reduces the event itself to the role of an anecdotal device (Boltanski in Bourdieu 1965,178).

Boltanski further explains that a news report is never the work of one or more journalists; instead it is the result of a multiplicity of interventions according to the hierarchy of the media outlet (in Bourdieu 1965, 179). The news report is delivered as a coherent and univocal production that can be achieved only when all the participants have a certain level of knowledge of the style, expectations, and restrictions of the news outlet. In Boltanski's view, the news report is a systematic organized system of rhetoric. By participating in the creation of news reports, journalists are actually immersing themselves in the system of norms of the news outlet. In that sense there is a standardization of messaging within media outlets.

Epistemological Scrutiny of the Words We Use

It is a daunting task to make sense of current events without the distance that is so often intrinsic to the depth and clarity of historical analysis. In a fascinating exchange with the French historian Roger Chartier, the sociologist Pierre Bourdieu described the difference in approach between history and sociology. Bourdieu explained that because history often deals with necrologies, the historian works to discover the hidden relations or "liaisons between historical figures." Bourdieu believes that in history, the temporal distance has a "virtue of neutralization" of the heated nature of consequential current events. In sociology, though, "we are always on a burning terrain, where things that we are discussing are alive; we are not dead and buried" (Bourdieu and Chartier 2010, 23).

On one hand, these limits make social sciences more vulnerable to bias from a variety of sources. On the other hand, studying these developments in real time can be empowering to those in dominated positions, because it provides an opportunity to biopsy "symbolic aggression and symbolic manipulation" (Bourdieu and Chartier 2010, 24) by professional producers of cultural goods such as media outlets. Bourdieu gives an example of election-night media coverage when pundits and political scientists are invited to comment on journalistic reporting on polls and politicians, leading to a "meta discourse" about the event. But people are not always duped by the media discourse, as they hold "instruments of passive resistance," or spontaneous methods of escaping the influence of specific television programs, the remote control being an effective example (Bourdieu and Chartier 2010, 51).

Bourdieu argues that the vulnerabilities of audiences to symbolic violence in all of its forms is an extremely important subject. The social sciences, he argues, have a duty to study these vulnerabilities in a sensible way, as they are consistently ignored by journalists, pundits, and social commentators (Bourdieu and Chartier 2010, 25). Like Norbert Elias, Johan Goudsblom, and Abram de Swaan, Bourdieu urges historians to act more like sociologists, and sociologists to act more like historians. With that in mind, this study of Al Jazeera places a strong focus on the long-term historic perspective of Elias and the "longue durée" of Fernand Braudel, and combines them with reflexive sociology in order to explain the complexity of social reality in the Arab world in all its facets. Since all notions and concepts are historic, special attention is given to Bourdieu's advice: "We should keep in mind the discontinuities and the genesis of discontinuity in order to detect anachronisms" (Bourdieu and Chartier 2010, 85–86). This advice is particularly relevant to an examination of the widespread disruption of a regional power structure that remained strong for more than half a century. Since the Arab Spring is well on its way to being considered a historic event, all concepts that are used to analyze it as a social phenomenon should be carefully examined as "historical notions or historically constituted." This couching of the Arab Spring within a broader historical concept is already apparent, as the terminology of a revolutionary "spring" has deep historical origins going back to the 1848 revolutions in Europe.

Bourdieu and Chartier's invitation to adopt a more reflexive attitude underpins the author's own work on Al Jazeera. Chartier warns against what he calls the "nominalism trap," which makes it easy to create categories that are intended to be universal and unchangeable, but instead mask the component parts and historical variations of the object (Bourdieu and Chartier, 2010, 30). Two other traps, identified by Bourdieu as anachronism and ethnocentrism, are also relevant here. The trap of anachronism is more common among historians, whereas ethnocentrism of class is a common pitfall of sociologists. The former is a tendency to analyze social phenomena through an outdated lens. The latter is a tendency to draw universal conclusions from the attributes of a single case or example. For example, the term "pan-Arabism" has been reified by many political actors and lost its historical context to become an ambiguous term. Its use often reflects the nominalism and anachronism traps when applied as a blanket term to cover both Nasser's calls for Arab unity as a means of political reform and Qaddafi's appeals to Arab identity as a hegemonic tool. These comparisons tend to ignore the complexities inherent in the application of nation-state governance to the post-imperial region, which brought about various strains of pan-Arabism to begin with. Pan-Arabism is also often treated as a unique and exclusive ideology to be examined as a phenomenon entirely different from that of past instances where nations have used linguistic identity to create larger conglomerations of states. This line of thinking clearly meets the definition of the ethnocentrism trap.

Pan-Arabism should not be inextricably linked to its nationalistic or negative connotation, but rather should be seen as a concept that has taken on multiple transformations and meanings over time. Al Jazeera gives us an interesting example of how these transfigurations of meaning have taken place. The worldview advanced by Al Jazeera can be described as a reconciliation between pan-Arabism and Islamic solidarity. Pan-Arabism, as conceived and propagated by Nasser, increased its galvanizing effects through radio (Voice of the Arabs), pan-Arab projects, and wars. Islamic solidarity as a doctrine was created in the 1960s by the Saudi–Wahhabi alliance (made up of Saudi Arabia, the Gulf Arab nations, Jordan, Morocco, and Pakistan) in order to counterbalance Nasser's pan-Arab movement (Mouline 2011, 2015). Thanks in part to the influx of oil money and Nasser's high-profile military failures, Islamic solidarity won out over pan-Arabism. But pan-Arabism remained a simmering force. The victory of Islamic solidarity found its zenith in Black September of 1973 when the oil powers threatened to cripple Western economies. This, in hindsight, was also one of the most harmful events for immigration relations from the Arab world and Africa to Europe (Cherribi 2010). Amid the climate of illiberalism and autocracy, as well as the Iranian revolution, this victory also put radical political Islam on an upward trajectory. It is in this context that "Islamized pan-Arabism" should be understood as a marriage of convenience between two ideologies that need each other to survive the rise of radical Islamic groups. Al Jazeera's promotion of a watered-down version of Gulf-region Wahhabism is a sign of the network's success in marrying the two ideologies.

This aspect of Al Jazeera's programming is representative of another theme that runs throughout the analysis of the network's recurrent frames, *khaljana* (domination by Arab Gulf ideas and culture). This may be a problematic term in English for the growing cultural and religious influence of the Gulf countries in the Arab world. Therefore, this book will emphasize the increasing focus on and projection of the culture and views of the Gulf states over those of the Levant countries and the Maghreb (northern Africa) as the expanding Arab Gulf identification frame. This epistemological scrutiny in the use of concept is important in order to escape the traps of nominalism, anachronism, and ethnocentrism.

There is a clear structure to the ideological positions of Al Jazeera, from the choice of visual themes, to the topics covered, the ads between segments, the tone of the delivery, the logo, and so on. In spite of its ecumenical outlook (it airs the views of political Islamists, liberals, and socialists), Al Jazeera has a specific message that reverberates throughout its programming. This work examines the production mechanisms of this ideological underpinning of Al Jazeera's continuous discourse. The consistency of the message is as important as the repetition of words in a specific context and specific historical conditions. Words stressing pan-Arabism, Islamic solidarity, days of rage, and *tahweed al-Quds* (the Judaization of Jerusalem) all have a history. Therefore, this book is extremely careful regarding ascribed "anterior or posterior" meaning of the words employed by the network. In other words, epistemological vigilance is needed in order to identify interpretations of events that conjure up a "mythical" past reactualized by Al Jazeera by injecting old meanings into descriptions of new events. For example, when the leader of the Tunisian "Islamist" party, Ennahda (Renaissance), returned from his London exile to Tunis, he was welcomed with a song that the *ansar* (supporters of the Prophet Muhammad in Medina) sang when the Prophet emigrated from Mecca to Medina. Al Jazeera made a parallel between Rached al-Ghanouchi's exile and return with the *hijra* (migration of the Prophet) giving the man a holy aura and anachronistic mandate (Bourdieu and Chartier 2010, 32).

Bourdieu gives as an example the French Revolution, an event from the past that is often evoked as if it were a part of the present, making it an eternal issue of political struggle. "One of the principles of the political struggle is to struggle for common words: for example, who is republican? [In France] everybody is republican; at election times, people talk of republican discipline, republican solidarity, etc. Everybody is in the center. . . . In short, there are words that we know owe their price in the struggle to the fact that they are objects of struggle" (Bourdieu and Chartier 2010, 34). There are "key words that are the point (focus/locus) of struggle in the universes" (2010, 34) that are mapped through observation and analysis of Al Jazeera in this book.

Pierre Bourdieu explains that, from the time of our birth, social pressures and constraints are so intense that we have only a very small chance to become free. In other words, we live within the intellectual boundaries of a worldview provided to us by others and generally lack the imagination and fortitude to become sovereign individuals. Bourdieu argues that illusions of liberty and freedom ubiquitous in cultural goods ranging from television shows to political discourse are themselves the building blocks of the very determinism that imprisons us. Bourdieu argues that this focus on liberty is a sociological paradox. In this view, even intellectual freedom is sometimes an illusion. Bourdieu doesn't believe in the idea of an objective, impartial intellectual as Karl Mannheim does. Instead he warns of the illusion of self-conscience (Bourdieu and Chartier 2010).

The prestige of this illusion comes from the intellectual's ability to master history as his or her own truth. Al Jazeera anchors like Faisal al-Qasim and others believe in their own intellectual independence and sell their truth as unbiased, free, and pure. Bourdieu's take makes us aware of the trap of the independence illusion in any work of journalism (Bourdieu 1998; Bennett 2011). Bourdieu doesn't promote pessimism, but rather advocates a constant awareness of our own biases and the biases imposed on us. Bourdieu attempts to show that behind the facade of freedom there are chains of determinism. This is personified, for example, by intellectuals confident that their university affiliation frees them from influence or constraint. Bourdieu argues that this very confidence may confine them to a field of discourse and thought even more rigid and regimented than that of their counterparts with entrenched political affiliations and allegiances. Bourdieu explains how professors and academics are more vested in academic interests than purely political interests. Journalists, he writes, are susceptible to the same sort of intellectual and professional morass (Bourdieu and Chartier 2010, 40). Al Jazeera presents itself as the network of "the opinion and the other opinion," the channel of freedom. The network is loath, however, to subject itself to the sort of public scrutiny it applies to other arbiters of power. The network, for example, stood mute in the face of criticism leveled at it by international news agencies for failing to cover uprisings in Bahrain (Erdbrink 2011).

If we understand the ideological motivations behind Al Jazeera's frames, such as pro-rebel Arab Spring coverage, we can understand the symbolic power and the symbolic domination of al-Qaradawi's proclamations about Al Jazeera's programming. The mechanism of delivery of al-Qaradawi's (and by extension Al Jazeera's) dogma is an organic outgrowth of its environment. Distinctions between groups, positions, and issues are routinely given a religious or spiritual foundation by muftis on Arab television. al-Qaradawi is only one example. What sets the Global Mufti apart from his peers is an intense charisma and the unprecedented reach his position on Al Jazeera provides him. He acts as an almost prophetic figure, answering crucial moral questions of life and death, sanctioning protests against el-Sisi in Egypt and attempts on the lives of Qaddafi in Libya and Assad in Syria. By providing him airtime, Al Jazeera legitimizes al-Qaradawi. In turn, al-Qaradawi legitimizes the network with his fatwas.

This weaving together of culture and religion to create a strong social fabric is not a new phenomenon. In his seminal work "La Distinction," Pierre Bourdieu contends that culture in European and Western societies is a "locus of sacredness and production of sacredness" (Bourdieu 1979). In this situation, he claims, the shaming resulting from a cultural gaffe is equivalent to the stain of sin. He explains the primacy of family religious practice in the intergenerational transmission of religious belief. There is a transmission of convictions from father and mother to daughter and son. As this transmission disappears, religion disappears. David Voas calls this "fuzzy fidelity," with each generation becoming less religious than the previous one (2009,167). However, when culture becomes intertwined with religion on television, the media outlet creates a charismatic illusion. Lizbeth van Zonen put a spotlight on the television's ability to absorb and reorder cultural norms (Cherribi 2010). In the case of al-Qaradawi's program and those like it, television becomes the religion and vice versa. But preaching to a devout congregation is not necessarily the same as preaching to viewers whose hands are resting on the remote control. Al-Qaradawi essentially acknowledges the conflict inherent in serving the dual masters of religion and television when he speaks about the politics of piety. Bourdieu explains that a great deal of suffering could be avoided if there were a better understanding of how culture functions and, in this case, how the culture of TV warps the cultural function of religion (Bourdieu and Chartier 2010, 45).

Methodology and Evidence

This book's analysis of Al Jazeera's Arabic-language news coverage *Harvest of the Day* and four of its most popular current affairs programs (*Sharia and Life, Talk of the Revolution, Without Borders*, and *The Opposite Direction*) during the pivotal events of the past decade will provide answers to the key questions posed later in the chapter. The following paragraphs, organized by each data source, provide a succinct overview of the author's research and data collection strategies.

First, an examination of Al Jazeera's coverage of the forty-five days of sit-ins during the month of Ramadan, discussed extensively in chapter 6, is based largely on ethnographic research conducted by the author. This research consisted primarily of side-by-side daily coverage by Al Jazeera and Al Jazeera Mubasher in the summer of 2013. Al Jazeera provided researchers an ideal opportunity to follow, minute by minute, the activities of protestors in Rabaa via a camera fixed on the central stage of the square. The live footage provided an informative look at the daily activities of a cohesive protestor community, supported by rituals and symbols. The comparison between Al Jazeera Arabic and the network's local Egyptian Mubasher station offers further insights into the objectives of the network, as revealed by its different approaches to reporting based on its specific audience.

Second, analysis of Al Jazeera's coverage of the Egyptian and Tunisian revolutions is based primarily on the author's analysis of two hundred news reports and program episodes from January and February 2011. Transcriptions of these programs were used to reconstruct Al Jazeera's narrative of the Arab revolutions, as well as the role played by journalists and anchors in the unfolding of the narrative.

Third, in order to understand Yusuf al-Qaradawi's influence on Al Jazeera, the author quantified into a viable dataset every appearance on *Harvest of the Day* by al-Qaradawi during the height of coverage on banning of the veil (2003–2004); the 2005 Paris riots; backlash over the Danish Prophet cartoons and statements by the pope in 2006; and all appearances between December 2010 and August 2013. This dataset also includes all of the episodes of *Sharia and Life* from 1996 to 2013, coded according to each show's dominant frame. The map in chapter 2 of the geographic locations, frequencies, and affiliations of al-Qaradawi's guests on *Sharia and Life* establishes some of the major themes and frames that are central to the mufti's discourse. Frequent appearances by representatives of Ennahda, the Nation of Islam, and the International Union of Muslim Scholars tell us a great deal about al-Qaradawi's ideological sympathies. The recurring connection with prestigious geographic locations, meanwhile, reinforces Al Jazeera's image as a transgeographic capital for Arab and Islamic thought and discourse, by placing it alongside the world's cultural and political capitals. Finally, by using *Sharia and Life* as a communications hub for these various groups and locations, al-Qaradawi expands the identification frame of a worldwide Islamic community, or *umma*, united by Al Jazeera.

Fourth, the dataset that includes the network's coverage of the French riots comes primarily from the author's 2005 research based on keyword searches of Al Jazeera's Arabic-language site, for the terms "riots," "French riots," and "riots in France," to identify relevant news stories. The following current affairs programs were shown to provide the most extensive commentary on the riots and were thus used as the basis for data analysis: *The Opposite Direction, Reporters, From Europe*, and *Al Jazeera Forum*, as well as *Sharia and Life*.

Fifth, the author has topically mapped nearly all episodes of the following popular Al Jazeera Arabic programs since their launch: *Sharia and Life* (*Sharia wa al-hayat*), *Without Borders* (*Bila hudud*), *The Opposite Direction* (*al-Itijah al-muakis*), *Today's Meeting* (*Liqa'al-yawm*), *Talk of the Revolution* (*Hadith al-thawra*), *From Washington, Witness to the Times* (*Shahidun ala 'asr*), *In Depth* (*Fi'l umq*), *Hotspot* (*Nuqta sakhina*), *A Private Meeting* (*Liqa' khas*), Friends of The Arabs (*Asdiqa' al-Arab*), *Barred* (*Mamnu'un*), *Veterans* (*al- Muharibun al-qudama*), *A Rendezvous with the Diaspora* (*Maw'idun fi al-mahjar*), *Their Archive, Our History* (*Tarikhuna wa archifuhum*), *Pioneers* (*Ruad*), *Prison Literature* (*Adab a-sujun*), and *More than Opinion* (*Akthar min ra'y*). This selection contains programs that are current as well as those that have been discontinued. In addition, specific episodes were selected, based on their titles, for deeper examination in order to compare the author's observations of daily news segments with commentary shows. Among these are episodes of *In Depth* and news bulletins from *Harvest of the Day* (including the Maghreb edition of it, entitled *al-Hassad al-Maghribi*), *Sharia and Life*, *Talk of the Revolution*, and the *Opposite Direction*.

Sixth, in addition to the topics described above, the author conducted research on Al Jazeera's coverage of events and issues from the past decade, including the 2007 twentieth anniversary of the founding of Hamas, the 2008 Gaza crisis, the 2008 focus on corruption in Arab countries, the 2009 discussions of the future of the Muslim Brotherhood, the 2009 Dubai satellite launch, the 2010 focus on the rise of Shiites in Sunni states, the 2011 focus on South Sudan, the 2011 reform program in Bahrain, and the 2011 debate between Al Azhar University and the Vatican.

Seventh, the author followed Robert Entman's technique in studying pivotal events, issues, and actors (such as 9/11) in order to come up with a codebook, which is concerned primarily with the focus and the function of Al Jazeera's framing techniques and consequences: defining problematic effects/conditions, identifying causes, endorsing remedies, and conveying moral judgments (Entman 2003, 24). Roberto Fransozi's idea of relational scheme, previously used by Charles Tilly to code locations, events, and people, facilitates the forging of a connection between the research subject, action, and object of the codes themselves (Fransozi 2004, 39). In summary, the analysis of Al Jazeera follows a methodology that strikes an appropriate balance between quantitative and qualitative approaches to data gathering and analysis in order to maintain the integrity of the dataset.

The entire theoretical framework is built on systematic observation, content examination, and an extensive analysis of Al Jazeera's news coverage during recent pivotal events in the Arab world that have had the most significant international impact. I define such events using the work of Roberto Fransozi in *From*

Words to Numbers: Narrative, Data, and Social Science (2004) and the work of Pierre Bourdieu in *Distinction: A Social Critique of the Judgment of Taste* (1984). Fransozi explains that although a mere cataloging of events can tell a complex story, that is not the goal (2004, 82). What is even more important are those things that contribute to the making of an event, narrative, or a story (Fransozi 2004, 31). Fransozi agrees with Gallie, who says that "all history . . . is basically a narrative of events" (1963:69, in Fransozi 2004, 190). Thus, the narratives assembled and framed for the publics by Al Jazeera are able to shape or promote a certain interpretation of the history of the Arab world. As Fransozi explains, a story is "a sequence of actions performed or suffered by certain actors." I want "to follow stories that enable us to understand history" (2004, 190). This volume is an attempt to understand history as it is narrated for the Arab publics by Al Jazeera Arabic and thus to deconstruct events in the Al Jazeera narrative.

Many types of events constitute social reality. However, not all events are equally newsworthy (Fransozi 2004, 168), crucial, or pivotal. By pivotal, I mean the events that are in some way contentious, dramatic, or highly significant for the Arab publics, and often the rest of the world. Fransozi quotes Weber regarding the infinite richness of such events, writing, "The quality of an event as a 'social-economic' event is not something which it possesses 'objectively'. It is rather conditioned by the orientation of our cognitive interest, as it arises from the specific cultural significance which we attribute to the particular event in a given case" (Weber 1949, 64 or Franzosi 2004, 188). Bourdieu speaks about the difference between collective events such as wars, crises, and the like versus individual events such as personal encounters. Collective events remain in the collective memory and have the potential to change the collective consciousness. Activation of these collective memories can serve as a mechanism for mobilization (Bourdieu 1979, 110). To paraphrase Bourdieu, this work does not focus on ephemeral or superficial events. The impact of events here is measured by their contentious nature— not necessarily as real-life events but as galvanizing or divisive forces—that is, their salience for social reality.

Braudel, in his book *On History*, explains that "we can see in advance which events are important, which ones will have consequences. Which ones will affect the future" (1982, 84). He adds that exceptional events have an impact on the order of events (1982, 99–136). An "event," for the purposes of this book, can be defined as a happening that occurs in a specific context that can lead to, as Braudel wrote, "a whole chain of events" (1982, 28). In the 1950s, Eckstein devised twelve measures of event characteristics on domestic conflict from his study of 113 countries, based on the New York Times Index: "internal warfare, turmoil, rioting, large-scale terrorism, small-scale terrorism, mutinies, coups, plots, administrative actions, quasi-private violence, total number of unequivocal acts of violence

(UE), and total number of unequivocal plus equivocal acts of violence" (cited in Franzosi 2004, 37).

Drawing on the author's dataset, the analysis in this chapter seeks to answer the following questions:

1. **What was the role of Al Jazeera in paving the way for the Arab Spring uprisings?**
   Al Jazeera spent more than a decade before the Arab Spring building an atmosphere of vigorous debate in a region notoriously intolerant of dissent. Amid this debate, the network presented its own alternative to military authoritarian rule in the Arab Mediterranean, a sort of Islamized neo-pan-Arabism.

2. **How did the network's involvement change during its coverage of the revolutions?**
   To report on the unexpected rash of liberalization movements amidst significant government pushback, the network had to devise innovative reporting methods. Additionally, it faced the jailing and killing of its journalists at the hands of the governments they were reporting on.

3. **How do Al Jazeera's unconventional origins inform its conception of pan-Arabism, its motivations, and its unique power as the strongest media voice in the Arab world?**
   The network's unusual founding and ongoing political and financial alliances, this book will argue, have more to do with its current project of democratized pan-Arabism than has been presumed by prominent observers of the network.

4. **What is Al Jazeera's role in shaping the internal dynamics of the Arab world and the diaspora?**
   The network's programming betrays a worldview that includes a strong current of *khaljana*, domination by Arab Gulf ideas and culture over those of the Maghreb (northern Africa).

5. **What bearing does Al Jazeera's newfound political influence have on the world—namely, through the lens of global Islam and international relations? What does Al Jazeera have to say, directly or indirectly, about the rise of Islamic fundamentalism, the victory of Islamist parties in the first democratic elections after the Arab Spring, the Islamic diaspora and non-Muslim political actors in the West, the US "war on terror," and the Arab–Israeli conflict? In what ways does Al Jazeera function as an incubator, domesticator, and protector of Arab democracy? What implications**

does the involvement of this new global player hold for foreign policy? How does Al Jazeera envision its own future and the future of the Arab World amid the global power structure?

What is meant by "new pan-Arabism," "Islamized pan-Arabism," and *khaljana* of the Arab world? Is Al Jazeera not only a pan-Arab network, but also a pan-Islamic network? Is the influence of Sheikh Yusuf al-Qaradawi, through his weekly program and other appearances, enough evidence to classify Al Jazeera Arabic as an international Islamic television network with an Islamizing impact?

This may be a controversial question; however, the data collected in the course of this study provide sufficient evidence to expand this argument, which is the same argument made by the author in an earlier article (Cherribi 2006). It is an argument that is gaining traction of late, and it is increasingly being pointed out and supported by others (Talon 2011; el-Qadiri-Issa 2008).

The manner in which Al Jazeera framed the Arab Spring and employed a recently developed "political agenda" worried oppositional networks in the Arab world and in several Western countries. Al Jazeera has won nearly every major battle it has fought. It deflected the harsh criticism of President George W. Bush's secretary of defense, Donald Rumsfeld. It survived verbal attacks and political pressure from former French president Nicolas Sarkozy. It thrived during more direct crackdowns by the Arab world's most ruthless rulers and dictators.

Al Jazeera is entering a new phase of its existence—one in which the vast majority of politicians and activists see substantial benefits in maintaining an accord with the network, and consequently eschew overt attempts to undermine it. The current Egyptian regime is a notable exception. The el-Sisi government has shut down Al Jazeera's headquarters in Cairo, jailed the network's journalists and sentenced in absentia its religious voice, Yusuf al-Qaradawi, to death. Yet, true to form, Al Jazeera continues its broadcast in Egypt via a secured satellite presence.

From Friday Marches to Million-Person Marches

Naming Fridays is a tradition that was established by Al Jazeera. The first "day of rage" of the Arab Spring occurred in Egypt on Tuesday, January 25, 2011, and was followed three days later by a "Friday of Rage," called for by Yusuf al-Qaradawi, on January 28, 2011. The evolution of the convention of naming Fridays as days of rage and anger, of occasions for peaceful demonstrations, is significant for what it can tell us about the entity from which it originates. The named Friday protests began during the Arab Spring as demonstrations with universal appeal that were inclusive of both religious and the secular factions. They became progressively more religious in tone, which helps explain, in part, the emergence of the parties of political Islam at the helm of revolutionary movements. Finally, they became vehicles of democratic deliberations, especially in Syria where protesters agreed on using social media to name Fridays.

Syria has been the site of more named Fridays than Egypt. Between 2012 and 2013, the frequency of demonstrations remained steady in Syria while declining in Egypt. An explanation for this could be that religious leaders did not call for demonstrations during the Muslim Brotherhood's rule. Days of rage returned with el-Sisi's rise to power, with a Friday of Rage organized as recently as August 7, 2015. The data urge us to ask how it is possible that the peaceful demonstrations in Syria turned into a civil war, while Egyptian protests resulted in a regime change. However, this is unfortunately not a question that this book can answer.

In Egypt, peaceful demonstrations toppled the Mubarak regime, but they would also serve as justification for the reestablishment of military rule. Following the ouster of Mohamed Morsi, the naming of Fridays took a new turn. The Muslim Brothers' civil rights organizations and the military, under General el-Sisi, both participated in named Friday demonstrations. Fridays became an instrument of protest and contestation for both secular and religious causes.

Similar tendencies exist in other countries, like Tunisia and Syria, where pro-regime forces also named their own Fridays. The data show that under the Morsi regime, Friday demonstrations in Egypt were almost exclusively carried out by anti-Muslim Brotherhood protesters. However, a significant intensification of daily and Friday demonstrations by both pro- and anti-Morsi groups followed the June 2013 ouster of the Morsi government, along with marathon sit-ins in Rabaa. It was at this point that *milyoniya* (million-person march) became part of the contestation lexicon of the Friday marches. This is often referred to as the Milyoniya-t-jumu'a-t-al-ghadab (the Friday Million March of Rage). Even in Tunisia, a small country, protests took on the title "million march of thousands of people [*sic*]." On June 30, 2013, General el-Sisi of Egypt spoke about *milyoniyat*, "million-person marches," in the plural. The response of the Muslim Brotherhood was to call for daily *milyoniyat* during the holy month of Ramadan, which was a daunting and impressive task, since the protesters could not drink or eat between sunrise and sunset. These sit-ins continued for forty-three days until the security forces' crackdown. The naming of Fridays for protests and demonstrations is now an established tradition throughout the Arab world, except for in Morocco, where demonstrations more commonly take place on Sunday. As demonstrated in figure 1, there is a frequency of secular versus religious slogans during protests, by country, across the Arab world between 2011 and 2013. As shown in the chart, secular slogans outnumbered religious slogans in all countries, with the exception

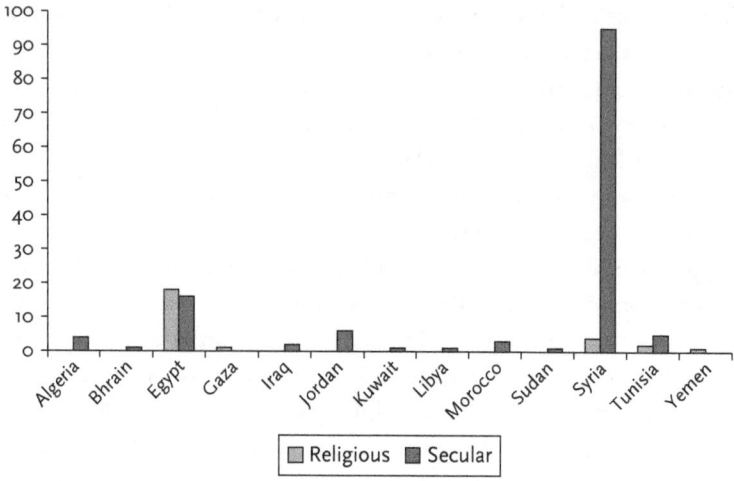

FIGURE 1 Secular versus Religious Friday Protest Slogans, 2011–2013

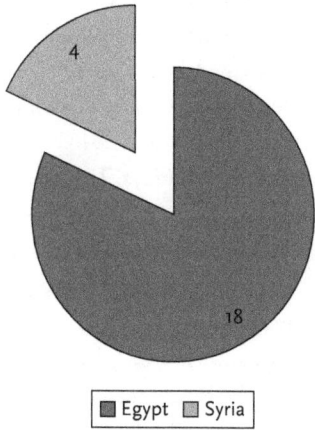

FIGURE 2 Number of Religious Protests in Egypt and Syria, 2011–2013

of Egypt, where religious slogans were slightly more prevalent. In Syria, by contrast, secular slogans dwarfed appeals to religion.

The day of rage was not invented in Egypt, though. According to the data, the first time a protest was labeled as such was during the Intifada of Al Aqsa in Jerusalem, on October 6, 2000. May 15, 2004, saw another Arab day of rage against Israel, followed by an Afghani day of rage against the US Army on May 29, 2006. In 2006, a day of rage was organized for Al Aqsa Mosque. That same year, days of rage were organized against Pope Benedict XVI as well as the Dutch *Jyllands-Posten* cartoons. Despite this legacy, the day of rage in Egypt served as a signal of a new day, the day of rage became a founding moment in Egypt's history, as represented in figure 2.

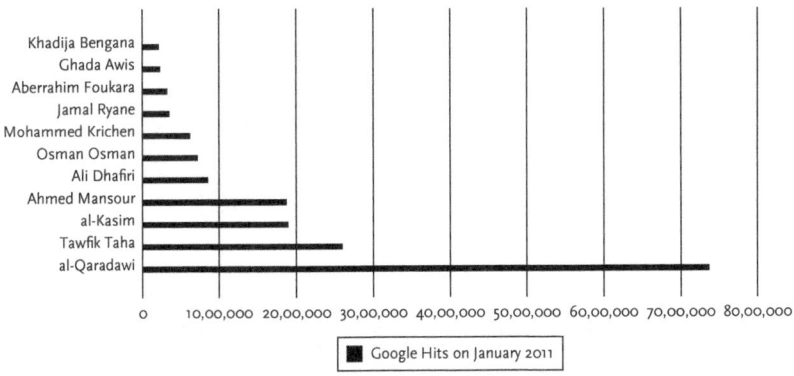

FIGURE 3 Google Hits of Al–Jazeera Contributors, January 2011

Anchors and Presenters

While it is helpful to identify Al Jazeera's most influential programs, it must be noted that the network's influence also rests on the popularity of its individual personalities. Figure 3 lists Al Jazeera's ten most popular anchors and presenters, as well as Yusuf al-Qaradawi, ranked by the number of Google search results for their names. These results come from a larger table of forty presenters and anchors. The names of correspondents are not included in the table, because their occasional use of pseudonyms makes it impossible to directly compare their name recognition in this manner. Al-Qaradawi nets nearly three times the number of results as the next person on the list. There is also a notable drop-off in popularity after the top three presenters, Tawfiq Taha, Faisal al-Kasim, and Ahmed Mansour. Saudi-born Ali Dafiri follows this group with less than half the number of search results netted by Mansour. The first female anchor on the list is Ghada Awis, from Lebanon, with a little more than a quarter of the hits of Dafiri. The Algerian star Khadija Ben Gana, who became world famous after she decided to wear the veil in her interview with a French minister at the height of the controversy over the French veil legislation in 2003, is the second most popular women, rounding out the bottom of the ten most popular presenters and anchors (again, the list has a total of eleven names, as al-Qaradawi is neither a presenter nor an anchor). Of the forty anchors and presenters who commonly appeared on Al Jazeera during the periods described in this book, thirty are men: eighteen from the Mashreq, six from the Maghreb, five from the Khaleej, and one from sub-Saharan Africa. Of the ten women, five are from the Mashreq and five are from the Maghreb (figure 4).

Frequency of the Topics by Program

Al Jazeera content in the dataset was analyzed via categorization. For Al Jazeera programs, excluding *Sharia and Life*, the categories consisted of political conflict,

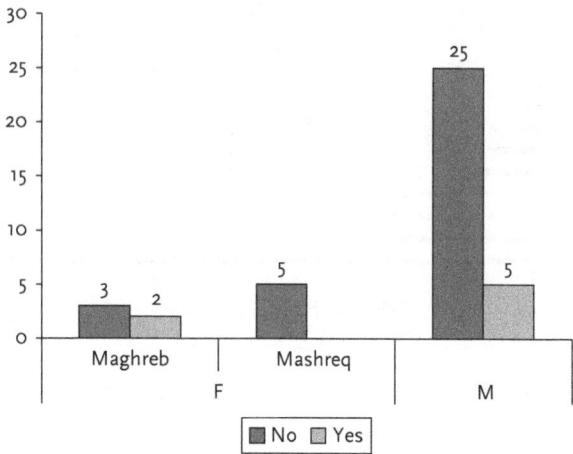

FIGURE 4 Veil (Women) and Headgear (Men) by Anchor on Al Jazeera

the Arab Spring, Islamists or political Islam, the Muslim world and the West, general interest, Islamic banking and economy, women's issues and inequality, and minorities. Gaza was added to this list after it became apparent that there was a marked shift of attention by the network from the West Bank to Gaza after 2005. The same categories were applied to topics of *Sharia and Life*, in addition to Sharia, Islamic rituals and morals, spirits and the unseen, and democracy in the Arab world (figure 7).

Arab Spring

The Arab Spring was the most common topic of *Talk of the Revolution* during 2011 and 2012, spotlighted in 323 episodes (223 in 2011 and 100 in 2012). During this period, *In Depth* covered the Arab Spring 53 times, *Without Borders* 44 times, and *Opposite Direction* 53 times. These programs generally air 54 times per year, meaning more than half of all episodes were devoted entirely to the Arab Spring. *Talk of the Revolution* is a newer program that aired almost daily and sometimes twice a day or more during this period. The program is a talk show about the revolutions, which explains the concentration and the focus on the Arab Spring. Figure 7 shows the percentage of Al Jazeera's Arab Spring coverage represented by each of the major shows that frequently reported on the revolutions.

During the months of January to May 2011 the total number of shows focused on the Arab Spring peaked, as shown in figure 5. After this period, Syria remained a major focus of the network's coverage. However, revolution and resistance in the rest of the Arab world declined in frequency as a topic, especially after the Muslim Brotherhood gained power in Egypt. The diminished airtime devoted to Egypt was marked by predominantly favorable coverage for the new Muslim Brothers'

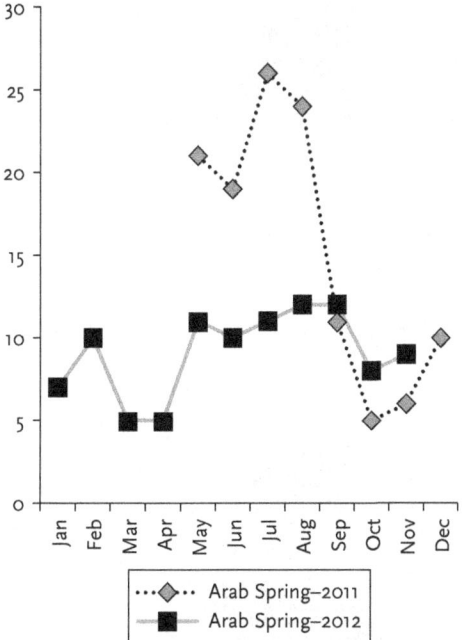

FIGURE 5 *Talk of the Revolution* Episodes Focusing on Arab Spring, 2011 and 2012

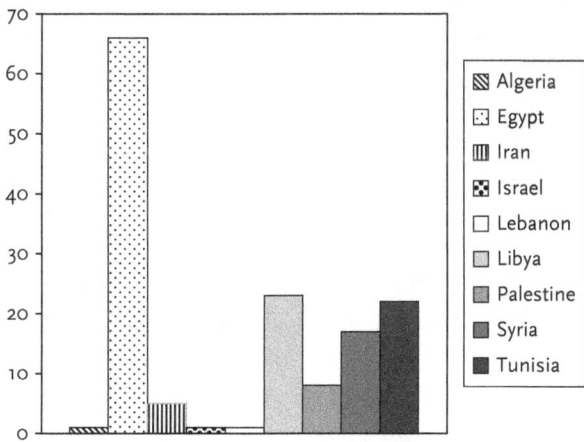

FIGURE 6 Revolution as a Topic per Country on Al-Jazeera, 1997–2012

government, a notable departure from the network's doctrine of focusing on antigovernment or antiestablishment messages. Despite this change following the fall of the Mubarak government, figure 6 shows that revolution was a far more common topic of coverage in Egypt than in any other country during the period observed.

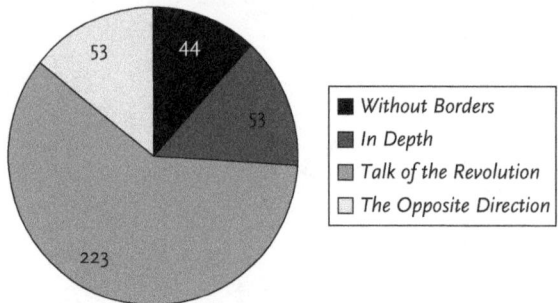

FIGURE 7 Number of Arab Spring Topics on Four Popular Shows, 2010–2012

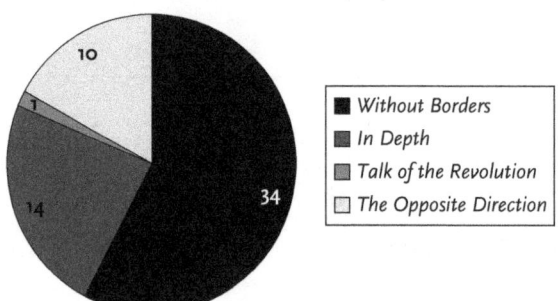

FIGURE 8 Number of Episodes Dealing with Political Islam by Show, 2011–2012

Political Islam and Political Conflict

From the early years of Al Jazeera, topics such as *qahr* (oppression), political conflict, and political Islam played a major role on the network. *Without Borders*, hosted by Ahmed Mansour, focused thirty-four of its episodes on political Islam in 2011 and 2012.

As shown in figure 8, this represented a majority of the network's coverage of political Islam during this period. *In Depth* aired 14 episodes on the topic, followed by *The Opposite Direction* with 10. Although *qahr* has been referenced by Al Jazeera programs since the network's inception, *The Opposite Direction* was the first program to make *qahr* a major topic of debate. The presenter, Faisal al-Kasim, continuously drew a link between the dictatorships of the Arab world and the marginalization of Arab countries. This focus on *qahr* mirrors al-Kasim's focus throughout 2006 and 2007 on the link between a lack of democracy and stagnation in Arab countries. Focus on each of these topics peaked during this two-year period. *Talk of the Revolution* had the least number of episodes on political Islam in 2011 and 2012. However, the program's 2013 format was devoted almost entirely to political Islam, with 90 percent of the episodes focused on the

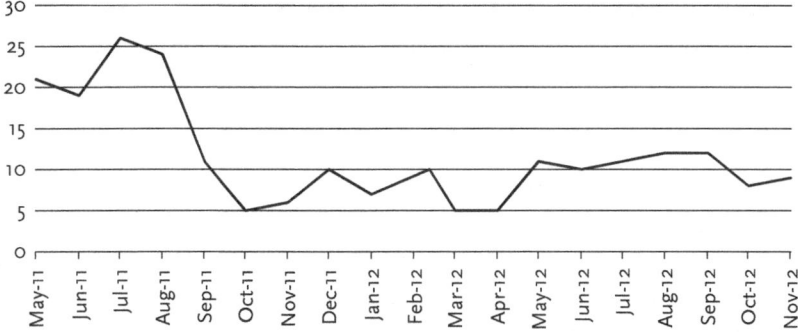

FIGURE 9 Number of Episodes Dealing with Political Conflict by Show, 2011–2012

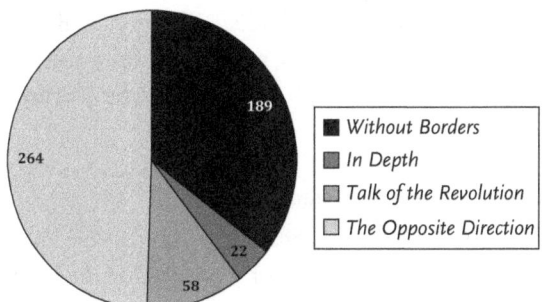

FIGURE 10 Number of *Talk of the Revolution* Episodes Focusing on Arab Spring, 2011–2012

Muslim Brotherhood. *The Opposite Direction* aired 264 episodes on political conflict during the period observed, followed by *Talk of the Revolution* (58) and *In Depth* (22). Figures 8–10 illustrate these trends.

Islam and the West

Islam's role in Europe peaked as a topic in Al Jazeera's programming in 2006 and 2007. This spike in coverage can be attributed largely to the Danish cartoon controversy and the "anti-Islam" statement of Pope Benedict XVI.

Islamic Banking

Islamic banking peaked as a topic on Al Jazeera's shows in 2008 and continued to receive steady attention in the years after, driven by the economic crisis in the West, which had little negative impact on Islamic banking. Islam in the West and Islamic banking have been dominant topics throughout much of Al Jazeera's history. Before the Arab Spring, Islamic banking was as important as political conflict on *Sharia and Life*. But beginning in 2011 the Arab Spring and political conflict became the main issues, at least for all the episodes featuring al-Qaradawi (the vast majority of the show's episodes). Figures 11–14 demonstrate the interdependence between the topics of *Sharia and Life*, Islamic banking, and political conflict.

Maghreb, Mashreq, and Khaleej

In the dataset from 1998 to 2012 there were 313 episodes devoted entirely to the Mashreq region, 72 to the Maghreb region, and 28 to the Khaleej region (figure 15). The Maghreb and the Mashreq were also topics of news and news reports. However, a count of these occurrences would be redundant, as the main news bulletin, *Harvest of the Day*, deals specifically with news in the Mashreq and Khaleej regions, with only sporadic focus on the Maghreb during times of major events. There is a special news bulletin for the Maghreb called *Harvest of the Magreb* that airs after the main news program in the Maghreb market. This division demonstrates the marginal position of the Maghreb in Al Jazeera's programing.

Gaza and Al Aqsa Mosque in Jerusalem

In 1998 the number of episodes solely about Gaza was very low. By 2006 it had grown to 18 percent, then 31.5 percent of shows during the Israeli siege of Gaza in 2008 and 23 percent in 2012. Many episodes were devoted to the Al Aqsa

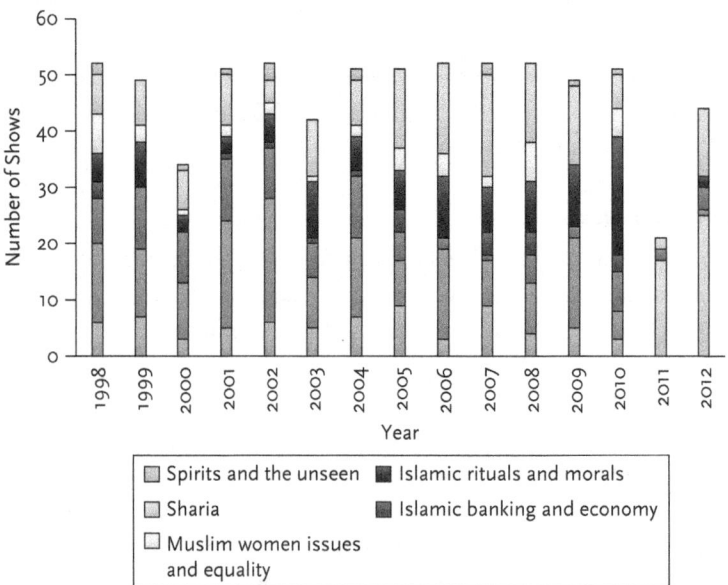

FIGURE 11 Episodes on Islam in the West versus Islamic Banking, 2006–2012

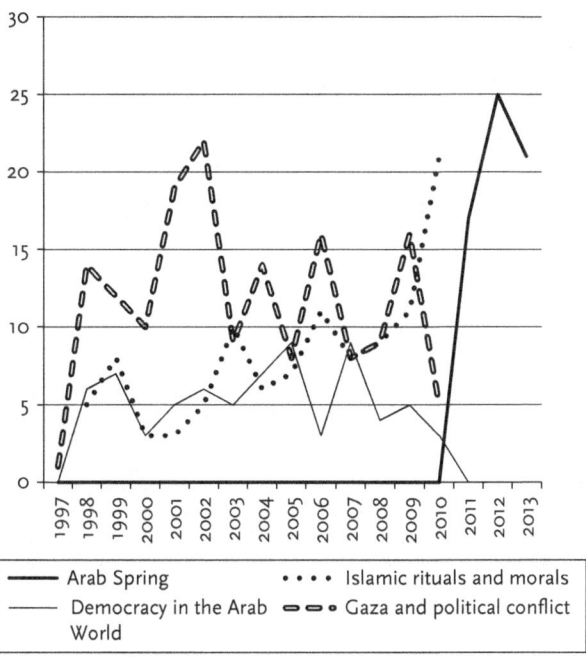

FIGURE 12 Focus of *Sharia and Life* Shows on Islamic Banking versus Democracy, 1998–2010

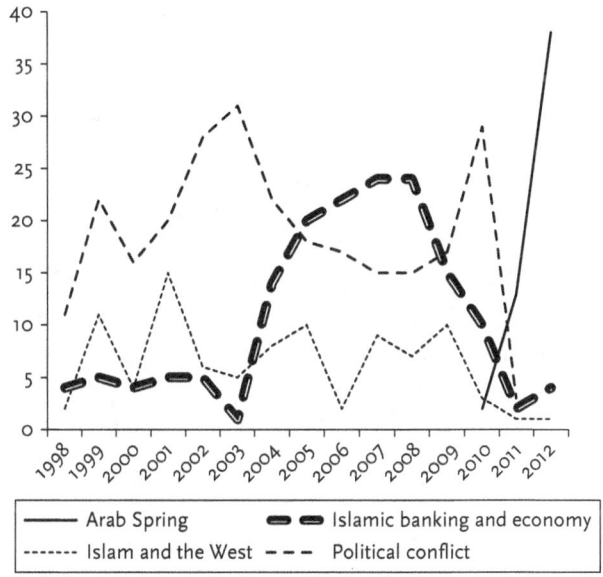

FIGURE 13 *Sharia and Life* per Topic, 1998–2012

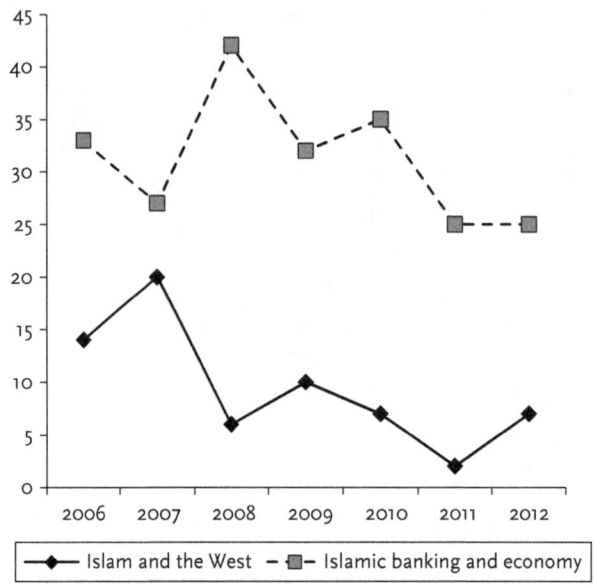

FIGURE 14 *Opposite Direction* Topics Compared, 1997–2013

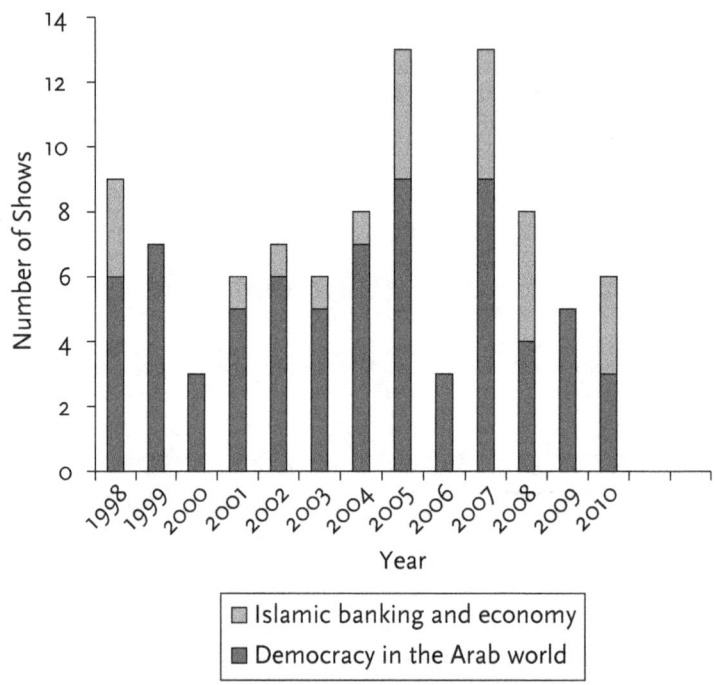

FIGURE 15 *Opposite Direction* Topics Compared, 1998–2012

Mosque and the dangers of Israeli excavations under the mosque that could lead to its total destruction. There was an annual commemoration of the burning down of the Al Aqsa Mosque beginning in 2004. Many episodes of various programs featured official visits to the mosque by Arab political or religious leaders as a symbol of support for the Palestinians or alternatively as recognition of the state of Israel. Figures 16–18 represent the production strategies of Al Jazeera with respect to Israelis and Palestinians.

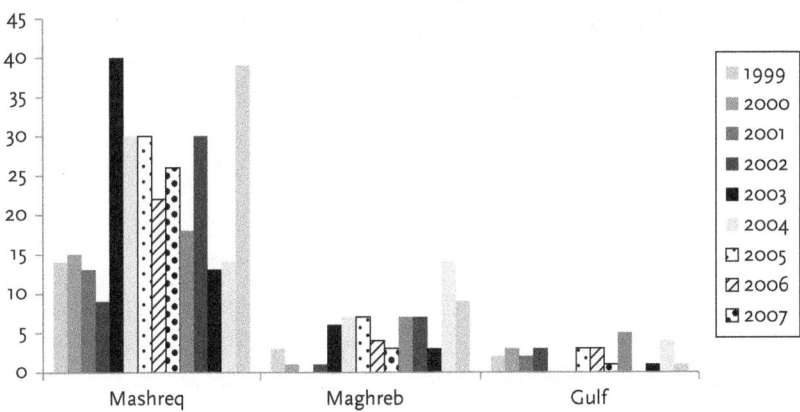

FIGURE 16 Weight of the Mashreq as a Topic on Al Jazeera Shows, 1999–2007

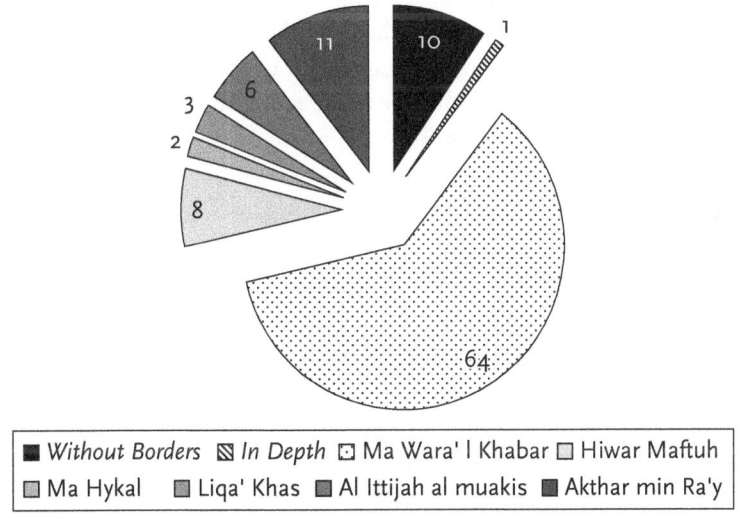

FIGURE 17 Number of Shows about Palestine on Al Jazeera, 1997–2013

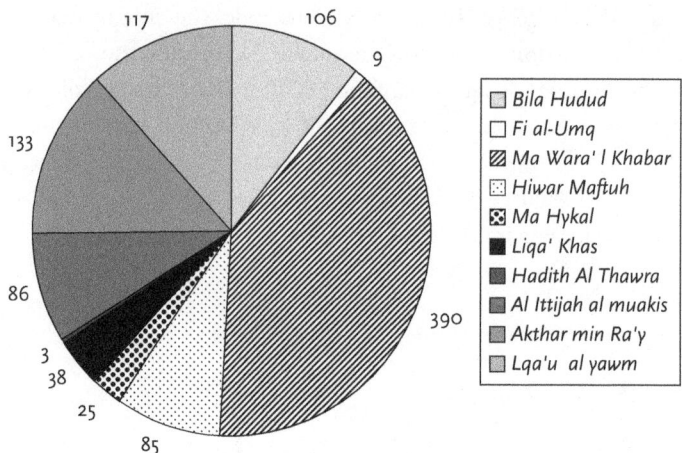

FIGURE 18 Percentage of Gaza Episodes on Popular Shows, 2006–2013

Minorities in the Arab World

Most of Al Jazeera's programs covered minorities in Iraq, Syria, and Turkey (mainly with reference to Kurds). However, neither Berbers nor Copts were identified as minority populations. More than six episodes of *What's Behind the News* (*Mawara' al khabar*) dealt with the refusal of Kurds to accept the Arab and Islamic identity of Iraq in 2005. Since 2010, episodes on minorities have dealt predominantly with the autonomy of Kurdistan and the crisis between Turkey and the Kurds. The conflict between Shia, Sunni, and Kurds appeared on Al Jazeera as a topic beginning in 2005. In 2006, Al Jazeera staunchly supported Hezbollah, portraying Nasrallah as a hero. Later coverage, especially after the start of the Syrian conflict and civil war, became more clearly critical of the Shia and portrayed Hezbollah as the pawn of a demonized Iran. Even the Global Mufti, Yusuf al-Qaradawi, renounced his previous support for Hezbollah, saying that he had believed the group would be inclusive of the Sunni perspective. He praised the *ulama* (Religious scholars) of Saudi Arabia as less naive than Egyptians like himself when dealing with Iran, due to familiarity and close proximity.

From 2001 to 2010 there were programs about Berbers in Algeria's Kabylie region, the conflict between Berbers and the Algerian government, and the Berber revolution, which never turned into a Berber Spring. In 2010 there was a focus on the Berber languages of the Maghreb and the consequences of having a Berber language spoken on TV in the Maghreb.

The Crisis of the Veil and Headgear

As noted earlier, thirty of the forty anchors and presenters examined in the author's analysis of Al Jazeera are men and ten are women. Only five of the thirty men wear any sort of headgear—three from Qatar, two from Saudi Arabia, and the Egyptian-born al-Qaradawi, who —who wears the Al Azhar University robe and headgear. Of the ten female anchors, only three wear a veil. Two are from Algeria and one is an Egyptian who moved to Al Jazeera Mubasher in Egypt and became an important anchor on the channel. She became the subject of international news when security forces stormed her studio while she was broadcasting live, just hours after the speech by General el-Sisi that marked the fall of President Morsi. This reveals that wearing headgear or the veil is not of significance for Al Jazeera's anchors.

Qatar in the News

Qatar was systematically reported on but never within the political conflict frame, except regarding the border programs with Bahrain and a crisis between Jordan and Qatar. The rest of the episodes dealt with the future of politics in Qatar and the activities of the emir of Qatar in the world, most often his charitable work in Gaza. The abdication of the emir in the summer of 2013 garnered much attention. The active involvement of Qatar in the Arab Spring has been heavily reported on since 2011, mainly in Tunisia, Egypt, Syria, and Gaza.

These data show that criticism of Al Jazeera as *not* being critical of Qatar is not completely accurate. Indeed, Qatar has never been portrayed negatively, but honest questions about the role of Qatar have been asked when ministers or even the emir were interviewed. Also, the website, aljazeera.net, is full of comments criticizing Qatar. The thesis of Talon's book about the lack of news about Qatar on Al Jazeera does not appear to match up with the data.

The dataset (1998–2013) shows that Al Jazeera focused most of its attention on Egypt, Tunisia, and Gaza throughout the period. Syria became a major focal point after the Arab Spring. Similarly, Iraq was an important topic during the Iraq war. The life cycles of Al Jazeera's major conflict topics show Al Qaeda as an important topic until the death of Bin Laden, Iraq between the invasion and the drawdown of US forces, and Hezbollah during its war with Israel in 2006. However, Egypt, Tunisia, and Gaza received constant attention throughout the sixteen-year life span of Al Jazeera. Short-term attention was given to Libya, Yemen, and briefly Bahrain during the Arab Spring. Syria, on the other hand, has captured the network's full attention since its first clandestine protests against the regime. At that time, Al Jazeera had difficulty finding footage of the demonstrations. Now the network is constantly with the free army and the rebels. As shown in figure 19, Al Jazeera prioritizes coverage of certain countries while deemphasizing Gulf state countries.

The map of the topics featured on Al Jazeera programs over a long period of time (1996–2013) reveals both moments of hostility and moments of peace and friendship, between Qatar, Saudi Arabia, the Muslim Brotherhood, and other Gulf countries. There is a noticeable discontinuity in the friendship between the Muslim Brotherhood and Arab Emirates, compared with a very warm relationship with Qatar and ambiguity with Saudi Arabia. In the past, exiled Muslim Brothers tended to enjoy influence and sanctuary in only one or two countries. For example, Azzedine Ibrahim went to the UAE, al-Qaradawi to Qatar, and Said Ramadan to Switzerland.

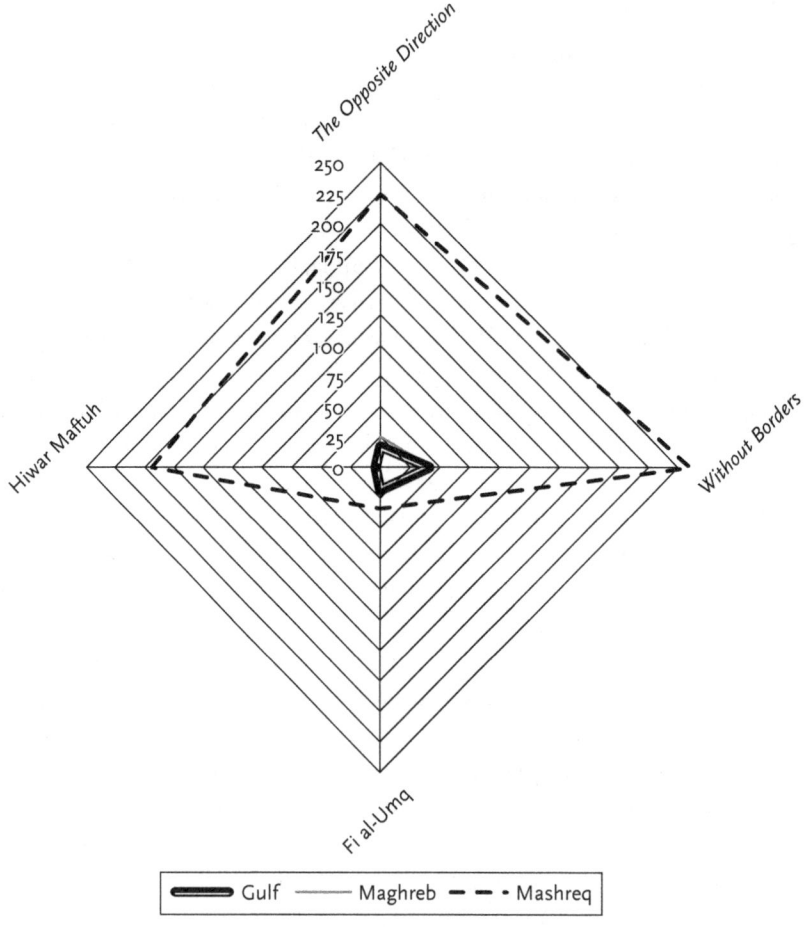

FIGURE 19 Gulf Cities under the Radar of Political News, 1997–2013

Recently, the relationship between Qatar and Saudi Arabia has been improving. The chair of the board of Al Jazeera, Sheikh Hamad bin Thamer al-Thani, visited Saudi Arabia in 2007 to help thaw the chilly relationship between Al Jazeera and Saudi Arabia. This marked the start of a period where Al Jazeera toned down its criticism of the kingdom. After Sheikh Hamad bin Khalifa al-Thani abdicated and transferred the throne to his son, Tamim, weeks before the deposing of President Morsi, the warm relationship between Qatar and the Muslim Brothers, Yusuf al-Qaradawi, and Ahmed Mansour did not suffer as Gulf newspapers had predicted.

Three chapters of this book focus on Al Jazeera's coverage of Tunisia and Egypt. Yemen, Bahrain, and Syria are referenced *en passant* throughout the book in order to maintain the focus on the Al Jazeera–Arab Spring nexus. Because of the overwhelming and rapid changes in the political situation, it became necessary to compress chapters dealing with less recent events in order to give more space to recent developments. This was especially true regarding the fluid situation in Egypt. This work analyzes the widely perceived failure of Al Jazeera to cover events in Bahrain and the decidedly partisan coverage of Syria. In fact, many Al Jazeera interviewees complained about biased coverage of the Bahrain uprising, and at least three Al Jazeera journalists resigned because they felt growing bias had undermined the organization's journalistic mission. The same happened in Egypt after the takeover by General el-Sisi.

The Roadmap of the Book

This book is divided into two parts, based on the unifying and divisive impacts of Al Jazeera on the Arab world. Part I focuses on the unifying momentum Al Jazeera has supplied in the Arab world.

The present chapter discusses the dataset for all Al Jazeera Arabic programs from 1998 to 2013, as well as the theory, concepts, and methods used in the analysis of the data.

Chapter 2, "The Symbolic World of Al Jazeera," explores Al Jazeera's origins in a failed partnership between the Saudi government and the BBC, and its emergence as the Arab world's preeminent international news network, funded by the emir of Qatar. The chapter details the importance of complex symbolism in building the network into a cyber homeland for disaffected or regionally dispersed Muslims.

Chapter 3, "A Tinderbox for the Revolution: Subjectivity and Resistance," deals with the self-immolation of the Tunisian fruit vendor Mohamed Bouazizi as the catalyst for the revolutionary wildfire that swept across the Arab world. The chapter discusses Al Jazeera's initial struggle to cover the event amidst a regime-ordered media blackout and its instrumental role in covering the events that would lead to the fall of the former president Ben Ali. The chapter also notes the evolution of Bouazizi's death in the popular mind from profane suicide to sacred martyrdom. This is an early example of a theme that would become common throughout the Arab Spring movements, where secular and formerly profane acts were ensconced in religious terminology, while religious activists co-opted the secular language of young demonstrators.

Chapter 4, "Gaza: A Perennial Arab Spring," deals with Al Jazeera's long history covering Gaza, Hamas, and the Palestinian question. Al Jazeera's reporting on leaked Palestinian Authority documents diverted the network's attention from the revolutionary environment in North Africa just as the Jasmine Revolution was reaching its climax and the Egyptian revolution was nearing a boiling point. The network's preoccupation with a story that served little more purpose than to embarrass the Palestinian Authority is exemplary of the network's solidarity with Hamas, which appears to trump the network's dedication to other Arab and Palestinian social movements. In the democratically elected, theologically driven Hamas government, one can see a beta version of the democratic Islamist political ideal that the network would openly advocate in postrevolutionary Tunisia and Egypt.

Chapter 5, "Secret Mission: Shining a Spotlight on Tahrir Square," traces the crucial events in Al Jazeera's coverage of the Egyptian revolution. This includes the closing of Al Jazeera's Cairo bureau on January 30, 2011, and the network's subsequent round-the-clock coverage of protests in Tahrir Square. The chapter draws on transcripts of interviews and television segments to illustrate how the network acted as a rallying force for demonstrators. We also see how Al Jazeera's embrace of the revolution brought with it an infusion of religious language and imagery to a movement that had previously communicated in a predominantly secular language. This is exemplified by the series of fatwas and appearances by Yusuf al-Qaradawi, the religious voice of the network.

Part II of the book discusses Al Jazeera's position at the center of a number of global fissures and sources of discord. As established in the preceding chapters, Al Jazeera is a strong force in promoting identification frames within the Arab Gulf. The network is also a force for the *khaljana* effect on the Muslim diaspora around the world. For Arabs living in Europe, Al Jazeera offers a picture of a unified Arab identity associated predominantly with the religious and cultural norms of the Gulf region, to the exclusion of the customs of the Mashreq and the Maghreb. Al Jazeera's advocacy of a unified—and arguably quite homogenized—Arab world has thrown regional and global relations into turmoil. In part II, these divisive global impacts are explored in Muslim communities abroad, particularly in Europe and the United States.

Chapter 6, "Exile on Paradise Square," details how Al Jazeera turned a negative situation following Mohamed Morsi's ouster into an advantageous one. How can losers set the political agenda for the winners in the eyes of the Arab publics? On July 3, 2013, the Egyptian general Fattah el-Sisi seized power from Morsi following popular demonstrations against the democratically elected leader. Al Jazeera Mubasher and many religious media outlets were shut down and many of their journalists arrested. This chapter details how Al Jazeera's coverage, along with the authoritarian tactics of the el-Sisi government, served to sanitize the image of the Morsi administration and reframe the Muslim Brotherhood as, above all else, a force for democracy in Egypt.

Chapter 7, "Bullets of Truth and Media Martyrdom," explores the "insurrectional moments" of the Arab Spring that contributed to refining and expanding the repertoire of frames that Al Jazeera developed to perfection in its fifteen years of existence preceding the Arab revolutions. The chapter illustrates how recurring use of imagery and catchphrases such as "bullets of truth," "dark blood," "Fridays of Rage," journalistic martyrdom, and international Islamophobia supports an array of narrative tropes, which combine to form the network's overarching frame of *qahr* (oppression).

Chapter 8, "Islam Near and Far," focuses on the influence of Al Jazeera in Western Europe and the United States. In 2007, some Arab intellectuals in Europe launched a campaign to stop Al Jazeera from being broadcast in Europe, accusing the channel of fostering extremism among Arab youths and supporting terrorism in Europe. What has happened to these opposing voices in the diaspora and what is likely to happen in the future? By looking at Al Jazeera's involvement in global controversies surrounding the issue of legislation banning the veil in France, the Paris riots of 2005, the Danish cartoon scandal, the pope's 2006 lecture at Regensburg, and the 2012 attack on the offices of *Charlie Hebdo* in Paris and the controversial movie, *Innocence of the Muslims*, in the United States, the chapter explores how Al Jazeera has been instrumental in transforming localized debates regarding immigration, assimilation, racism, and integration into major global controversies between the Arab Islamic world and the West. As noted by Al Jazeera's opponents in Europe, such media explosions and their social fallout may hold serious implications for Islamic extremism throughout the world.

Chapter 9, "The Emancipation of Political Islam?," deals with Al Jazeera as an incubator of Muslim democracy in the Arab public sphere. This chapter examines how media power set up Al Jazeera and Qatar as the brokers between Arab publics desperate for political change and political Islam as a potential alternative to the status quo of autocratic governance. In offering Islamist leaders not just a platform, but also a public forum for debate, Al Jazeera helped smooth the rough edges of political Islam. The network acted as a mirror for Islamist leaders, who might have otherwise been relegated to preaching to the converted amidst the repressive atmosphere of the totalitarianism of the Maghreb. Al Jazeera's success in breaking the coercive monopolies on communication held by Arab dictators and its claim as the voice of the champion of the Arab street can be described as the first revolution in the twenty-first century in the Arab world. The network's spread of the ideology of pan-Arab unity and democracy can also be described as a revolution against submission. Finally, the network's domestication of political Islam can be described as a revolution of the contentious relationship between Islam and democracy. These three revolutions changed the dynamics of power relationships in the Arab world.

2 THE SYMBOLIC WORLD OF AL JAZEERA

It took me more than two years of contemplating which media outlet I should talk with, whether Al Jazeera or the other Arab channels, before I read in some newspaper that Bush was against Al Jazeera. I knew then that what doesn't fit Bush, fits me.

—Muhammad Hassanein Heikal (Al Jazeera, July 8, 2004)[1]

This phenomenon, the Al Jazeera effect, is reshaping the world.

—Philip Seib (2008, xii)

A clear path can be found from Al Jazeera's founding in 1996 to the events of the "Arab Spring" of 2011.

—Philip Seib (2013, vii)

This chapter focuses on the way Al Jazeera uses media frames to construct an alternative to the dominant narrative in Arabic culture. This alternative narrative undermines the importance of historic mandates or geographic holdings as the sources of regional power in favor of debate, logic, and religious devotion. It advocates a symbolic weakening of the borders between Arab states and the development of a transnational community based on shared culture, religion, and values. This chapter also examines the parallels between the growing influence of Al Jazeera and the Qatari government since the network's inception in the mid-1990s, including links between Al Jazeera's interests and the interests of its benefactor. However, in most matters, Qatar does not need to exercise overt control over editorial content, so long as the interests of the news network and the Qatari government are aligned.

Al Jazeera's story is the story of Qatar's ascension on the global stage. Set afloat by its oil-rich patron, Al Jazeera successfully rode the late-twentieth-century tech-driven wave of globalization to a position of international prominence. Al Jazeera's rise to dominance of the Arabic-language news market can be seen as the successful conversion of Qatar's natural resource wealth into cultural, political, economic, and symbolic capital. These forms of capital are the new sources of influence in the Arab world and beyond.

Qatar became the strategic fulcrum of the region by exploiting both its liquefied natural gas wealth and its crucial geographic location at the fault line between the Sunni and Shia worlds. Qatar sits wedged between Saudi Arabia, the custodian of the two holy mosques and de facto leader of the Sunni world, and Iran, the leader of the Shia world. Qatar's distinction in the Arab world stems from its willingness to use its almost limitless wealth to upset the status quo throughout the region. Consequently, the nation is the target of the slings and arrows of the entire Arab world. El-Nawawy Iskandar (2003), Aidi (2003), Lamloum (2004), and el-Oifi (2015) have all written about the effect of Qatar's funding of Al Jazeera on its diplomatic standing with its neighbors. Through its funding of the antiestablishment Al Jazeera Arabic, Qatar has stood in contrast to Saudi Arabia, which has invested in maintaining stability in the Sunni Middle East, as evidenced by its backing of Egypt's military rulers amidst crackdowns on Islamists (Nordland 2013). Al Jazeera's power rests in its ability to create a symbolic world where the region's multitude of contradictions and rival factions can interact in relative harmony. Qatar is home to the US Central Command (CENTCOM), the United States' regional military command center for the Middle East. It maintains friendly diplomatic relationships with Iran, Israel, and the Taliban. It serves as a safe harbor for leaders of political Islam who are personae non gratae in their countries of origin. Qatar's powerful presence in the media landscape through the Al Jazeera phenomenon and savvy development as an international banking hub has earned the tiny nation an outsized level of global attention and regional influence (Shadid 2013; Mehdi Lazar 2014).

Once known as a destination for regional investment, Qatar has grown into a source of funding for ventures throughout the developed world. These include European soccer teams (Paris Saint Germaine and FC Barcelona), car companies (Volkswagen), and banks (Barclays). Qatar is scheduled to host the 2022 FIFA World Cup, the preparations for which have already attracted increased attention, both positive and negative, to the country.

Qatar is the richest country in the world in terms of per capita GDP. Only a fifth of its population is native-born (Al Jazeera, October 12, 2004). This native population of roughly 250,000 constitutes a dominant minority, in the words of Amy Chua (2003), amidst a majority immigrant population made up largely of Indian, Pakistani, Egyptian, Jordanian, and Iranian nationals.

In eighteen years since the televised peaceful coup d'état of 1995 by Emir Hamad bin Khalifa al-Thani against his father, Qatar has become the envy of the world in terms of wealth as well as cultural and symbolic power, with Al Jazeera as the jewel in the crown. In addition to the country's high per capita GDP, Qatar's cultural and symbolic power is evidenced by the nation's role both as host of the 2022 FIFA World Cup and as home to and major stakeholder in the region's most influential news network.

The network originated as a British–Saudi project, but a dispute over British asylum granted to the political dissident Mohammed al-Massari led Saudi Arabia to withdraw from the project (el-Oifi 2004, 649–660). Qatar stepped in to take the Saudis' place, and the network began broadcasting from Doha just over a year into Hamad al-Thani's reign. The emir, who funded the launch of the Middle East's leader in international news, oversaw Qatar's rise as a regional cultural and diplomatic force. He made one of his wives, Sheikha Mozah bint Nasser al-Missned, the symbol of Arab feminism in a Gulf region dominated by conservative Wahhabism. In 2013, he abdicated to his younger son Tamim, perhaps in the fashion of a great soccer player leaving his career while still at the top of his game. Amidst the turmoil of the Arab Spring, Qatar saw a transition of power free from a coup or bloody revolution.

The symbolic world of Al Jazeera has four aspects. First, Al Jazeera is the new symbolic pearl of Qatar's trademark export industry, satellite television. Second, Al Jazeera promotes itself as the face of a new Arab journalism competing with world media outlets for status and credibility. Third, by making Mecca Time its operating time regime, Al Jazeera has fashioned Doha, the capital of Qatar, as a new, symbolic Mecca. Fourth, Qatari support for Arab revolutions and the prominence of political Islam on Al Jazeera are manifestations of Qatar's embrace of a new pan-Arabism that marries moderate political Islam and old pan-Arab ideology.

The following sections break down these aspects of Al Jazeera's symbolic world and analyze what they can tell us about Al Jazeera as a major driver of opinion in the global media landscape. Additionally, this chapter examines Al Jazeera's role as a transactional platform for cultural debate and how this reflects the evolution of Qatar under Emir Khalifa al-Thani as a transactional state for political, cultural, and financial interaction.

Al Jazeera: Qatar's Pearl of Rage

The logo of Al Jazeera is fascinating. A white pearl plunges with enormous speed into the turbulent blue waters of the Gulf region, the pearl loses its shiny coat when it touches the bottom of the sea, and then rises again to the surface, transformed into a pearl-shaped earring with the name "Al Jazeera" spelled in Arabic calligraphy.

Adnan Sharif, who was a general director of Al Jazeera between May and October 2003, speaks about the evolution of the logo over time: "I am proud that I designed the logo of Al Jazeera, which resembles a ball that resembles a pearl that goes into the water and comes out as Al Jazeera. Al Jazeera surpassed Arab media and Western media. The big challenge is that Al Jazeera came from an

Arab country, speaks Arabic but a different and unusual Arabic, something very unusual in the West" (Al Jazeera, October 29, 2011).

Al Jazeera pays tribute to the pearling tradition of Qatar, whose government founded and holds ownership of the network. The established tradition of pearling on the Pirate Coast and surrounding seas came to an end after the Great Depression (1929–1939) and with the rise of cheap cultured pearls from Japan, which came to dominate the world market in the following years (Lamloum 2004). But with the first oil concession in 1935 and oil production in 1949, Qatar bade farewell to the old tradition of pearling and joined the community of modern states. Toward the end of the twentieth century, Qatar began investing its accumulated oil wealth in a renewed tradition of pearling. Rather than gathering rough-shelled oysters from the depths of the sea and exporting the polished gems found within, this new industry would gather news and opinions from throughout the tumultuous region and export a polished, regionally distinctive and visually compelling product via the unending blue skies to all corners of the world. The success of Al Jazeera's business model triggered widespread competition for news in the Arab world, as evidenced by the multiplication of private and public satellite television networks since Al Jazeera's launch, a sort of twenty-first-century pearl rush. A natural pearl, no matter how well polished, is the result of its environment. Similarly, the news gathered by the Arab world's burgeoning satellite news industry can be likened to pearls that have gestated in their individual environments for years, if not decades. Despite varying degrees of private or state-led pressure on the slant of satellite media, a common trait of the news throughout the Arab Mediterranean has been rage toward authoritarian governments. Where local state-sponsored media might have concealed these pearls of rage, Al Jazeera brought them to market, for local and international appraisers alike to behold.

The World Watches CNN, and CNN Watches Al Jazeera

In the Qatari capitol of Doha, in a quiet residential area, the building that is home to the headquarters of Al Jazeera stands out in a markedly Western way. It could easily blend into any upscale business park in the United States. A white building with clean and boxy lines, it is surrounded, as is everything in Qatar, by palm trees. Its lobby might well be any lobby in any corporate headquarters in the Western world except for one overwhelming feature, a huge poster that reads "The world watches CNN, and CNN watches Al Jazeera." Although the building is less than a quarter of the size of CNN's Atlanta headquarters, the bold words resonate far beyond their surroundings. (Lamloum 2004)

It is interesting to draw a parallel between the histories of CNN and Al Jazeera. The story of CNN and its extraordinary founder are practically matters of

American lore. Ted Turner, the bombastic son of a wealthy, southern advertising maven, survived a lonely, emotionally dry childhood to become "Captain Courageous," winner of the 1977 America's Cup, the uniform-wearing owner of the Atlanta Braves, and the mastermind behind the world's first international cable television network. CNN's rise was, in fact, intrinsically linked to events in the Middle East. It was CNN's coverage of the first Gulf War that marked the network's transformation in the public mind from a media oddity to a "global news leader" (Lamloum 2004).

Some think it odd to compare the emir of Qatar and CNN's founder, Ted Turner. However, there are parallels in the creation of these two media giants. Even if Al Jazeera's staff came predominantly from the BBC, and Al Jazeera implemented BBC protocols, Al Jazeera followed CNN's model of using war reporting as a path to prominence. In the second Gulf War, Al Jazeera gathered more news from the front than CNN (el-Oifi 2011). Al Jazeera's reporters were in fierce competition with those of CNN.

Around the same time that CNN was gaining dominance of the news sphere, a young Qatari named Hamad al-Thani was defiantly carving out his place in the world. Al-Thani's family was a tribe not traditionally affiliated with the Prophet's lineage, but it nonetheless had a long history of influence in the region (Lamloum 2004; el-Oifi 2011). The family's history of Machiavellian political and diplomatic strategy dates back to its 1916 collaboration with the British against the Ottomans, followed by decades of shifting alliances with the Saudis, Iraqis, and Iranians, and would continue with the young crown prince. While Turner had bested his father in business, al-Thani bested his father, Emir Khalifa bin Hamad al-Thani, in politics. He led an unpopular but bloodless coup to become the emir of Qatar in 1995 and founded Al Jazeera shortly after his ascension to the throne (Al Hurra, June 25, 2013). He had CNN's example to follow, and his aim was to re-create the American network's international scope and reach in a distinctly Islamic image. However, with much of the network's early staff made up of former BBC employees, much of Al Jazeera's early coverage mimicked the BBC style more closely than that of the American news network (el-Nawawy and Iskander 2003; Lamloum 2004).

But al-Thani's vision of a network catering to an international Islamic community came with a price for the Arab status quo, particularly regarding the secular military governments of the Mediterranean. By embracing an Arab identity based on pan-Islamism, Al Jazeera's viewpoint would erode the multicultural, multinational, and multireligious facets of the existing Arab identity, while also undermining the multiethnic character of Islam around the world (Lamloum 2004; el-Oifi 2015). This would serve as a major factor in the growth of pan-Arabism and notions of democracy in the Arab world, both of which will be covered in later chapters.

Some now characterize Al Jazeera as the CNN of the Arab world (Amin Maalouf, France Culture, March 24, 2009), but this is not the case. As the following chapters will illustrate, Al Jazeera is not a "liberal" or "neutral" channel. Rather, it is a religious news channel that also airs occasional neutral or liberal-leaning viewpoints (Kepel 2012; Fandy 2007). If the news broadcast on Al Jazeera is pluralist, the religious message that it disseminates almost daily is mono-denominational. For example, Al Jazeera's coverage of the veil in France communicates a clear message connecting Arab and Muslim identity to a distinct interpretation of Islam, constructing an imagined transnational Muslim community (Cherribi 2006).

From its inception and launch in 1996, Al Jazeera Arabic was aimed at Arabic-speaking audiences in countries around the world. With nearly 50 million viewers worldwide, its largest audiences reside in Arab and Muslim states, followed by Europe and North America. As one might expect, much of Al Jazeera's most notable reporting has come from Arab and Muslim-majority countries. In 2003, more than a decade after CNN became the world news leader with its reporting on the first Gulf War (Talon 2011; Lamloum 2004; Kepel 2013), Al Jazeera earned global recognition for its reporting in Afghanistan and Iraq, punctuated by access in the two war zones that went far beyond that of Western media organizations. When the Taliban granted only one reporter exclusive rights to report from Kabul for two weeks, it selected Al Jazeera's Taysir Allouni. Meanwhile, Western news organizations had to depend on Al Jazeera to report statements made by the Taliban leaders. The exclusive material and interviews with Bin Laden dating back to 1998 brought Al Jazeera notoriety in Western countries. But the fact that the channel is financed primarily by the emir of Qatar and his holding companies, and that advertising sales do not cover Al Jazeera's operational costs, prompts questions regarding Al Jazeera's objectivity. Al Jazeera's reporting on the issue of the veil in France, in particular, reveals an underlying agenda.

Al Jazeera would be comparable to CNN or other US news networks if one were to remove the religious overtones from its broadcasting. The constant religious messages in its current affairs programming, including daily advertisements for the veil and an incessant drumbeat of off-the-beaten-path stories regarding the veil in Al Jazeera's daily news program, clearly distinguish Al Jazeera from its US counterparts. Al Jazeera's relentless coverage of the veil is particularly revealing. The veil is a sign of distinction—a cultural and religious symbol belonging to the imagined transnational community, the *umma*, and a "civilization message" that Al Jazeera works to construct daily by delivering certain programs and views to a wider Muslim and Arabic-speaking audience. The veil is a recognizable symbol of otherness: non-Muslims do not wear it. Consequently, Al Jazeera sees the veil as a major issue and seeks out news on the veil that often fails to appear in other news outlets. Even when Al Jazeera is not explicitly reporting on the veil, the veil appears regularly in its advertising. The author published a lengthy article on this topic (Cherribi 2006), as discussed in greater detail in chapter 8.

On April 1, 2004, Sheikh Yusuf al-Qaradawi devoted an entire one-hour episode of his show *Sharia and Life* to the prohibition of the veil in France. By focusing his program exclusively on this topic, al-Qaradawi gave religious affirmation to the view that the issue was not just a concern for Muslims in France, but a controversy demanding the strict attention of Muslims around the world. In this instance, Al Jazeera's own religious leader was validating the network's extensive coverage of the issue, enhancing the network's reputation as a watchdog for the international Muslim community. Within France and the West, the controversy over banning the veil in French schools provoked debate over the merits and limits of *laïcité*, the long-standing French policy of staunch public secularism. For viewers of Al Jazeera, especially those outside of France with no local sources of information, France's ban of the veil in schools could be understood as an act of French persecution of Muslims, another column in a Western war against Muslims that also included the US invasion of Afghanistan and Iraq (Cherribi 2008). By framing the legislation against the use of religious symbols in schools as an "invasion" of the Muslim community in France, Al Jazeera's news and current affairs programs intimated that the entire Muslim community had a duty to respond. In the words of Al Jazeera news analyst Maher Abdalah, "If you touch one finger, the whole body will react as one" (Al Jazeera, December 23, 2002).

The format of al-Qaradawi's program is common in Arab television. An imam (in this case, al-Qaradawi) discusses with laypeople or other imams questions about Sharia or the Quran's interpretation of current issues. The network is not diverging from regional media norms in offering such specifically religious programming. However, for a station that defines itself by bucking the status quo while closely adhering to Western principles of journalism, the choice to conform to this convention is in itself revealing. Al Jazeera's projected image of offering "the opinion and the other opinion" is really trompe l'oeil, a cover-up of its larger religious message. If CNN had an extremely popular Christian minister each week host a one-hour program live during prime time, offering his judgments, his prohibitions, and his pronouncements on what those in the audience may or may not do, then CNN would be approaching a Christian version of al-Qaradawi's program. The patriotic, combative, and energetic formats on Al Jazeera resemble those of Fox News, and the coverage is laden with opinion, but the similarities end there. Unlike Al Jazeera, the leading Fox current affairs program does not feature a religious leader who tells 10 million religious viewers how to interpret religious laws and is often called upon as a religious authority to speak on world affairs during the nightly evening news, as did Al Jazeera, for example, during the Paris riots in November 2005 (Cherribi 2006). With its underlying agenda and religious overtones, Al Jazeera cannot be considered the CNN, or even the Fox News, of the Arab world. The map shown here represents the global reach of al-Qaradawi's show, with an emphasis on the frequency of guests commentators from specific locations.

In its Arabic form, Al Jazeera presents Islam as an alternative to established elite, Westernized, and secularized governments, which seem to lack the home-grown credibility of more intrinsically Muslim power structures. One could argue that the pan-Arab social movement failed in the 1950s, 1960s, and 1970s largely because the various Arab states, in the absence of a faith-based approach, lacked adequate common ground to pursue a unified vision (Kepel 2013; Lamloum 2004; el-Oifi 2015). Al Jazeera has not made the same mistake. It pushes a neo-pan-Arab social ideology, undergirded by the commonality of Islam in much the same way that the neoconservative social movement in the United States is undergirded by evangelical Christian principles.

In fact, Americans might best understand the trajectory of Al Jazeera's Islamic message by comparing it with the trajectory of the neoconservative message. The neocons came sweeping into power via 1994's Contract with America, mas-terminded by Congress's social movement and Newt Gingrich because many Christians felt that the conservative power structure had neglected their interests (Cherribi 2012). Christianity, they felt, was under attack; they were oppressed by a non-Christian society. The conservative message of fiscal stringency and boot-strap social advancement was too easily portrayed as a mantra of callousness and greed. By piggybacking on evangelical Christianity, the conservative social move-ment adopted a religious vehicle for its message of conservative social policies, a vehicle that was naturally suited to "spreading the word" (Cherribi 2012).

Similarly, in the Middle East and North Africa, many religious Muslims felt abandoned by their nominally Muslim leaders. With the Waterloo of the pan-Arab social movement—the Six-Day War, which left Israel the victor over an alli-ance between Syria and Egypt—and the death of Egypt's Gamal Abdel Nasser, the idea of a unified Arab front languished, kept alive only by the Palestinians, who, because of close proximity to the victor, may have felt more compelled to do so. In Palestine, pan-Arabism remained a popular social theme, nourished by a new infusion of Islam tinged with the zealotry often found where religious individuals are oppressed. Across the Mediterranean, as communities of Muslim guest workers in Europe grew in size and number, the "othering" inherent in such waves of immigration fueled a growing perception of Islam as a religion oppressed by surrounding secular cultures alongside the kind of nostalgia for the homeland that is found only among exiles. Together, these two developments gave rise to an Islam-fueled neo-pan-Arab social movement. And all the while, the seeds were

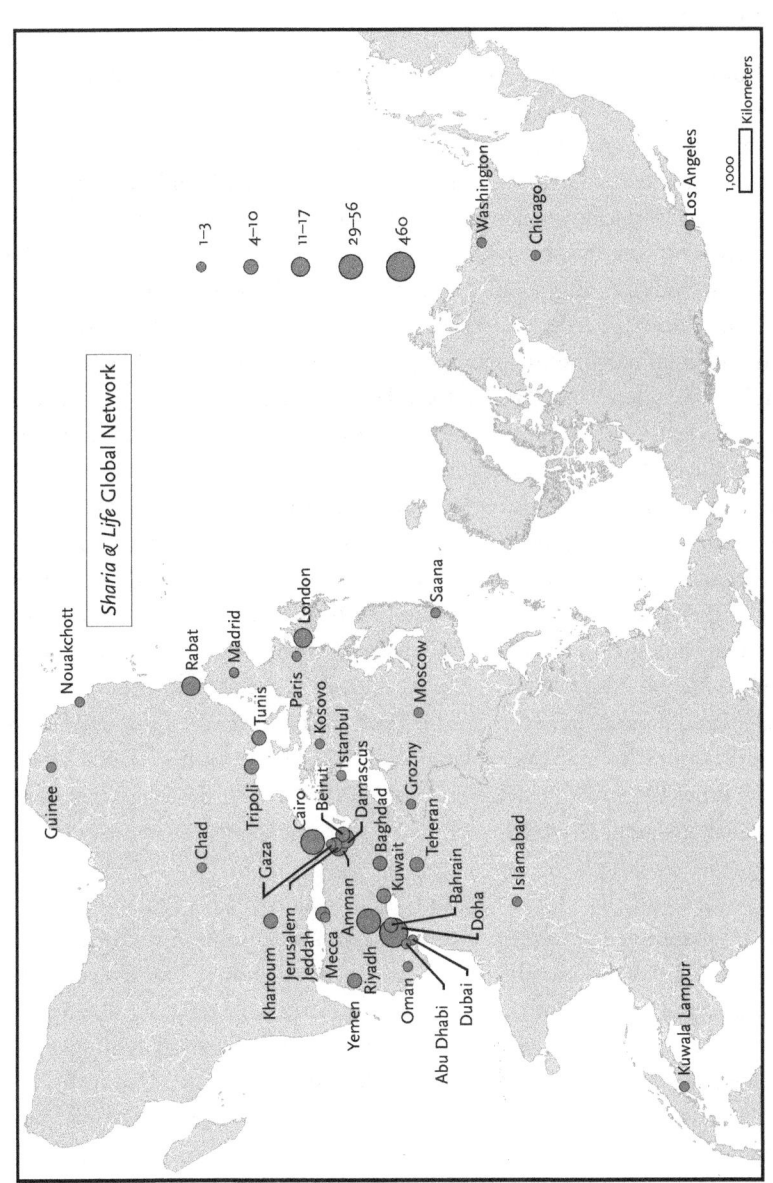

Map of *Sharia and Life* Global Network (all calculations performed by the author from the dataset)

being sown for Al Jazeera: a new voice that could broadcast the message of a neo-pan-Arab social movement to the world.

Mecca Time Regime

Efforts in the Middle East to subvert the dominance of Western culture have long included a drive to replace dominant Western indicators with cultural norms and institutions of more indigenous significance. On a cold Amsterdam day in the summer of 2011, the Dutch sociologist Johan Goudsblom recalled Khomeini's 1979 attempt to come up with an alternative system of time in Iran, to dispense with the European-influenced model, forgetting that the idea of a twenty-four-hour day originated in the Middle East, specifically in neighboring Iraq. Today efforts to replace Greenwich, UK, with the holy city of Mecca as the international baseline time zone represent similar efforts to de-Westernize cultural norms. Clerics like Yusuf al-Qaradawi have made direct appeals for such a change in the Islamic world. Meanwhile, the construction of the Abraj al-Bait, a massive tower that dwarfs London's iconic Big Ben, serves as a symbolic challenge to an international time regime that orients the entire world toward the United Kingdom. Al Jazeera has embraced this effort wholeheartedly, announcing its broadcasts in "Mecca Time," which also happens to be the same time zone as that of Doha, home to Al Jazeera's international headquarters. This focus on Mecca Time not only helps reinforce Al Jazeera's theme of a transnational Arab/Islamic *umma*, but also frames the network itself as the vehicle through which geographic boundaries between Muslims and the holy city are eliminated. This accessibility goes hand in hand with the Qatari description of Doha as the "Mecca of the vulnerable," accessible at all times via satellite broadcast regardless of financial, geographic, or other obstacles that might separate believers from the city of the Prophet.

Al Jazeera and the House of Saud are not alone in recognizing control over the measurement of time as a source of symbolic power. David Christian (2005) argues that time regimes are a new form of power that coerce individuals to agree to a certain rhythm of social, cultural, or religious life. When Al Mayadeen and other media outlets (such as the Hezbollah-aligned Al Manar) choose Jerusalem as the basis for their standard operating time, they are politicizing a landmark in Islamic culture through its cultural and symbolic power. Norbert Elias argues that time is not a natural given; rather it is a means devised by humans for comparing processes of various speeds and durations. "As such," he writes that the measure of time "is a function of 'timing'—an activity which is inherently place-bound. Four phases can be distinguished in the development leading up to universal global timing. In phase one, there are no instruments for dividing the day into clear-cut intervals such as hours. Phase two brings various instruments such as sundials and water clocks with which the day is divided in 24 hours of unequal length. In phase three, the mechanical clock makes standardization of the hour possible. In phase four, the world is divided in 24 time zones, with a synchronized schedule of hours, minutes and seconds spread globally as an invisible net" (cited in Goudsblom 1995, 22).

According Johan Goudsblom, one of the most important aspects of globalization is the widespread use, by almost all countries, of a unitary time regime. This makes it possible to calculate, with high precision, the time in any city in the world, facilitating the complicated logistics of international communication, travel, and shipping (Goudsblom 1995, 20). Goudsblom explains that coordinated universal time (UTC) standardizes the time of day but leaves in place differences regarding the measure of months or weeks based on religious, political, or cultural conventions at the local level. At the international level, the Christian model dominates.

The formation of standard time was introduced in England at the end of the eighteenth century in order to increase the efficiency and reliability of postal traffic. London was the natural central location, since it was the home of the Greenwich Observatory, which had specialized in determining time to facilitate the growth of railways since 1675. Other countries soon followed the British example (Goudsblom 1995, 32). During the International Meridian Conference in Washington, DC, in 1884, twenty-five countries agreed on today's familiar system based on a prime meridian passing through Greenwich (Goudsblom 1995, 35). In Paris in 1913, standard time was determined in its current form the Bureau International de l'Heure. The uniform time is linked to the long-term time division of the Christian era as measured by the Gregorian calendar (Goudsblom 1995, 35). The timetables do not represent an objective measure of time, but rather a regime that exists because of human coercion (Goudsblom 1995, 39).

In 2012 the Saudis built the largest clock in the world, a symbolic challenge to London's Elizabeth Tower, more commonly referred to as "Big Ben." *The Week* magazine gives the following description of the Abraj al-Bait, or Royal Mecca Clock Tower:

> Not only is it by far the world's biggest clock tower—six times larger than London's Big Ben—but at a height of 1,970 feet, it is also the second tallest building in the world. The clock's four faces stretch 151 feet in diameter, and are each inscribed with huge Arabic words reading, "God is greatest." Five times a day, 21,000 green and white LED bulbs flash as a reminder to pray, and its spire is topped with a 75-foot wide golden crescent moon. (April 13, 2010)

In the United States, the *Washington Times* took a less nuanced view of Saudi Arabia's construction of the imposing tower:

> Islamic scholars have proposed that the Royal Mecca Clock Tower supplant the observatory in Greenwich, England, to set the new global standard time. It is the latest form of Muslim global outreach—taking control of time itself.
>
> The Mecca clock is as much propaganda as it is a timepiece. Its purpose is to proselytize. "In the name of Allah" is written in Arabic on the clock face, and tens of thousands of green and white lights will flash five times a day to remind people when to pray. (August 11, 2010)

The Qatari government appears to support this notion of the Abraj al-Bait as a symbolic challenge to British primacy in the international time regime. The government, with cleric Yusuf al-Qaradawi, hosted a conference on April 19, 2008, called "Mecca, the Center of the Earth, Theory and Practice," advocating the adoption of Mecca Time over Greenwich Mean Time (GMT). "Mecca is the center of the universe," al-Qaradawi exhorted. Referring to Islam's geographic origins between the old worlds of Asia, Africa, and Europe, al-Qaradawi continued, "Islam is a religion of the center." He described the *qibla* as one of the most important aspects of unity among Muslims, saying, "God has made the best house established for people on the earth, the Kaaba that all Muslims face for prayer five times a day" (*Sharia and Life*, 2010).[2]

Al-Qaradawi's website offers further arguments for the universal adoption of Mecca Time. The site credits Yasin al-Shouk, a Palestine-born French national, with establishing Mecca as the center of the earth on a scientific basis. Al-Shouk asserts that the location of the *qibla* can be determined from anywhere in the world and that the city of Mecca aligns perfectly with magnetic north. He even invented a wristwatch with the hands moving counterclockwise to mimic the direction of the *tawaf*, or circling, of the Kabaa, which is described as the natural direction of other significant rotations, including the movement of the planets around the sun, the rotation of galaxies, and the circulation of blood in the human body. Accepting the logic that Mecca is the center of the world, the website contends that Mecca Time is a more logical choice as the global standard time than GMT. The website urges participants in the conference to work toward mainstreaming the idea of Mecca Time as the standardized time for all Arab countries, contending that Mecca is a more worthy and "scientific" chronological baseline than Greenwich. The site describes the Royal Mecca Clock Tower as a step on the road to reviving Islamic knowledge drowned out by Western thinking (Qaradawi.net).

Construction of the Abraj al-Bait coincides with efforts across the Muslim world to synchronize the timing of Ramadan and other religious holidays according to the moon as seen over Saudi Arabia rather than as it appears in individual countries, depending on the effect of weather conditions on visibility. In 2013, the entire Arab world started Ramadan on the same day. Previously, Saudi Muslims might begin the month of fasting two days before worshippers in Morocco or a day after those in Pakistan. This emphasis on Mecca as the center of the Islamic world is framed as an important mark of Islamic identity.

Doha, meanwhile, is described by the emir of Qatar as the "Mecca of the Vulnerable." With this overt Qatari aspiration to transform Doha into a new Mecca, Al Jazeera became the first global Arabic satellite television channel to use Mecca Time systematically. In every news bulletin, the anchors say, "The news is according to the blessed Mecca Time." On-screen, Mecca Time and GMT are displayed alternately. The distance between Mecca and Doha is 798.6 miles. However, both cities are in the same time zone. By claiming global synchronicity between Doha and the holy city, Al Jazeera incorporates the Qatari capital within the holy city's symbolic limits, despite the geographic distance separating the two. As Hugh Miles describes, "Forthcoming features are advertised using Greenwich Mean Time and New York time, but Al Jazeera's principal operating time is Mecca Time. Exactly the same, Al Jazeera is broadcast all over the world at the same time, there are no regional differences" (2006, 1).

Saudi Arabia clearly understands the value Al Jazeera derives from appropriating Mecca in this way. In 2002, the kingdom denied Al Jazeera permission to cover the pilgrimage in Mecca. Saudi advertisers were encouraged to boycott Al Jazeera (el-Nawawy and Iskandar 2002, 211). Meanwhile, CNN was given the right to report live from the site of the Hajj. The move was a clear attempt by Saudi Arabia to establish its leverage against Al Jazeera's growing influence.

Al Jazeera's adoption of Mecca Time represents a merging of media time, social time, and religious time for Arab publics. The rhythm of the clock acts as a metronome, setting the pace of the day around calls to prayer, when the geographic orientation for all Muslims is synchronized toward Mecca. The adoption of Mecca Time adds another layer of synchronicity to the lives of Muslims and further establishes the holy city as the central point around which life revolves. Norbert Elias explains the symbolic power of the clock in making invisible time measurable (in Cipriani 2013, 14). In that spirit, Al Jazeera makes time and its tangible representation in the clock symbols of Mecca's uncontestable sanctity.

But while most Muslims will not visit the holy city more than once in their lives, Al Jazeera and its twenty-four-hour broadcasts in "Mecca Time in Doha" are accessible to viewers at all times. This is the institutionalization of Doha as a symbolic new Mecca, not confined by geographic barriers. Elias would say that this phenomenon is acquiring "the characteristics of a mobile social [and in this case, religious] symbol . . . placed within the communicative circuit" (in Cipriani 2013, 22). By invoking Mecca Time as an operating time regime, Al Jazeera goes beyond giving information via its newscasts, by regulating it religiously. Elias stresses that when "symbols reach a high level of conformity with reality, it becomes very difficult for human beings to distinguish symbols from reality" (in Cipriani 2013, 14). According to Elias, the question of time is the question of knowledge (in Cipriani 2013, 22). The word "time" is rich with meaning in Arabic. It can be translated as *waqt, tawqeet, sa'a* (clock) or *zaman, zamaan* (period).

The Birth of an Arab Transactional State and the Rebirth of Pan-Arabism

Al Jazeera functions as a marketplace of ideas and opinions influenced by different cultures and nationalities. However, its coverage has a central message, whether presented from a North African or South Asian point of view. This cultural exchange beneath a unified set of cultural assumptions is part of the transactional function that Al Jazeera serves for Islamic and Arab publics. Likewise, over the reign of Hamad al-Thani, Qatar's growing influence has rested largely on its emergence as a transactional state. This is most literally true in the banking sector, where Doha serves as an international hub. However, it is also true in the diplomatic sphere. Sitting between two regional titans and the de facto leaders of Islam's two major denominations, Qatar has managed to maintain a level of invested neutrality amidst regional disputes and conflicts. Most notably, in this role Qatar has served as a diplomatic hub where the Arab world's elite meets with groups who wield influence but lack legitimacy. It is specifically this position as a regional diplomatic arbiter that has gained Qatar a seat at the table in some of the region's most important international discussions.

Al Jazeera, with its focus on offering "the opinion and the other opinion," has built itself into a transactional space that is a mirror image of the Qatari state. Qatar presents itself as a neutral ground for monetary, cultural, and diplomatic transactions while using its position at the center of these transactions to advance its own interests. In the same way, Al Jazeera, by offering representatives of all viewpoints a seat at the table, maintains control over the field of play in the Arab world's most important debates. This position as arbiter leaves Al Jazeera well positioned to advance its own worldview, as will be examined throughout this book. Critics have described Al Jazeera as a diplomatic arm of the Qatari government. But this is an inaccurate and simplistic view. Al Jazeera has earned much of its success on the strength of debates between political rivals on controversial issues. Further, Al Jazeera's journalists exert significant control over the subject and scope of their reporting. In a France Culture interview, Mohamed Krichen, a Tunisian presenter often critical of Al Jazeera, was clear that there are distinct limits on Qatari influence over the editorial content of Al Jazeera. The data collected by the author back up this assertion. Qatar has certainly had some influence on Al Jazeera's content but not in the caricatured way portrayed by critics. Qatar's ownership has not diminished the professionalism or dedication of the network's journalists. The network is highly professional, with a staff of three thousand people (Nabila Amel, France Culture, October 7, 2011). To treat Al Jazeera as a state apparatus of Qatar is to ignore these aspects of the network .

As outlined in the literature review in chapter 1, the use of Bourdieu's concept of the field is well suited to the study of Al Jazeera. In Al Jazeera's reporting there are a number of field effects, some of which can be interpreted as pro-Qatar but others of which signal independence. Al Jazeera and Qatar have both parallel and intersecting interests. However, it cannot be ignored that Emir Hamad al-Thani's elimination of the Ministry of Information came around the same time Al Jazeera was brought online (Lamloum 2004; el-Oifi 2015). Many of the major themes in Al Jazeera's programming are in striking alignment with Qatari foreign policy. These themes include consistent support of democratic Islamist movements, a noncombative stance toward extremist groups, and the propagation of a rational Wahhabi-lite worldview that undercuts the Saudi-dominated fundamentalist Wahhabism which holds a strong influence over much of the Sunni world. Both Al Jazeera and Qatar use their positions as neutral outsiders to position themselves at the junction between old-guard powers and ascendant counterbalancing forces. This positioning emancipates both the network and the nation from hegemonic influence, while engendering dependence among upstart powers and admiration among onlookers unhappy with the status quo.

Al Jazeera has been famously brazen about delivering reporting that flies in the face of Western tastes. This was never more true than during the broadcast of Al Qaeda tapes, which gained the network infamy in the West. The network has also aired tapes from numerous other radical groups. This airing of radical messages could be interpreted as a symbolic transaction between Al Jazeera, Qatar, and radical groups like Al Qaeda. There is a benefit to Qatar and Al Jazeera in having a terrorist organization trusting, even relying on, the media outlet to get its message out. Al Qaeda has never launched an attack in Qatar, despite the fact that the US. Central Command is located within its borders and the terrorist group is strongly opposed to any non-Muslim military presence on Islamic soil. Lamloum (2004) and Moghadam and Fishman (2011) cite the presence of Al Jazeera as a possible reason Qatar has stayed out of Al Qaeda's crosshairs. The only major terrorist incident Qatar has suffered took place in 2004 when a bomb exploded in Doha, killing a Chechen refugee, for which two Russian nationals were eventually prosecuted (Myers 2004). Meanwhile, a willingness to broadcast statements from the most hated enemy of the United States only reinforced Al Jazeera's reputation as a free and open forum for even the most extreme opinions, as well as a voice of rebellion against Western dominance.

There was a symbolic transaction between Al Jazeera and Al Qaeda during the height of the monopoly on the broadcasting of videotapes of Al Qaeda. This symbolic transaction was a result of the interaction between the two during a time when only Al Jazeera correspondents had access to Al Qaeda leaders for interviews, in the period around 9/11. Many books and writings in Arabic, such as *The Invisible Hands Behind the Al Qaeda Tapes* of Suhaila Zainal Abidin Hammad (2011), made claims that Al Jazeera has some complicity with terrorism, but those claims are not supported by evidence. However, evidence of a symbolic transaction is supported by two factors: the language used to describe Bin Laden and terrorism, and Al Jazeera's exclusive access to the extremist tapes. First, Al Jazeera describes Bin Laden as "sheikh" and his right-hand man al-Zawahiri as a "doctor" (Al Jazeera, 2001–2006). Also, Al Jazeera continues to call terrorism "the so-called" terrorism. Second, since the 9/11 attacks Al Qaeda has produced more than thirty audio- and videotapes, and in 2005 and 2006 the number of videos produced by Al Qaeda "quadrupled" (Al Jazeera.net, 2010). One of the tapes, an interview of Bin Laden by Al Jazeera, was broadcast by CNN without permission and caused a major dispute between CNN and Al Jazeera. The tape was about banning the killing of innocent civilians (*Guardian*, February 1, 2002). Al Qaeda tapes were exclusively shown on Al Jazeera first, as the premier media outlet of choice of Al Qaeda. At that time, Al Jazeera was at the height of its popularity. Al Jazeera devoted many shows to discussions of the tapes' messages. On many occasions, such as the second and fifth anniversaries of the 9/11 attacks on New York, the same guests were invited to the show *Behind the News*, including Abdel Bari Atwan, the editor of the Arab newspaper in London. In other words, the symbolic transactions on both sides were not limited to the exchange of videotapes, but benefited Al Jazeera in terms of its notoriety, its presentation of breaking news, and its access to all the groups affiliated with political Islam. For Al Qaeda, Al Jazeera was the gateway to the world and the disseminator of its message. Al Qaeda's routine use of Al Jazeera to deliver its message was also one of the key factors in the professionalization of Al Qaeda's media arm: the self-declared a-Sahab (Clouds) (Seib 2012). The process of professionalizing Al Qaeda and its affiliate seemed to be unstoppable and led to a flurry of new online magazines and sophisticated media production spread via social media. In the age of social media and mobile technology, al Qaeda and its affiliates, such as ISIS, professionalized and took steps toward a more autonomous production of primary sources.

While Al Jazeera's value to Al Qaeda lies in the network's willingness to provide coverage of the group and broadcast its statements, the network's coverage of political Islam has amounted to outright cheerleading, as will be shown in later chapters. This favorable coverage helped bolster political Islam movements in Morocco, Tunisia, Egypt, Libya, and Gaza. Additionally, visits by the former emir and Sheikh al-Qaradawi to Gaza amidst heightened tensions with Israel added legitimacy to the Hamas government in the face of harsh criticism of the group in the West. Despite its own authoritarian government, Doha has established itself as the host of the negotiation table between political Islam, regional leaders, and Western democracies.

Both Qatar and Al Jazeera have been actively involved in efforts to tame political Islam as a palatable democratizing force in the Arab world. Al Jazeera serves as a regular platform for the speeches and fatwas of Yusuf al-Qaradawi, a Sunni scholar and member of the Muslim Brotherhood. Al-Qaradawi is president of the International Union of Muslim Scholars and has a broad network of Muslim scholars and preachers who appeared weekly on his program, *Sharia and Life*, for the majority of Al Jazeera's time on air. Al Jazeera has also long played host to leaders of outlawed political Islamic parties like Ennahda and the Muslim Brotherhood, which formed the backbone of opposition to the Arab regimes before the eruption of the Arab Spring. Many of these prominent Islamist leaders found refuge in Qatar, including al-Qaradawi; Abassi Madani, leader of Algeria's Islamic Salvation Front; and Abassi Madai of Sudan Hassan al-Turabi. Saudi-based Al Arabiya has directly accused Qatar of arming Islamist extremists (Al Arabiya, September 9, 2014). Wadah Khanfar, Al Jazeera's longest-serving managing director, grew up in 1980s Jordan and belongs to a generation for whom political Islam as a form of resistance, particularly the Muslim Brotherhood, was a powerful influence (el-Oifi, *Le Monde Diplomatique*, September 2011). In 2011, Khanfar (2011) wrote an article for the *Guardian* titled "Those Who Support Democracy Should Welcome the Rise of Political Islam."

In supporting Islamist political movements and the notion of a transnational *umma*, Al Jazeera has succeeded in creating a new model of Islamic society to compete with those underpinning the power structures of traditional regional leaders, Saudi Arabia, Iran, and Egypt. This ideology can be described as a marriage between watered-down Wahhabi beliefs, Islamist calls for rebellion against secular dictatorships, and democratic notions of popular rule. Support for this Wahhabi-lite ideology helped emancipate Qatar from the dominant Saudi cultural and religious frame, while allying it with the anti-Mubarak Muslim Brotherhood in Egypt. The emancipation started in earnest in 2003 when Saudi Arabia and the United States increased pressure against Al Jazeera. In response, Al Jazeera became more hostile toward Saudi Arabia, while simultaneously softening its hostility toward the United States. Al Jazeera took the opportunity to challenge Saudi Arabia's status as the emblematic leader of Sunni solidarity (Lamloum 2004; el-Nawawy and Iskandar 2003).

Al Jazeera's main challenge to this old-guard Saudi dominance is its message of Arab unification, with cultural norms determined via free market ideology. This can be seen as an effort to displace the individual founding mythologies of the different Arab countries, from the pharaohs of Egypt to the Carthaginian and Berber heritage of the Maghreb, with the unifying concept of the *umma*. The deconstruction of these founding myths levels the playing field between historically dominant cultures, the Arab diaspora, and the newly ascendant cultural forces of the region.

This attempt at cultural unification can be seen as a revival of the pan-Arabism championed by Egypt's Gamal Abdel Nasser. Nasser envisioned a kind of confederation of Arab nations under a supernational leadership (provided by Egypt's secular military government) to create a greater "Arab nation." The pan-Arabism of the mid-twentieth century relied on the binding force of Nasser's charisma and political power. Rather than any one persona, Al Jazeera's revived pan-Arabism relies on an enduring faith in Islam to unite Muslims throughout the Arab world.

Yusuf al-Qaradawi plays a major role in bringing religious clout to Al Jazeera's message of Islamist pan-Arabism. Al-Qaradawi's show, *Sharia and Life*, is one of the most popular programs in the network's history. Additionally, al-Qaradawi has served as a regular guest on the network's other programs to offer religious opinions. The opinions of al-Qaradawi as the religious voice of the network are closely entwined with the worldview that underlies the various frames of Al Jazeera's programming. As noted earlier, this worldview tends to favor a new international community over traditional hegemons and power brokers. Al-Qaradawi describes the spread of Western cultural norms as a burden that Muslims must escape. Meanwhile he has been uncanny in his ability to portray himself as a foil to those at extreme ends of the theological spectrum. Western observers such as Lynch (2006) and Kurzman (1998) have described al-Qaradawi as a liberal voice, while (Machari Daydi, *Asharq al-Awsat*, August 18, 2014) and (Tarik al-Hamid, *Asharq al-Awsat*, May 14,2014) insist that he is a conservative. He has warned followers against the fatwas of other imams who promote excommunication from the Muslim community. However, he himself delivered such fatwas during the Arab revolutions (Talon 2011,189). Al-Qaradawi's role on Al Jazeera has also allowed the network to imbue its programing with enough religious heft to resonate with devout viewers while also commanding the credibility inherent in the principles of secular Western journalism to which it claims fealty. The religious perspective is ostensibly limited to *Sharia and Life*, but al-Qaradawi's words and judgments are often offered on other programs as the sole expression of religious authority. Meanwhile, the mufti's air of piety frequently seeps into the attitudes of the network's less religiously affiliated commentators. The host of *The Opposite Direction*, Faisal al-Kasim, set the tone for an October 10, 2000, broadcast by explicitly describing his Moroccan guest, Mohammed Fizazi, as a secular thinker. Without further fuel from al-Kasim, the discussion between Fizazi and his Salafi counterpart erupted into a blazing argument. The data corroborate claims by Lamloum (2004), Kepel (2013), and el-Oifi (2015) that such "othering" of secular leanings is common throughout Al Jazeera's programing. The unchallenged views of al-Qaradawi, presented on both his own show and other programs, as well as interventions by anchors and moderators like the one just described make it difficult for an observer or researcher to understand the network as anything other than a mechanism of power and domination. As detailed in later chapters, the imposition of an Islamic discourse on the Arab revolutions had the effect of Islamizing a revolution that began, according to most observers and scholars, as a nonreligious revolution (Olivier Roy, Gilles Keppel, and others); in that sense, Al Jazeera's editorial view must be seen as a deliberate policy of advocating a constructed ideology of Islamized pan-Arabism.

Like the cleric who serves as its religious voice, Yusuf al-Qaradawi, Al Jazeera has built up its own status by positioning itself between powerful factions and pushing out in all directions. The network has gained notoriety for decrying Western intervention in Middle Eastern affairs and stoking outrage over the treatment of Muslims in Europe. However, the network has not been shy about taking Middle Eastern leaders to task. During the Arab Spring revolutions the BBC adopted a neutral position, while Al Arabiya's reporting reflected the shifting political posture of the Saudi crown. Al Jazeera was the only satellite news network to offer staunch support for the Arab revolutions (Talon 2011, 192). Al Jazeera's updates on the uprising were accompanied by a triptych screen with images of Cairo, Benghazi, and Tripoli, heralding a domino effect of toppled Arab regimes. There was a patriotic verve to Al Jazeera's reporting, reflected in the use of the songs of Umm Kulthum and Abdel Halim Hafez as the soundtrack for the revolutions brought to the world by Al Jazeera's satellite broadcasts. The network's open support of Arab rebels only served to enhance its reputation on the Arab street. As Talon explains, Al Jazeera describes its reporting as objective, but not neutral. The network overtly pushes back against what it calls the hegemony of Western standards. However, the network's claims of objectivity have come into question at times. Many scholars, including Abdelwahab Meddeb (*Le Monde*), have denounced Al Jazeera's conflict reporting as a kind of pornography of violence. The use of macabre imagery, argues Meddeb, belies its claims of objectivity.

Despite these questions about its objectivity, Al Jazeera's prominent role in the toppling of governments in Tunisia, Libya, and Egypt has caused the West to take notice of the powerful role of satellite television in the Middle East. Barack Obama did not give his first Arab media interview as president to Al Jazeera, but instead spoke to the Saudi-owned Al Arabiya. Media experts in the Arab world saw this as a faux pas, considering the gap in regional credibility and viewership of the two networks. However, the fact that the US president would give a personal interview to an Arab satellite network was also seen as a shift from the Bush administration's blanket snub of Arab media. Further, that snub could be seen as a reprimand of Al Jazeera for its negative reporting on US war efforts in Iraq and Afghanistan. This shift was indicative of a recognition by Western powers of the importance of Arabic media as a tool for winning the hearts and minds of Arabs. Secretary of State Hillary Clinton would later offer a gesture of endorsement to Al Jazeera by appearing on the network. In the summer of 2013 Al Jazeera entered the US media landscape by launching Al Jazeera America . It was an entirely different entity than Al Jazeera Arabic, with its own editorial leadership and a focus on US national news. In April 2015, however, it closed down its operations. According to the AJAM CEO, Al Anstey, the decision to do so was "driven by the fact that our business model is simply not sustainable in light of the economic challenges in the U.S. marketplace" (Al Jazeera, May 16, 2015).

While Al Jazeera takes aim at the status quo, leveling the playing field for cultural, religious, and financial upstarts, Qatar invests heavily in improving its position on this playing field, particularly in sports, finance, and media, the key areas where it has focused on building symbolic capital (Ennasri 2013). Qatar's investment fund invests heavily in sports teams and television rights for sporting events, including those featuring Qatar Stars League, the country's top football league. This concentration on athletics as an investment in cultural capital is perhaps best evidenced by the placement of Qatar's name on the jerseys of FC Barcelona, one of the most popular teams in the world's most popular sport. Additionally, Qatar has invested in economic events (the Doha Rounds), political Islam summits, and a media-training center for journalistic excellence. These pillars of soft power—media, finance, and athletics—have been central to Qatar's strategy of expanding its influence in the Arab world (Da Lage et al. 2013; Chesnot and Malbrunot 2013). But Qatari ascendance is not limited to the Middle East. Five books came out in the summer of 2013describing the rise of Qatari influence in France.[3] Qatari investments in the French *banlieues* and in the construction of various European mosques were the subject of numerous radio programs on France Inter and France Culture. These programs advanced the view that Qatar targets only investments that promise a big media impact, such as cultural activities in the Mosque of Paris and its contribution to the construction of one of the biggest mosques in Europe, Centre An-Nour, located in Mulhouse, France. In this view, Qatar does not invest in neighborhood mosques. Instead, it promotes identification with an Arab-Islamic *umma* mainly through a limited number of conspicuous projects and Al Jazeera (France Culture, October 3, 2013).

The soft power bestowed on Qatar by Al Jazeera has helped transform the small nation into an important voice in matters of international diplomacy. The emir of Qatar played an active role with French president Nicolas Sarkozy and British prime minister David Cameron in planning the international effort that would lead to the ouster of Muammar Qaddafi. It was not only Qatar's wealth that earned it a seat at the diplomatic table, but also its symbolic capital, emanating from the influence of Al Jazeera (Jean Ping, *Le Monde Diplomatique*, August 2014).[4]

Reforms in Qatar and the New Arab Political Order

Many scholars have questioned whether it is possible for Al Jazeera to act as a harbinger of democracy while operating out of Qatar, a prosperous but by no means democratic nation (e.g., Lamloum 2004; Lynch 2006; el-Oifi 2011; Kepel 2012; Talon 2011). Qatar set out on a path toward political reform in 1998, two years after the launch of Al Jazeera. The Ministry of Information was abolished, touching off a wave of media liberalization that would bring Qataris access to the *New York Times*, the *Times Magazine*, the *Financial Times*, and other newspapers. Reporters Without Borders and other international organizations were welcomed into the country to help boost its reputation as a favorable environment for international media (Talon 2011, 9). At the same time as the dissolution of the Ministry of Information was shut down, a plan to extend universal suffrage for citizens aged eighteen in addition to creating a committee tasked with drafting a new constitution were announced. The aim was to create a parliament with two-thirds of its members chosen by popular election. The reforms were adopted in a 2003 referendum and ratified by the emir in 2004. Only in 2005 was the parliament created, giving Qatari citizens the right to participate in national politics. The minister of interior and the minister of foreign affairs created a special bureau for human rights in 2005. A cassation court and a supreme council of family affairs were created, and numerous other reforms were implemented. Initiatives to promote democracy in the Arab world were also undertaken. In 2007, Sheikha Mozah, wife of the emir of Qatar, oversaw the creation of the Arab Democracy Foundation. In 2007, Qatar was admitted to the UN Council on Human Rights. On the whole, the reforms undertaken by Sheikh Hamad al-Thani were unprecedented in both the country and the region, with freedom of the press representing the area of greatest liberalization (Talon 2011; Lamloum 2004; Kepel 2012). The expansion of media freedom in Qatar was billed as "the manifestation of the personal will of the new Emir to reform the political system and a sign of democratization in Qatar" (Talon 2011). As of 2016, there have been no signs of elections being held.

The Arabian Peninsula has long been dominated by powerful families through a system of clientelism (patron–client relationships), tribal politics, and polarization (Talon 2011, 10–11). Despite the political reforms just described, this ruling order remains in Qatar. The new constitution encourages political participation but does not in any way limit the royal family's monopoly on political power, nor does it add new powers of scrutiny to the government. The authority of elected officials is limited predominantly to municipal and agricultural issues. Meanwhile, the election of members of the parliament, the Majhlis Ashoura, required under the new constitution, has been postponed since 2005. International organizations must obtain official government permission to operate within Qatar's borders. This strict control over NGO activities stems largely from the Qatari government's determination to maintain control over how it is portrayed to the rest of the world. Despite a number of reforms that opened up access to outside sources of information, the media code of 1997, which treats criticism of the state as a criminal offense, remains in place. The code also gives the prime minister the means to introduce new restrictions and sanctions. The state strictly controls licensing for foreign publications as well as access to the Internet (Talon 2011, 12). This regulation of the press is implemented in a way that strictly limits production of both traditional and digital media content in Qatar. The Qatari government has even more effective tools to exert influence over foreign journalists, an important point since foreigners account for about 90 percent of media professionals working in Qatar. Indians dominate the English-language media, while Egyptians disproportionately make up the Arabic media. Foreign journalists must be accredited by the Foreign Information Agency or another local institution that sponsors them. Until 2009, their passports were held by these agencies, and they needed to ask for an exit permit to leave the country. Talon questions how it is possible that Al Jazeera has so enthusiastically supported the democratic aspirations of the people of the region, playing an important role in the Arab democratic revolutions that shook the Middle East, without destabilizing the state of Qatar (Talon 2011, 15). Has Al Jazeera turned a blind eye to the internal affairs of Qatar? Talon explains that local society does not recognize itself in the narrative that Al Jazeera has constructed, nor does the reality that it promotes accurately reflect life in Qatar.

Qatar's monopoly on the media differentiates it from other Gulf states. Saudi Arabia, despite its tight control over all aspects of social life and funding of the spread of Wahhabism internationally, does not have a true system of media propaganda to promote its ruling ideology. In Saudi Arabia and the Gulf, local media are strictly controlled. However, the scope of the state-run media is not sufficient to crowd out dissenting views (el-Nawawy and Iskandar 2003; el-Oifi 2015). The paradox of an authoritarian state promoting democracy and freedom has been addressed by a number of authors (Talon 2011; Lamloum 2004). The key to Al Jazeera's relationship with its Qatari royal backers appears to be the latitude granted (either implicitly or explicitly) to the network in its critical coverage of Qatari government policy, which falls far short of its critical coverage of other governments in the region. The author's data show that Al Jazeera has been selectively critical of Qatar in the area of foreign policy while remaining largely mute regarding its domestic policies.

Pacification of Political Islam

Al Jazeera has created a symbolic world where neoliberalism, political Islam, and pan-Arabism revolve around a Mecca Time regime, centered paradoxically in Doha. Additionally, Al Jazeera acts as the arena in which the symbolic world is pitted against opposing worldviews in a contest that will determine the architecture of a new transnational Arab social construct. As will be shown throughout this book, Al Jazeera serves not only as the medium but as the message for an Arab cultural transformation that eschews traditional pillars of power.

Talon describes three important distinguishing themes of Al Jazeera's programming: an anti-Western media standard, a constant focus on war and conflict, and the portrayal of Al Jazeera journalists as fighters and martyrs. These will be recurring themes in the coming analysis of Al Jazeera's coverage of the Arab Spring revolutions. Stated another way, these overarching themes give the observer a clearer understanding of the story told by Al Jazeera's broadcasts: The Western world is an alien force, intent on controlling God's pious worshippers. The Muslim world is engaged in a war against tyranny, both foreign and domestic, and enemies of a society that is based on principles of peace and justice promised by Islam. Al Jazeera is the first line in this battle, fighting on behalf of the embattled Arab people against the entrenched influence of an illegitimate power structure.

From its infancy, Al Jazeera has worked to round the sharp edges of political Islam while Qatar provided safe haven to its most controversial leaders (Talon 2011; Lamloum 2004). By providing a platform for activists who were subject to censorship and persecution by their own leaders, the network also built its own image as both providing a professional contrast to state-controlled media and serving as a champion of the vulnerable and the voiceless. In this sense Al Jazeera becomes, like Doha, the satellite channel of the disenfranchised, a Mecca for the vulnerable.

The network's anti-Western rhetoric and reliance on conflict frames play an important role in enhancing Al Jazeera's negotiating power with the West. By promoting a unifying frame for an Arab and Islamic *umma*, Al Jazeera creates a market for its own cultural goods. On the global stage, the *umma* serves as a constituency for Qatar and Al Jazeera, in the same way that groups united by regional or religious affiliation support politicians at the national level.

It should be noted that, for a number of reasons, Al Jazeera English is not capable of facilitating the same sort of cross-cultural dialogue with the West that Al Jazeera Arabic promotes. Al Jazeera English is a completely different animal than its Arabic-language counterpart. Talon (2011) describes Al Jazeera English as more theater than a marketplace of cultural ideas. Al Jazeera, by creating new channels in languages like English, Turkish, and Swahili, is reaching out to new audiences and building new markets for the Al Jazeera brand. This does not mean that the ideological framework on display in these foreign-language products is representative of what one would find on Al Jazeera Arabic programming.

Cross-cultural dialogue with the Arab public must begin with a neutralization of the mechanisms of exclusion that have been reproduced and perpetuated through Western media coverage of the region. This should include an analysis of international affairs as they affect people of the region rather than in terms of their potential fallout in the West, a narrative of the Israeli–Arab conflict that acknowledges the suffering of displaced Palestinians, and a portrayal of Islamic practice that goes beyond scrutiny and criticism. Cross-cultural dialogue with the West has nothing to do with language or cultural barriers, but rather with the ideological frames through which reporting is presented. Al Jazeera's ideological frames specifically counter what are seen as typical Western frames.

While Al Jazeera's reporting creates a symbolic world for its Arab audience, this world is also shaped by the experiences of those who produce the channel's content. It may be helpful, at this point, to provide descriptions of the network in the words of its own members. The words of Al Jazeera's anchors, presenters, editors, reporters, and camera operators offer useful insights into the network's mission, as well as a sense of the experiences that have influenced their judgments and attitudes while providing coverage of tumultuous events. In October 2011, Al Jazeera aired a retrospective on the network's first fifteen years. Journalists who worked for the network gave their own account of some of the defining moments in the network's history. These testimonials offer more than a narrative history of the network. They provide insight into the ways that conditions on the ground, ranging from technical limitations to the emotional toll on journalists reporting from a war zone, affected the network's coverage of important events. Most of the following quotes are translations of statements taken from Arabic transcripts of the retrospective, originally aired on October 10, 2011. Other sources are noted as well.

Editors in Chief

Salah Najm was Al Jazeera's first editor in chief, serving from 1996 to 2001, and was later appointed director of news at Al Jazeera English, in 2009. He is well known for his statement, during a November 5, 2011, interview with Paloma Haschke, that "[Al Jazeera] follow[s] the British and the American ethical broadcasting codes. Our policy is to be ethically correct but not politically correct. We empower the people with knowledge. This is our job. We give them information" (Haschke 2012).

He went on to say, "Al Jazeera doesn't like prepared answers from leaders, because they are superficial. We can't compare Al Jazeera to any other channel that came before it because they were all entertainment [channels]. Qatar had no influence on our editorial freedom." Regarding the future of the network, he said, "The future of media is online. We already have an online stream, but in ten years reporting for Al Jazeera will require multimedia skills to produce not only video reports but also digital media products on a variety of multimedia platforms. The network also has a research and development center and media training to improve its strategy and competitiveness. Right now, we are focusing on the launching of three new channels in different languages: Turkish, Swahili, and Bosnian. The Al Jazeera network is also elaborating a rebranding strategy to modernize its image for the next ten years" (Haschke 2012).

Ibrahim Helal was the editor of Al Jazeera from 2001 to 2004. He speaks of the difference in orientation between Al Jazeera and the BBC: "When we came from the BBC to Al Jazeera we never thought that Al Jazeera would come out in [BBC's] image" (Al Jazeera, October 10, 2011).

Ahmed Sheikh was the editor from 2004 to 2010. "From the beginning there were no limits to the political margins in Al Jazeera," he says. "We were free in our editing. The only limits are the limits of true journalism. We discarded every political position from other countries. Al Jazeera is very wise to be in Sudan and in many wars around the world. Al Jazeera covered famine in Niger, civil wars in Congo, the drug cartels in Colombia, the tsunami in Japan. We were the first to report on the earthquake on Aceh" (Al Jazeera, October 10, 2011).

Mustafa Sawak, editor from 2010 to 2011, offers some insight into the important role Qatar's royal family plays in supporting the network. "Al Jazeera has three pillars. The first one is the emir of Qatar, the second pillar is the professional management of Sheikh Hamad bin Thamir al-Thani, and the third one is the staff and journalists" (Al Jazeera, October 10, 2011).

Anchors and Presenters

According to the Tunisian presenter Mohamed Krichen, one of Al Jazeera's founding journalists, "[The history of] Al Jazeera can be described as an epic that became more attractive over the years. It started modestly, with a small margin of freedom. But from the first month we knew that the channel was here to stay. I am proud that Al Jazeera succeeded in resisting a huge number of hidden frustrations and overt pressures. With the help of Qatar we succeeded in enduring [under difficult conditions] until Al Jazeera moved on from the phase of childhood. Al Jazeera succeeded in breaking the official Arab discourse based on propaganda and lies and [the notion] inculcated in the Arab mind, the Arab citizen that nobody can change the status quo. When it comes to the West, Al Jazeera courageously imposed its achievements and [showed] that the truth will not start or end in the West. I am grateful to Al Jazeera for putting me on the map of presenters and linking their faces to important events in the Arab world" (Al Jazeera, October 10, 2011).

The Palestinian Jordanian journalist Jamal Rayyan started his career in 1974 as a news reporter and presenter for the Jordan Radio and Television Corporation in Amman. He worked in Korea, at the BBC in London, and for Abu Dhabi Television Network before joining Al Jazeera. He is well known for not being able to hold back his tears during a massacre of children and civilians. As he describes the network, "Al Jazeera is a new service, its origin is Arabic, its orientation is international, its motto is 'the opinion and the other opinion.' It is a plural form that desires truth and adheres to the principles of professionalism in an institutional framework. . . . Al Jazeera is the most important boon to my professional career. It helped me to become an international star. In many markets in China, people stopped me to show me their admiration" (Al Jazeera, October 10, 2011).

The Iraqi presenter Jamil Azer relates, "When I came to Al Jazeera I was asked to come up with a slogan that could represent the identity of the channel. After two days, I came up with 'the opinion and the other opinion.' Al Jazeera was distinguished by its language and its style from its first week. . . . Al Jazeera's neutrality via-à-vis regional conflicts, including the Arab–Israeli conflict, is superior to that of other Arab media outlets" (Al Jazeera, October 10, 2011).

The Syrian Faisal al-Kasim recalls, "Al Jazeera gave me fame, something I couldn't have dreamed of before. I admit that I had a PhD diploma before coming to Al Jazeera but I wasn't an intellectual; I was just a learned person. Because of Al Jazeera and my program [*The Opposite Direction*], I began to read and to know the world. Al Jazeera gave me [the opportunity] to become one of the fifty most influential journalists in the world. . . . I am proud of belonging to Al Jazeera. . . . My name was put on black lists of the Arab world, I am not allowed to visit many Arab countries, and my brother was expelled from Egypt" (Al Jazeera, October 10, 2011).

Managing Directors

The first managing director of Al Jazeera was Jassim Al Ali (1996–2003). "Arab journalists thought that Al Jazeera would be a failure, since we broadcast twenty-four-hour news, while other Arab channels broadcast entertainment," he says of the network's early years. "They said that Al Jazeera is an Israeli channel, an American channel, a Bin Laden channel, an Intifada channel, and this is, I think, why Al Jazeera is very successful" (Al Jazeera, October 10. 2011).

Wadah Khanfar is a Palestinian managing director who started as a reporter. Under his leadership, Al Jazeera became a global network with multiple languages and channels on which it aired a variety of programs, from news to sports, children's programing, and documentaries. Khanfar was the network's longest-serving managing director, occupying the position from October 2003 to September 2011. He resigned a couple of months after the victories of the Arab revolutions in Tunisia, Egypt, and Libya and after the "scandal" that erupted between Hamas and the Palestinian Authority (Al Jazeera, October 10. 2011). Al Jazeera and the *Guardian* published leaked documents implicating the Palestinian Authority in a collaboration with Israeli-targeted assassinations of Hamas members (Seumas Milne and Ian Black, *Guardian*, January 24, 2011). Opponents saw Khanfar as having Islamist sympathies. However, Khanfar states, "Al Jazeera became a distinguished school internationally based on professionalism, courage, and truth" (Al Jazeera, October 10, 2011).

Khanfar was replaced by a member of Qatar's royal family, Sheikh Ahmed Bin Jassim bin Mohamed al-Thani, in September 2011. "What attracts me to Al Jazeera is the triangle of truth, impartiality, and courage accompanied [by] investigative reporting based on 'the opinion and the other opinion,'" he says (Al Jazeera, October 10, 2011).

Reporters and Camera Operators Riding Pivotal Events

Dramatic events helped Al Jazeera grow.[5] The network proudly touts its reporting on major events and its effect on the Arab media landscape. Al Jazeera frames its effect on competing media as a major achievement and doesn't miss an opportunity to display the success and heroism of its reporters and camera operators. In the following paragraphs these staff members describe some of the important events that shaped the history of Al Jazeera.

Operation Desert Fox, 1998

Mohamed Bourini and Shaker Hamid describe how the dedication of reporters enabled a fledgling Al Jazeera to deliver strong reporting despite limited resources during the 1998 bombing of Iraq. They recount using rudimentary supplies and modest logistical innovations to package exclusive reports. In one instance, two cameras with a scooter engine were tucked to the belt of the cameraman Khalid Salman,. This was challenging, because the fuel from the engine was hot and could have burned Salman's skin. They relied on a 1976 Mercedes that had to be pushed in order to start. Al Jazeera's crew in Iraq was sixteen strong. In comparison, CNN had eight correspondents and fifty-two other crew members to manage numerous cameras, a huge car fleet, and a logistical supply line bringing water and food from Jordan (Al Jazeera, October 10, 2011).

Mohamed Bourini recalls, "During the war I didn't sleep for five days and I never took off my shoes. Once I almost fainted when sitting on an iron chair, but I woke up after hearing a siren when Tomahawk cruise missiles hit nearby. I remember that CNN offered us money and cameras but our editor rejected that idea" (Al Jazeera, October 10, 2011).

The Second Intifada, 2000

Walid Al Umari, an Israeli Palestinian, covered the Second Intifada for Al Jazeera. "With very modest means during the beginnings of the Intifada, we tried to get to the location of the events," he remembers. "We succeeded in making three reports daily. It was difficult because we had to cross a checkpoint at Bayt Hanun into Gaza. Sometimes I didn't sleep for three nights in a row, and we didn't see our families and children. We were the only journalists who got into the Janine Camp during the Intifada. Israelis cut off the road many times. Our bureau in Ramallah was invaded by Israeli soldiers. I was expelled twice from Arafat's office, and my colleague Shireen Abu Akala was expelled once. In spite of the difficult conditions, and because of our professional convictions, we continued to work" (Al Jazeera, October 10, 2011).

The Afghanistan War, 2001

Taysir Allouni, a Syrian-born Spanish citizen, was a correspondent in Kabul during the coalition invasion of Afghanistan. In 2005, he was convicted of terrorism because of his interview with Al Qaida leader Osama bin Laden after the terrorist attacks of 9/11. While Allouni served a jail sentence in Spain, Al Jazeera undertook a long campaign to prove his innocence. Allouni describes his work in Kabul: "We didn't sleep for many days. I didn't change my clothes for more than two weeks; I didn't take a shower. We were working under bombing conditions. We understood the danger of our work, but we felt the responsibility of bringing the news to the whole world. The crew was very small. We had a guard, a technician, a cameraman, and a cook. The work we did was five hundred times more than the size of our crew" (Al Jazeera, October 10, 2011).

Abdel Sadah, a colleague of Allouni's, worked as a correspondent based in Kandahar during the US invasion. "There was an agreement between Al Jazeera and CNN, but the CNN workers didn't help me by giving me a place to stay," he remembers. "In the end they let me sleep in the bath in the bathroom. For three weeks, I slept, worked, and ate in that room with an Afghan translator. It was difficult because of the anti-Arab sentiment at that time in Kandahar. But we succeeded in covering the news every time there was an event" (Al Jazeera, October 10, 2011).

The Iraq Invasion, 2003

Majed Abdelhadi is a Palestinian whose war reporting has a distinct literary style focusing on the color of blood. He covered the Second Intifada in 2000, Tora Bora in Afghanistan, the inspection of Iraq and the search for weapons of mass destruction in 2002 and 2003, the Arab summits of 2002, 2004, and 2006, and the elections in Lebanon in 2005 and 2009. He delivered live reports on the assassination of Prime Minister Hariri of Lebanon and covered the presidential election in Yemen in 2012, the Egyptian presidential election in 2012, and the protests in Egypt in 2013. Abdelhadi was a news producer in Iraq in 2003. "I remember the first day of war," he says. "I was on the roof of my bureau at 5:35 a.m. when I saw a missile hitting the ground. I started to scream six times. I was scared and confused. This situation continued for the whole period of our coverage of the war in Iraq. Our protection gear was not enough to protect us. I would sleep on a couch with my protection gear. I slept between missile attacks" (Al Jazeera, October 10, 2011).

The Lebanese War, 2006

Ghassan Ben Jedou is a Tunisian star journalist who resigned from Al Jazeera in 2011, citing the network's lack of objectivity in its coverage of the Arab Spring. Ben Jedou was the director of the Al Jazeera bureau in Beirut. "We were working for twenty-four hours nonstop," he says. "Our crew . . . was very simple and at the most there were twenty-five journalists. We succeeded in being everywhere at all times. We never had more than a three-man crew covering an event. And this is . . . almost a miracle in television work. We wanted to minimize the human costs if a crew was hit by an attack. Al Jazeera was distinguished by its accuracy and quickness, accurate and comprehensive newsgathering. We brought the images from Israel and Lebanon to the Arab public with courageous and hardworking journalists. We tried to give balanced news without forgetting any political opinion. We gave the human dimension fifty percent [of the coverage]. I lost fifteen kilos during the war. I didn't sleep for six days. One morning the director of the Al Jazeera channel ordered me to go to sleep" (Al Jazeera, October 10, 2011).

In 2012, Ghassan Ben Jedou helped launch a competing satellite television network called Al Mayadeen (Squares), serving as board chair. The motto of Al Mayadeen, which operates on Jerusalem time, is "reality as it is." On March 7, 2015, the network celebrated one thousand days of existence. On this occasion, Jedou exclaimed, "Al Mayadeen came out of the womb of nothingness." Implicitly ribbing his competitors and former employer, he crowed, "We never got involved in sectarianism or inciting religious or national division, or lying to the people, or getting involved in projects that caused bloodshed or plotting, internal wars or terrorist propaganda. . . . We didn't sink into the quagmire of political discourse and cheap language, or religious discourse of blood, or insulting others or news bulletins based on lies" (Al Mayadeen, March 7, 2015).

The Arab Spring

Correspondent Bibih Ould Mhadi said in 2011: "I want just to stop briefly to talk about the Libyan experience, since it is one of the most dangerous ones. . . . Al Jazeera's coverage from the start of the revolution on February 17, 2011, until the fall of Qaddafi was successful and distinguished in its activities, reporting, photographers, and technicians. Al Jazeera in Libya is the same Al Jazeera in Egypt, in Yemen, and where the events take place" (Al Jazeera, October 10, 2011).

Said Thabit Said, who became the bureau chief in Yemen in 2011 recalls, "When the Arab revolution started to bloom . . . the regime in Sana'a started a hostile propaganda campaign against Al Jazeera, blaming it for igniting the revolutions in Tunisia and Egypt. The Al Jazeera workers were threatened and were denied work [but succeeded in covering the events in a hostile environment]" (Al Jazeera, October 10, 2011).

Abelfattah Fayed, bureau chief for Egypt, recalls, "On January 29, 2011, we said on TV, to the world, that Egypt had its Friday of Rage [January 28, 2011] and it was a real catastrophe—hundreds of dead and thousands wounded. The regime spoke of one dead in Cairo and one in Suez. The former minister of information called me and said that he would close the Al Jazeera bureau in Cairo. I answered that the bureau was closed already, since there was no Internet and all the landline phones were cut off just before our cell phones also were cut off. The minister said, 'We are going to close the building, so you will have no place to sit.' I warned him that Al Jazeera was not impressed, and this meant that we had more than a thousand correspondents instead of three or four. And this is exactly what happened. All the Egyptians were in direct contact with Al Jazeera. When the police came and closed the bureau and stripped us of our media license, the TV outside of our building showed Al Jazeera reporting directly from Tahrir Square. The police looked everywhere but couldn't find the source of the broadcast. The police force was looking everywhere [in the studio] for the hidden camera but couldn't find it. They even looked in the toilet" (Al Jazeera, October 10, 2011).

Conclusion

This chapter argues that even if Qatar's financial and material wealth is the foundation of Al Jazeera's symbolic world, that wealth is merely a facilitator of a broader cultural force. Al Jazeera sprang from an already existing capital of talent incubated and nurtured in a rich media tradition of an established institution, the BBC, and the rich pluralistic backgrounds of journalists who came from different Arab countries with unique social, cultural capital and also different editorial ideologies and biases. They shared a professional habitus based on their adherence to Western journalistic norms. These talented journalists had cultivated their own aura through years of broadcasting in the Arab world (Lamloum 2004). They also shared a collective habitus of independence and freedom in their news reporting.

The financial capital of Qatar facilitated the harnessing of these journalists' energy into what eventually became Al Jazeera. Despite their wealth, Qatar's neighbors have not managed to create a similar apparatus for cultural promotion. Al Jazeera shook the foundations of the pan-Arab media field, breaking the monopolies of the established media systems of each Arab country. Empowered by new communication technologies Al Jazeera became the Arab face of globalization.

The acculturated Arab journalists from the BBC who made up the earliest corps of Al Jazeera journalists also functioned according to a new logic of dual culturalism. They acted as Arab voices, catering to Arab audiences. But they also reported as Western journalists, undeterred by government opacity and confident that the European passports the majority of them held would serve as a shield against arrest by abusive regime forces.

This duality of being in and out, of being insider and outsider, also characterizes the power of the symbolic order that Al Jazeera created. The European passport had significant advantages (although these did not extend to the journalists who were detained in Egypt after President Morsi was ousted). Ahmed Mansour, the Egyptian star journalist, was arrested in Germany in June 2015, but was released after three days when it was discovered that he was British. Dual citizenship was almost a necessity for excelling in the world of Al Jazeera and avoiding censorship and prison.

Journalists with only Qatari passports did not have as many advantages as the British, the Dutch, and the German Arab journalists. The example of the presenter of *Sharia and Life* who was denied excess to England is a clear example. Al

Jazeera profited enormously from the professional capital of BBC and CNN—from their examples as international news agencies, the training their former employees brought to Al Jazeera, and the freedom enjoyed by journalists who had earned status as dual nationals while working for the Western press. All of these factors helped Al Jazeera to build its reputation and to create notoriety, foundations of the network's symbolic world.

Another element that adds to Al Jazeera's notoriety is its success in linking its journalists to dramatic events. Al Jazeera claims to represent the voice of the Arabs, another foundational piece of its strong symbolic order.

The energy of Al Jazeera, in addition to the strategic thinking behind it, led to the phenomenon of Al Jazeera operating on Mecca Time, linking the network to an audience of 350 million people who are predisposed to consuming religious messages or references to the Prophet's place of birth. The religious input of Al Jazeera doesn't stop at adopting Mecca Time; it also attempts to inject religious identification into this pan-Arab media field by taming the forces of political Islam or at least making their voice part of the Arab public sphere, which has been shaped by Al Jazeera. Al Jazeera has not tamed all the forces of political Islam, as many radical terrorist forces are untamable and, as Kepel (2013) noted, Qatar itself is involved in a game that nobody understands.

In sum Al Jazeera built a symbolic world that, until the Arab Spring, functioned smoothly. The turning point came after the network began watering down its principles of adherence to Western journalistic norms. Sympathy and enmity toward the subjects of its reporting on the Arab Spring eroded the network's veneer of objectivity. Now Al Jazeera is, in spite of relative dominance in the world of news, seeing cracks in the foundations of its symbolic world.

This book details the rise and fall of this symbolic order with concrete examples in which ethnographic details are used, as Loic Wacquant would say, to find the way to understanding the unthinkable and the invisible (1995, 660).

3

A TINDERBOX FOR THE REVOLUTION

SUBJECTIVITY AND RESISTANCE

In spite of the censorship in Tunisia, young people succeeded in showing that the Internet is a space without limits.

—Al Jazeera (January 15, 2011)

We must question both the political and subjective dimensions of this sudden revolution.

—Fethi Benslama (2011)

This chapter focuses on Al Jazeera's early coverage of the Arab Spring in Tunisia. The protests, which began in Sidi Bouzid in December 2010, became a prominent focus of Al Jazeera's news reports and talk shows, beginning roughly a week after the start of protests against the Ben Ali regime. Subjectivity stands out in these reports as an important means of telling individual stories through simultaneous image and sound transmitted via the Internet. In contrast, bureau reporters had been forced to deliver their live reports by telephone. This binary approach to reporting, imposed by circumstances on the ground, resulted in phone communication being reported separately from video footage, which would characterize all Al Jazeera news reports from December 25, 2010, through January 14, 2011—the day Ben Ali was ousted.

Online activism was the crucial factor in the success of Tunisia's Jasmine Revolution. Young people posted pictures and video footage online exposing the violent efforts of police to quell protests against the government. The constant updates spurred the Tunisian people to action and prompted international media outlets to pay attention to what was transpiring under the watch of the dictatorship. Stars of the newly termed Arab Spring used technology to outfox attempts by the government to censor them through traditional channels.

Using multiple aliases and screen names to disseminate their message, the youth in some ways paralleled the scrappy revolutionaries of *Star Wars: Episode IV—A New Hope*, with the Tunisian desert doubling as the terrain of the distant planet Tatooine. Cyberspace, rather than outer space, was the setting for this battle between poorly equipped, ideologically driven forces and a seemingly invincible juggernaut of establishment power. The surge of subjective news and updates on the protests posted by Internet activists, bloggers, and Facebookers served as the main resource for international media outlets trying to get information from behind the wall of government censorship surrounding the unrest. These images helped bolster calls for spontaneous strikes, demonstrations, and ultimately the "Jasmine Revolution." The pictures of police brutality outraged the Tunisians, who had a reputation for being open, peaceful, and tolerant. Decades of domination by President Ben Ali, widely recognized as a despot with French government backing, had clearly stretched the people to their breaking point. The dissemination of anger-inducing images empowered by distribution through satellite television channels reached large audiences throughout the Arab world. Online activists reigned supreme over both local and international media in their coverage of events during Tunisia's revolution (Al Jazeera, December 25, 2010).

Online sources became the de facto news agencies of the Arab revolutions. Photos and videos transmitted via cell phones shaped public awareness of the revolutions, and the Internet opened a new space for the expression of opinions and attitudes. Al Jazeera praised this online activism for its ability to escape the censorship of the traditional news media and become the first link between on-the-ground events and traditional media outlets.

The dramatic self-immolation of Mohamed Bouazizi, the fruit vendor in Sidi Bouzid, was not initially reported by a single media outlet. It was met by a media blackout imposed by the regime. It was only when the pictures of the protests, in the middle of the country's agrarian region, were put on the Internet that Bouazizi's self-immolation and subsequent protests became a media event.

Even Al Jazeera was taken by surprise when the early Tunisian protests in Sidi Bouzid broke out. It was the sort of event that Al Jazeera had been yearning to cover. Years earlier, in 2008, Al Jazeera had announced that miners' strikes in the southern part of Tunisia, which were met with unprecedented brutality, could lead to popular uprisings and had the potential to spark additional revolutions in Morocco, Algeria, Egypt, and other countries. The host of *The Opposite Direction*, Faisal al-Kasim, spoke of *thawrat jiyya*, the coming revolution of the hungry. He said that bloggers had written on *"Luqmat aysh* that the hungry cannot fear anything or anybody since they have nothing to lose" (Al Jazeera, June 26, 2013). But the simmering unrest didn't reach a full boil until after December 17, 2010. It was on that day in Sidi Bouzid that Mohamed Bouazizi, a twenty-six-year-old fruit vendor, set himself on fire in the street after the government seized his produce because he lacked the proper vending permits.[1]

Improbably, it was almost a week before Al Jazeera began covering this defining event in the Arab world. By 2010, Al Jazeera had gained a reputation for being the first on the scene of breaking stories across North Africa and the Middle East. Its reporting was frequently quoted by world media outlets like CNN and the BBC, which were consistently slower to pick up on stories of importance in the region, but during the first week following Bouazizi's dramatic act of protest Al Jazeera was forced many times to base its news reports from Tunisia on sources like Reuters, BBC, and Tunisian newspapers, in addition to the online sources that would eventually provide the basis for most of its reporting. When Al Jazeera finally began delivering substantial original reporting on the revolutionary events in Tunisia, it relied heavily on subjective sources: photos taken with cell phones, social media, and blog posts. These activist bloggers and cell phone documentarians were suddenly the most important link in the information chain between streets filled with protesters, the rest of the country, and the outside world (Al Jazeera, December 29, 2010). It was largely thanks to this new approach to reporting that Al Jazeera was able to take the global media lead from within an almost hermetically closed country until the eventual departure of Ben Ali.

It was not until the day Ben Ali left office that the revolution became a live event, aired on various media outlets. Cameras were everywhere, registering every movement, every face, and every interaction. An unprecedented wave of euphoric imagery and sound from a Tunisian public astounded by the outcome of its struggle washed over the global public.

It was the freedom to use a camera without the threat of having it confiscated that struck Lotfi Hajji, the bureau chief of Al Jazeera in Tunis. "January 14, 2011, was a different day," he would later recall. "I appeared for the first time on Al Jazeera TV as a correspondent of Al Jazeera for Tunisia" (Al Jazeera December 11, 2011).

"At last we have Lotfi Hajji in voice and image," Hajji's colleague Said Dosri exclaimed during the network's first live broadcast from the ground during the Tunisian Revolution.

"I couldn't find a better response than the Quranic verse 'We bring these days to men by turns, and that Allah may know those who believe and take witnesses from among you' [3.141]," Hajji recalled of that first broadcast, adding, "I also said, 'I am on Al Jazeera TV live from my country. Ben Ali denied me access to my country and now he is somewhere in the sky trying to find a country who can give him shelter.' "

Ben Ali had spent hours "up in the sky," aboard his jet, awaiting responses to his petitions for asylum. As Ben Ali left Tunisia, Al Jazeera came in. Hajji's recollection of the challenging reporting environment created by the Ben Ali regime sheds light on how images and video provided by citizen-journalists came to characterize Al Jazeera's reporting on events in Tunisia, as well as the rest of the Arab Spring uprisings. "The conditions were certainly difficult because of the censorship," he recounted. "We were not allowed to film and any company we approached to help us was subject to sanctions, so we used the work of bloggers who published images on the Internet, including the work of activists and lawyers who were also bloggers."

The strict controls imposed by Ben Ali's regime during the revolution necessitated the development of an underground web-based communication network, which started in Sidi Bouzid. The circumstances also gave rise to a unique kind of "collective courage," which made this development possible.[2]

"There is a long list of bloggers who helped me," Hajji said. These bloggers helped Al Jazeera report on the daily demonstrations in Tunis, eventually spreading the spark of revolution as far distant as the town of Thala in the governorate of Kasserine and on to the rest of Tunisia's cities. The courage of Al Jazeera's reporters and its stable of affiliated stringers, bloggers, and citizen-journalists, Hajji said, "became the courage of all the people who started to contact me and give me some Internet links with photos to highlight the statements of political leaders, trade unionists, and protesters. And everybody started to post news updates on the Internet. In those moments they were very important for our coverage, especially in the last minutes of the revolution. We benefited a lot from the courage of these Tunisians" (Al Jazeera, December 11, 2011).

Al Jazeera's Ahmed Mansour, who has conducted more interviews on the Arab revolutions than any other Al Jazeera journalist, explained that the bloggers represented an entirely new brand of revolutionary messenger, relying on innovative campaign methods to build support for the revolution, turning the disinterested into supporters and supporters into participants. Where earlier popular revolutions had succeeded by turning poor agricultural and industrial workers into guerrilla soldiers, the face of the Arab Spring movement was that of revolutionary citizen-journalists. These teams of largely untrained reporters explored new ways of leveraging social media and consumer electronics to deliver their message to a growing international audience. The result was a constant stream of reporting that not only offered a novel form and perspective, but was also nearly impossible for government forces to stamp out.

"The Tunisian Revolution was the beginning of this new kind of journalism in the Arab world," said Mansour in an interview with Hajji.

"Exactly," Hajji agreed. "It was a difficult task for the regime of Ben Ali to suppress all means of communication after the spread of the images and the multiplication of the websites" (Al Jazeera, November 11, 2012).

Blogging to Freedom

In May 2012, the celebrated revolutionary Tunisian blogger Lina Ben Mhenni spoke on the Al Jazeera program *Witness of the Era* (*Shahidun ala asr*) about her blogging history. Long before the Jasmine Revolution, Ben Mhenni had spent nine months teaching Arabic as a Fulbright scholar in Boston. She returned home to Tunisia because she couldn't "get used to life in America and closed [herself] to social life" (Al Jazeera, July 25, 2012). Upon her return to Tunisia, she participated in demonstrations in support of Gaza. As in many Arab countries, she explained that the only demonstrations allowed by the Tunisian regime were those in support of the Palestinian cause. After this show of support for Gaza, which often serves as a rite of passage for Arab activists, Lina Ben Mhenni spent most of her spare time away from her teaching obligations at home.

Eventually, though, she discovered an outlet for social interaction online. By keeping in touch with friends and family through Skype or Facebook and following the latest news from home in Tunisia, Ben Mhenni was able to stay socially connected from the confines of her home. She began a blog in 2007, around the same time that she opened her Facebook account. Quickly drawn into the blogosphere, she started reading feminist and avant-garde blogs like *Code Fatima Arabica, Normal Land*, and many others. She joined in the activities of the Tunisian *mudawineen* (bloggers) movement amidst the 2008 general strikes at the phosphate mining basin in Gafsa, which met with government repression and outbreaks of violence. The regime of Ben Ali crushed protests by mineworkers demanding better wages and better living conditions. Hundreds were imprisoned (Sonia Chamkhi, Emory University, September 21, 2011). Ben Mhenni's active participation in the cyber protest activities in support of the mineworkers helped gain her a reputation and following as a respected blogger.

In January 2010, one of Lina Ben Mhenni's female students, a supporter of the regime, was insulted to find her teacher among a group of protesters the student was photographing. As the interchange between teacher and student became heated, a police officer in civilian garb called Ben Mhenni by name, saying, "You are well known to us."

"They used all kinds of tactics to pressure me," Ben Mhenni recalled during her interview with Ahmed Mansour on *Witness of the Era*. Mansour asked her if her online activism was a form of expression, an outlet for her rage. She nodded yes.

On May 21, 2010, Ben Mhenni released an antigovernment video on the Internet from a cyber café that was quickly taken down by the government. She later recalled being very frightened the next day when online activists called for a protest. The participants wore white T-shirts and carried white jasmine flowers, a symbol of innocence and trust. The popular response to this single act of censorship would forever attach the name "Jasmine Revolution" to the movement that eventually deposed Ben Ali.

The call for protests was heard by a mass of people, all wearing white shirts and holding small bouquets of jasmine flowers. Protesters on Habib Bourguiba Avenue were beaten and harassed by government security forces. Anyone wearing a white shirt was instructed by these forces to leave the avenue. Ben Mhenni's participation in an Al Jazeera interview about the protests earned her the attention of the regime and constant monitoring by police.

Mohamed Bouazizi was not the first Tunisian street vendor driven to suicide by police harassment. A month before Bouazizi immolated himself, setting off intense protests, another young man named Abdul Salam Trimch set himself on fire in the city of Monastir when the municipal police confiscated his cart. However, his act of immolation didn't lead to the same outpouring of anger as had the actions of Mohamed Bouazizi, who held a university degree. Lina Ben Mhenni remembered the sting she felt upon hearing of Bouazizi's act: "It pained me. I was at a friend's house, a lawyer; we posted the news to Facebook" (atunisiangirl.glogspot.com).

The Internet Is Not Tunisia

In a second interview on *Witness of the Era* in July 2012, Lina Ben Mhenni warned people not to make the mistake of assuming Internet activists were representative of all Tunisians. "The Internet is not Tunisia," she said. Only a small segment of the Tunisian population (10 percent) has access to the Internet. However, Ben Mhenni argues that the Internet was crucial in encouraging activism; many new online users posted their photos and profiles and were not afraid to say, "*Ben Ali Degage*" (Get Out, Ben Ali). They asked others on the Web to do the same and to show their solidarity with the cause by attending the anti-Ali demonstrations. At the request of Mansour, Lina Ben Mhenni recounted her participation in the demonstration on the Friday following Bouazizi's act of protest:

> On Friday I started from the Place Mohammed Ali, in front of the trade union [building]. We moved forward slowly, and eventually we reached the front of the Interior Ministry. What stuck in my mind was that when we were all shouting the slogan "*Ben Ali Degage*," waving our hands, there were personal things at stake for me. I had not seen my family during that time, I avoided going home, so they did not know where I was. (Al Jazeera, July 25, 2012)

She went on to explain that her mother was concerned and had called her, asking where she was, but in order to protect her family and herself, Ben Mhenni couldn't tell her family where she was.

Ahmed Mansour systematically framed his questions using Friday as a religious identity marker to stress victory against oppression. This can be seen, for example, in the conversation leading up to Ben Mhenni's description of the protests. As Ben Mhenni began to recount the events, Mansour interjected, asking "On Friday?"

"Yes," Ben Mhenni replied, "on Friday in front of the Ministry of the Interior."

"What was on your mind that Friday?" asked Mansour.

Ahmed Mansour also had the opportunity to retell the story of Sidi Bouzid, filling in the information left by previous reporting, on his show *Talk of the Revolution*. This was a common narrative tool used by Al Jazeera when the network was unable to report facts from the ground, as with war reporting in Afghanistan, Pakistan, and Iraq. Sidi Bouzid was certainly a place where Al Jazeera was unable to deliver firsthand reporting. The network was also absent from the 2008 strike and sit-ins by the mineworkers in Gafsa, which led to clashes and riots between the police and the mineworkers. But Gafsa was disconnected from the rest of Tunisia, located 229 miles from Tunis in Tunisia's politically and economically marginalized south. Even the bloggers and Facebookers who wrote of the protests did not write from firsthand knowledge of the event. The Gafsa events, for all involved, can be seen as a rehearsal for the much more traumatic events that would take place in 2010 and 2011. In 2008, Faisal al-Kasim the host of *The Opposite Direction*, predicted a "revolution of the hungry" in Egypt, Morocco, Algeria, and Tunisia spurred by poverty, hunger and *qahr* (oppression), asking, "Didn't some Tunisians declare that hunger drove them to eat animal feed?!" (Al Jazeera, June 19, 2008).

In spite of its inability to report live from Tunisia during the Ben Ali era, Al Jazeera presents itself as a major, authoritative voice that reported on the oppression of the Ben Ali regime and spurred on the Arab Spring. Al Jazeera's drumbeat against Ben Ali, no doubt, contributed to civil unrest in Tunisia and other Arab countries. The French political scientist Gilles Kepel calls Al Jazeera's coverage an igniter and extinguisher of Arab revolutions (Kepel 299, 2013). Al Jazeera's talk shows devoted much of their time to the unrest in Tunisia. The concept of *qahr* was discussed in more than 104 talk shows and news reports. *Qahr* became a powerful media frame for describing the brutality of Ben Ali's regime, as well as similar regimes in the Arab world. The word *qahr*, according the Tunisian psychoanalyst Fethi Benslama, "summarizes everything," meaning it is inclusive of all kinds of domination and oppression undertaken by the regime. Bouazizi, for example, has been seen as a martyr, an oppressed person—he was identified as a hero. Bouazizi, however, didn't consider himself a martyr when he burned himself to death. He was not a "suicide bomber" who believed in his cause. He chose to engulf himself in flames not as a mode of destruction but as demonstration of rage.

Maqhur is an extremely powerful word in Arabic describing a total lack of options, even a lack of means to protest. It conveys Bouazizi's despair—his sense that he was at the end of his rope. He wanted to defeat his oppressor, and since *qahr* is linked to this feeling of having no way to act on one's own behalf and an extreme dependence on the "other," self-immolation, according to Benslama, is the last resort in breaking the chain of *qahr*. Al Jazeera developed a whole lexicon around this concept of *qahr*: practiced *qahr*, the period of *qahr*, cultural, social, and economic *qahr*, the stick of *qahr*, the force of *qahr*, under *qahr*, the extent of *qahr*, the situation of *qahr*, absolute *qahr*, fighting *qahr*, transforming *qahr*.

A Painting of *Qahr*

Tunisian attorney and activist Khaled Awyneh from Sidi Bouzid, who was a guest on Ahmed Mansour's *Talk of the Revolution*, compared the *shahid* (martyr) Bouazizi to a matchstick whose flame had ultimately spread throughout the autocracies of the Arab world, burning away the barriers of fear and *qahr* that had previously insulated leaders from their oppressed subjects. Before Bouazizi, he explained, a terrible climate of fear had suppressed a powerful undercurrent of hostility toward the government. Activists, members of trade unions, and lawyers, who were "militating" for a viable civil society, used the opportunity to confront the state over its practice of *qahr*. A half hour after Bouazizi was enveloped in flames, Khaled Awyneh and others gathered around the regional government building) to watch as the "martyr Bouazizi" was transported in an ambulance to a hospital close to Sidi Bouzid.

The gathering in Sidi Bouzid soon developed into a demonstration, a confrontation of the *qahr* imposed by the state. Trade union members, lawyers, and others continued to join the demonstration in the hours after Bouazizi's immolation. Tension in the crowd increased as the number of (mostly young) activists grew. Khaled Awyneh described talk within the crowd as centering on what drove Bouazizi to burn himself to death. Questions were asked about who should be held responsible and about the state of *qahr* in Sidi Bouzid that led young people to throw the remaining oranges from Bouazizi's cart at the state headquarters in the regional government building. At that moment, fear vanished from the residents of a nation built on fear.

"With our blood we will redeem you, Mohamed," the demonstrators began to chant, as citizens spontaneously assembled before the regional government building. When news came that Bouazizi was still alive and might have been transported to Sfax, 120 kilometers away, or to Tunis, 350 kilometers away, young people tried to force their way into the building. These attempts only increased after the governor (*wali*) refused to talk with the protesters. Minor confrontations occurred between protesters and police. A picture taken at the protest was posted on Facebook and led to another demonstration in front of the regional government building the next day.

Photos and descriptions of the protest at the regional government building quickly reached Tunis and the rest of the country via Facebook. The story of Bouazizi's dramatic protest against the state, against corruption, bribery, and the misuse of the wealth of the country were the subjects of Facebook comments posted by users throughout Tunisia.

After two days of protests, on Saturday, December 18, 2010, the people of Sidi Bouzid were surprised by the regime's use of brutal force against them. The police came with sticks, tear gas, and trucks to shut down the protest. The demonstrators cleverly used an iron wire to knock police off their motorbikes, giving protesters the opportunity to take their gear. Demonstrators who were chased into a small side street by police succeeded in taking a tear gas gun and a protective shield from their pursuers. Awyneh described the event as a true battle between police and demonstrators that continued into the late hours of the night. More security forces arrived in Sidi Bouzid the next day, December 19. A group of lawyers, trade unionists, doctors, and activists from Sidi Bouzid formed a committee to protect vulnerable people.

"We marched to the area of the security forces, chanting the slogan "*Shedin, Shedin*" [We strongly demand the release of the prisoners]," recounts Awyneh. The demonstrators were attacked again with tear gas and clubs. Demonstrators who were caught taking pictures were brutally beaten by the police. Nonetheless, notes Awyneh, "a single photograph" of Bouazizi's act was successfully posted on the Internet. The young person who took the photo was arrested the next day. In Awyneh's words, "Sidi Bouzid became a city under siege."

Awyneh explains that Facebook and social media helped spread the image and the word of the protests. "Our big sit-in in front of the court was reported on French TV and Al Jazeera [thanks to photos shared on social media]."

Awyneh praises the attorneys who made the footage available for social media and television use. Once the international media and Al Jazeera started paying attention to the events of Sidi Bouzid, "everywhere in the country sit-ins were organized. Our sit-ins were cloned." Some of the chants by demonstrators demanded an end to the regime: "The regime needs to fall, along with its collaborators and followers."

Awyneh notes that the protesters seemed to work in shifts, a tactic that exhausted the security forces. Young people were active mainly at night. During the day attorneys, trade unionists, doctors, and other activists came out to voice their frustration. With each passing day, the spontaneous demonstrations became better organized.

With a state stranglehold on the media, there was a nearly total media blackout on reporting of the protests. Many outlets did not even report that there had been a disturbance in Sidi Bouzid. "The only thing we wanted to do was to bring a picture to the world in order to feel that we were breathing," explains Awyneh. Tunisians working for French broadcasters, the BBC, and Al Jazeera were able to break the media blockade and bring news of the unraveling events in Sidi Bouzid to the world (Al Jazeera, May 24, 2012).

The revolution came from the most unexpected of locations at the most unexpected moment. Media, intellectuals, and politicians all seemed to underestimate the potential impact of the demonstrations in Sidi Bouzid. This can be attributed to the city's location along Tunisia's poverty belt and a population made up largely of poor families who had migrated from the southern part of the country. Intellectual assumptions that only an educated and politically engaged middle class could drive political change had led the poverty belt to be forgotten. This is not a new story, of course. Nearly all popular revolutions start in unexpected places, driven by ordinary people.

The lack of transparency of the regime and its news outlets following Bouazizi's act of protest fueled the revolutionary atmosphere in Sidi Bouzid. On December 24, the security forces killed another "martyr," the protester Menzel Sidi Bouzayène. To quell the unrest, eight thousand policemen were deployed to the city, firing *rasas al-hayy* (live bullets).

Soon after the announcement of Bouazizi's death, the revolution caught fire in Gasrin, Thala, and Tunis. On December 28, 2010, Ben Ali made a speech based on *tahdid and takhwif* (promises and threats). Young people responded by burning tires on the main streets. Thala became the city of martyrs. Twenty "martyrs" died in the city of Gasrin alone.

Awyneh was present at the funeral of Bouazizi. "I delivered a eulogy at the cemetery, and I said that the legal community offers the deepest condolences to Mohamed Bouazizi's family. Bouazizi's [sacrifice] gave us a beautiful painting, one that nobody could decode, one whose symbolism no one could understand ." he said. Awyneh added that Bouazizi's actions had brought to light problems more disturbing than the burning of a body. "It is the crisis of options that are flawed from the very beginning," he said. The people in Sidi Bouzid and across the poverty belt looked to Tunis, waiting for an answer to their demands for change (Al Jazeera, May 24, 2012).

Whirlpool of Rage versus Timid Reporting

Al Jazeera began its first rudimentary coverage of the Tunisian protests as early as December 25, 2010. The network reported the killings in Menzil Bouziane, the protests, and the spread of sit-ins to different cities. The tone of the report was that of measured concern over secondhand accounts of the developing situation. On the same day, Al Jazeera reporter Nabil Rahani spoke about a "polarization of social conflict" after the killing of new protesters.

Two thousand young people demonstrated in Menzil Bouziane after the killings. Al Jazeera reported, "According to the German news agency (Deutsche Presse Agentur), a youngster was killed by National Guard bullets, and [as a result] the youth took out their rage on the police cars. The report showed burned cars. A young man, a university graduate, set himself on fire. Another joined him [in committing suicide], spurred by the impossibility of leading a decent life" (Al Jazeera, December 25, 2010).

The "killing with live bullets" constituted a dramatic turning point in the events of Sidi Bouzid. Voices from inside and outside the country began to demand justice. Al Jazeera called the protests an "intifada" (uprising or resistance). Lacking images or on-the-ground reporting from within Sidi Bouzid, Al Jazeera filled its December 25 report with a graphic listing the projects Ben Ali had recently announced on Tunisian national TV, including programs to spur job creation and more government spending in economically vulnerable regions. "There are no target dates for the realization of these projects, say the critics," Rahani told viewers of Ben Ali's promises. "[They say] these are only calming pills and not real medicine." Rahani also noted criticisms of the *langue de bois* (wooden language) of the government response to citizen outrage.

External sources, including Reuters and the BBC, were credited with providing the reporting that was aired on the segment. At the same time, Al Jazeera noted that other Tunisian media were singing the praises of economic gains and infrastructure improvements achieved by the government. These local outlets placed the blame for disruptions in the street on the people of Sidi Bouzid. The demonstrations in Sidi Bouzid, Rahani concluded, had disturbed the picture of an economic paradise put forth by the Tunisian government, a picture impoverished Tunisians had seen only on television.

On December 26, Al Jazeera reported that a confrontation between security forces and residents in the province of Sidi Bouzid had taken place. The report described the clash as a crackdown in the form of an overnight raid on protesters. The network described the protests, now spreading to Tunis, as social and focused on unemployment and poverty rather than political issues. For this segment, the network managed to obtain footage of the regional government building, but the footage was shaky. The network reported that the protests were entering their ninth day, that one person had been killed and another wounded. Al Jazeera's coverage stressed the solidarity among protesters throughout different regions of the country.

On December 27, Al Jazeera announced that the protests had spread across Tunisia. The Tunisian media, network anchors reported, had been silenced by the severe censorship enforced by the government. Al Jazeera reporters offered effusive praise for social media and the young Tunisians who were using it to feed Al Jazeera and other networks sound and images of the protests, however rough they might have been.

On the same day, another report described more demonstrations of solidarity with Sidi Bouzid's citizens in every city in Tunisia. There were marches everywhere in the north, south, and east. Crediting various sources with providing information for the report, Al Jazeera's video consisted largely of previously aired footage of trade unionists in front of the regional government building.

On the December 27, Al Jazeera also aired a critical analysis of reporting on the protests by Tunisian television stations and newspapers. According to the analysis, citizen-journalists were vastly superior to the "submissive media." Al Jazeera contrasted the traditional Tunisian media, maintaining their well-funded status and security at the end of a government leash, with the army of regular citizens, using cell phones to challenge government power and show the world what the established media refused to turn their cameras on. The analysis laid bare both Tunisian submission to government censorship and the impotence of that censorship in the face of new technology.

As it had with demonstrators in the streets of Sidi Bouzid, Al Jazeera's examination of Tunisian media stressed the apolitical motives of the citizen-journalists responsible for much of the news coming from within Tunisia. They were described by Lotfi Hajji, the bureau chief of Al Jazeera Tunisia, as seeking "partnership in the development of a true media in Tunisia" (Al Jazeera, December 10, 2014).

Clips from Tunisian news programs illustrated the failure of the local press to report on what was potentially the nation's most earth-shattering news story in more than two decades. In one clip a female news anchor dismisses the events in Sidi Bouzid, referring to the protests as stemming from "the unverified interpretations that some people are using to explain what happened last week in Sidi Bouzid."

One Al Jazeera correspondent, Mohamed Krichen, bemoaned the fact that this willful ignorance of the reality of *qahr* was representative of the conditions that protesters in Sidi Bouzid and the rest of the country were rebelling against. The correspondent went on to explain that even the independent newspaper *Al Sabah*, in an article entitled "In the Heart of Sidi Bouzid," had downplayed the unrest. Then, the following bullet points were displayed on screen, which outlined Al Jazeera's stance on the unrest:

- Opinions . . . are unanimous that the social conditions are problematic and that development is limited and access to privilege is closed.
- The situation of Bouazizi is similar to [that of] other youth in the region. They suffer from unemployment and marginalization.
- The suicide [self-immolation of Bouazizi] was a result of the behavior of civil servants in the region who denied the victim self-expression.

Al Sabah wrote, according to Al Jazeera, that the regional employment union of Sidi Bouzid had petitioned the regime to free all of its detainees. It quoted a representative of the Human Rights Organization in Tunisia descrying the opportunism of radical parties in the region and the unpredictability of the street. A spokesperson for the Popular Unity Party was also quoted: "We all are responsible [for the unrest]." The coverage of another newspaper, which was closely tied to the government newspaper, *Shuruq*, was similar to that of the independent newspapers; the newspaper *Al Watan* of the Democratic Union Party had almost identical coverage.

Al Jazeera exposed the Tunisian regime and media outlets as conspirators in a propaganda war against the Tunisian people. Reporting that stressed shared responsibility for the unrest and the presence of actors with ulterior motives was a precondition for the easing of government censorship of select publications. The segment concluded with what would become a common refrain in Al Jazeera's reporting on the unrest—the assertion that independent news reporting in Tunisia was made impossible by the alliance between the media and the regime. This alliance was again contrasted with the protesters and citizen-journalists: "The demonstrators didn't care about and didn't pay attention to the official media or semiofficial mediators, or even the correspondence of satellite TV [including Al Jazeera]." They relied on their cell phones and updates from their social media cohorts. As Al Jazeera put it, "They were the event, and they were the reporters of that same event" (Al Jazeera, December 27, 2010).

Al Jazeera news reports on the protests featured a photo of the regional government building in Sidi Bouzid as a symbol of the origin of people's rage in Tunisia. "The Internet doesn't know censorship," commented one Al Jazeera reporter. "They gave us audiovisual material that no single satellite channel could find an alternative for in order to cover the events in Tunisia" (Al Jazeera, December 27, 2010).

This praise for the courage and ingenuity of citizen-reporters versus the malaise of government-controlled media would serve as a recurring frame that would go stronger with each use. During the Egyptian revolution, an Al Jazeera program spotlighted this dereliction of duty in clips from a Tunisian talk show in which ephemeral topics took precedence while the growing social unrest was ignored. Al Jazeera would offer similar critiques of both independent and state media in its coverage of other Arab Spring nations, especially post-Morsi Egypt.

On the same day, another Al Jazeera news report aired, narrated by a female reporter whose name was not given. On-screen, previously shown photos of trade union demonstrators are shown as the reporter says that the "ceiling of demands" is getting higher and that they are changing from "social demands to political demands." Protesters were now demanding more freedoms and new limitations on mandates from the president. The report stressed the continued peaceful nature of the demonstrations and the continuing attempts by security forces to crush them. The news report ends with the words "A demonstration started over a slice of bread, but it remains unclear as to where it is going."

The next day, December 28, Al Jazeera reports described a growing intensity in the demonstrations, which seemed to lack any kind of "visible hand" organizing or guiding them. As in the previously described news reports, Al Jazeera's coverage framed the demonstrations as "social, without any political intention to destabilize the regime." Most of these reports were filed by reporters who identified themselves as Nabil Raihani and Bibe Uld Mhadi. Under later scrutiny, these names were found to be fabricated.[3]

The news report showed protesters holding signs made on A4 paper expressing support for Sidi Bouzid. Rows of attorneys in their robes stood in front of the Palace of Justice holding signs saying "Justice, Justice, Justice." Again, the report stressed that these demonstrations were spontaneous and had not been organized by political parties or organizations. They were fueled, the anchor Mohamed Krichen explained, by independent ideology.

The secular character of the protests in Tunisia was very clear. However, this Al Jazeera report focuses on the only veiled woman among the attorneys. It's an attempt to show the pluralistic nature of the protests, but it's also an Islamizing lens.

The scene cuts to a crowd shouting, "With blood and life we will sacrifice ourselves [ya Sidi Bouzid]," a slogan borrowed from Palestinian demonstrations against Israel. As the reporter asks questions about the "whirlpool of rage," pictures of the 2008 mineworker demonstrations in the south fill the screen. "The expression of pain doesn't need a leader," says the reporter. "The knot in [the people's] tongues has disappeared, and now the public square showcases their own leadership skills."

On the same day, December 28, another Al Jazeera news report delivered by Nabil Rahani warned about the increasing intensity of the "demonstrations of rage." "The protests are entering a tunnel, a point of no return, a phase nobody has any interest in getting into," Rahani said.

The word "rage" would come to be used with ever increasing frequency during Al Jazeera newscasts about the protests during the Arab Spring, including the many "Fridays of Rage" during the Egyptian revolution and counterrevolution. The following day, Mohamed Krichen dedicated an entire episode of his talk show to the Tunisian crisis. On December 30, an Al Jazeera news report began with footage of two blue trucks closing off an important artery of Tunis to block protesters. President Ben Ali was also shown, appearing on Tunisian national television to accuse extremists of manipulating the demonstrations. The report detailed the wave of ministerial changes and letters from political parties and organizations expressing support for Ben Ali. It is a common convention in Arab and African countries for radio and TV presenters to read such letters aloud (Al Jazeera, December 28, 2010).

On December 31, Al Jazeera reported on developments in Mohamed Ali Square in Tunis. A representative of the Tunisian Workers' Union had urged demonstrators to support Sidi Bouzid's demands, according to the report, which cited widespread marginalization and economic inequality in the country as the source of union anger. Al Jazeera's footage was taken from a hidden camera in the crowd. Security forces had closed all the passages to Mohamed Ali Square, making it impossible for a broadcast team to gain access to the protest area. The shaky images showed union members chanting antigovernment slogans. But there was not enough demonstration footage to fill the entire report. The image of a press release signed by six trade unions calling for a demonstration by all workers provided a visual background for the report. It was dated December 27 and adorned with old-fashioned rubber stamps. The Al Jazeera segment referred to the Tunisian newspaper *Al Sabah*, whose reporters had been on the ground during the demonstration. According to the newspaper, the slogans shouted by protesters were "very controversial." The newspaper also reported that the political demands made by the trade unionists had to do with more than just labor statutes. Al Jazeera also turned to Tunisian national television for coverage of the demonstrations. The secretary general of the trade union appeared on the national network, saying his trade union had not called for any demonstrations in Mohamed Ali Square and that his Tunisian Central Trade Union desired a "rational solution" to problems with the government. Another union spokesperson downplayed union involvement in the protests, saying, "The slogans [of protesters] don't involve the trade union."

Aside from the surreptitiously filmed, handheld footage in Mohamed Ali Square, Al Jazeera showed only still photographs of the demonstrations. One photo showed a man holding up a French baguette, offering a coy nod to the French Revolution in the face of a North African dictator's tanks. Al Jazeera reporter Lotfi Hajji continued to allude to past revolutions, asserting that the "man of the street" should be acknowledged and helped to attain "his" basic demands for "bread and freedom," a subtle nod to the Bolshevik Revolution. In hindsight, the conventions and frames that emerged during Al Jazeera's coverage of the protests in Mohamed Ali Square were the same that the network would use in its coverage of protests in Tahrir Square in Egypt, several months later. Mohamed Ali Square was portrayed as a sort of boxing ring, where the opposing forces of Tunisian protesters and their government would fight it out in a contest to decide who would chart the course of the nation's future. For fans of American pop culture, the square would seem aptly named for such a purpose, though it should be noted that the square is named after an attorney-activist prominent during the preceding century rather than the legendary American boxer.

In previous days, demonstrators had been equipped with small signs—just an A4 or slightly bigger sheet of paper. Slogans were written with ordinary felt-tip markers, with the exception of the attorneys' slogan, "Justice," which was printed on signs in typeface.

On the same day, December 31, another surprising piece of news broke. Libya officially announced it would lift all administrative fees and constraints on Tunisians wishing to enter and work in Libya. It seemed Tunisia's neighbor to the east was attempting to help calm the growing unrest. News reports described a phone conversation between Libyan leader Muammar Qaddafi and Ben Ali, where the two discussed a framework for consultation and coordination between the two countries in an effort to respond to the protests. Al Jazeera reporters described Qaddafi's intervention in a Tunisian social crisis unprecedented.

Also on that day, Al Jazeera reported that Ben Ali had fired three ministers and governors, including the governor of Sidi Bouzid. Over blurry video footage of the streets of Tunisia, the network's reporters described widespread protests that continued despite the concessionary effort by the government. Al Jazeera announced the killing of another young person, Chokri Belahdar, when *rasas al hayy* (live bullets) penetrated his spine.

In the streets, the people's shouts had evolved into a direct demand that Ben Ali step down from power. In response, Ben Ali appeared on national television to deliver a statement tinged with assurances and threats: "The law will be applied *wa'ada wa'tawa'da* [with all rigor, with all rigor]," he told the nation.

Al Jazeera described Ben Ali's response to the demonstrations as increasingly characterized by a "policy alternating between soft and hard approaches." Ben Ali had told his civil servants to take the demands of the citizens seriously. The network showed the famous photograph of Ben Ali visiting an essentially mummified but still living Bouazizi in the hospital. Al Jazeera commenters suggested that Ben Ali was trying to contain unrest by pursuing programs to stimulate regional development. The same people who were quick to recognize Ben Ali's earnest attempts to mollify an unhappy public, though, were equally quick to note that security forces had acted quite differently.

The person giving the December 30 news report on Tunisia is unequivocal about his admiration for the protesters, opining, "The demonstrators refuted all the prejudice about this country that had developed during the twenty-three years of Ben Ali's rule." The report emphasizes the government's wish "to return to order and stability before Monday, the day when the students will go back to school. Schools are full of young people who are without job opportunities and don't know what destiny awaits them. The authorities are afraid that the youth will join the demonstrations sparked by the flame that came one day from Sidi Bouzid."

Al Jazeera promoted a specific interpretation of the events in Tunisia, presenting its reporting through explicitly antigovernment and antiestablishment frames. On New Year's Day, 2011, Al Jazeera's report on Tunisia, delivered by Besam Bounini, focused on the expressed concern of the United Nations, United States, European Union, and United Kingdom over the excessive use of force in Tunisia. The following day's news report highlighted the failure of the Tunisian media, public and semiprivate, in dealing with the Sidi Bouzid case.

The "nonexistent local media," according to Al Jazeera, reinforced the opacity and hegemony of the government's "wooden [empty] language . . . aggrandizing" the leader. Clips taken from various Tunisian television outlets were offered as evidence of this failure by the local media. The critique was a less than subtle attempt by Al Jazeera to take a metaphorical sledgehammer to the remnants of the media–government conspiracy in Tunisia.

Al Jazeera's efforts to draw a stark distinction between its "highly engaged" reporting and that of the local media were essential to the blossoming of the Jasmine Revolution. This focus on building a distinct identity within the Arab media landscape was a constant theme for the network throughout the Arab Spring. Al Jazeera built a niche for itself by portraying its role in unfolding events as that of not only a news network but also an engaged participant on the side of the people against oppressive regimes and sycophantic media. In the case of Tunisia, as well as Egypt, Al Jazeera demonstrated the strong link between local media and the autocratic regime. Government control did not end with its ability to muzzle negative reporting, but extended so far as to allow the government to use local media as a conduit for state propaganda. The simultaneous chorus of mea culpas by Tunisia's local media over their failure to cover the events in Sidi Bouzid served as evidence of the strong media–government link. "Everyone at the same time!" exclaimed the reporter providing the voiceover for the news report.

The local Tunisian media responded to the unfavorable coverage with their own criticism of the satellite network. Al Jazeera, in turn, doubled down on its war of words, describing pushback against its coverage in the local press as a "coordinated attack on Al Jazeera." Network commentators described "a permanent crisis of media in Tunisia and a permanent offense and attack on foreign media outlets." The lone exception to this was the "youth media in Tunisia," described as the only media presence with any level of engagement or sense of objectivity and independence in its reporting on the unrest spreading throughout the country.

The Al Jazeera news report on January 6, 2011, focused on the funeral of Bouazizi. The report functioned as a sort eulogy for the young fruit vendor from Sidi Bouzid. "Bouazizi protested against his conditions twice," intoned the reporter, "first by selling fruit and vegetables as a university graduate, and second . . . by burning himself, which ultimately turned into something that set Tunisia alight as well." The report stressed the courage of the "enraged" youth following the self-immolation of Bouazizi. The report also covered news from the rest of the Arab world. Algerian police had intervened to disperse protests in Algiers.

Hiba Harbi, the secretary general of the Tunisian democrats, was shown criticizing the Tunisian media for ignoring the demonstrations, creating explosive situations, and denying the stifling of Tunisian expression. He also called out foreign media, mainly Al Jazeera, for adding fuel to the fire of discontent. The anchor described Harbi's comments as "scapegoating" the innocents.

The segment gives way to footage of demonstrators participating in what is described as "a spontaneous gathering to express rage." On-screen, a car is shown burning in front of the closed doors of the regional government building, with the commentator stating that no government officials would speak about on the demonstration without written permission from the ministry in Tunis. The report ends with the commentator saying that invisible hands, perhaps those of the government, still prod the *"jamra* [burning charcoal] beneath the ashes" in Sidi Bouzid.

By January 14, 2011, it had become clear that Ben Ali was having real trouble finding a country that would grant him asylum. In France, which considered Ben Ali an ally, the sizable North African community voiced staunch opposition to granting the Tunisian leader safe haven. The French minister of foreign affairs, Michèle Alliot-Marie, had resigned earlier that week in response to pressure from the North African community.

Meanwhile, Al Jazeera's news coverage focused on criticism from the United Nations, France, Germany, and other countries leveled at the violence of the Tunisian authorities in dealing with protesters. The anger stirred by these reports in Europe kept the pressure high on European governments to deny Ben Ali refuge in their countries. Al Jazeera reporters described efforts by Western leaders to distance themselves from Ben Ali as indicative of a major swing in their attitudes, driven by the crisis, from praise for the Tunisian model to an increasingly anti–Ben Ali atmosphere throughout the West. Al Jazeera commentators stressed the role of the Arab diaspora in Europe in bringing about such a radical change in attitudes. Outside of the Tunisian Embassy in Paris, European Tunisians were shown chanting in a demonstration against Ben Ali.

The day's second report was drastically different from previous Al Jazeera reports on the Tunisia crisis. It was the moment that Al Jazeera had been waiting for: a live report without the use of hidden cameras or other clandestine means of covering the events. The newscast came live from Tunis, where the editor in chief, who had been working under trying conditions and in hiding, couldn't control his emotions of joy and disbelief. Apparently fighting off tears, he tells the audience, "I am reporting from here, my country, Tunisia." The report became, in essence, its own subject, highlighting the departure of Ben Ali as a watershed, allowing Al Jazeera (and other media) much more freedom to report without fear of government interference. With Ben Ali's departure that day from Tunisia, the Al Jazeera news reports became live and well documented.

Can Al Jazeera's coverage of the Tunisian demonstrations be credited with leading the revolution? It was not the mere presentation of images that produced a revolutionary atmosphere; it was instead the production of meaning relating to *qahr* (oppression) that led to the eruption (Benslama 2011, 10). Al Jazeera's news reports were well crafted and focused on specific frames that created a coherent meaning beyond the simple facts of the story, and it was these that encouraged revolt. Al Jazeera's images and words during the Tunisian revolution and the rest of Arab Spring consistently advanced an antiestablishment message that chipped away at the legitimacy of the ruler.

On January 15, 2011, a dispatch from Al Jazeera reporter Fawzi Bashri began with video footage of Ben Ali saying, "I understood you," but the reporter answers him, boldly saying, "It is already too late." Bashri explains that the people want a dignity that can't be realized without freedom. Text on Al Jazeera's screen indicates that "Ben Ali arrived in Jeddah." People can't survive on bread only, Bashri says, stressing that the spirit of revolution "never dies, in spite of repression." The famous photograph of Ben Ali and Bouazizi lying in a hospital bed, covered in bandages, is again displayed. The following comment is paired with this face-to-face confrontation between Bouazizi and the man who took away his dreams: "Mohamed dies, but the Tunisian people live through him." This sentence echoes the words of the first caliph after Prophet Muhammad's death, who said, "Muhammad died, but Islam does not die." By starting the report with a dismissal of Ben Ali's apology, "I understood you," and displaying the photo of Bouazizi and Ben Ali, the reporter Bashri poses as the voice of Bouazizi and the triumph of the Jasmine Revolution.

Al Jazeera's cameras filmed freely in the wake of Ben Ali's departure, showing things the network had never before been able to show. A woman in European clothing sits on the shoulders of another protester holding a sign that is illegible in the shot. Next to her is a man holding a sign in English: "Yes we can!" a nod to Barrack Obama's first presidential campaign. Other slogans read "*Degage*" (Get out) and "Ben Ali wanted to be president for life, but the people said, 'Life is for me.'"

"The sky [for Ben Ali] is too small, the earth is getting smaller, and between the sky and the earth the dictator has nowhere to go," Bashri says over a photo montage of past dictators whose reigns ended in a search for exile: the Iranian shah and his wife, who found the doors of the United States closed to them after the revolution; the former dictator of Sudan, Numeri, ousted in 1985 and living in Cairo; and finally the dead and muddy body of the Romanian Communist leader Nicolai Ceausescu. "France has already said no [to Ben Ali's request for asylum]." The euphoria on the streets of Tunisia jumps from the screen—even policemen are crying with joy. The news report reiterates the sentiment expressed by the mufti al-Qaradawi: revolution must not be stolen. "Ben Ali the individual left, but Ben Ali the regime is still there," the anchor says.

The Al Jazeera news reports summarized in the following paragraphs document the key points in the history of the popular uprisings in Tunisia. They show brutality by the police, expose the blackout of local media, and praise the work of the youth who used the cameras on their cell phones and social media to spread news and awareness of the events taking place. They also reveal how Arab governments (chiefly in Tunisia) blocked websites, mimicking the Iranian model of censoring Internet activism during the Iranian elections of 2009, when access to YouTube and the websites of activists was blocked. Tunisia was near the top of Reporters Without Borders' list of the world's worst offenders in the realm of government censorship, topping all other Arab countries. But ultimately, the Tunisian bloggers outsmarted the censors. As one Al Jazeera reporter put it, "In spite of the censorship, the inventive young people succeeded in proving that the Internet can be a space without limits." Al Jazeera added a mythical dimension and air of romance to online activism.

On January 16, 2011, Al Jazeera praised the dynamism of Tunisian society, including the spread of community activist groups throughout the neighborhoods of Tunis. The news report also noted the embarrassment of French president Nicholas Sarkozy, who had been "severely criticized" by the French press for his long-standing support of Tunisia's dictator, but Sarkozy was able, at least marginally, to "redeem himself" by refusing to grant asylum to Ben Ali. New footage of the demonstrators, including women in European clothing without veils or headscarves, accompanied the report. People held signs reading "*Tunis hura,*

hura" (Tunis, free, free). Members of the Tunisian diaspora abroad were another focus of the segment. Many French cities displayed solidarity with Tunisia by hoisting the Tunisian flag.

News reports on the following days showed continuing marches and sit-ins across the country. Al Jazeera regularly broadcast portraits of the Tunisian people, describing their vitality and high spirit. The narratives that Al Jazeera crafted around the tragedy of Bouazizi were largely responsible for establishing the story in the context the deeply ingrained collective memory of the Arab publics. During the demonstrations people chanted:

> When people choose to live in freedom,
> Destiny will respond and take action,
> Darkness will surely fade away,
> And the chains will certainly be broken.

These words, spoken by Tunisian youth nearly eighty years before, would become the resounding rallying cry of the Tunisian youth of 2011 who chanted in the streets as the despotic regime of Ben Ali was overthrown. The words of the Tunisian poet Abu al-Qasim al-Shabi would also be invoked during the revolutions that followed throughout the Arab world and would become part of the new national anthem of Tunisia. Abu al-Qasim al-Shabi became an icon of the Tunisian Revolution. Demonstrators learned his verses by heart and chanted them in the streets.

With the fall of the Ben Ali regime, plans by the Islamist leader of the Ennahda (Renaissance) party, Rached Ghannouchi, to return from exile in London emerged as one of the most important news stories about the future of Tunisia. On January 31, about two weeks after news of this planned homecoming surfaced, an Al Jazeera news report aired. The segment began with video footage of Ghannouchi leaving his house in the suburbs of London on his way to Gatwick Airport with other members of the Ennahda party. "His return comes at a crucial moment for the country," the commentator says. The camera zooms in on the plane before cutting to a close-up of Ghannouchi's face.

"I am going back with a big dream," says Ghannouchi. "This blessed revolution carried out by the youth of Tunisia and made possible by the blood of martyrs succeeded in ousting a harsh dictator. Now we want to create a just system where there is a balance in development between regions with real urbanism and regions that have been destroyed by poverty, like Sidi Bouzid and other places."

In Tunisia, as Ghannouchi descended the steps from the plane, a large crowd was gathered on the tarmac. Thousands of supporters cheered inside the Cartago airport, holding small, simple welcome signs made with felt-tip markers. Men and women wore the Tunisian flag around their shoulders or their waists. In order to show that Ghannouchi was welcomed not just by bearded Islamists, Al Jazeera interviewed a clean-shaven man who said, "This is a feast for the Tunisian republic. . . . Look at all these people who love him."⁵ A veiled woman with over-size black sunglasses offered a different opinion: "He had to return because he was forced to leave [the United Kingdom]." Another voice rang out, "We die but the nation lives." A bearded man, introduced as Chokri Mazuli, recited a verse from the Quran saying that prophets are often called liars, but in the end they are granted victory from Allah. He seemed to have chosen the verse as an implicit comparison of Ghannouchi's arrival to the Prophet's return to Mecca after a long exile in Medina.

On February 1, 2011, Al Jazeera reported troubling violence against businesses, doctors, and attorneys —all of it lingering in a Tunisia without Ben Ali. The report ends with a woman, whose face is somewhat obscured, telling a reporter that she had lost a son to the revolution but that she had other sons she would readily sacrifice for freedom and dignity. The camera then focuses on a dead body covered in blood as the commentator's delivers his last sentence: "[There is] no stepping back in demanding justice, whatever the sacrifice may be."

In Al Jazeera's coverage of post–Ben Ali Tunisia, one gets the sense of an almost deliberate search for religious symbolism. A February 25 Al Jazeera news report exemplifies this trend. The segment focuses on a Friday religious service where worshippers had spilled into the streets because the mosque was overcrowded that day. The day was termed "Al Juma' Al 'Adhima" (the Great Friday). From this date onward, Al Jazeera's reporting on Tunisia would take on an increasingly religious focus. The coverage casts an Islamizing aura over seemingly secular events, saturating the reporting with images with strong Islamic connotations, like the headscarf, the veil, bearded men, and Friday congregational prayers.

In addition to this Islamizing lens, another ingredient in Al Jazeera's framing repertoire was its positioning of the West as an enemy of the Arab world and Islam. The network was quick to point out the West's failure to stand up for the rights of the Tunisian people in the same way it had worked to liberate Eastern Europe from Communist domination.

On March 1, 2011, Al Jazeera's news report focused entirely on the portrayal of the Arab revolutions by Western media. Coverage of Georgia's "Revolution of the Roses," where the return of President Saakashvili from the United States was "portrayed romantically for almost nine days," served as a contrast to the dis-interest of these same outlets in Arab and Muslim struggles for freedom. Heavy media coverage of Ukraine in the lead-up to the "Orange Revolution," devised by Western leaders in search of an ally in the East, served to drive home the link between the interests of Western leadership and ostensibly independent Western media. In the case of Tunisia, though, "the West didn't pay enough attention to the Tunisian revolution [because] it didn't believe in the power of the 'submissive' Arab people." Footage of Tony Blair, in which he said he didn't "believe in the revolution," was used as a case in point, although Blair also said, "There will be change."

"Tony Blair spoke about the danger of change to the security of Israel," the reporter says. "Tony Blair couldn't say this if Western media took Arab nations as seriously as they did Georgia." The report ends with pictures of harmonious protests in Georgia sarcastically compared to "an orchestra or symphony." The news report chastises the West for failing to take Arab democratic aspirations seriously.

Al Jazeera's monolithic portrayal of the West as disregarding the human rights of the Arab and Muslim world is common in the network's reporting, but it ignores the fact that many Muslims living in Western Europe enjoy a far greater level of freedom than those in the Maghreb or Mashreq.

Another common theme of Al Jazeera's reporting is "Western hostility" to Arab awakening. This includes Western and Israeli warnings about the marginalizing effect of political Islam on minority communities. As the impresario of political Islam in Tunisia, the network set out to gauge how the Jewish community in Tunisia had fared after the fall of the secular dictator Ben Ali. On May 28, 2011, Al Jazeera aired a segment on the Tunisian Jewish community in Djerba. The report opens with images of the beautiful synagogue of Djerba and a Tunisian reading from the Torah. The narrator says that many fewer believers and tourists come to the synagogue from Tunisia and abroad than they did some years before. The Jewish community, according to the report, says that nothing has changed for them since the revolution, and they will not leave the country "even though Israel might try to seduce them" into migrating and "to scare them" with the threat of rising political Islam. The president of the Jewish community, Perez Trabelsi, says, "We were a little bit scared in the beginning, but this is my country." A bearded Muslim says on camera, "We have excellent relationships [with the Jewish community]." The camera settles on a sizable Star of David, followed by a number of empty places of business. A young man in a Diesel Jeans T-shirt says, "There is less work [than before the revolution]." Another man named Zaen Haddad says, "Business is dead for ninety percent [of us]." The underlying message appears to be that people are more concerned with their ability to earn a living than with petty religious differences. Over video footage of schoolchildren wearing kippahs, the report ends with the comment, "Between the things that are constant and the things that are changing, the Jewish reality in Tunis is impacted just as much as everybody else in Tunisia. Good and bad things have effects on the community, but in spite of hidden plans to uproot the Jewish community from Tunis they say, 'We are here to stay.'" The choice of wording reveals the underlying frame, that outside forces—mainly Israel—hope to uproot the Tunisian Jewish community that has been living in the country for centuries by frightening them with stories about the dangers of political Islam. In other words, Al Jazeera portrays Israel as a bigger danger than political Islam.

The Jasmine Revolution in Review

Al Jazeera's coverage of the Tunisian revolution was itself a major news story. It had a significant impact on the direction, the energy, and the actions of people throughout the course of the revolution. Tunisia's revolution was sudden, and it occurred in an unexpected, remote location.

Consequently, Al Jazeera's coverage of the developing events began with cautious reporting efforts based on the limited secondhand sources at the network's disposal. Al Jazeera heaped credit on the young bloggers and online social networkers for serving as the most important link between Tunisians living under repression and the outside world. As Al Jazeera gained a firmer grasp of the events, its reporting grew stronger, more engaging, and, perhaps most important, more engaged. Al Jazeera employed a team of Tunisian correspondents who knew the country well and who used their networks of friends and family to help them provide bold reporting while the regime was still in power and shutting down all but a few hand-selected media outlets.

It wasn't until the day Ben Ali was ousted that Al Jazeera deployed its full capabilities to report live from Tunisia. While the revolution was still ongoing, it expanded its *qahr* (oppression) frame as the ultimate lens through which to view the oppression that had existed under Ben Ali (who had left the country) and continued under what remained of the Ben Ali regime, despite the expulsion of its leader. Al Jazeera constructed a heroic narrative around the "sacrifice" of Bouazizi, painting him as a passionate and honorable martyr for his people, while becoming ever more aggressive in its approach to reporting news about the unrest. Al Jazeera positioned itself on the side of the people rather than on the side of the remnants of a regime that had been forced to adopt reforms in the hope of remaining in power. Al Jazeera had one thing in mind, helping political Islam to victory. This preliminary conclusion is consistent with my findings over time (see chapter 1). Especially, after the return of Rached Ghannouchi from exile in London on January 30, 2011, the coverage took on an Islamizing tone. Al Jazeera described Ghannouchi's Ennahda party as an alternative to a scattered left-wing and liberal opposition. The network claimed that Ghannouchi had a strategy for eradicating all forms of *qahr*—a coherent vision, a solid political program, and a loyal cadre and base he had been developing for more than twenty years. The demonstrations shown on Al Jazeera evolved and became better organized over time, as protesters mastered the art of making protest signs. Before Ben Ali left, they were written by hand and were the work of amateurs.

Even though Al Jazeera forewarned of a possible revolution in Tunisia in 2008, when it described the events of Gafsa in the southern part of the country as a "revolution of the hungry," the network itself wasn't prepared for the Jasmine Revolution in Tunisia. Its suddenness was mediated by the quick response of a globalized, tech-savvy group of young Tunisians who had mastered the art of mass communication through social media and blogs, largely updated with mobile devices. The Tunisian writer, poet, and journalist Abdelwahab Meddeb argues in his book *Printemps de Tunis: La métamorphose de l'histoire* that what characterized the Tunisian revolution was its element of surprise. "C'est arrivé par surprise," he wrote. Meddeb and the French Algerian historian Benjamin Stora compared the youth of the Tunisian revolution to the youth who overcame the fear on November 9, 1989, during the dismantling of the Berlin Wall. Meddeb also referred to July 14, 1789, when the divine monarchy was brought down in France. In terms of a revolution, suddenness and surprise are linked to speed; therefore, many authors discussed the acceleration of Arab history making and change during this period (Stora 2011; Meddeb 2011, 10).

Al Jazeera developed a *qahr* frame, focusing on years of repression by an aging dictator and widespread nepotism and corruption cultivated by his family. Tunisia became synonymous with the broader situation of *qahr* afflicting much of the Arab world. However, the Tunisian uprising took Al Jazeera by surprise , possibly because it originated on the periphery and most of the network's correspondents were located in the urban areas of Tunisia. The Tunisian psychoanalyst Fethi Benslama argues in his book *Soudain la Révolution!* that the concept of revolution had become "inconceivable" in Tunisia because it had disappeared from the common lexicon. For many, it took time to believe that it had really happened. Benslama recalled that after the revolution someone "really exceeded the dream" by taking down the street sign for November 7th Square (a reference to the day Ben Ali had become president). According to Benslama, the Tunisian revolution went beyond reactivation because it was actually reinvention. The word "revolution" had disappeared from daily usage, but when revolution actually came it was hard to believe it was really happening (Benslama 2011, 9–16). In contrast, Al Jazeera had used the word "revolution" liberally and almost systematically since 1997.

Benslama offers an interesting analysis that is helpful for linking two prominent aspects of Al Jazeera's reporting: the *qahr* media frame and the explosion of subjectivity in the cyber activities of the youth. "Subjectivity" refers to how each individual sees or takes his or her place in the social world. An individual opinion or perspective can affect behavior, beliefs, or actions regarding various issues. Subjectivity is way of understanding and interacting with the social world (Lawson and Garrod, 2001, 242). It is impossible to be completely immune to subjectivity, and the Internet is a medium that is capable of increasing the reach, volume, and intensity of subjectivity. Al Jazeera, since its launch, has opened a new horizon of subjectivity in the Arab world via talk shows and its interactive website (www.aljazeera.net), which became a true space of trans-Arab and global expression for Arabic speakers. Real people are the driving force of this process of subjectivity. In Tunisia, life was unbearable for the majority of people, and they wanted to change their conditions.

When people discovered the Bouazizi story, they encountered an event that had meaning for them and enlarged their scope of identification. Several people even tried to imitate Bouazizi's self-immolation. As the Al Jazeera reports revealed, some were successful in their attempts, while others failed. Identification with Bouazizi actually went far beyond Tunisia. It happened, too, in Egypt, Morocco, Yemen, Saudi Arabia, and Syria. It also happened in countries outside the Arab world.

Bouazizi's self-immolation had meaning, says Benslama, even though it took place in a very small city, far away from the capital. Sonia Chamkhi, a Tunisian filmmaker, noted that before Bouazizi, other people had burned themselves, but their acts of protest hadn't had the same effect that Bouazizi's achieved. Benslama compared this act in a small city to the wings of a butterfly setting in motion a chain of unforeseen events that might cause a hurricane thousands of kilometers away. He explains that the Tunisians constructed a story around Bouazizi that was stronger on symbolism than fact. Bouazizi was made out to be an exceptional man, a gifted man, which is actually something of a myth. Contrary to what has been said, Bouazizi was not a university graduate. He had been humiliated many times—the last incident, which resulted in his self-immolation, was not the first time his cart had been confiscated by authorities (Benslama 2011; Kepel 2013). Utter despair drove the twenty-six-year-old fruit vendor to engulf himself in flames. He experienced the governor's refusal to meet with him as yet another affront after all the other injustices he had suffered over the years. Pundits capitalized on the fact that a policewoman had slapped him in the face, speculating that Bouazizi lived in a culture that sees humiliation by a woman as the most extreme form of *qahr*. This synergy of different logics of oppression—including those of class, gender, and authority—leads to different interpretations. The honor codes of Arab societies—even the most open of them, like Tunisia—led the unhappy Bouazizi through a passivation process (Benslama 2011, 19–20). The status of *shahid* (martyr) that Bouazizi achieved erases all of these logics and paints him as a model of honesty, honor, and righteous rage. This makes it even more interesting that the story popularized by Al Jazeera and other news outlets about this small-town fruit vendor does not always stand up against the facts.

Hearing the Al Jazeera reporters speak Bouazizi's name brings to mind the mystical undertones of his name in Arabic. Benslama deconstructed the name "Bouazizi" into two parts, *bou* meaning "father" and *azizi* meaning "my dear." Aziz is one of the names for Allah, the most "powerful and merciful."

Benslama, like the Algerian philosopher and historian Mohammed Arkoun, invites us to examine the power of myth in history using the work of French anthropologist Lévi-Strauss. The spread of the myth was the tipping point for the objective conditions that facilitated its creation; neither alone was sufficient to spark a revolution. The myth of Bouazizi is now a powerful, widely recognized, and highly empathic fiction, and it was put to work extensively during the Tunisian revolution. It comes as no surprise that Al Jazeera was instrumental in promoting that myth. Many of the books written about Bouazizi perpetuated inaccurate details that had made their way into the narrative surrounding his life. The myth was never challenged or journalistically investigated until Gilles Kepel's *Passion Arabe* (known in English as *Diaries of the Arab Revolution*). Kepel reveals that Bouazizi was not in fact university-educated, a misconception that had helped engender the middle class's empathy for the poor street vendor. According to Kepel, when the policewoman confiscated his scale, he asked her, "How do you want me to weigh the fruit, with your boobs?" In this telling, the slap on the fruit vendor's face came in response to a remark about the policewoman's breasts rather than a plea on behalf of his livelihood (Kepel 2013, 248). Kepel adds, in the same vein, that Bouazizi was probably drunk before he burned himself. This is not an attempt to besmirch the dead or to belittle the frustration of a man who clearly felt his options in life had run out. Rather, it is meant to illustrate how the narrative of Bouazizi's life was dramatically transformed to represent the myriad frustrations of a varied public. Bouazizi's expression of frustration is the founding myth of the Jasmine Revolution. As such, the symbolic truth of his life and death have grown larger than their reality.

Were Al Jazeera's footage, images, and coverage enough to single-handedly lead to a revolution? As mentioned earlier in the chapter, Benslama argues that it wasn't the simple accumulation of images that led to the protests—Bouazizi's actions just created a moment that produced larger meaning. Al Jazeera framed the self-immolation of Bouazizi as being a result of the extreme humiliation he suffered, a blatant example of institutionalized *qahr* and *rujula* (emasculation). Benslama uses the Arabic expression *kharj a'la nifsou*, or "exiting from the self," a *sortie hors de soi*, more an ejection than subjection, a movement of extermination (Benslama 2011, 17). This is the moment of rage when someone behaves erratically, as though he or she has become a totally different person. The frame of *shahid*, martyr, used by Al Jazeera and others belongs to a theological repertoire. A repertoire is a set of frames based on performances by people or individuals, a definition inspired by the work of Charles Tilly (2007, 13–14; Tilly and Lesley Woods 2012). This reference to a theological repertoire alters the religious meaning of martyrdom. Benslama argues that it led to a complete rupture within the traditional concept of martyrdom, as it has been (mis)used by suicide bombers. The use of the term "martyr" in the case of Bouazizi and his imitators can be seen as a secularization of a theological term. The likely reality was that he was concerned only with his personal situation and did not commit suicide for a specific cause. This becomes a subjective interpretation of how to defy *qahr*. This secularization is responsible for what Rene Girard calls the "mimetic echo" in the Arab world that led to many subjective "micro-revolutions." Another interpretation could be that the self-immolation of Bouazizi was a way to conserve the humanity and honor of young people, since honor equals humanity (Benslama 2011, 75).

Bouazizi does indeed seem a desperate and frustrated subject of *qahr* and despair. But Bouazizi's story has been reconstructed as a heroic narrative. Although he died in the hospital, his revised story did not die in the memory and imagination of Tunisians—he is still alive for them. The media and Al Jazeera showed Ben Ali, the most powerful man in Tunisia, visiting this common man in the hospital—wrapped in so many bandages that he looked like a mummy—and bending down to meet the man's gaze. That act of the president bending to Bouazizi on his bed has been interpreted as Ben Ali's bowing in front of Bouazizi and by extension all other Tunisians stifled by *qahr*. Benslama calls this moment an act of compassion on Ben Ali's part since the president and his advisers actually believed it was an act of compassion, but that the big man would bow before the little man was seen by the people as an act of weakness. The little man held the whole regime at his mercy. Benslama said that these analyses don't conform to economic rationality in the sense that calculated actions can have a boomerang effect: there are moments when people don't back away from tragic scenes. Ben Ali's gesture was like King Creon's kneeling before Antigone.

Benslama explains that another aspect of the mythologized Bouazizi story is the development of a new subjectivity stemming from the proliferation of online social media. It forms a kind of rupture with classical political discourse and the established traditions in Tunisia, and even within the revolutionary utopia. The current generations of youth tend to see less difference between the virtual and the real than earlier generations did; the lines are more blurred. For them, there is more reality on the Internet and more virtuality in reality. The role that the Internet played in the Arab Spring revolutions confirms the existence of a new subjectivity empowered by technology that is transforming modes of being in society. Benslama thinks that this new subjectivity holds a fascinating possibility, which is that people can have multiple identities on the Internet while maintaining their own nonvirtual identity. They can call themselves Robocop or Hannibal or Jedi Knight or whatever they want in this alternate existence. Benslama calls this an experience of plurality. Olivier Roy calls the predominantly youth-dominated revolution a generational phenomenon, since Arab youth are less invested in political Islam than older generations were. The instantaneity of cyber activism also adds a dimension of ubiquity to revolutionary situations. This ubiquity comes from the rapid response to pivotal events. The Bouazizi myth shows that what we must believe is not predetermined. The Bouazizi story stresses, according to Benslama, the dimension of contingency as an expression of extreme subjectivity. Benslama describes the subjective act of self-immolation by Bouazizi and how the Tunisians perceived it as love at first sight. It was an event that altered drastically one individual life and shaped the collective life of the Tunisian people. And these events are contingent, says Benslama; they are not subject to calculations, equations, statistics, or any kind of measurement. Al Jazeera's news reports sang the praises of Tunisia's ubiquitous, globally oriented young generation.

Al Jazeera gave rappers such as El Général ample room in its news reports, and the popular rapper's songs contained many words referring to the Islamic identity of all Tunisians. For example, he used the word *shahada* (confession of faith). Abelwahab Meddeb, a Tunisian scholar and presenter of the well-known program on French Culture, *Cultures d'Islam*, sees "Islamist substance" in his lyrics. He explains, though, that his gestures are those of a globalized rapper but that his words are colored by an Islamist ideology. Meddeb describes rappers like El Général Psych M (100,000 friends on Facebook) as disseminating a kind of schizophrenia that prospers only in milieus of the forbidden (Meddeb 2011, 119).

Al Jazeera's coverage of the events following the ouster of Ben Ali favored Islamic connotations through images of the veil and the headscarf, while the overwhelming majority of the protestors did not make use of religious slogans or symbols (Chamkhi 2011). Meddeb is intransigent about the Islamizing effect of Al Jazeera coverage. He cites the words of the Al Jazeera superstar preacher, Yusuf al-Qaradawi, as an example of this. The preacher used only Quranic categories to explain the events of Tunisia, though these events happened predominantly outside the religious sphere (Meddeb 2011, 116–118).

4 GAZA

A PERENNIAL ARAB SPRING

The four letters of Gaza trigger a lot of emotion and passion.

—Jean-Pierre Filiu (2012)

We support the Palestinian people in Gaza.

—Sheikh Hamad bin Khalifa al-Thani (Al Jazeera, September 7, 2011)[1]

Tarnishing of the Palestinian Authority

The scholars Olivier Roy (2012) and Gilles Kepel (2013) have argued that the Arab world pushed the Palestinian question to the back burner during the Arab Spring. They appear to be correct in that none of the slogans and rallying cries of the protesters in Tunis and during the first weeks of protests in Tahrir Square included any reference to Palestine. But this was not entirely the case for Al Jazeera during that time. The network's coverage of the Palestinian Authority nearly eclipsed that of Tunisia's Jasmine Revolution on January 23, 2011, a major inflection point of the revolution. Just days after the ouster of President Ben Ali, when Tunisian protesters were challenging the interim government–imposed curfew and the events that would lead to the Egyptian revolution were just getting under way, Al Jazeera announced a major news scoop. The network revealed during its main evening news bulletin, *Harvest of the Day*, that it had obtained access to documents outlining a secret Palestinian–Israeli collaboration against the Islamist Hamas government in Gaza. It was a major story that seriously damaged the credibility of the Palestinian Authority. The breaking news, which was simultaneously published by the *Guardian*, was a bombshell in terms of the consequences for the governing party in the West Bank.

Voices on Al Jazeera demanded abdication by the Palestinian Authority of its leadership role in the West Bank, and the network spent almost six days providing analysis of the documents at the expense of coverage detailing the apparent success of the revolution in Tunisia and the rumblings of a new revolution in Egypt. Al Jazeera's preoccupation with Palestine at the time provides some explanation as to why the overthrow of Mubarak came as such a surprise to the international community. News of the "collaboration" with Israel, as relayed by Al Jazeera, outraged the Palestinian Arab street, especially after the disclosure of substantial concessions the Palestinian Authority had made to Israel. The sixteen hundred documents, which totaled more than sixty-five hundred pages and dated from 2005 to 2006, were made available online and became the subject of intense daily analysis on Al Jazeera. But why exactly was the leak of documents about that specific period from 2005 to 2006 so crucial and significant for the Arab publics, beyond the apparent damage inflicted on the Palestinian Authority's reputation?

An epistemological disclaimer may be necessary regarding the following paragraphs. This chapter is information-dense and has the feel of a very long chronological bullet list. It references just one source, Al Jazeera, in order to illustrate the network's narration of the history of resistance in Gaza through the eyes of Hamas founder Sheikh Ahmed Yassin. In addition to describing Al Jazeera's coverage of pivotal events, the chapter attempts to explicitly link the causality of one event to another, where applicable. The report just referred to focusing on the leak of sensitive documents incriminating the Palestinian Authority just days after the Tunisian revolution serves as a starting point for this analysis.

The focus by Al Jazeera on years-old events in the midst of two major revolutions illustrates the network's embrace of its role as newsmaker rather than news reporter, its traditional gatekeeper media role, and its tendency to draw the attention of its audience to news events that advance a broader narrative of the state of affairs in the Arab world. The network bolsters this narrative with a set of recurring frames and narrative conventions that consistently reinforce the worldview of Al Jazeera leadership and blur the lines between reporting and analysis.

A few facts are important for understanding the regional narrative of Al Jazeera's Palestine coverage. The first is Al Jazeera's portrayal of the relationship between Israel and the government of Qatar (the network's owner) as one of mutual enmity. The emir of Qatar explicitly supported this characterization in a 2011 Al Jazeera interview (September 7, 2011). Second is the network's characterization of Qatar as playing a leading role during the 2011 eruption of the Arab Spring through its participation in the Arab Peace Initiative and its hold on chairs of UN discussion sessions regarding the uprisings. Third is the fact that Al Jazeera's positive coverage of Hamas directly reflects the emir of Qatar's view of the group as an instructive model of democratic governance by homegrown Islamist parties in Arab nations. Fourth is the close political relationship between Wadah Khanfar, the managing director of Al Jazeera, and Hamas during the Arab Spring and Khanfar's strongly sympathetic slant on political Islam in general (el-Oifi 2011).

With these facts in mind, what should be made of Al Jazeera's Palestine coverage in light of the Arab Spring? At what point did Gaza rise to its current level of importance in Al Jazeera's news coverage? Why does Al Jazeera consistently frame Palestinian Authority rule in terms of failure? Conversely, what drives Al Jazeera's positive coverage of Hamas? Finally, how has Al Jazeera's reporting affected international attention on the Gaza Strip and the West Bank?

Arafat and Yassin

Yasser Arafat, the historic leader of the Palestinian Liberation Organization (PLO) and Palestinian Authority, died on November 11, 2004, just eight months after the killing of Sheikh Ahmad Yassin on March 22 of the same year. Yassin was the founder and religious leader of the Islamist movement Hamas. Less than nine months later, in August of 2005, Prime Minister Ariel Sharon withdrew Israeli settlers and defense forces from Gaza, putting an end to thirty-eight years of occupation.

From the start, Gaza was a magnet for conflict—it had taken Israel four years to gain control of Gaza at the start of the occupation, and the price in human lives was very high (Filiu 2012, 158). After Israel's withdrawal, Hamas became the dominant political force in the region, contesting the Palestinian Authority and launching an Islamic alternative to the secular Fatah party (the largest faction descending from the PLO). Hamas's overwhelming victory in the 2006 elections in Gaza was hailed by Al Jazeera as a "victory for political Islam," serving as inspiration for other Islamist movements to pursue the same path of perseverance to reach power. Al Jazeera had given Hamas and its leaders (mainly Sheikh Yassin) significant exposure since as early as 1997—something that will receive further discussion in the following pages.

In August 2010, Al Jazeera spearheaded additional in-depth investigative reporting that discredited the Palestinian Authority. One such project was a nine-month investigation into the death of Yasser Arafat, which entailed digging into the Swiss forensic report provided to Arafat's widow and conducting DNA tests in a Swiss laboratory. Al Jazeera claimed that Arafat's widow, Suha Arafat, had given the network a duffel bag filled with personal belongings of the Palestinian leader. Al Jazeera's speculation that Arafat had been poisoned with radioactive polonium-210 eventually led a French prosecutor to open a murder inquiry into his death. The findings by French doctors regarding Arafat's alleged stroke were not conclusive, putting pressure on the Palestinian Authority to authorize the exhumation of Arafat's body (*Guardian*, August 28, 2010). The controversy drove a wedge between the memory of Arafat and the political party that he had helped to found.

Al Jazeera devoted substantial airtime from 1997 to 2012 to discussion of the failure to establish a Palestinian state since the defeat of Arab forces in 1967, despite multiple resolutions and accords that attempted to do so (see chapter 1).[2] Following its victory in Gaza, Hamas assumed the role as face of the Palestinian cause, and the Palestinian Authority was forced to take a back seat.

Al Jazeera had previously obtained controversial Palestinian Authority documents that had been provided to the network in 2007 by Hamas sources and aired on the show *Without Borders*. Al Jazeera journalist Ahmed Mansour introduced the news of the 2007 documents thus: "When the Islamic resistance movement Hamas dominated the Gaza Strip in mid-June of 2007, it surprised the world with a treasure trove of intelligence documents regarding the Palestinian security forces. . . . I was not alone, and perhaps dozens of journalists like me around the world sought the right to be the first to publish these documents, and I was the first one of those who initiated contact with the leaders of Hamas in Gaza in order to inform Arab viewers about plans by Dayton and Eliot to bring down Hamas." For the Palestinian Authority and its president, the report was damning. Viewers and readers were horrified by the news that Palestinian leaders might have conspired with Israel against a rival Arab faction.

When Al Jazeera broke the news of its new information on leaks about Israeli–Palestinian Authority relations on January 23, 2011, it would take the outbreak of revolution in Egypt to shift the network's attention from its exhaustive, six-day-long coverage of the leaks. The frames used in the coverage became an integral part of Al Jazeera's antiestablishment repertoire, which spurred a number of significant events that still affect the future of Gaza and its Islamist leadership today.

Release of the papers was a major development in the relationship between the Palestinian Authority and Hamas from which future attempts at cooperation between the two entities could never be divorced. The leaked documents implicated Palestinian Authority leaders in a secret collaboration with the United States to delay progress of the Goldstone Report, a UN Security Council investigation into allegations against Israel in Gaza. Additionally, the Palestine Papers describe an Israeli minister sharing details of a possible Israeli attack on Gaza with Palestinian Authority chief negotiator Saeb Erekat and informing him that Hamas would "be taken care of" (*Guardian*, January 26, 2011).

On January 26, three days after Al Jazeera broke the news of the leaked Palestine Papers, Saeb Erekat was the featured guest of Al Jazeera's *Without Borders*. His encounter with Al Jazeera's Ahmed Mansour on air was uncomfortable, even by the standards of Al Jazeera's often confrontational interviews. The visibly flustered Erekat verbally flailed during questioning by the well-prepared, articulate, and composed host, who further frustrated the diplomat by interrupting his answers. Erekat, that same day, had denied all accusations of involvement in "backdoor dealings" with Israel when he was questioned by the international media. However, on the show, he notably "fail[ed] to repeat his previous claim that the documents—obtained by Al Jazeera TV and shared with the *Guardian* [were] 'a pack of lies'" (*Guardian*, January 26, 2011).

The following excerpt from Mansour's introduction to the show provides a sense of Al Jazeera's angle on the story, as well as the gravity its presenters and reporters attempted to convey regarding the Palestinian Authority's ability to lead, in good faith, the Palestinian people:

> Almost all observers concur that the Palestinian issue will take on new dimensions now that Al Jazeera, along with British newspaper the *Guardian*, reported on Sunday the story of more than sixteen hundred [leaked confidential] documents, including the minutes of meetings and agreements reached between the leadership of the Palestinian Authority, the Israelis, the Americans. and other parties over the past six years. . . . The documents exposed by Al Jazeera are, according to many observers, hundreds of times more serious and dangerous than the WikiLeaks documents.
>
> Tzipi Livni, the former Israeli foreign minister, said to the *Jerusalem Post* on the 31st of December [2010], "We negotiated with the Palestinians in closed rooms and this is the best way to achieve the interests of Israel. We have been in control and we have the initiative and use appropriate tactics and techniques." But leaks to Al Jazeera during the past few days . . . reveal what was going on in those secret meetings or at least much of it. . . . Al Jazeera will continue to broadcast Part Four [of its report on the secret documents] tonight. Although Dr. Saeb Erekat agreed [to appear] several weeks before Al Jazeera broke [he uses the word *tafjir*, "to make something explode"] the story of these documents, it was our agreement to broadcast the show today from Brussels, where he made a speech before the European Parliament, and I also needed to do some work in France. But because of the developments that have taken place due to the breaking of [the news of] this affair by Al Jazeera, we agreed that the appropriate venue is [Jordan]. (Al Jazeera, January 26, 2011)

Mansour, sure of himself, and equally confident in the explosive documents in his possession, does not hesitate to press hard and push Erekat onto the hot seat. Mansour reads from one of Erekat's portions of the secret minutes: "I lie and I lied during the last few weeks. I was in Cairo, I was in Jordan, I was in America; everyone asks me what is happening in Israel, what will Olmert [the Israeli prime minister] do?"

Mansour then addresses Erekat, "Yossi Gal [the Israeli ambassador to France] told you [Erekat]—and repeated it to everybody—that 'we are on the verge of success. I told you and I always tell them that this would be an internal Israeli issue, and I continue to lie; if a person sneezes in Tel Aviv, I catch a cold in Jericho and I have to lie.'

"All I want from you, before we embark upon this episode that everybody is waiting for," Mansour tells Erekat, "is please don't lie" (Al Jazeera, January 26, 2011).

Saeb Erekat, somewhat flabbergasted, answers, "I did not expect this *waqaha* [insolence]. I do not lie, and did not lie. This statement is true in the document, and this sentence in particular—I said that when Olmert has been subjected to a scandal and people ask me about the politics in Israel, I answer, 'This is an internal Israeli matter,' and this is a lie because if somebody sneezes in Tel Aviv we catch the flu in Jericho. But this is your usual way of dealing with what I say—to take what I said out of context and modify it. I asked you to give me just five minutes at the start of the episode."

Ahmed Mansour interrupts, "Listen to me, I didn't modify a thing. I took you literally. Aren't these your words?"

"No," Erekat responds. "But the text [as you read it] paints me as a traitor and you paint me as a liar by asking me not to lie; *khalina shwayya* [just cool off]."

Ahmed Mansour again cuts in, "Didn't you say that you were lying in the documents?"

The remainder of the interview would continue in this fashion, with Erekat clumsily attempting to provide context to seemingly incriminating statements read by Mansour. At one point, Erekat accused Al Jazeera of employing former members of the CIA and British intelligence. Mansour laughed off the accusation and quickly moved forward with his questioning.

When Erekat attempted to explain that references in the leaked documents to the "killing [of] Palestinians" by the PLO were meant to unite Palestinians against Israel, Mansour again pounced.

"You admit to the killing?" asked the host.

"Please," Erekat barked, trying to regain control of the conversation.

"Recognition of murder! It's necessary to highlight it."

"Give me a minute and let me finish my sentence," the frustrated diplomat growled.

Through his own verbal fumbling, and despite the host's interruptions, Erekat eventually managed to explain that his reference was to an accidental killing of three members of Hamas, which he had warned colleagues was a threat to the solidarity of the Palestinian Authority.

"You just admitted the killing!" was the host's incredulous response.

At this point the exchange ceases to be an interview, continuing on as a succession of insults and accusations hurled back and forth. Mansour calls Erekat a murderer and accuses him of handing Palestinian land over to the Israelis in an effort to serve the interests of Israel. Erekat accuses the Egyptian Mansour of being ambivalent about the right of Palestinians to have their own state. He also accuses the Qatari government of bribing one Palestinian leaker with a lucrative job working for the emir. The interview ends with Erekat threatening to sue both Mansour and Al Jazeera in an international court.

Fifteen of the ninety comments on the webpage concerning this episode of *Without Borders* are from Palestinians who disagree with Mansour's style of questioning and accuse Al Jazeera of tampering with the documents (Al Jazeera, January 28, 2011). But the full impact of Al Jazeera's reporting on the documents was evidenced by the thousands of Palestinians who took the streets to protest against the Palestinian Authority's Mahmoud Abbas. Al Jazeera was instrumental in setting the agenda for all Arab media outlets, including its direct competitor, Al Arabiya, which followed Al Jazeera's reporting with its own extensive coverage of the leaked documents (Jallad 2011).

Hamas, the Undisputed Victor

Five months after the Palestine Papers were released, Ahmed Mansour interviewed Khaled Meshal (the political bureau chief of Hamas, who had formerly worked from Damascus) while they were both in Cairo. The interview was about the recent truce between Fatah and Hamas and the new spirit of collaboration between the two Palestinian organizations. The interview ended with a discussion about the positive role of the Arab Spring and especially the new leadership role of Egypt in achieving democracy and helping the Palestinians to achieve independence and live "in dignity" (Al Jazeera, July 7, 2011).

After that, the stock of Gaza and its leaders continued to rise on Al Jazeera. Nine months after the Tunisian revolution, on September 20, 2011, Wadah Khanfar, the managing director of Al Jazeera, stepped down. Most news outlets reported that his resignation had to do with the December 2010 WikiLeaks controversy, in which US diplomatic cables described Al Jazeera as a foreign policy "bargaining chip" for Qatar (BBC News, September 20, 2011). Strangely, nobody discussed the possible link between his resignation and the Palestinian Authority's outrage over the release of the Palestine Papers, which had seriously undermined its authority in the ongoing struggle with Hamas. This possibility should be considered as an equally likely cause of Khanfar's departure.

On November 14, 2012, Israel launched "Operation Pillar of Defense," an offensive that included the assassination of Ahmed Jabari, the leader of

Hamas's military wing. After eight days of escalation, Hamas and Israel agreed to a ceasefire on November 21. The deal was brokered by the new Egyptian president, Mohamed Morsi. Hamas declared victory in Gaza while Palestinian Authority members prepared a bid for statehood through the United Nations. On November 29, 2012, the UN voted to recognize Palestine as a non-member observer state, the same status afforded the Vatican. While Al Jazeera trumpeted the Gaza treaty as a mark of legitimacy for Hamas, the network's response to UN recognition of Palestinian statehood was lukewarm.

The escalation of the Israeli–Hamas conflict, which directly preceded the Palestinian Authority's bid for statehood and an upgraded status with the UN, was short and less costly in terms of human life (162 Palestinian deaths) than the conflict in 2008, which had resulted in 1,400 fatalities. However, as Al Jazeera pointed out, "Since the first Qassam rocket fell on Israel in April 2001, there have been 59 Israelis killed [compared with] 4,717 Palestinians" (Belen Fernandez, Al Jazeera English, December 22, 2012) Here again, during the 2008 Gaza conflict, Al Jazeera enjoyed a level of access to information unique among international media networks. Consequently, when the world's attention turned to the Middle East, its eyes turned to Al Jazeera. The same had been true in Afghanistan during the era of post-9/11 Bin Laden tapes in the early 2000s. Al Jazeera commanded an overwhelming 53.4 percent of the Palestinian audience during the Gaza conflict, with Palestine TV running a distant second place with 12.8 percent and Al Arabiya trailing with 10 percent during the Gaza conflict (Bosney and Koogler 2010). The network's label for the conflict, "Attack on Gaza," encapsulates the overarching frame through which Al Jazeera covered the conflict from December 2008 until January 2009.

As Shereen Tadress, who reported from the front in Gaza, later described it, "We were living through the first week of the war on Gaza in 2008. The Israelis call this week the first phase, in which the international media was denied access to Gaza. I found myself with my colleague Mohiddin reporting the news for Western viewers. When the bombing intensified at night, we tried to get everything to our viewers. One night, as I tried to sleep in our bureau in Gaza with one of our colleagues from the Al Arabiya channel, his five-year-old nephew called on the phone to ask, 'When is all this going to end?' The little boy was crying. It was night, dark, and the image was horrific. This phone call gave us the idea to report to our European viewers something nobody knew about the Israeli attacks—that they were targeting children and women who are no different than our viewers and their families. The next evening, we decided to spend the night with a family in Gaza in order to experience every moment of their fears through the night. Israel destroyed Gaza in all possible ways. The siege was not enough—Israel [also] wanted to deny Gaza even the basic necessities of life like electricity. Gaza slept under a heavy cover of darkness, where the simple pleasures like TV or games were not accessible" (Al Jazeera, October 11, 2011).

A second Al Jazeera correspondent in Gaza, Tamer Al Mishal, looked back at the days of crisis in Gaza in 2008. "The camera of Al Jazeera didn't stop following the story of the little boy named Firas, whose doctor decided that he badly needed treatment in a hospital outside of Gaza. And after many phone calls, one of the Israeli hospitals agreed to treat him . . . and when we wanted to go with the family to the checkpoint, the Palestinian hospital called us to say that Firas was dead. . . . The story of Firas was transmitted on Al Jazeera on May 13, 2009, and it made everybody cry" (Al Jazeera, October 27, 2011).

Another Al Jazeera correspondent, Yasser Abu Halala, added this to the story: "The images of the bodies of the children were like they were sleeping—not dead. It gave an angelic look to the scene. The shelter didn't protect them from the Israeli air attacks. The shelter became a big tomb. I will never forget the little boy with his red sports pants. He would un-dust himself from the [debris of the] destroyed shelter. In the midst of such a scene it is difficult just to carry a plastic camera. It is difficult just to be a journalist reporting the event. You wish you were the president of a big country who could protect helpless kids against injustice. The minimum you could wish for is to open up the rain of your tears and crying" (Al Jazeera, October 27, 2011).

In that period of the Israeli–Hamas escalation, streaming video exceeded 600 percent of normal broadcast viewership, and Al Jazeera Arabic and English were the most heavily viewed channels in that month (Surk 2009, cited in Jalad 2011). The French Tunisian scholar and journalist Abdelwahab Meddeb voiced outrage over the twenty-three days of violence in Gaza that started in December 27, 2008, blaming first Hamas and Israel: "The horror of those who present themselves as victims in an intolerable way. The horror of those who wage abstract electronic war to preserve themselves from guilt over the death they inflict." He also expressed disgust with Al Jazeera for sensationalizing and exploiting horrific images of suffering and violence (including crying and slain children), deeming such imagery "war pornography." He remarked, "The horror fueled by Arab television networks (in particular Al Jazeera) which complacently zoom in on bloody and disfigured faces, which are sometimes contorted with pain and sometimes inert. These images succeed each other according to the morbid logic of editing designed to excite Arab opinion." Meddeb explained that Hamas encourages "collective martyrdom" to promote its cause. But he was also critical of all actors in the global political scene, including the EU, the United States, and the UN (*Le Monde*, January 12, 2012). The visual frames portrayed a human tragedy, a humanitarian crisis of Gazans in the depths of bloody suffering. The *New York Times*, by contrast, recounted a "lethal" escalation of the conflict where

Gaza militants fired missiles into Israel and Israel responded with airstrikes and sent armored vehicles into Gaza (Isabel Kershner and Rick Gladstone, *New York Times*, November 22, 2012).

In a 2009 PhD dissertation devoted to the Gaza conflict, Farah Fakhri Jallad compared Al Jazeera English and Al Jazeera Arabic coverage of Gaza during this period of violence and came to the following conclusions. For Al Jazeera Arabic, more than 60 percent of the stories came from the war front, while the least number of stories came from the West bank. Stories foregrounding violence (violence frames) made up 40 percent of the coverage, and the antiwar frame was present in fewer stories in the first stage of the war, but peaked at a higher frequency than in Al Jazeera English during the third week of the war. Also, Al Jazeera Arabic focused more on casualties and showed dead faces (44 percent vs. 23 percent for Al Jazeera English). More than 53 percent of the sources of Al Jazeera Arabic's stories were Palestinian, compared with only 19 percent Israeli. These are very interesting statistics and merit more than just a single sentence of general analysis. What is Al Jazeera up to here? And why? It would seem that only by dramatizing the Gaza tragedy to the maximum could Al Jazeera Arabic cater its message of Islamizing pan-Arabism to large Arab publics. In sum, Al Jazeera Arabic was more sensational than Al Jazeera English (Jallad 2011).

Gaza, Al Jazeera, and the Making of Hamas

Gaza gave Al Jazeera the golden opportunity to coin, establish, and perfect the framing repertoire that would serve it throughout the Arab Spring. As the birthplace of the Intifada, it gave Al Jazeera the frame of defiance against Israel. The small size of Gaza—just 360 square kilometers tucked between the Mediterranean, Israel, and Egypt with more than 1.5 million people living daily in "the biggest prison in the world" (Filiu 2012, 11) gave Al Jazeera a compelling frame of resistance, where the Gazans were portrayed as resilient to pressures from Israel and "backstabbing" by the Palestinian Authority. The defeat of Fatah by Hamas in 2007 and the dismantling of the Palestinian Authority in Gaza gave Al Jazeera two frames: the antiestablishment frame and that of Islamism as a viable alternative to the status quo. The 2008 raids by Israelis and the economic sanctions that failed to lead to the weakening of Hamas (Filiu 2012, 11) gave Al Jazeera the frame of dignity and identification with the *umma* (the collective Islamic community). The ongoing escalation of conflict between Israel and Gaza gave the mufti of Al Jazeera the frame of an International Day of Rage as a show of "Islamic solidarity" rather than "Arab solidarity."

Other frames that can be detected in Al Jazeera's news stories include the Judaization of Jerusalem (*tahwid al-Quds*), which relies on a narrative of Israeli attempts to erase the Arab presence in Palestine. Arab silence (*assamt al Arabi*) is another common frame used by the network to decry the passivity of Arab states and governments toward the processes of "de-Arabization" of "Arab land." The remove the blockade/siege (*raf' al hisar*) frame describes a heroic resistance by the Gazans against the state of siege imposed by the embargo and sanctions enforced by the Israeli Army. The Gaza's holocaust (*mihraqat Gaza*) frame describes Gaza as a massive concentration camp where innocent children and women are trapped behind walls and deprived of their human rights. The relief (*ighatha*) frame describes efforts by Gazans, with the help of Qatar and Turkey, to break or end the siege of Gaza. The injured of Gaza (*jarha Gaza*) frame describes the daily resistance of Gazans to the "arbitrary" occupation of the region. The suffering and steadfastness (*shuhada' Gaza* and *mu'anat wa sumud*) frames expand on the previous frame of permanent resistance and resilience. Gaza and the events taking place in the region have been inextricably linked to Al Jazeera's rise to international prominence.

It was, in fact, Al Jazeera that first gave a face to Hamas in much of the Arab world. In April and May 1999, Ahmed Mansour organized for the program *Witness to the Times* (*Sahidun ala ala asr*), a series of seven interviews with Sheikh Yassin, the founder of Hamas. Yassin's vision, positions, and teachings were at that time still largely unknown to the majority of Arab viewers. In addition to the segments aired on Mansour's show, the interviews were released in full in a publication produced under the umbrella of Al Jazeera.

Two additional interviews followed in September and October of the same year, with Sheikh Yassin as a guest on Ahmed Mansour's other program, *Without Borders*. On September 9, 1999, Ahmed Mansour explained that Yassin had been invited back on the network to answer questions that his previous comments had raised among important players in the negotiations over the Palestinian quest for sovereignty.

Unlike Mansour's Erekat interview the following decade, the discourse between the journalist and the revolutionary would remain cordial. Mansour began the program by promising to confront Yassin with diverging viewpoints in the form of newspaper and media stories published from London to Tel Aviv. He would deliver on this promise. But unlike the intense grilling Mansour would later administer to the Fatah negotiator, his treatment of the Hamas leader allowed Yassin space to respond at length to various areas of criticism. Over the course of the interview, Yassin was given a platform to define the ideology and goals of his militant group, using the friction of third-party criticism as a means to sharpen his arguments.

Touching on the broader theme of Al Jazeera's utilization of Islamizing frames, it bears noting that Mansour opened his interview of the Islamist leader with his usual salutation, steeped in language Western readers will identify as clearly religious in tone, saying, "Peace, mercy and blessings of God, and welcome to a new episode of the program *Without Borders.*"

In Mansour's questions about the stringent criticism leveled at Nasser by Islamists, Yassin took the opportunity to summarize the injection of religious frames into Arab nationalism that would come to define the identity of Hamas and other Islamist political movements. "We can't close our eyes to the good deeds of Nasser, who ignited a spirit of resistance and furthered the struggle and persistence of the Arab world," Yassin said. However, he continued by recounting the Egyptian leader's poor human rights record, specifically regarding his suppression of the Muslim Brotherhood. Asked whether his description of Nasser's human rights record inaccurately conflates Nasser's persecution of political opponents with persecution of Islam, Yassin ducks the question without admonishment from the host, saying, "Our role as Muslim Brothers and Muslims is to invite the rulers, the regimes, and all the people to Islam, and ask them to apply [Islam to governance]."

The digression allowed the Hamas leader to explain the link between the Muslim Brotherhood and his organization. "We, Hamas, were educated with [the Muslim Brotherhood], living, eating, learning, and talking with the Brotherhood as members of the community," Yassin told Mansour. "We are an extension of the Muslim Brotherhood in all the world. . . . We have support from all the Muslim Brothers in the world."

Turning to the more contentious issue of the descriptions of his group as a terrorist organization, Yassin fired back, "We are not terrorists. . . . We fight for the cause of a Palestinian homeland and a people, and when one of the sons of the Palestinian people collaborates with the enemy and reveals the secrets of [our] fighters and attempts to eliminate them and kill them and bring them down with immoral distractions, adultery, homosexuality, opium, and hashish, we need to nip it the bud. . . . Compared with other revolutionary groups, we give fairer treatment to collaborators."

In the second interview, on October 13, 1999, Yassin spoke with Mansour via satellite, opening with what can be seen as a mission statement for the militant group:

> The Hamas movement is *harka mujahida* [a militant movement] for the land of Palestine. . . . The movement is a popular movement scattered both here and across the Arab and Muslim world. It has its supporters and its soldiers and leaders and its thinkers. So if one office is closed down, it does not mean we are in crisis. Our strength derives from an active role on the ground and an active role in the life, in jihad and politics, and our relation to the Arab people and Muslims everywhere, and the Palestinian people first and foremost.

Again, the Hamas leader managed to expertly use the interview as a platform to shape the narrative surrounding his group. Yassin described the widespread jailing of Hamas members, and the progress of the Oslo peace negotiations between Israel and the Palestinian Authority, which at the time did not include Hamas, as sources of braggadocio rather than as evidence of a decline in Hamas's relevance. According to Yassin, the two developments demonstrated a concurrent strengthening of Hamas and weakening of the Palestinian Authority. "History shows that the blows of the past, and [time spent in] prisons and jails, give the sons of Hamas a forcefulness and resolve . . . and strengthens our front against the oppressive enemy," Yassin told Mansour. "Oslo," he said, "is not a peace process but the process of surrender to the Zionist enemy. . . . It's the process of liquidating the Palestinian cause, the refugees. [It is the] sale of land and Jerusalem to settlers."

The interview continued, with Yassin describing the dire economic situation of occupied Gaza, the failure of past peace negotiations to deliver promised lands back to Palestinian control, and his belief in an Israeli goal of economic domination of the Arab world. Yassin described the only true choice in the Palestinian–Israeli conflict as one between "occupation and no occupation." He said, "The day that the occupation of Palestinian land ends and the Palestinian people go back to their land, we can talk about peace."

Yassin stressed that he did not see all Jews as enemies. "We do not resist the Jews because they are Jews, nor do we make a call to fight the Jews, in any place, because they are Jews," he explained. Rather, he said, Hamas's fight was only against "the Jews that raped our land and made us homeless."

Yassin's appearance was a hit with Al Jazeera audiences. It encompassed the same frames of oppression and rebellion against established powers that would help Al Jazeera expand its audience exponentially in the following decade. Someone who called in to the show described the Hamas leader's wheelchair as "superior to all the thrones of [leaders of] cowardly states" (Al Jazeera, June 4, 2004).

The interviews, nine altogether, allowed Yassin a transnational platform to counter portrayals of his militant group as a bloodthirsty terrorist organization. His own description of Hamas as a politically engaged group of freedom fighters reached an international audience of a scale that would not have been possible with various state media apparatuses that were more likely to see the radical leader as a threat than an ally. In what would turn out to be the last five years of his life, Yassin saw awareness of his message grow internationally. Yassin would again receive dense coverage from Al Jazeera following his 2004 assassination in Gaza by an Israeli Hellfire missile. As the Palestinian Authority stumbled in the wake of Yasser Arafat's death later that year, Hamas would come to serve as the popular alternative to the seemingly ineffectual Fatah leadership.

A Friday of Rage for Gaza

On his program *Sharia and Life*, al-Qaradawi called for making Friday, January 9, 2009, a day of rage in order to gain victory in Gaza against Israel (Al Jazeera, February 1, 2009). Gaza became a kind of catalyst of anger in the Arab street, even more so than the West Bank did. A brief history of Gaza is important for understanding the sociogenesis of anger in the Arab world. In his book *History of Gaza*, the French historian Jean-Pierre Filiu explains that the history of Gaza is also the history of Pax Romana, Pax Islamica—and the many other transitions that this port city has undergone as the last piece of land tucked between the Levant and Egypt (2012, 29).

Gaza is a historically cosmopolitan city that, since antiquity, has had a substantial Arabic-speaking community. It resisted conquest by Alexander the Great. It was also an important hub for caravans traveling between Egypt and the desert cities of Arabia. Caravans from Syria and Palestine came from the tribe of Qureish (the tribe of the Prophet Muhammad). One of the most important businessmen and a notable citizen of the city of Qureish, Hashim Ibn Abd Manaf, dominated the oasis of Mecca but died in Gaza at the age of twenty-five. One of his sons, Abdel Muttaleb, had six daughters and ten sons in Medina. One of those sons, Abdellah, married Amina, and around C.E. 570, their son Muhammad was born. The Muslim tradition portrays Hashim as a descendant of Ishmael and his father, Abraham, who is symbolically the grandfather of all Arabs. This tradition unifies the three major clans of the Arabian desert, the Qureish, the Abasiddes, and the Elaids. The Hashemite dynasty claims descent from this prestigious lineage, which reigned over Mecca for centuries (Filiu 2012, 31). In Arabic literature, Gaza is designated as Gazzatu Hashim. The second caliph, Omar Ibn Khatab (591–644), also a renowned businessman and negotiator, similarly has links to Gaza (Filiu 2012, 32). The founder of the Al Shafi'i school was born in Gaza in C.E. 767. The Pax Islamica continued for more than a century and a half before tensions between Egypt and the Middle East made their impact on Gaza (Filiu 2012, 33). First, the Abbasside caliphs of Baghdad launched their conquest of the Nile valley from 899 to 905 via Gaza. In 969, the Fatimid dynasty of Tunisia invaded from the west, this time to conquer the Nile valley, where they founded Cairo (meaning "the victorious"). Between Baghdad and Cairo, and between the two caliphates, the geopolitical importance of Gaza grew. During the Crusades, the Omar Mosque in Gaza was converted to a church by Western occupiers (Filiu 2012, 34). The Islamic conquest by Saladin in 1170, however, led to the re-Islamization of Gaza.

Gaza was important during the Mamluk era and essential for Ottoman control of Damascus and Egypt (Filiu 2012, 35). Napoleon Bonaparte, before invading Egypt, sent an expedition from Gaza to Port Said via the Sinai Desert in 1789 (Filiu 2012, 42). In November 25, 1946, Muslim Brothers launched their Gaza chapter in the movie theater Samer (Filiu 2012, 62). Gaza had been the subject of an Egyptian diplomatic public relations strategy since the late nineteenth century.

The region held symbolic significance for revolutionaries and renowned intellectuals of the twentieth-century Left. Che Guevara visited Gaza in June 1959 and in March 1967 Jean-Paul Sartre and Simone de Beauvoir visited, accompanied by Egypt's most well-known journalist, Muhammad Heikal, who continues to make waves in the Arab media (Filiu 2012, 134).

Sheikh Ahmed Yassin was approached many times by the Palestinian resistance movement Fatah in the 1960s. By 1965, Yassin was seen as the most important Islamist personality in Gaza. He refused to support any secular alliance against Israel. The Islamist pamphlets and media outlets saw in the defeat of Nasser in June 1967 a punishment for those aligned against Muslim clerics and against Islam (Filiu 2012, 143). In 1967, the population of Gaza was estimated to be 356,200. This number had fallen to 324,900 by early 1968 due to the occupation of Gaza by Israel (Filiu 2012, 148). On January 2, 1971, Ariel Sharon, after an incident that resulted in the deaths of Israeli soldiers, moved to dissolve the municipality of Gaza and disconnected it from Israel's national electric network. A total of 209 people with Egyptian passports were forced to return to Egypt, and since then the people of Gaza have lived under a state of siege (Filiu 2012, 154). Sharon, who became minister of agriculture, in 1977 "proceeded with a policy that doubled the number of Israeli settlements in Gaza" (Filiu 2012, 179). The Camp David Accord between Israel and Egypt did not involve Jordan or the Palestinians (Filiu 2012, 182). In March 1979, US president Jimmy Carter and Menachem Begin concluded the Camp David meeting; however, Teheran replaced the Israeli Embassy with PLO representation (Filiu 2012, 184). Around the same time, the Muslim Brothers in Gaza celebrated the ouster of the shah of Iran. Regarding the Camp David Accord, Sheikh Yassin did not speak out against Sadat, but he did benefit from the resulting crisis in Egypt and the isolation of Sadat. Because students from Gaza could not travel to Egypt from Gaza, the first Islamic university was created inside Gaza. The Islamic university of Gaza adopted the institutional framework of Al Azhar University and benefited from a donation by the Organization of the Islamic Conference in Jeddah of €150,000 (Filiu 2012, 185). On June 6, 1982, Israel invaded Lebanon, and the images of the massacres of Sabra and Shatila refugee camps in Beirut had a strong impact on Gazans (Filiu, 2012, 193). Sheikh Yassin was detained by Israel, touching off a wave of anti-Israel activism in Gaza. Even at this time, there was a deep divide between Islamist and secular resistance to Israel. Sheikh Yassin compared cooperation with Fatah to the *haram* (illicit or forbidden) acts of eating pork and drinking alcohol (Filiu 2012, 203–208). On December 14, 1987, the Muslim Brothers in Gaza called for an end to the Israeli occupation (Filiu 2012, 209). Sheikh Yassin announced his affiliation with the founder of the Muslim Brotherhood, Hassan al-Banna (Filiu 2012, 220). Yassin admitted to having authorized the killing of collaborators with the state of Israel (Filiu 2012, 223).

Yasser Arafat became very aware of the rising power of Hamas in Gaza and tried to neutralize it through division and co-optation (Filiu 2012, 245). However, as the heirs of the PLO legacy leaned toward a strategy of diplomatic dealings with Israel, Hamas gained traction by taking a militant stance against the Israeli occupation. In 2002, the Brigades of Saladin and of the Martyrs from Al Aqsa launched kamikaze attacks on Israeli settlers in their settlements (Filiu 2012, 279). Hamas bragged about the production of its own improvised rockets. Sheikh Yassin rejected the Oslo Accords, which he said imperiled the Palestinian Authority (Filiu 2012, 298). Hamas, however, was not incapable of pursuing diplomatic means to achieve its ends. It put pressure on the more radical and older Islamic jihad movements to stop launching rockets on Israel around 2007 (Filiu 2012, 327). The Hamas prime minister, Ismael Haniyeh, asked the Palestinian Authority on June 23, 2007, for inter-Palestinian dialogue (Filiu 2012, 343). This represented a dialogue between Gaza's "crushed generation and the generations of the intifadas" (Filiu 2012, 353).

Today, more than 1.5 million men and women live in a daily impasse. In 2011 the youth of Gaza demonstrated that they will no longer accept the status quo. Like Al Jazeera, the French historian Filiu believes that it is in Gaza that Israel must negotiate for a durable peace. Gaza is the birthplace of the Intifada, says Filiu.

According to the American Palestinian scholar Edward Said, "On the West Bank, the emergence of Hamas has much to do with the results of the Peace Process, the results of the intifada, the results of the occupation. Ninety percent of what Hamas does is not, in fact, to produce terrorism but [to create] economic opportunity through education and so forth, through daycare centers, through food supply. That's how they develop. Islamic fundamentalism begins as a protest and then takes on a life of its own" (Said and Viswanathan 2001, 275). Said argues that Hamas and Islamic jihad are "violent and primitive forms of resistance" (Said and Viswanathan 2001, 417). About the sociogenesis of Hamas and Islamic jihad, he believes that they "arise out of two principal factors. One is corruption. . . . The other is the resistance to hegemony of the U.S., which supersedes the influence of regional powers Egypt, Israel and Saudi Arabia (Said and Viswanathan 2001, 417).

John Mearsheimer and Stephen Walt describe this resistance as steadily growing since the early 1990s, writing, "Arab and Islamic anger has grown markedly since the end of the cold war, and especially since the second Intifada in 2000, in part because the level of violence directed against the Palestinians has been both significantly greater and more visible. The first Intifada (1987–92) was much less violent and there was relative calm in the occupied territories during the Oslo years (1993–2000). The development of the internet and the emergence of the alternative media outlets such as Al Jazeera now provide round-the-clock coverage of the carnage" (2007, 68). Not only is Israel "inflicting more violence" on its Palestinian subjects, but Arabs and Muslims around the world can see it with their own eyes (2007, 68). However, the long and bloody Syrian civil war has presaged a change in perceptions of the conflict in Gaza. Gaza has fallen into the background when it comes to media attention because Libya, Syria, and Egypt are on fire!

Conclusion

The questions asked at the beginning of this chapter are crucial to making sense of Al Jazeera's coverage of the Palestinian conflict. First, Al Jazeera's interest in Gaza and Hamas has a long history. It did not arise overnight. Second, Al Jazeera has worked to tarnish the Palestinian Authority in order to give more leverage to Hamas. Third, portraying Hamas in a positive light allows the network to use it as a model for the type of democratic political Islam the network has advocated for in other Arab nations. Fourth, by constructing Gaza as the heart of Palestinian resistance and martyrdom, Al Jazeera paints the Islamist government's mere survival as a success compared with the secular Palestinian Authority's capitulation to Israel's "Judaization" of Jerusalem.

The encounter between the chief negotiator of the Palestinian Authority and the star presenter of *Without Borders*, Ahmed Mansour, shows how Al Jazeera actively sought to direct the rage and anger of Arab publics toward the Palestinian Authority. The Palestinian interviewee Erekat was truly also enraged. The timing of the interview was not well chosen, as shown by the unfolding events in Libya and Egypt, discussed in chapters 6 and 7. The Arab Spring was a blessing and a curse for the Palestinians in general. Immediately after the Tunisian uprising, young people in Gaza called for an Arab Spring in Palestine by calling for a unity government. At the same time the Palestinian question lost some of its urgency for Arabs outside of the immediate region, who were suddenly overwhelmed by their own local struggles. Al Jazeera, like many international spectators, was taken by surprise when countries like Egypt, Libya, and Syria followed in the revolutionary footsteps of Tunisia. The network continued to give prominence to the Palestinian question, and mainly Gaza, under the assumption that it would continue to represent the pivotal international story in the Arab world.

A miscalculation perhaps? Maybe the network underestimated the power of local problems to eclipse pan-Arab issues such as the Palestinian question. However, Al Jazeera remained consistent in pursuing the issue of Gaza during and after the start of the Arab Spring.

Al Jazeera seems to favor Hamas because its aims ring true to the network's mission to function as the voice of an Arab people who are abused by their regime and to spread a philosophy that marries pan-Arabism with a democratic form of Islamism. In order to position itself as the voice of the people, Al Jazeera crafted anti-regime frames that eroded the legitimacy of the Arab establishment. These frames have been employed with some degree of success in almost every country in the Arab world, but most notably in Tunisia and Egypt, the birthplaces of the Arab Spring. By mounting pressure against Arab governments, including the Palestinian Authority, Al Jazeera has acquired for itself significant political leverage within the region.

Al Jazeera's main objective in favoring Hamas is to show that political Islam can be democratic, since Hamas was democratically elected. By focusing on positive framing of Hamas, Al Jazeera promotes the credibility of political Islam as a means of voicing the Arab people's aspirations for freedom, dignity, development, and independence. Qualitative and quantitative reviews of the author's dataset show that Al Jazeera functioned as a campaign machine for Islamist parties throughout the Arab Spring.

In contrast to the way it has portrayed Hamas's leadership, Al Jazeera has painted the Palestinian Authority's rule as one of failure and even treason because it has not achieved what it was elected to do, establish an independent state. Al Jazeera devoted many programs in 2014 (the fiftieth anniversary of the formation of the PLO) to the sixty-six years of the *nakba* (disaster or catastrophe) beginning with the 1948 exodus of more than 700,000 Palestinians from Israel.

Both Hamas and the Palestinian Authority (represented mainly by the rival Fatah party) were weakened by the events of the Arab Spring, which sparked a continuing civil war in Syria and the establishment of an Egyptian government that is staunchly anti-Hamas. Hamas, after a short moment of victory during the Muslim Brotherhood rule in Egypt, has since been totally paralyzed by the anti–Muslim Brotherhood government of el-Sisi in Egypt. And in spite of the Palestinian Authority's success in attaining observer status at the United Nations, Mahmoud Abbas has received little credit for his leadership of the Authority. Al Jazeera's reporters and commentators, for example, rarely note the difficulty Mahmoud Abbas faces as he attempts to navigate between the intractable hazards of Hamas and Israel. The difficulty, explains Agnès Levallois (France Culture, May 20, 2014), is that Israel saw Arafat, Abbas's predecessor as lacking credibility and reliability as a negotiation partner, favoring Abbas. But once he attained power, Abbas was also discredited because he could not chart a course capable of appeasing both Israel and Hamas. Hamas explicitly refuses to recognize Israeli legitimacy, while Israel demands that Hamas ban what Levallois called its "mantra of the destruction [of Israel]." Any concession to one party will invariably anger the other. Levallois explains that in the past Israel supported Hamas to weaken the PLO, failing to anticipate the rise of Hamas as a powerful enemy (Thierry Garcin, France Culture, May 20, 2014). Al Jazeera's role has been to empower Hamas to the extent that the Palestinian Authority must coordinate with the group. Their working together would allow Hamas to implicitly recognize the state of Israel without explicitly abandoning its anti-Israel platform. Al Jazeera's ubiquitous reach allows it to exert pressure in Gaza, Israel, and the West Bank, undermining all parties except for Hamas.

The electoral victory of Hamas in June 2006 was a watershed in the history of Palestine, but it was also greeted with distrust by the international community. The timing of the victory came amidst the US wars in Afghanistan and Iraq and tensions between Israel and Hezbollah. The Palestinian question had been put on the back burner of the Arab and international agenda. The ensuing tensions pitting Gaza against the West Bank changed the international dynamic of the Palestinian question. Events now seemed to turn on a bipolar axis with Iran and Syria aligned with Hamas and Saudi Arabia and Egypt supporting the Palestinian Authority (Filiu 2012). Backed by regimes with a reputation for spitting in the face of Western hegemony and suddenly faced with international economic sanctions, Hamas in Gaza bolstered its image as a force of resistance (Mohamed Juma, 2006–2007).

The response of Qatar and Al Jazeera to Hamas's rise to power helped fill a void left by the Saudis and Egyptians, who showed extreme fatigue over the Palestinian question. The network played an important role in pressuring Arab countries to build their relationships with Hamas as it transitioned from a resistance movement to a governing political party. Because historically, many Palestinian leaders were refugees living in Lebanon, the proximity to Syria fostered a close relationship between Syria and Hamas until the Arab Spring, when Hamas leaders had to choose between supporting the popular uprisings or the Syrian government. The victory of the Muslim Brotherhood in Egypt made it easy for Hamas to realign with Cairo and leave Damascus. The leader of Hamas, Khaled Meshal, currently lives in Doha, Qatar. In 2012, the emir of Qatar visited Gaza, as did Prime Minister Erdogan of Turkey. Al Jazeera showed Gaza in a festive light, with the emir of Qatar painted on the Palestinian flag. The network trumpeted the announcement that new homes would replace those built by Israeli settlers.

Three important events characterize the relationship between Al Jazeera and Hamas. First the January 2011 leaks, the 2013 leaks, and the 2013 results of the nine-month investigation by Al Jazeera that concluded Arafat had been murdered by poisoning. On the pan-Islamic level, the developments in Egypt that led to the banning of the Muslim Brotherhood created new alliances between Saudi Arabia and Egypt and pushed Qatar, Hamas, the Muslim Brotherhood, and Turkey closer together, fracturing relations between the major Sunni powers. The dramatic developments of the Arab Spring led to a rapprochement between Hamas and the Palestinian Authority in 2014. In this atmosphere of conflict and confusion, Al Jazeera continues to provide comprehensive coverage of Palestinian developments to Arab publics that are largely oversaturated with local problems in the aftermath of the Arab Spring.

Qatar and Turkey, along with some international activists, have tried to break the blockade of Gaza without success. Instead the blockade appears to be growing stronger, with the closing of borders and tunnels between Gaza and Egypt. Control of the tunnels was an important source of money for Hamas that has now dried up. Despite help from Qatar and Turkey, Hamas increasingly sees itself as financially unable to effectively govern a region widely viewed as the world's largest prison, walled off by a hostile Israel on one side and a blockaded sea on the other. This situation of impasse in addition to the failure of Islamist parties in Tunisia and Egypt to remain in power leave Hamas with little choice but to pursue the formation of a unity government with the Palestinian Authority.

The West Bank and Gaza are as ideologically divided as they are geographically divided. The divide is maintained by a total lack of communication between the secular Palestinian Authority and Islamist Hamas. In a way Al Jazeera was the only line of communication in this bicephalous leadership configuration. The network brought the voice of Hamas not only to the Arab public but also to the Palestinian Authority. Just as the collapse of the Muslim Brotherhood government in Egypt undermined Hamas, Israeli nonchalance toward the Palestinian Authority, the failure of the 2005 roadmap for peace, and an overall failure by the Palestinian Authority to achieve independence for Palestine have pushed the two entities closer to something resembling an accord. With each party having demonstrated an inability to attain its goals independently, the reconciliation efforts of April 23, 2014, seem to be the only hope for the weakened parties.

Hamas's failure, though, should not be seen as a failure of Al Jazeera's activist journalism. The network has made Gaza, where all historic leaders of Palestine have come from, including Arafat, the face of the Palestinian struggle in the popular mind. In the past, Jerusalem served as the epicenter of the conflict, but Al Jazeera has recast Gaza as the symbol of Palestinian resistance, with Hamas's victory as a necessary precondition to stopping the "Judaization" of Jerusalem. In July 2014, a third "war on Gaza" erupted. Bloody images filled Al Jazeera's account of the retread of 2008 and 2012 armed conflict. The network pointed an accusatory finger at Arab regimes (mainly Egypt) that kept their distance from the conflict, as well as the international community and what it called the heartless Israeli government and its army. Al Jazeera presented a narrative of the conflict as an Egyptian and Israeli conspiracy to break Hamas. In the end, Hamas was portrayed as the winner of the conflict, though. Al Jazeera's reporters appeared inside tunnels that remained "intact," contradicting the official claim of Israeli prime minister Benjamin Netanyahu that most of the tunnels used by "militants" in Gaza were destroyed. Despite this portrayal of Hamas emerging as the noble and embattled victor, this most recent eruption of violence only serves to show that despite financial support from Qatar and unconditional positive coverage by Al Jazeera, the dual identity of Hamas as both government and resistance movement has not enabled it to alleviate the immense suffering of the Gazans, who are paying a high human price.

5

SECRET MISSION

SHINING A SPOTLIGHT ON TAHRIR SQUARE

The Egyptian regime exerted all sorts of pressures and [employed many]
tactics to prevent the coverage of the revolution and its Fridays [of protest].

—Mohamed Krichen, anchor (Al Jazeera, June 28, 2011)[1]

Each successful revolution legitimates itself, but legitimates, too, revolution
as such.

—Pierre Bourdieu (1996,125)

Al Jazeera's role in empowering and facilitating the Egyptian revolution was considerable. After spending more than a decade building its
symbolic and financial capital through resourceful and daring reporting, Al Jazeera had considerable resources to devote to covering the
Arab world's biggest cultural and political shock in a generation. Not
content to serve as the Arab Spring revolutions' preeminent documentarian, the network applauded its journalists as they became increasingly immersed in antigovernment movements, especially in Egypt.
Rather than fading into the background as the story of the Arab
Spring unfolded before them, Al Jazeera's cameras became the focus of
the coverage. More than professionalism or objectivity, retrospectives
by the network would stress the heroism of its reporters, presenters,
and camera operators in their support of the revolutions.

Meanwhile, the network's religious voice and biggest star, Yusuf al-
Qaradawi, played an active role in the revolution. The mufti delivered
a series of televised fatwas sanctioning acts of rebellion and pressuring Egyptian president Hosni Mubarak to step down from power, a
pattern he would echo when commenting on rebellions in Libya and
Syria. In the wake of Mubarak's ouster, al-Qaradawi returned to Egypt
after a forty-year exile, injecting powerful religious rhetoric into the
discussion about post-Mubarak Egypt. With Al Jazeera covering his
every word, al-Qaradawi would advance his vision of an inclusive yet
undeniably Islamist Egyptian democratic government, which clearly
mirrored the Muslim Brotherhood's campaign platform in the democratic elections that followed the revolution.

This chapter recounts the most vivid moments of Al Jazeera's involvement in the Egyptian revolution—in the words of the Al Jazeera journalists and commentators who were there when possible—from inspired acts of journalism to chest thumping over its own role in what appears to have been a brief flirtation with democracy. An examination of Al Jazeera's coverage of Egypt between the first "day of rage" demonstrations against Mubarak and the fall of the dictatorial regime reveals the network at its most resourceful and effective. In its reporting on Egypt, the network would lean on improvised tactics that had brought it through previous challenging situations, including the use of user-generated content, international shaming of repressive regimes, and a tireless devotion to watchdog journalism. However, Al Jazeera's coverage of Egypt's transition from Mubarak to Morsi to el-Sisi also serves as an example of the network's drift from "journalism with a point of view" to partisan press, which will be a recurring theme in the second half of this book. Recollections by the journalists who covered the Egyptian revolution for Al Jazeera reflect a shift in self-perception, as revealed by their comments regarding coverage of the Tunisian revolution. During the events in Tunisia, journalists spoke as sympathetic documentarians, unabashedly proud of their resourcefulness in bringing the story of the revolution to the world. Recollections by veteran journalists of the Egyptian rebellion, though, evoke an image of comrades in arms of the revolution.

The network's own descriptions of its work reveal three categories of frames that shaped its reporting on the Arab Spring in Egypt. The first category can be described as a constellation of frames used throughout the network's Egypt coverage. These consist of the heroism frame (*butula, basala*); the resistance and defiance frame (*muqawama wa tahadi*); the outsmarting the regime frame (*ghalb nidam*); the secret mission frame (*muhima siriya*); and the bricolage frame (*ma fi mutanwili al-yad*), meaning the use of any available resources to achieve the goals of both covering and supporting the revolution. The second category can be described as an array of frames related to expressions of anger. There are the anger frame (*ghadab*) and the mobilization frame (*irhal*). Religious frames make up the third category. These include the righteous punishment/reward frame (*uquba saliha wa mukafa'a*), as when Friday sermons implored Allah to intercede in the unfolding events; the pharaonic frame (*fir'awn*), used to portray leaders who overstep their boundaries; the absolute oppression frame (*taghiyya*); the military rule frame (*hukm al askar*); the fatwa frame (fatwa), which attaches a religious opinion from al-Qaradawi to every event; the impurity frame (*najassa*), relegating Mubarak to the level of sewage; the martyrs' frame (*shahid*), which bestows high religious rank on any activist who dies in support of the revolution; and the injustice frame (*zulm*).

Hanging a Lamp over Tahrir Square

Al Jazeera's Cairo bureau, situated in the capital's bustling downtown area, served as Egypt's most prestigious Arab news hub prior to the revolution. Mubarak's police forces closed the bureau on January 30, 2011, during the protests in an attempt to gain control of the news coming from the city and particularly from Tahrir Square. Journalists and reporters were driven from their workplaces, their press cards confiscated. Satellite broadcasting was effectively shut down. However, Al Jazeera's coverage from Tahrir Square inexplicably continued around the clock.

When authorities realized that Al Jazeera was still delivering coverage from within Cairo, Egyptian police scoured the city trying to track down Al Jazeera's video cameras—they even dismantled the bureau's office toilets in their search for hidden cameras. None were found. Ultimately, the decision to close the bureau didn't yield positive results for Mubarak's regime in terms of silencing "the rebel," Al Jazeera. In fact, it did quite the opposite.

Abelfattah Fayed, the bureau chief of Al Jazeera in Cairo, said in a 2011 retrospective episode of *Without Borders* that for him one of the most dramatic moments was his secret communication with Egypt's former minister of communication. "When he told me he planned to close down the bureau, I told him clearly, 'You are closing an office where four correspondents work,'" said Fayed. "[In doing so] you will open a new bureau as large as all of Egypt itself, with millions of [citizen] correspondents.

"I speak all this for the first time," said Fayed. "[There are still] many secrets that nobody knows about the bureau of Al Jazeera in Cairo and about Tahrir Square. While the screen of Al Jazeera may have been closed down in the Cairo office, another much bigger screen was opened on Tahrir Square, created by the protesters themselves—we had no role in it. First the protesters created a screen opposing the regime, and second they tweeted breaking news on Al Jazeera moment by moment. . . . The government's decision to close the Al Jazeera bureau came at a time when the bureau was, for all practical purposes, almost closed anyway" (Al Jazeera, November 12, 2011).

This is exactly what happened. The Egyptian people became unofficial correspondents and reporters for Al Jazeera, and Tahrir Square was transformed into a citizen-powered news bureau. The newsroom was moved from an office building to the streets of the revolution to powerful effect. The potential for greater direct involvement in the events heightened the Egyptian people's sense of investment in the revolution. As media scholar Mohamed Zayani argues, "Social media captured the unfolding of events and provided a constant stream of images, videos, reactions, and statements. Transnational media like Al Jazeera moved the material into a compelling narrative" (Zayani 2015, 189).

"[Mubarak's security forces] were *al udda tua'd* [making preparations],"[2] recalled Mohamed Fayd, "to challenge the Egyptian revolution by removing Al Jazeera from the immediate scene. Just before January 25, they cut all the phone lines and we initially thought it was accidental. The next day, the Internet began to cut out, and then it disappeared. As you know, the building was full of big companies that use phone lines and Internet regularly, and there are even other satellite TV organizations within the offices there—it is a building that was made especially for this purpose with all the built-in capabilities necessary for TV broadcasting. But nobody knew anything about the cutting off of Al Jazeera's communication capabilities. And this had nothing to do with our intention to intensify the coverage. They cut off all means of communication for us. On January 28, 2011, the Friday of Rage, when we started filming and covering the event, they even closed off the communication link that we had with Qatar, which meant that no images could reach Al Jazeera. . . . Before, we were at least able to film and then later send comments via phone or Internet. But by then, they had cut off everything. At the end of the day, when they closed down all the cell phones, there was total paralysis. When the communication minister spoke with me on January 29 and said, 'We are going to close the Al Jazeera bureau,' my first thought was, 'Well, the bureau is already essentially shut down.' The bureau was little more than a furnished room at that point."

Recounting the story of the bureau closure with Fayed was Ahmed Mansour, possibly the most overtly aligned with the Muslim Brotherhood of any Al Jazeera journalist. His habitus is formed by religious sympathy to the Muslim Brotherhood and adherence to solid journalistic standards. He has been consistently open regarding his bias against secularism.

"How is it possible after all this that Al Jazeera was the strongest TV channel present in Egypt covering the revolution?" Mansour interjects. "The closing of the bureau was a kind of curse for the regime, and it was good for Al Jazeera and good for the revolution. . . . When the authorities came to the Al Jazeera bureau they were looking for cameras, but they could not find a single one. They were even looking in the toilets. I asked one of them, 'What are you looking for?' He said, 'We are looking for cameras.' I said, 'There are no cameras.' He said, 'But why is Tahrir Square on Al Jazeera? You are on the air.' I asked him, 'Did you think Al Jazeera only comes from this bureau?' I told him that Al Jazeera comes from many places. They had forgotten that Al Jazeera is an international network that has correspondents everywhere and is capable of reporting events from more than one place. With social media, all citizens can participate in broadcasting breaking news."

Another journalist from the Al Jazeera Cairo team, Abdel Azim Mohamed, recounted his experience during that period on the *Without Borders* retrospective about the Egyptian revolution. "The most difficult moment was when tear gas bombs were everywhere and we couldn't even breathe. We didn't eat for almost twenty-four hours. A colleague ventured out on a scooter to get us macaroni his wife had made for us. . . . There were a large number of people who came to support us when they heard the Al Jazeera bureau was closed down. They gave us Pepsi Cola to clean our eyes and vinegar to put on our clothes in order to help us breathe again. Many of these colleagues were arrested and taken from their hotels" (Al Jazeera, November 12, 2011).

Abdel Azim recalls that ordinary citizens were able to "supply raw images that, given the circumstances, proved to be more efficient and also demonstrated that their courage was similar to that of the journalists." He argued that the first images of the revolution were disturbing: "I can't see young people dying in Tahrir Square, and I was just a spectator. I gave the Al Jazeera administration the option to choose whether I should cover Tahrir Square as a reporter or whether I should go there as a demonstrator. They told me to go undercover, as a citizen-journalist on a secret mission in Tahrir Square."

Muntaser Muarai, a Cairo bureau reporter who was sent on the same "secret mission" explains that the mission's goal was to create a point of transmission so that news coverage could continue in the event that the Al Jazeera offices were closed down or the camera operators could no longer film inside Tahrir Square.

"Even the manager of direct transmission didn't know that I was traveling to Cairo," Muntaser said in his interview on the *Without Borders* retrospective. "Not even those who were with me in the plane to Cairo knew of the mission. I told them I was going to visit my family. Upon landing, I was able to pass with some difficulty through Egyptian security carrying the basic means for broadcasting. . . . We succeeded in penetrating all these barriers with a set of devices that would give us broadcasting capabilities. It is said that when the thief steals, he doesn't steal only in the dark. We were keen to keep the camera rolling to serve as a lamp hanging over Tahrir Square so as not to strengthen the hands of the thieves of the revolution [i.e., the thugs of the regime who were planted among the protesters]" (a reference to the words of al-Qaradawi) (Al Jazeera, November 12, 2011).

The host, Ahmed Mansour, asks, "Where did you put the camera?"

"In the middle of Tahrir Square," Muntaser answers, "where we felt a kind of security after what happened during Harb al-Jamal [Battle of the Camel].[3] We were at risk of being exposed, since the people didn't [necessarily] know that the camera belonged to Al Jazeera. We were trying to keep the mission secret, saying that we were just a news agency that provides news to other stations. And this was true—we were not lying. After the battle of the camel, this very difficult day, we positioned the camera above a shop that sold bags, called the Star of Tahrir [Najma]. We put a small camera there, though we didn't have a microphone."

Ahmed Mansour interjects, "Your live video feed came from the roof of the shop?"

"We were sleeping holding the camera," Muntaser replies, "and we had only this one small camera that brought all of this broadcast coverage to the whole world. And we had a small broadcasting device that we were holding, too. If that device had been taken away, then the sole news camera focused on Tahrir Square would have been turned off, too. [He holds up a photograph.] This was our ladder, our ladder that linked the earth and the sky. Sometimes people used our ladder to suspend banners of the revolutionaries, and sometimes we didn't eat or drink or even talk to our guests [on camera]. Thank God, we managed to keep our live camera the whole time."

"The revolutionaries protected you well," Monsour says.

Muntaser replies, "The rebels became part of the team when they moved spontaneously to protect us. I want to thank them. And at times I was alone, without my team, and somebody was holding my microphone or otherwise helping me without interfering in the coverage. Thank God, who allowed us to bring you the images [of the revolution]" (Al Jazeera, November 12, 2011).

Echoes of the Revolution in Alexandria

Egyptian revolutionaries saw Al Jazeera as an ally. The network warned Tunisians and Egyptians to be vigilant about the future of their revolutions. Throughout the revolution, Al Jazeera assured protestors that they were right to be angry and that they should show their anger in their public demands for change. The following segments focus primarily on Al Jazeera's use of frames centering on anger and rage in its coverage of the Egyptian uprisings.

While the revolution raged in Cairo, demonstrators in Alexandria also took to the streets to raise their voices against the regime. Ibrahim Mohsin, a Lebanon-born Al Jazeera reporter who covered Alexandria during the revolution, would recall that the daily demonstrations in Alexandria were a challenge, especially around mosques. Mohsin describes attacks by thugs against him and his colleagues (Al Jazeera, November 12, 2011).

Mohsin recalls reporting from the Al Kaid Ibrahim Mosque in Alexandria on the Friday Mubarak was ousted. The demonstrators in Alexandria were more mobile than those in Cairo, who tended to stay within Tahrir Square. "That day, we were with our English and Arabic teams filming from a central point for the demonstration," says Mohsin. Normally, the demonstrators would turn right and go down the street, but this time they turned left toward Tena Palace. A few of the protesters told us that they had an apartment overlooking Tena Palace where we could film. When we went there, [but] we found it was too far away to get a shot of the palace, and many people armed with knives and swords were surrounding the building. Shortly after, we reached an agreement with the owner of the building that we would turn off our cameras and go away. The walk back to our car was the longest and most dangerous four hundred meters of my life. We were walking through two rows of people carrying swords. What they didn't see was that our colleague stayed behind with another camera in the building, and this is how we succeeded in covering that event" (Al Jazeera, June 28, 2011).

The run-up to Tuesday, January 25, 2011, the landmark day of rage in Cairo, diverted attention from the heavy coverage and the euphoria that had been sparked by Al Jazeera TV. The daily live coverage intensified on January 28, the day that was proclaimed the "Friday of Rage." These days were named, respectively, the "Tuesday 25th Day of Rage" and "Friday of Rage (28th)."

The daily twenty-four-hour news operation was punctuated by a barrage of images, text, and publicity ad spots announcing the fall of the old regime and proclaiming the new Arab dawn and spring. Many episodes of Al Jazeera's popular programs devoted time and attention to the "heroism of Al Jazeera" and its journalists, camera operators, and technicians for their astute tactics, which kept live coverage of the revolution on the air, in spite of the substantial difficulties they faced. These episodes also focused on Al Jazeera teams' innovative and savvy use of social media to help guide revolutionaries to the epicenter of the Arab tsunami: Tahrir Square.

Baltajiyya and the Battle of the Camel

Without Borders was far from the only program to devote episodes to Al Jazeera journalists' accounts of their Arab Spring coverage, including the famed Battle of the Camel. In the immediate wake of the revolution, most of Al Jazeera's shows were celebrations of the heroism of Al Jazeera. This made sense, particularly since the Arab Spring coincided with the celebration of the fifteenth anniversary of Al Jazeera's founding. These episodes were hosted by Al Jazeera star anchors, hosts, and reporters. Like the Egyptian journalist Ahmed Mansour, the heralded Tunisian journalist Mohamed Krichen also described the severe conditions under which journalists had to do their work during that time in their respective countries, Egypt and Tunisia: "Ahmed Mahmud was the first colleague in our profession of troubles [journalism] who was killed during the spring of the Arab revolution. Unfortunately, he was not the last one. A bullet fired by an officer near Tahrir Square killed a photographer who wanted to document the events of the Fridays of Rage, and he passed away on the twenty-eighth of January, 2011" (*Spring Revolutions and the Media Spotlight Gap*, May 3, 2011).

In another broadcast Krichen went on to say that many journalists' credentials were withdrawn and the regime used *baltajiyya* (thugs) to attack Al Jazeera staff members along with tactics similar to those employed during the Tunisian revolution by the ousted Ben Ali to prevent the provision of images and news to the global viewing public. This all came after decades of blockades of the media. "But those weapons of censorship are obsolete," he went on. "The world saw footage of the protests in Tunisian cities and the violent response of the Tunisian security forces, thanks to broadcasts via YouTube and Facebook. We see now, from the unprecedented events and demonstrations in Syria, that the regime in Damascus preferred to replicate the unsuccessful experiment of the failed regime in Tunisia" (Al Jazeera, September 18, 2011).

The Pulpit of the Revolution

Along with the talk about heroism and sacrifice by Egyptians and Al Jazeera journalists, the network managed to inject its commentary with religious imagery and symbolism. The technique of split screens, zooming in on signs of religiosity, intensified the religious flavor of protests, which at first had a more secular air. By linking democratic aspirations to Islam, Al Jazeera presented a new model for Arab countries, a new order. The following paragraphs deal with the third category of frames identified earlier that Al Jazeera employed during the Tunisian and Egyptian revolutions: the couching of revolutionary developments in religious terms.

In Cairo, demonstrators found encouragement on Al Jazeera during the Friday of Rage, especially when the mufti of Al Jazeera, al-Qaradawi, transformed the TV screen into a pulpit, praying for the "martyrs" and promising them a better life in the heavens while simultaneously forecasting defeat on earth and damnation in the hereafter for Mubarak and his supporters.

Al-Qaradawi began issuing religious decrees regarding the revolution, almost from the outbreak of protests. Only two days after the start of the revolution, al-Qaradawi issued a fatwa forbidding the use of bullets against the peaceful demonstrators (Thursday. January 27, 2011). He prayed publicly for the "martyrs of the day of rage," who died on January 25, 2011. His first article on Egypt's protests appeared in *Ashuruk* on the first Friday of Rage, on January 28, 2011. On this day, al-Qaradawi appeared live on Al Jazeera to describe the conditions under which disobeying a ruler is *halal* (licit). On Saturday 29, 2011, al-Qaradawi spoke live on Al Jazeera, addressing first the Egyptian people, second, the Egyptian Army, and third, the Egyptian regime and its president.

On January 29, 2011, the Saudi presenter of the program *In Depth*, Ali Dafiri, introduced Yusuf al-Qaradawi, saying that many imams and Islamic scholars were praying "with us, with our people in Egypt, and they ask all of you to offer prayers for them and for us all. Everybody is watching and listening to Al Jazeera in Tahrir and many other squares." The anchorwoman then dramatically interrupts, "And now we are expecting a new Friday, called the 'Friday of Departure.'"

Al-Qaradawi's framing strategy was very effective in demolishing the image of the regime. The success is reflected in the fact that al-Qaradawi was mentioned or cited in media across the entire Arab world. Al-Qaradawi has said that prayers are the weapons of the Prophet. He opened his January 29 appearance by quoting the Prophet: "God answers the prayers of people in need or in distressing situations." He prayed, "God, help our brothers in Egypt; God, protect our brothers the protesters from injustice and hatred; God, help them; God, give them victory; God, don't give victory to the enemies; God, make our brothers strong; God, help them with your soldiers. . . . These innocent youth, these sacrificing *mujahid* [fighters for jihad]. . . , al-Qaradawi asks God to defeat the tyrants, the pharaohs" (*Harvest of the Day*, January 29, 2011). He continues:

> I would like to say this to the Egyptian people whom I am greeting now, with their blessed intifada, revolting against the dire conditions of their lives after being very patient so as to put an end to poverty, hunger, and unemployment: Others are enjoying the wealth of this country, monopolizing our resources and land and [exploiting] all the people and their patience. The patient [people] will say, one day, "Enough." The people went to the streets in a peaceful manner—in demonstrations, in protest, without sticks, but with prayer beads or Qurans, refusing to leave this life, wanting dignity and freedom and *halal* [fair] wage. But the security forces countered their protest with live bullets. . . . We saw yesterday dozens of martyrs falling and more than a thousand wounded. This is what eventually led to some aggression toward the property of the state. I want to stress that the youth who were in the intifada didn't participate in any looting, however. I call on everybody—do not touch anything that belongs to the state, public or private—that is *haram* [forbidden]. I ask the people to continue their intifada—continuity is the only way to secure your rights, *Inshallah*. This is what I ask the great people of Egypt to do. I say this to my friends, to my children, and to my grandchildren—to continue the intifada. . . .
>
> To our beloved army, I say that the army's purpose is to protect Egypt in the period to come, a very crucial period. But I ask them not to govern. I don't want to go back in history to another time, to the time of military rule [*hukm al askr*]. We want the civilians to govern. We want a civilian governance, and if people of the military want to run for office, they

should take off their military uniforms and engage in political competition with other civilians according to the rules of the Republic and democracy. I watch the army now on Al Jazeera while talking [on Al Jazeera]. The people see the army taking the wealth of the country, monopolizing the land, and the people are patient, and patient—but patience cannot go on indefinitely. What I want to say to the Egyptian regime and especially to Mubarak: I regret to see a regime that is blind and can't see, deaf and can't hear, stupid and can't understand.

Eighty years ago the prince of poets, Ahmed Chawki, said when the world was stunned and surprised to discover the wealth of Tutankhamen after an archaeological discovery, "The age and time of the individual, O Pharaoh, is done. The state of authoritarians is gone and the ruled are now equal [with the rulers]." This is what the prince of poets said eighty years ago, but the pharaohs of today don't understand. I was hoping that President Mubarak, from whom reasonable discourse has long been expected, would be aware of this, but he spoke like someone who lives in a different world, not our world. He doesn't feel [the suffering that] is going on in the Egyptian streets. He doesn't feel and see the martyrs; he doesn't feel the wounded; he doesn't feel the hungry; he doesn't feel the suffering of the people. All he said was that he was going to dissolve the government [laughing]. He didn't say what needed to be said. He didn't say that he failed to solve the problem of succession or that he would dissolve the parliament that had been subject to the highest level of corruption in the world. He didn't say that he would abolish the emergency laws that had ruled Egypt for decades and inflicted a lot of pain on the people. This regime doesn't understand. It is not reasonable, and it didn't learn anything from history's lessons, even though the lesson of Tunisia is still alive. I advise the president to leave office and to leave Egypt. There is no solution other than his departure [rahil]. In just a handful of days, Egypt lost billions of pounds—the Egyptian pound is now at its the lowest rate ever. The economy and jobs are stagnating. Thirty years are [long] enough. . . . Take what you have and leave in order to limit the damage done to Egypt. You killed dozens in one day, dozens who went to demonstrate and wanted only their rights. Where is social justice? Where is dignity? Where is humanity? Where is the luqmat halal [piece of bread]? But your security confronts [these protesters] with live bullets in their chests. You can't stay anymore, Mubarak.

O Mubarak, learn from Ben Ali, leave on your own feet, before you are forced to leave. I don't want the crowds to judge you. I want for you a fair civilian trial. I don't want you in a military tribunal, the ones you use to oppress the people with unfair sentences. I want you to leave on your own feet and leave the people *idalin nihaya* [to the end, a popular term in Egyptian movies] and your *nihaya* is now. The winds of change are here and when the winds of change come from the people, no one can stop them. . . . You can't fight destiny, you can't fight dawn. God doesn't help bad people [*yumhil wa la yuhmil*, a recitation from the Quran]. I say to you now, on behalf of the children of Egypt, who are all calling and praying for your departure; I say to you on behalf of all the *ulama* [scholars] of Egypt—hundreds of thousands of Al Azhar *ulama*—I say on behalf of all the *ulama* of the world, who are far greater in number than the ones of Egypt: I ask you in the name of all these people to have mercy on your country, to have mercy on your people. If you have one grain of mercy in your heart or one grain of intelligence in your head, I ask the mighty God for the sake of our beloved Egypt, Egypt of Islam, Egypt of Uruba [Arabness], the Egypt of history, Egypt the civilization, Egypt of the present and the future, I ask God to make our [present] day better than our past, and our future better than our present. I ask the children of Egypt to continue in their pacific movement, pacific *istimarar* [perseverance], and the victory of God is coming soon.

The Moroccan anchor acknowledges al-Qaradawi as *shukran fadilat al sheikh* (president of the International Union of Muslim Scholars at the end of the speech.

On January 30, 2011, Al Jazeera announced on its main evening news the declaration by the International Union of Muslim Scholars, signed by al-Qaradawi, supporting the "Egyptian intifada" and blaming the Egyptian government for the widespread poverty, poor governance, and marginalization of the Palestinian struggle. The "people have lived in a big prison ruled by emergency law for decades. They do not possess true political freedom, have no right to form political parties, no right to oppose state policy, no access to military tribunals for civilians, an absence of religious freedom. The government controls the mosques, the pulpits and the Friday sermons. Mosques have to be closed after prayer" (Abu Zeid 2011, 47).

On February 2, 2011, al-Qaradawi signed another declaration on aljazeera. net, stating that both Egyptian and Qatari newspapers had placed the responsibility for ousting the oppressive ruler on the shoulders of the *umma*. He outlined the severe conditions under which the use of arms against rulers is legal in Islam. One condition is that the violence must not lead to blind *fitna*, where people die without hope of freeing themselves from an oppressive ruler. Al-Qaradawi called on the Egyptians, *jamahirina al mu'mina*, or the "faithful public," to peacefully go out on the streets on the Friday of Decisiveness). Al-Qaradawi gave a fatwa marking the demonstration on Friday, February 4, 2011, as the last day of Mubarak's reign. The demonstration was a religious duty (*wajib Shari'*) for everybody who could walk to the gathering. He gave Mubarak an ultimatum to leave with the increasing number of "one hundred and fifty martyrs." Al-Qaradawi asked the army to meet this historic challenge before an "angry Egyptian people" and a president who had lost his legitimacy (Al Jazeera, February 4, 2011).

Al-Qaradawi asked the *ulama* and *khutaba*, the scholars and preachers of Al Azhar and Dar al-ulum (the House of Sciences), to join the demonstrations and to distance themselves from the *ulama sulta* (scholars who serve those in power). He asked preachers at the mosques to direct the *musalin* (those who pray) after the Friday prayer to join the *masirat shabia* (popular marches). From Muslim communities around the world, he asked for a show of solidarity with the oppressed Egyptian people. He also asked them to protect the churches in order to avoid *fitna* caused by the regime.

That same day, Al Jazeera interrupted its live coverage of the Tahrir Square uprising in Cairo to cut to the reading of a fatwa from al-Qaradawi, its resident mufti, which it billed as breaking news. Yusuf al-Qaradawi delivered an emotionally charged fatwa condemning Mubarak and calling for solidarity among rebel Egyptians. Following a brief salutation praising God and the Prophet, al-Qaradawi said:

> In reality I follow this *masira* [march] and the demonstrators with utmost pride. These young, free, honorable *shuhada'* [martyrs] have a degree of faith and morals and *muru'a* [humanity] such that they are free of violent aggression.
>
> Mubarak is *najassa* [an impurity]. He cuts the throats of his people. How can he butcher these people? You are doing exactly what the pharaoh did before you, dividing the people into factions against each other.
>
> We want to address the Egyptian people to tell them they didn't commit wrong. All they want is to make their voice heard and to lift up the [reputation] of their country and protest against injustices that have gone on for many long years, for thirty years. Maybe the early years [of Mubarak] were [characterized] by less injustice, but [injustice] has risen . . .
>
> Any excess is compensated for by its opposite, Arabs say. In these demonstrations they [the demonstrators] didn't harm anybody. They didn't harm any public or private property, but they were a living example of generous morals. Nine days. Yesterday there was a march, or marches, of millions. Some estimated the number of demonstrators in different parts of the republic as being up to eight million.

Al Qaradawi then directs viewers to go to Tahrir Square with "everything that can help people: emergency kits and bandages for the wounded, and things people need like food and water and blankets." He goes on:

> You should go in groups so as not to [be attacked]. Go in groups to support your brothers who are part of this people. We ask the whole Egyptian people to stand beside these young people who are setting an example by sacrificing themselves for all that is dear to them. I ask everybody: the judges, the lawyers, the journalists, the scholars of Al Azhar University, and religious scholars—and especially the religious scholars—to stand behind their brothers. Sheikh al-Azhar, I already wrote a letter to him to stand behind the people. It's a pity that he just made a declaration today accusing the demonstrators, who have been [subject to] injustice.
>
> The demonstrators want their rights. They want the *halal* life. Freedom, they ask for dignity. . . . We ask our brothers the Azhar scholars to come to the streets with their gowns and headgear and to stand behind the people, especially on Friday. We ask the imams and preachers of the mosques to go with the worshippers to the street. To go to the street. I ask the entire people of Egypt to stand behind the demonstrators, who defend the entire people. I salute these young people who refused to leave their positions [in the streets or Tahrir Square] until they get their legitimate rights even if they fall as martyrs; a hundred and fifty have fallen. Not one single policeman has died, because these young people don't carry arms. But one hundred and fifty martyrs of these young people have fallen and more than four thousand are wounded and dozens of them were disappeared or [kidnapped] in unknown places. . . .
>
> I want to address one steadfast word to the Egyptian army. We are used to the Egyptian army as the arm and the pride of the people. . . . Your attitude is noble, you prevent the killing of the children [demonstrators]. . . .
>
> I want to address a third word to President Mubarak himself. I addressed him some time ago, but I will repeat what I said . Haram[forbidden in the religious sense], O Mubarak, to kill your people. If you are a good and responsible shepherd, you should protect your people, not kill them. The herder is turning out to be the wolf. . . . You can't leave the people to the looters and criminals.

The delivery of the fatwa was a powerful moment for al-Qaradawi. From the safety of a television studio, he managed to portray himself not only as one with the protesters, but as a leader of all parties, offering marching orders to protesters, the army, and the president. Meanwhile, his use of the religiously charged word *najassa* (feces, body fluid, or other impurities) in his condemnation of Mubarak sent a very powerful message. Before praying, reading the Quran, or stepping into a mosque, every Muslim is required to cleanse him- or herself of *najassa*. In applying this term to Mubarak, al-Qaradawi implicitly excluded the leader from the realm of purity, the Quran, and the mosque.

The statement suggested that Mubarak was unfit even to pray. Muslims must perform two kinds of purification before praying. First, they must cleanse themselves of the impurities of urine, feces, and sex with water. This is called the *tahara al kubra* (great ablution). Then they must perform the *wudu'* (a small ablution) each time they pray. To call Mubarak *najassa* is to say that the ablution cannot make him clean, because he himself is the impurity that must be removed, in this case through revolution. Presented in this frame, the revolution is a form of ablution, cleansing Egypt of impurities, and it is not only religiously permitted but a requirement for good Muslims. Al-Qaradawi declared that the regime represented thirty years of impurity that "is Mubarak." For such an impurity to soil Egypt, home to the most important sites of Sunni Islamic knowledge in the entire world, would be a disgrace and, moreover, a sin.

By relegating Mubarak to the realm of impurities, al-Qaradawi also positioned himself as the voice and defender of purity. By offering guidance to the demonstrators, he positioned himself as an adviser to and leader of the uprising. It would not be an exaggeration to say that the Arab Spring was, in a sense, co-opted by the mufti of Al Jazeera. Thus, by proxy, the victory of the Arab revolutionaries was also seen as the victory of Al Jazeera, which had distinguished itself by airing breaking news several times a day during the Arab Spring uprisings. The British anthropologist Mary Douglas explains in her book *Purity and Danger* how the impure are seen as outsiders. In this sense, al-Qaradawi is drawing boundaries between the out-group, or those in the realm of impurity where Mubarak and his supporters belong, and the in-group of those in the realm of the pure (Entman and Rojecki 1999, 50). This looming threat of the out-group remained even after the ouster of Mubarak in the form of plotters against the revolution and later the military government of Abdul Fattah el-Sisi.

The airing of the fatwa was superbly timed, occurring at the precise point when Arab rulers could no longer count on support from their long-dominated citizens. Introducing fatwas from al-Qaradawi during pivotal Arab and Muslim events became a strategic pattern in Al Jazeera's news coverage. The network used these impromptu statements from al-Qaradawi to communicate clear messages denouncing the deposed Ben Ali, Mubarak, and Qaddafi. Al-Qaradawi's live interventions promoted frames with elements of patriotism, as well as pan-Arabic and Islamic fervor. These elements were centered on courage, solidarity, and deep faith in God. In sum, they were rallying and unifying frames.

The Journey of Rage

The journey of rage that led to the ousting of Mubarak was debated heavily by experts on Al Jazeera—for example, in a three-part series of interviews with the iconic Egyptian journalist, Muhammad Hassanein Heikal, on his show *With Heikal* (*Ma' Haykal*).[4] Heikal has been a journalist since 1942 and has incredible access to confidential information. In the interviews, Heikal refutes the popular notion that the revolution was a complete surprise, saying, "At the beginning of the revolution, I didn't think that the revolution was a surprise. The only one who knew the size of the problem was Mubarak. People think that the military forced Mubarak to pronounce the magic word before February 25, 2011, two or three days before he resigned. . . . According to valid sources, President Mubarak asked the general to protect the legitimacy of the state, or *ya shil e' shila*, which was, I guess, the keyword" (Al Jazeera, October 29, 2011).

Mohamed Krichen stops him. "What does that mean?"

Heikal answers, "This is an Egyptian expression that means 'carry the weight and the responsibility in this situation of impasse.'" Heikal continues, "January 25 brought the dream of democracy to the people of Egypt, but nobody understood three important needs: the need to understand what we did to ourselves for thirty years, what others did to us for thirty years, and what the Israelis and their intelligence did to us for thirty years."

Heikal explains that the director of the Israeli military intelligence said to him, "What we did with Egypt! Even if they [the Egyptians] want to repair it, it won't be easy to do it."

Krichen asks many questions over the course of the interview about the role of the army and whether the army's power poses an obstacle for the future. Heikal argues that the army is not the problem and that the military dictatorship of the Mubarak regime had already long outlived its years by the time of the revolution. "What was surprising," he says, "and it was not a secret, was that when the young people, the youth went out on the streets, people thought it was the end of the regime. I wrote a year and a half before the revolution that we were at the end of an old era and that we needed to think about the transition, but Mubarak and his family were talking about succession scenarios" (Al Jazeera, May 3, 2011).

Krichen notes that the statement led to a big controversy resembling *qamat al qiyyama*, or the day of the resurrection. Krichen continues, asking about the role of the Americans in the power struggle in Egypt. Heikal explains that the Americans didn't see the son of Mubarak in any future scenarios. "There were many scenarios," he says. "The father had his own scenario. The son had his own scenario. The Americans had their own scenarios, and there was also an unknown scenario. Most of the youth came up with a totally different scenario."

"But, sorry," interrupts Krichen. "The army had a scenario, too?"

"Not at all," Heikal responds. "The army wanted one thing. The army had one basic need, to not support any scenarios against the people when it came to succession by the son of Mubarak . . . [and] that the military would not be used against the people."

Heikal recounts that on February 10, 2011, something strange happened in Tahrir Square, a meeting between the army and the youth. "Everybody was asking about all the scenarios [for succession], and Omar Suleiman, the vice president, was still the [the most likely candidate]. General Hassan Ruwaini, a member of the Supreme Council of the Armed Forces, spoke to the youth with enthusiasm and said that their demands would be met." According to Heikal, the Americans called to ask about what was happening on Tahrir Square half an hour later, when they saw the news on satellite TV.

Krichen moves on, asking, "The principle force in Egypt is the Muslim Brotherhood?"

Heikal responds with a serious look: "The biggest problem of the Muslim Brotherhood is their organization, their origin in a secret environment. . . . It is not their fault . . . they were severely hit and their ideas were disseminated among other chapters outside the country. The Islamic movements used the Muslim Brotherhood. However, the Muslim Brotherhood in Egypt is the most important fundamental organization even though it found itself the weakest member of this Islamic organization as a whole."

Heikal explains that the Muslim Brotherhood was not ready to govern because of its heavy weight of its history and its lack of experience with democracy. Staring down Krichen, the Tunisian star journalist, Heikal laughs at Tunisia, saying it is a tiny country, and stressing the impossibility of comparing Tunisia to Egypt, with its 88 million people and long history of regional importance.

"How big is the population of Tunisia?" Heikal asks.

Krichen answers, "Eleven million."

Heikal continues to explain that the leaders of the Islamists in Tunisia spent more time in Europe learning about European democracy. This, he says, was not the case for the Muslim Brotherhood, bluntly concluding that the Muslim Brothers "don't have any expertise in foreign policy."

"There is high religiosity in Egypt," continues Heikal. "There are high religious values, but you can't impose Islamic values on the large Coptic minority."

"Professor Heikal," Krichen responds. "To be frank, when I hear you, I feel a kind of fear because the institution of the army is not ready to run the country, and there is no obvious alternative. The Muslim Brotherhood is not ready yet, and the youth is not ready yet. What to do?"

"I don't have a solution," Heikal answers.

"Aren't you afraid that some mistakes could kill [the democratic process]?" Krichen asks.

"Yes," answers Heikal. "I am afraid of deadly mistakes in the coming period."

The Revolution Will Be Islamized

"Take care that your revolution doesn't get stolen from you," al-Qaradawi warned protesters during the revolution in Tunisia. Those words spread like ripples from a stone dropped into still water. Many who have echoed these words have no idea that they are those of the mufti of Al Jazeera. The French philosopher Bernard-Henri Levy's movie, *Le serment de Torbrok*, portrays rebels in Benghazi proclaiming their vigilance so that the revolution "does not get stolen" from them. Levy (2012) took this as an authentic, original sound bite of the rebels. Journalists, politicians, and revolutionaries have adopted the phrase as well (Saad Al Din Ibrahim 2013; Abdelillah Belkeziz et al. 2012). The spread of this now-pervasive phrase has outpaced its link to the man who originated it. This is just one example of the wide-ranging impact of the Global Mufti's well-crafted and brilliantly framed fatwas. The former Egyptian minister of culture, Jaber Asfour, rather ironically used the mufti's own words three weeks after the revolution in a comment in the magazine *Rosa al-Yūsuf*: "When I saw Sheikh Yusuf al-Qaradawi praying in Tahrir Square, I realized that the revolution had been stolen" (October 25, 2012).

In February 2011, Cairo's Tahrir Square was transformed into a live studio. Two million demonstrators served as the live audience for an episode of Al Jazeera's popular program *Sharia and Life*, broadcast from the epicenter of the antigovernment protests that had recently helped oust Egypt's decades-old military government. The event, which marked the homecoming of al-Qaradawi, was emblematic of Al Jazeera's emersion in the Arab Spring revolutions; the charismatic appeal of its star preacher; and the network's role in injecting a religious flavor into popular demands for civil liberties and political openness.

As the first waves of protest spread through Cairo in January 2011, Yusuf al-Qaradawi could be described as both outsider and native son to Egypt and its nascent revolution. Born and educated in Egypt, he represented a voice of dissent against the nation's military dictatorship, not only throughout Mubarak's reign, but also during the rule of his two predecessors. However, he had not set foot in Egypt in more than forty years. As news of anti-Mubarak demonstrations in Cairo spread across the globe, the rebel mufti would join the revolution, already in progress, from a studio in Doha. Additionally, the social media–connected protestors chanting secular slogans in the squares and streets of Egypt stood in stark contrast to the politically organized, religiously driven gospel preached for decades by al-Qaradawi and his Muslim Brotherhood compatriots.

Al-Qaradawi's appearance in Tahrir Square came at a time of unparalleled excitement, amidst a revolution half-completed. With Mubarak having already conceded defeat, Egypt's future remained in flux. In this sense, al-Qaradawi's return to the country of his birth invites comparisons to Khomeini's 1979 arrival in Tehran or Lenin's 1917 return to Petrograd. Like Khomeini and Lenin, al-Qaradawi brought a laserlike ideological focus to a revolution composed of various loosely united interest groups. The former exile delivered a broadly inclusive sermon that nonetheless tied wholesale disgust with autocracy to an embrace of the pragmatic Wahhabism endorsed by Qatar and embodied by the Muslim Brotherhood in Egypt.

Al-Qaradawi's dual role as both an Al Jazeera television star and a Muslim Brotherhood–aligned political and religious force in post-Mubarak Egypt highlights both the power of Al Jazeera as a cultural force and the contradictions inherent in the network's claim of objectivity without neutrality. Despite forty years of exile from Egypt, al-Qaradawi's prominent role on Al Jazeera earned him a level of recognition and popularity in his home country far greater than he might have reasonably hoped to achieve as an itinerate preacher inside its borders. The Global Mufti's celebrity and affiliation with the Muslim Brotherhood would provide him with the opportunity to directly challenge the state-sanctioned religious order he had chafed against from his time as a young religious scholar.

Al-Qaradawi retained his role as Al Jazeera's primary spiritual and moral adviser, despite his direct ties to current events in Egypt, on which the network provided extensive coverage. Al-Qaradawi offered religious justification for acts of protest and rebellion that offered a competing ideological narrative to establishment-aligned clerics who claimed that acts of insurrection were prohibited by Islam.

The Making of a Revolutionary Preacher

Yusuf al-Qaradawi was born in 1926 in Saft Turab, a poor village on the Nile Delta with no running water. The only sources of news were rumor and the government-owned national newspaper, *Al Ahram* (Shavit 2007, 127). This Egyptian village is known as the final resting place of one of the Prophet's companions during the Hijra (flight from Mecca) in the year 86 of the Muslim calendar. This association is rarely glossed over by al-Qaradawi's biographers.

The Egypt of al-Qaradawi's early life was at the center of a number of events that surely shaped the political and religious beliefs of the future imam, along with the rest of the Arab world. Egypt's ostensible ruler at the time of al-Qaradawi's birth was an Ottoman king who served as a puppet of the British Crown. The rise of British influence in Egypt and of Western influence throughout the Arab world had mirrored the slow decline of Ottoman power in the region. By the time the last vestiges of the Ottoman caliphate (Islamic state) were abolished by Kemal Ataturk in 1924, the entire Muslim world, from Indonesia to Morocco and from Azerbaijan to Kazakhstan, had fallen under Western control in the form of protectorate agreements, puppet governments, and outright colonization. Anger over Western domination was one of the key factors that led to the formation of the Muslim Brotherhood in 1928.

However, neither the Brotherhood nor its Islamist ideology would lead Egypt out from under British control. Instead, Gamal Abdel Nasser and his message of pan-Arabism would oust the British-backed monarchy and emerge as a guiding force in Egyptian and Arab politics for nearly two decades. Nasser's government was no more friendly to the Muslim Brotherhood than the monarchy had been. The group was outlawed and persecuted, as Nasser took a decidedly secular approach to rallying for independence from Western influence.

Amidst Nasser's rise, the creation of the state of Israel in 1948 would touch off the Arab–Israeli conflict that dominated regional consciousness into the following century. The conflict sowed the seeds of Nasser's undoing in the traumatic defeat of Egyptian-led Arab forces in 1967, which effectively brought to an end the Egyptian's status as a regional leader. For the Muslim Brotherhood, the defeat served as proof that the expulsion of Western influence (including that of the Jewish state) would have to be achieved through religious rather than geographic unity.

In the leadership vacuum left by Nasser's fall from grace, the oil-rich Gulf countries, led by Saudi Arabia, rose to prominence. Religious unity, labeled "Islamic solidarity," had been a natural tool for both the Muslim Brotherhood and the Gulf states to counter Nasser's message of secular pan-Arabism. In the wake of the Israeli victory, the region's military dictatorships maintained their political and coercive power. But with the sunset of pan-Arabism, there remained no other international cultural movement to compete with the ascendant Islamization movement.

Al-Qaradawi's personal life was as tumultuous as his country's political atmosphere during these years. His father died when he was two years old. Although he continued to live with his mother until her death when he was fifteen, he was raised largely by his uncle, a farmer. He attended a *kutab* (Quran school), where hundreds of children between the ages of four and six were gathered together in a single large room to receive instruction. When he fled to attend a different *kutab*, the wayward orphan had no way to pay the weekly tuition. It was not until the age of seventeen that he would attend public school for the first time. Despite his advanced age in comparison with his fellow students and the fact that he had received no formal schooling since the age of seven, he was able to gain admittance by demonstrating his memorization of the Quran. According to al-Qaradawi's memoirs, he proceeded to outpace his classmates in academic achievement throughout his secondary school years. Al-Qaradawi was then accepted for study at Al Azhar University in Tanta (Kassab 2007, 25). Today, he defines himself as Azhari (a scholar of Al Azhar). However, he was often critical of the university during his studies because of its lack of spirituality (Skovgaard-Petersen and Graf 2009, 90).

Al-Qaradawi joined the Muslim Brotherhood during his fourth year of study at Al Azhar, but the group's influence had been a presence throughout the life of the young mufti. Al-Qaradawi came into contact with the Muslim Brothers at an early age in the form of itinerant preachers. He fell in love with the personality of Hassan al-Banna (1906–1949), the Brotherhood's founder. In a time of colonialism, communism, liberalism, and Islamic Reformism, al-Banna provided a simple alternative to the hodgepodge of competing social and political theories that promised to alleviate the uncertainty and suffering in the region. Al-Banna's followers taught the young al-Qaradawi that strict adherence to Islam was the only cure for the ills of the region. Al-Banna's assassination by an unknown gunman in 1949 would have a major impact on al-Qaradawi's life.

There were, of course, other books, teachers, and intellectuals whose teachings helped steer al-Qaradawi's intellectual trajectory. While studying at a satellite school of Al Azhar in southern Egypt, he became fascinated by the work of the medieval legal expert, scholar, theologian, and Sufi imam, Abu Hamid al-Ghazali. Al-Ghazali had a primary influence on the early *usuli* (those wanting to go back to the fundamentals) (Arkoun 1984, 233–244). Despite al-Qaradawi's devotion to al-Banna, he has said he considers al-Ghazali (1058–1111) his sheikh and main source of inspiration. Al-Ghazali's book *Ihya 'Ulum al Din* (Revival of the Religious Sciences) was one of the few items he took with him to prison when he was arrested in 1949. The then-teenage al-Qaradawi was picked up as part of a large-scale imprisonment of Muslim Brothers following al-Banna's assassination.

Another major influence on al-Qaradawi was Said Ramadan, an Azhari professor and father of the well-known European scholar Tariq Ramadan. Al-Qaradawi has said of the elder Ramadan, "He was overflowing with emotional spirituality" (Graf and Skovgaard-Petersen 2009, 90). Ramadan wanted to reform Al Azhar in the same way al-Banna had. He was intent on reviving the religious sciences as described by his intellectual master, Mohamed al-Ghazali. Ramadan's focus on the shortcomings of Al Azhar would be echoed by his protégé, al-Qaradawi, who made the university one of his main targets of reform once he gained an international pulpit.

The sources of al-Qaradawi's way of thinking can be traced to a rigorous Sunni tradition that consolidated Quran and Sunna (the Hadith and practice of the

Prophet Muhammad) under Ibn Taymiyyah and further elaborated upon by al-Banna and Sayyid Qutb, author of the most influential book in the history of political Islam, *Milestones* (1964). The intellectual evolution of this ideology can be summarized by the following chain of thinkers: Ibn Taymiyyah (1263–1328), Hassan al-Banna (1907–1949), Sayyid Qutb (1906–1966), Mohammed al-Ghazali (1917–1996), and al-Qaradawi (b. 1926).

These intellectual influences were the foundation on which one of Al Jazeera's master framers would interpret religious, political, and social issues throughout his life. Al-Qaradawi's elaborate interpretation of the social world, in the form of fatwas—opinions pronounced by religious scholars based on their interpretation of the Quran and the prophetic tradition, *sunna*—relies on six primary assumptions:

1. Human reason is limited.
2. Only that which is based on reason can be attributed to God.
3. Early Muslim scholars avoided interpretation [of the Quran] because they were afraid that non-Muslims would misuse it.
4. The Quran and Muslim traditions are the right path.
5. The knowledge of the early Muslim scholars was based on unanimous agreement.
6. All new interpretations must be based on the previous ones. (Kassab 2007,122)

Following his studies at Al Azhar, al-Qaradawi campaigned in villages throughout Egypt, and later in Beirut, Damascus, Hums, Hama, Amman, and Jerusalem, on behalf of the Muslim Brotherhood. At the time, it was difficult for Azharites in Egypt to find gainful employment, and members of the Muslim Brotherhood were undergoing harsh persecution by the Nasser government. On September 12, 1961, al-Qaradawi emigrated from Egypt to Qatar, where he was able to both escape police harassment for his involvement with the Muslim Brotherhood and better his financial situation. In Qatar, al-Qaradawi was placed at the helm of the Secondary Religious Institute of Qatar, a malfunctioning religious education institute that had been launched in 1960 (Kassab 2007, 30–39).

In the 1970s, al-Qaradawi caught the attention of the emir of Qatar, who occasionally attended his sermons. His impression on the emir was strong enough to land the immigrant preacher his own program on Qatar's national television station, called Guidance of Islam (Hadiy l'Islam). The question-and-answer program was modeled on a common Arab television format whereby viewers would call in or send in letters with religious, social, and cultural questions. At first, al-Qaradawi's weekly program ran for twenty minutes. Then it was expanded to half an hour, then fifty minutes. This fatwa program became popular in the Gulf states, with a strong viewership in Bahrain and Saudi Arabia, in addition to Qatar (Lamloum 2004; Graf and Skovgaard-Petersen 2009, 151). When Qatar TV first aired in 1980, al-Qaradawi's status had grown to such a degree that the network arranged for him to tape his shows from Lebanon, his preferred vacation spot, and have them sent to Doha for broadcast.

Many Islamists see television as *haram* (illicit), but they still commonly use it to advance their cause. Al-Qaradawi has offered a more nuanced view, arguing that TV and radio take on the intentions of those who control them. "[Television] is like the sword in the hands of the *mujahid* [*fighter*]; it is an instrument of jihad. If television is dominated by criminals it becomes a means of crime. It depends how you use it" (Kassab 2007, 232). Throughout his illustrious career, al-Qaradawi has wielded his sword on the following television and radio programs:

1. *Light (Nur)*, which has been on the radio for seventeen years in Qatar.
2. *Talk of the Sunset (Hadith al-Maghrib)*, a radio program presented during Ramadan for five years just before the breaking of the fast, the regional equivalent of prime time and Sweeps Week.
3. *Guidance (Had'y al Islam)*, a TV show from Qatar.
4. *Sharia and Life (Sharia wa l'hayat)* on Al Jazeera.
5. *The Forum (Al Muntada)* on Abu Dhabi TV, a program that was discontinued after 9/11; since then al-Qaradawi has not been not allowed to come back to the United Emirates

Many programs were broadcast for a short time on religious occasions like Ramadan (Kassab 2006, 230; and www.alqaradawi.com).

Al-Qaradawi left Qatar for a brief period in 1991 to go to Algeria, where he joined a contingent of Muslim Brothers who had been expelled from Egypt during the Nasser years. There, he gained a substantial following as a preacher and mediator in the ongoing conflict between the Algerian government and the Islamic Salvation Front. He also worked to actively promote Islamic banking as an alternative to Western banking. The latter of these efforts helped build the preacher's reputation as an activist voice against Western hegemony in the Arab world while also endearing him to the Qatari royal family, who stood to benefit from increased international interest in their country's robust financial sector.

On November 30, 1996, al-Qaradawi's program, *Sharia and Life*, was launched. With the program's growing popularity and the spread of satellite TV throughout the Arab world during the mid-1990s, al-Qaradawi's celebrity grew from that of a regional phenomenon to worldwide popularity. Al-Qaradawi says that he accepted a position with Al Jazeera in order to bring his voice to fellow

Muslim Brothers in Europe and the United States (Kassab 2007). The mufti donates his Al Jazeera salary to charity (Kassab2007).

The format of *Sharia and Life* is similar to that of al-Qaradawi's earlier program on Qatar TV as well as Egyptian television shows going as far back as the 1960s. Programs interpreting the Quran or dealing with religious issues were popular from Morocco to Saudi Arabia. Each such radio or TV program would start with recitations of the Quran, followed by some interpretation of them by an eminent local mufti (Graf and Skovgaard-Petersen 2009, 152). On *Sharia and Life*, Qaradawi is a permanent guest who answers questions put to him by a rotating cast of hosts. He also answers viewer calls, emails, and tweets. *Sharia and Life*'s novelty is its global reach via the transnational Arab television platform and its courage in discussing hot-button issues in Arab, Muslim, and world politics.

The success of al-Qaradawi's program was important for Al Jazeera's growth, because it succeeded in breaking the monopoly of state radio and TV broadcasts of live Friday sermons and Friday prayers from the main mosques of the countries where the networks are viewed, including the most well-known broadcast of Friday prayers from Mecca and the annual Hajj via Arab satellite. The model was so successful that it has been replicated by the so-called new Islamic media (Graf and Skovgaard-Petersen 2009, 160). In that sense, al-Qaradawi is rightly seen as a global mufti, since his programs are widely followed and translated into many languages.

From Mubarak to Morsi

On February 11, 2011, aljazeera.net reported on al-Qaradawi's sermon in Doha. He warned of "revolution thieves" who would steal the work of the "honorable youth." The thieves, he cautioned, would reap what other good people had sewn. "I'm fearful for the Egyptian revolution and the Tunisian revolution," he lamented, "because of *al haramiyya* [the thieves]." These revolutionary hijackers, he said, would leave the land in the hands of new "*pashas* [aristocrats] and sultans."

On February 13, 2011, al-Qaradawi devoted a whole episode of *Sharia and Life* to the Egyptian revolution. He answered live questions taken by phone and via Facebook. Three days later, al-Qaradawi spoke at the Festival of the Egyptian Community in Doha, where he praised Al Jazeera and its efforts in spreading his word. "I will be candid with you," he said. "When I learned about the victory of the revolution, I called the emir of Qatar to congratulate him and thank him. He told me that I played an essential leadership role. I told him that if Al Jazeera had not been there, my voice would not have reached [Tahrir] Square and the people of Egypt (Al Jazeeera, February 13, 2014).

Al-Qaradawi framed the Egyptian revolution as an "extraordinary" experience in society and politics. This description helped him further formulate his *fiqh a-thawra* (jurisprudence of revolution). According to al-Qaradawi, this new *fiqh* was needed for two reasons. First, Egypt was a "religious nation" easily influenced by religious discourse. Second, the official religious institution was the biggest danger to the revolution because, by labeling the revolutionary youth "Kharijites," in search of *fitna* (discord), for revolting against the ruler, it could derail the revolution. The official view of the religious institution was supported by many Salafis and Sufis, he argued. The *ulama* of the official religious institution wanted the people to obey their ruler (Abu Zeid 2011, 7). Therefore, al-Qaradawi's participation in the revolution can be seen as an oral jihad. Citing the Hadith, al-Qaradawi contended, "The best jihad is the word of justice in the face of the oppressive sultan." Al-Qaradawi urged the security forces to take on more agency, arguing that excuses such as "I obey the orders of superiors" were against Islamic teaching.

After Mubarak's departure, al-Qaradawi stressed that the sons of the Egyptian people should be aware of the dangers of the *fulul* (remnants of the old regime), by voting down the presidential candidate, General Ahmed Shafik. Al-Qaradawi told his followers it was a *wajib ahar'i* (religious duty) to protect Egypt from the followers of the "impure" Mubarak such as Shafik.

Although focusing his criticism of Shafik on the general's ties to the old administration, he also made clear his aversion to an overly secular leadership for the postrevolutionary government. In a Friday sermon at Omar Bin al-Khattab Mosque in Doha, which was also partially aired on Al Jazeera, al-Qaradawi said, "We support the Islamists and do not accept those who refuse the Sharia Islamiyya (Islamic Sharia), because it is the reference point for Islamic rule. We do not want a religious bureaucratic rule where clerics govern. What we want is for the most capable to govern, whether they are people of the clergy or of the state, but their reference point must be Sharia Islamiyya. In the event that the second round of the elections is between two Islamists, Dr. Morsi and Dr. Abdul Fotuh, [we hope] that everyone will choose the worthier one, the one who can bring people together" (*Rosa al-Yūsuf*, May 16, 2012). A week later, al-Qaradawi asked Egyptians to support presidential hopeful Morsi. According to the Egyptian newspapers, al-Qaradawi's support for Dr. Morsi and Dr. Abdul Fotuh, his two preferred candidates in the first round, was a tactic to unite the Islamist vote in the first round and to make it impossible for non-Islamist candidates to make it to the second round. In political jargon, al-Qaradawi was working to establish himself as a kingmaker with the influence and currency to make or break politicians. Al-Qaradawi described voting, particularly during the democratic elections that followed the uprisings, as a "religious duty" (*Rosa al-Yūsuf*, May 22, 2012).

Revolutionizing Islam

After conducting the Friday prayer in Tahrir Square, three days after the fall of Mubarak, al-Qaradawi succeeded in making inroads with Al Azhar, the most prestigious and hierarchical institution in the Sunni Islamic world. Just as al-Qaradawi's fatwas and sermons injected religion into the revolution, his attempts to reestablish a relationship with his alma mater, Al Azhar, represented an attempt to bring the revolution to Egypt's state-sanctioned religious authority. Qaradawi had repeatedly questioned the legitimacy of clerics who initially spoke out against revolutionary activities, some of whom could be found at Al Azhar.

Al-Qaradawi's wish to visit Al Azhar and deliver the Friday congregational sermon met with some resistance. Many religious groups saw this as a move by a prominent member of the Muslim Brotherhood to seek *al imama*, or the leadership of the *umma* (*Rosa al-Yūsuf,* November 27, 2012). Dr. Ali Gomaa, the official mufti of the Republic of Egypt, warned clerics against mixing religion and politics. In response to al-Qaradawi's request to lead the Friday prayer, the mufti of Al Azhar criticized the star preacher's claim to an exclusive understanding of true Islam. "Those people [like al-Qaradawi] think that they are better defenders of Islam than others, that they are the only true Muslims and scholars and that others are not, and that every Muslim should follow their views and opinions with obedience." Sheikh Gomaa added that politicians, by nature, come and go, and therefore religion should stay away from political parties and their games. He attacked al-Qaradawi, questioning his ability to remain neutral while vocally supporting the Muslim Brotherhood and their candidate, Mohamed Morsi, saying, "In this sense you represent *al batil* [falsehood]" (*Rosa al-Yūsuf,* June 17, 2012).

After the election of Mohamed Morsi, the new government welcomed al-Qaradawi as a religious voice within the administration. The new Egyptian Ministry of Religious Affairs invited him to preach one Friday each month at Al Azhar. A spokesperson of the ministry criticized his detractors by saying that *fitna na'ima*, or "discord is dormant," and asserting that there was no compelling reason al-Qaradawi should not be active in Al Azhar. The Independent Union of Imams in Egypt voiced its rejection of the invitation of al-Qaradawi to preach at Al Azhar (*Rosa al-Yūsuf,* November 16, 2012). Al Azhar's case shows the lines of fracture within the faith and scholarly Islamic communities and the new lines of allegiance in the new government. The detractors had a slogan that rhymes well: "We have Gomaa this Jumaa," which means that they have this Friday a mufti called Friday, and that is enough. In the Egyptian dialect, the letter "J" is pronounced as a "G." The mufti of Al Azhar is called "Gomaa" (Jumaa), or Friday. Nevertheless, the symbolic importance of preaching in Al Azhar is unparalleled, and Al Jazeera has long made a practice of reporting only the victories of al-Qaradawi. All other media, including newspapers, gave a great deal of attention to the discord within Al Azhar. Al-Qaradawi was a celebrity who had refused many times to assume the responsibility of becoming the *morshid al-a'm*, or general guide of the Muslim Brotherhood. He was seen in the Egyptian media as posturing as the guide for the revival of the *umma*, acting as heir to the tradition of his intellectual master, al-Ghazali. After a meeting with Mohamed Hussein Tantawi, the previous mufti of Al Azhar, Palestinian president Mahmoud Abbas urged Egyptians not to heed the fatwas issued by al-Qaradawi and prohibited an official Egyptian delegation from visiting the Al Aqsa Mosque in Jerusalem. Abbas described the fatwas of al-Qaradawi as political in nature (*Rosa al-Yûsuf*, April 3, 2012).

Despite these criticisms, al-Qaradawi's association with Al Azhar would continue until the end of the Morsi regime. Al Jazeera's coverage of the February 11, 2013, election of Egypt's new official grand mufti at Al Azhar spotlighted al-Qaradawi's role in the election. The scene opens on the steps of Al Azhar University and soon cuts to a man inside dressed in a Western suit and passing around a transparent glass ballot box to the sheikhs of Al Azhar. The sheikhs sit in their traditional clothing and headgear around a rectangular table. "This is the first time that direct elections have been organized to choose the mufti of Egypt," Al Jazeera reporter Mahmoud Hisseen explains. The camera zooms in on al-Qaradawi, who is one of the many sheikhs voting. The president of the committee says, "After the secret ballot, a committee examined the results and determined that Professor Shawki Ibrahim Abdelkarim Allam won the majority of the votes."

"Dr. Shawki Ibrahim Abdelkarim Allam will be first mufti to be elected freely after the revolution," Hisseen says. "He is mufti number nineteen in the history of the House of Aifta, which was founded in 1895. Professor Abdelkarim Allam works on the Faculty of Sharia of the University of Tanta. He will occupy the chair as other scholars before him have, like Imam Mohamed Abdu and Sheikh Jadel Haq Ali Haq. The new mufti received the largest number of votes of all the candidates who met the criteria set by the committee." The camera zooms in on al-Qaradawi, who then explains the work of the committee. The microphones of many television stations, such as MBC and Al Hura, can be seen. Al-Qaradawi, shown standing, says, "The candidate is *faqih* [Islamic legal expert], busy with *fiqh* [Islamic jurisprudence], a graduate of the Faculty of Sharia, worked in the *fiqh*, published in the *fiqh*, and has been acknowledged by the peers. But he is also interested in public affairs."

Hisseen continues, "The committee will send its decision to Mufti Abdelkarim Allam, who will confirm his new role." The camera then moves to another sheikh, who says, "We are very happy with the independence of Al Azhar and the choice of the new mufti." There were nine candidates from Al Azhar on the ballot;

however, the list of names did not include anyone from the Muslim Brotherhood. Hisseen argues that many observers think that this initiative will counterbalance any accusation that the Muslim Brotherhood is trying to force a "brotherhood-ization" (*akhwana*), co-opt, or even infiltrate the institutions of the state. This move was intentionally set forth by the pro–Muslim Brotherhood government. Al Jazeera claims, "The independence of Al Azhar and the free choice of the mufti was one of the most important successes of the Egyptian revolution." Hisseen ends his news report saying, "Because the mufti was chosen freely, the position of the mufti is immune to any accusation of politicization of the religious institution, which is something that has happened in the past."

Conclusion: Revolutionary Impatience

Tahrir Square became the symbol of the Egyptian revolution and the epicenter of the Arab world. By literally and symbolically placing Tahrir Square under its lens, in a time when the Egyptian political field was hermetically closed off to the media and the regime was at the height of its brutality, Al Jazeera succeeded in stealing the show from other media outlets. Meanwhile, the failed efforts of the Mubarak regime to silence the network only served to enhance Al Jazeera's reputation as an indefatigable messenger of the revolution and a tireless voice for the disempowered.

Al Jazeera's coverage of the Tunisian revolution brought the network a new level of symbolic power, which only increased during the Egyptian revolution. The recollections of the revolution by Al Jazeera's journalists offer a revealing look at the framing that Al Jazeera has relied on in its reporting. A portrayal of the network's reporting as a search for answers to the ills of the world is one such common frame. Al Jazeera's reporting during the Arab Spring relied heavily on three interrelated categories of frames: those of heroism, anger, and religiosity.

Meanwhile, al-Qaradawi's fatwas provided support, encouragement, and religious endorsement for the revolutionary cause. His appearance at Tahrir Square in the wake of Mubarak's ouster established the mufti as a "symbolic fact." From the early stages of the revolution, al-Qaradawi's commentary strayed from that of support to that of potential leadership. Al-Qaradawi's roles as symbol, commentator, supporter, and ideological leader are emblematic of the unifying force of Al Jazeera for Arab people striving for change. However, the active role played by al-Qaradawi in steeping the revolution in the religious rhetoric of the Muslim Brotherhood, and his close relationship with the Morsi regime, are emblematic of the partisanship that would make both the mufti and Al Jazeera a divisive force at a time of regional uncertainty.

Al Jazeera, as a transnational media network dominating a national market, behaves in accord with the rules of the art or literary field described by Bourdieu, subject to action and reaction in an almost mechanical way. In spite of the effective language and visuals that Al Jazeera used to mobilize and demobilize zones of the revolutionary field, the network cast a kind of veil over the different revolutionary groups. Al Jazeera filtered its coverage of the emerging mass of young, engaged political actors through its own lens. The rhythm of the Egyptian, Tunisian, Libyan, Syrian, Yemeni, and Bahraini revolutions was so impressive that people had the impression that a "logic of a permanent revolution" had been imposed through these revolutions. They empowered all kinds of actors, from young liberals, trade unionists, and socialists to Islamists of all sorts (from Muslim Brothers to Salafis to violent radicals). However, the accounts by Al Jazeera's journalists that begin this chapter explain how the revolutions, mediated by Al Jazeera, advanced a new vision of the world that was accompanied by the trope of Al Jazeera's endeavors to help the Arab people. Through the process of framing, the many different actors coalesced into a single movement in support of this vision and the celebration of Al Jazeera and its staff as heroes. In this way, the social and political struggle of the Egyptians became a joint struggle of the Egyptians and Al Jazeera. This pattern of collaboration between the people of a country and Al Jazeera continued in other revolutions. The sound of young Egyptian voices demanding change has now been replaced on Al Jazeera by the voice of al-Qaradawi.

Managing the revolution from the studio in Doha was an impressive feat. But the flip side is that the Egyptian revolution was hijacked, absorbed, as it were, by Al Jazeera Inc. All the revolutionaries in Egypt and the various narratives of the revolution became part of one great Al Jazeera revolutionary narrative. In the Egyptian case, where the Muslim Brotherhood was not a factor in the first catalyzing days of the revolution, Al Jazeera wrote into the narrative a starring role for the group. Where Islamist forces played a less than decisive role in Tunisia's revolution, they were a driving force in Al Jazeera's version of history.

Through its distinctive coverage of the most defining events in the Arab world during the period of the revolutions, Al Jazeera itself became a major player in the unfolding of the story. Al Jazeera, as an external force representing a transnational media field, became a powerful player in motivating potential protesters and revolutionaries to take part in these revolutions. Al Jazeera effected a deep symbolic transformation in the fields of power, media, and religion. Al Jazeera's symbolic capital grew exponentially during the early revolutionary period. The network redefined the revolutions as more religiously motivated struggles than as movements in the pursuit of freedom and dignity. In the political and militant battlefields of the Arab Spring, Al Jazeera intervened as a media power, at times changing the course of events and even changing widely held beliefs about the ideological stakes of the contest.

The power of Al Jazeera lies in its direct and indirect moralizing effects, which are discussed in the upcoming chapters. In answer to Egyptian citizens' demands for freedom, Al Jazeera pressed forward on behalf of political Islam, offering it as the most appropriate path for democratic reform in the Arab Mediterranean. The struggle for freedom that Al Jazeera praises itself for is rather a struggle for its own freedom to promote a political agenda.

6 EXILE ON PARADISE SQUARE

If you haven't yet had the honor to sit in at Rabaa al-Adawiyya Square, let's
go. . . . It is a slice of paradise.

—Alaa Sadekof[1]

L'histoire inachevée n'impose pas de verité. (The incomplete story does not
require truth.)

—Raymond Aron (1970, 118)

Changing the past threatens to undermine our construction of ourselves,
while pressures to change our political identity in the present press us to
rewrite the past, that is to alter the symbolic construction of the past.

—David Kertzer (1996, 7)

The situation in Egypt was tenuous following the ouster of Hosni
Mubarak. Mohamed Morsi was demonized by major media outlets in
Egypt and Saudi Arabia as a "Muslim Brotherhood president" whose
allegiance lay first with his political movement rather than the nation of
Egypt (Stephane Lacroix, France 24, August 13, 2013; Assafir, February
5, 2014). However, Morsi enjoyed favorable coverage from Al Jazeera
Mubasher, a popular Al Jazeera station devoted entirely to coverage of
Egyptian news delivered mainly in Egyptian dialect. Even after Morsi's
popular electoral triumph, Al Jazeera's Egyptian coverage was seen by
many outside media pundits as biased, pro–Muslim Brotherhood, and
out of touch with evolving revolutionary sentiments.

From the early days of the pro-Morsi sit-ins, Al Jazeera's live news
reports from Egypt were dominated by events in Rabaa Square. At
crucial junctures, a split screen offered a view of Rabaa beside a live
feed from outside the Presidential Palace. Both sides, pro– and anti–
Muslim Brotherhood, were shown demonstrating in their chosen
squares, Rabaa and Tahrir, respectively. Noora, the veiled anchorwoman of Al Jazeera Mubasher, occasionally interrupted guests who
supported the military during interviews. "Let's not talk about millions opposing Morsi, because the supporters of Morsi say that they
have millions of supporters, too. Just say large numbers of supporters,"
she advised them.

Al Jazeera provided intense and continuous coverage of the events that followed the Egyptian military's removal of President Mohamed Morsi from power. In particular, the network provided extensive coverage of pro-Morsi demonstrations from their beginnings in a few squares and mosques in Cairo to the violent government crackdown that precipitated their end. As has become habitual for the network, coverage of these contentious events was presented through partisan frames intended to turn public opinion against the anti-Morsi camp. Unfortunately, the sit-ins in Rabaa al-Adawiyya Square, and the Al Nahda and Al Fath Mosques ended in a massacre. Despite Al Jazeera's efforts to shift the tide of Egyptian opinion during the events of 2013, pro-Morsi supporters didn't benefit directly or immediately from the network's support.

The political identities of the two camps—pro- and anti-Morsi—can be grasped through symbolic representations of pivotal events created by the media to cater to their audiences. It is intriguing how the media, religious, and political fields collapsed into a chaotic whirlwind in which only the symbolic realm lent meaning to the events of that summer.

David Kertzer describes the process of constructing symbols in order "to nourish the memory of sacred events" (1996, 1). The besieged Islamic movement (that of Morsi), the interim government, and the media were all fond of "naming names" in this way. The story of Rabaa Square is one of "political trauma," "human tragedy," and "personal dramas" played out in the public gaze through the media and especially the cameras of Al Jazeera, which were present for all that happened in the squares and mosques. Al Jazeera succeeded in framing Rabaa as a founding myth for the new square of resistance against oppression and Tahrir Square as having sold its soul to became the deep state. Claude Lévi-Strauss asserts that myths depend on the manipulation of symbols, which can occur in infinite variations (Kertzer 1996, 1; Arkoun 2008). Raoul Girardet outlines three critical elements in the construction of a political myth: the existence of an evil conspiracy, the existence of a savior, and then the arrival of a golden age (Kertzer 1996, 17; Giradet 1995, 37). Emphasis on the opposition between "saviors and conspirators" and the use of military metaphors to brand the different camps are effective means of building this symbolic construction (Kertzer 1996, 41–44). During this time, Egypt's opposing political movements began to portray each other in the same terms that Fascists in pre-war Italy had undermined the Communist Party: "The political opponents in Italy were simply branded 'reactionary forces in the service of foreigners,' in a discourse equating current domestic political adversaries with the foreign military adversaries of war" (Kertzer 1996, 45). The situation in Egypt during the sit-ins was framed in similar terms by a passionately divided media and public.

Given this situation it is useful, though challenging, to examine the role symbolism played in Egyptian politics and media and also "why [and] how it work[ed], and who it fail[ed]" (Kertzer 1996, 45). In sum, the power of Rabaa Square as a symbol of resistance to military rule transformed it from a simple city square into the core of a series of pivotal events that will have indefinitely long-standing consequences. Rabaa Square became a symbol of peaceful rage and purity of intention. It exuded the warmth of a cohesive community and functioned as a protective womb for the demonstrators who gathered there. It also played a role in the feminization of resistance, and ultimately became the site of a brutal human tragedy.

Relocating the Epicenter of Pivotal Events

Could the negative fallout from the dramatic ouster of Morsi be leveraged into an advantage for his supporters? Would it be possible for the losers to set the political agenda for the winners under the watch of the Arab publics? The answer to both of these questions appears to be yes. An Al Jazeera broadcast during the summer of 2013 described the situation in Egypt as follows: The Egyptian army, backed by "30 million" Egyptians, had pulled the plug on the "unpopular" Morsi, who according to the vast majority of the Egyptian media outlets was unfit for the presidency and had been steering the country toward an economic and political "disaster." On July 3, General Abdel Fattah el-Sisi presented the anti-Morsi demonstrations of June 30 as evidence of the people's overwhelming wish to remove a president motivated by Muslim Brotherhood objectives rather than the orders set out in Egypt's General Guide (Murshid al A'm). El-Sisi framed the protests as a widespread rejection of Morsi's attempts at *ikhwanization* of (imposition of Muslim Brotherhood doctrine on) the state apparatus. The dominant narrative in the Egyptian media was that the country risked civil war if the army did not intervene by suspending the constitution and appointing an interim government to lead until new elections could be held. The supporters of ousted President Morsi, it seemed, had suffered an insurmountable defeat. Their position only appeared to worsen as religious media outlets and Al Jazeera Mubasher were shut down and many of their journalists arrested. Morsi's supporters also faced hostility from local media and anti-Morsi demonstrators. The power of symbols, created by and transmitted through the media, played an important role in the mobilization of public opinion in both camps.

Bourdieu's concept of political capital includes the qualifier that it exists only "through representation." And so, along lines similar to those expressed by Kertzer, two questions about the situation in Egypt following Morsi's ouster might be posed: "1) How are the symbols underlying political life constructed and altered? And 2) By what process do people come to recognize some symbols and legitimate and others illegitimate" (Kertzer 1996, 5). Naming is thus a creative process, but also a dramatic one—particularly in the construction of contentious identities. In the case of the rise of General el-Sisi as the newest symbol of change, we can learn from what Kertzer says about the political leader in general: "The rise of his [the leader's] truly magical power over the group derives from faith in the representation he gives to the group. But how do people come to endow their leader's representation with their faith? The act of naming is central to the crisis" (1996, 5).

In the Limelight of Rabaa al-Adawiyya Square

When the anti-Morsi protesters, who, according to the *Guardian* and Al Jazeera outnumbered Morsi's supporters by millions (*In Depth*, May 30, 2013), claimed victory in Tahrir Square after the military stepped in, the mosque of Rabaa al-Adawiyya and its public square became the primary symbol of resistance for the Muslim Brotherhood and pro-Morsi protesters. The symbolic meaning of the Rabaa sit-ins was very important for the pro-Morsi protesters and Arab publics because of the square's mythical significance as a location of piety, solidarity, and loyalty to the ideals of the Islamic *umma* (community). Rabaa became a powerful symbol of piety, particularly during the holy month of Ramadan. Rabaa resides at the intersection of many major avenues and arteries close to the heart of Cairo. It is close to the National Guard Headquarters, to the Ministry of Interior, and to Al Fatah mosque, the site of a July 8, 2013, raid by Egyptian security forces. The geographic location of Rabaa was the main reason it was chosen as a place of protest, according to the Al Jazeera pundit Osma Farah. The Morsi supporters were not tolerated in the more popular Tahrir Square—they had essentially been exiled.

Rabaa Square turned into the site of the largest table in Cairo for breaking the fast of Ramadan. Tents were erected all around the square, but the scene remained that of an open sit-in, and protesters spoke about the sweetness of the nights there. The square turned into an unlikely stage for weddings, theater, interviews with visitors from the EU and Africa, and rap performances. It hosted civil organizations from all over the world that came to witness the events. Interestingly, Rabia is the name of an eighth-century Sufi who is well known in Arab history as the "Mother of Good."

During the forty-five days of sit-ins, Al Jazeera brought every move on and around the stage in Rabaa Square to its viewers in vivid detail. It was a unique situation for ethnographic study. In the meantime, anti-Morsi protesters were busy constructing a competing symbolic image of the Rabaa Square protests. The comedian Bassem Youssef referred to Rabaa as a mere intersection of streets, not a square. Amr Adeeb, the *enfant terrible* of the Egyptian media, called it "a center of backwardness and de-civilization." Others called it an arms depot and hideout for terrorists. In spite of this heavy criticism, the Muslim Brotherhood managed (with the help of Al Jazeera) to create a sensational new venue for its demonstrations, which reached unprecedented proportions replete with religious symbology, and to further galvanize its supporters.

Bloody clashes between the opposing camps broke out the day after Morsi's July 3 ouster, leading to dozens of deaths and injuries. On July 11, the military attempted to break up pro-Morsi sit-ins. And on July 26, anti-Morsi groups took to the streets a second time to support the marching orders of General el-Sisi, who was by then the head of state. General el-Sisi had requested a *tafweed*—a sort of carte blanche mandate backed by the people—to "fight terrorism." The situation seemed grim for the Muslim Brotherhood, which had been forced from its place at the epicenter of the Arab Spring. But the Muslim Brothers had two considerable assets that helped them counter the army's mighty claim of "fighting terrorism" and turn the tables on a generally hostile public opinion led by a decidedly anti–Muslim Brotherhood media. First, they had their faithful followers, and second, they had Al Jazeera's influence in the form of both Al Jazeera Mubasher and Al Jazeera News in Arabic.

It is important to note that Al Jazeera English offered a completely different angle on the events following Morsi's ouster than did Al Jazeera Arabic. Al Jazeera English described a fatigue associated with the pro-Morsi sit-ins, while Al Jazeera Arabic spoke of the untamed energy and dynamism displayed by Morsi's supporters. Al Jazeera, its pundits, and its guests described Morsi's removal from power as a military coup and suggested that General el-Sisi's catch phrases, "fight terrorism" and "the roadmap," were imported, and unwelcome, terminology from the Iraq War. El-Sisi couldn't have chosen worse terms, even with the overwhelming backing he had, at the time, from the Egyptian media. Al Jazeera employed all the tactics it had perfected during its long history as a critical media outlet in the Islamic world's most troubled areas. It rebranded Tahrir Square as Taharush (Harassment) Square and painted it as a place full of *baltajiyya* (thugs of the regime), *fulul* (remnants of the old regime), and molesters.

The masses of pro-Sisi demonstrators also came under the network's scrutiny. Al Jazeera raised doubts about the accuracy of claims coming from the anti-Morsi side of the conflict, calling them "bogus," at the least. While el-Sisi supporters were given airtime on Al Jazeera broadcasts, they were frequently depicted as imposters and supporters of the old regime who had succeeded in manipulating the young people of Tamrud into opposing the Muslim Brothers. Conversely, Al Jazeera presented Rabaa Square as a place of "piety," communal solidarity, a podium for "martyrs," true "democrats," and "selfless" patriots. Coverage of the square was continuous during Ramadan. This added an aura of the sacred to every activity that took place there in the nearly forty-five days before the third day of the Eid religious holiday. The square attracted the attention of the whole world, with visits from international political delegations, artists, and NGOs. Everything was covered on Al Jazeera—from interviews with European parliamentarians, preachers, and guests from other political parties and organizations to the daily prayers, the extra prayers during the nights of Ramadan, and special prayers for the absent (to honor martyrs). The podium was also transformed into a wedding venue and a place for tears, laughter, blessings, and poems. The square was truly multifunctional—it served as a school, a mosque, a stage, a kitchen, a dorm, a field hospital, and even a market, not to mention the center of the counterrevolution.

Rabaa: A Protective Womb

An important aspect of the square was its role in the strategic feminization of the protests. Women and children participating in the protests were often positioned at the front of the crowd. The Muslim Brothers were naturally accused by their detractors of using women and children as human shields, but with the help of Al Jazeera the prominent female presence was framed as an indication that Egyptian women were playing a prominent role in the pro-Morsi demonstrations. The visibility of women in the mosques, squares, and demonstrations broke down the wall of separation between men and women in a culture that highly values gender segregation. Their presence was also used tactically to generate news reports. One broadcast focused on how "embattled" General el-Sisi's enemies were laughing at the threat of a crackdown on the Rabaa Square protests. Contrary to Bouazizi's dramatic response to a policewoman's literal slap in the face, the women in Rabaa were laughing at General el-Sisi in defiance, said the news report. When the name of a new "martyr" was mentioned at the podium in the square and the audience was prompted to react, the result was a riot of high-pitched *yu-yu*s of joy from the women. This expression of joy—*zaghareed*—is a traditional part of Islamic rituals to help dead men leave the family house in a festive way in order to be welcomed by a *houri* (faithful Muslim virgin) bride in paradise.

Women also organized their own activities and speeches at the podium, many of which were aired live on Al Jazeera. During the sit-ins, Walid Al Attar reported from a funeral held for three women who had been active in the demonstrations: "In the midst of sadness and deep emotions people walked in the funeral procession, today, for three ladies who were killed. Every one of these women had left a family behind. Islam Mohamed and Ilham Mitwally were both mothers of four," Al Attar's voice intoned as the scene opened on three imams standing before microphones in a mosque adorned with Andalusian tiles. "God, make the killing of these pious women a curse on their killers," said one of the imams. People knelt in prayer before the cameras. "Hala Shisha was a seventeen-year-old student in the second year of high school. Her parents say that she had sworn the *shahada* [profession of faith] on her Facebook just days before she died, and she got what she wanted," Al Attar told viewers as the camera zoomed in on the body being carried into the mosque. "Why did they kill her?" asked the victim's distraught father, a bearded doctor with black sunglasses. "She was seventeen years old and she always had high scores of ninety-seven percent at school. Why!? Three bullets killed my daughter!" The camera zoomed in on a banner displaying the picture of a veiled woman named Hala, with the words "Martyr of Shar'iyya [legitimacy] and Sharia." Al Attar explained that the friends and family of the deceased women, who were protesting against the removal of Morsi in the city of Mansoura, believed that many *baltajiyya* (thugs) attacked them during a peaceful demonstration during the million-person march held on the Friday following the coup. The camera then zoomed in on a veiled woman in black.

"[The women] were supporting men in the demonstration without expecting to be attacked by *baltajiyya* who were helped by the security forces," Al Attar's voice continued over the footage. Some of the women in the crowd wore the *niqab* (face veil). Many carried Egyptian flags. The camera focused on the face of a woman in tears, totally exhausted, while behind her stood an unfinished brick wall in a poor neighborhood. "They killed her with bullets," she cried. "They killed my daughter, my love! My heart is bleeding. They killed her, they killed her! They killed her for no reason!"

"In spite of the sadness and the deep emotions, the demonstrators continue with their peaceful rage, calling the military coup a bloody action," Al Attar continued. Men with open hands prayed on-screen, begging God for forgiveness. A young reporter, in a red-and-white checkered shirt and black sunglasses, stood before the crowd of walking protesters. "The people here believe that this is a necessary price to pay in order to restore the legitimate power," he said, concluding the report. "Walid Al Attar, from the district of Tahalikya. Al Jazeera."

Shaytana and the Rumor Mill

Shaytana is an Arabic term that refers to the demonization of "the other." It derives from the word *Shaytan* (satan). *Shaytana* was frequently used on Al Jazeera to describe attempts by the Egyptian media and the newly established political elite to degrade pro-Morsi protesters. On July 30, 2013, Al Jazeera covered three major press conferences alongside its round-the-clock coverage of Morsi's supporters as they rallied in the "million-person march of martyrs."

The first of these press conferences was held in Tunisia, with the Tunisian minister of the interior speaking about the events in Egypt. The second took place in Egypt, held by the acting vice president, Mohamed al-Baradei and the European commissioner Catherine Ashton. The third press conference, in Gaza, was held by Hamas to offer the group's take on the situation in Egypt. Not surprisingly, Hamas's press conference was at the center of both Al Jazeera's news coverage and pundit commentary for the day. Al Jazeera's decision to focus its attention on Hamas is revealing, for one reason in particular. Hamas seized on the international attention focused on Egypt to unveil documents that, according to the group, proved the involvement of Palestinian Authority leaders and security agents, as well as Egyptian media, in driving a wedge between the Egyptian Army and Hamas by negatively depicting the Gaza leadership's "resistance against Egypt." Hamas had been accused of killing Egyptian soldiers in Sinai and was blamed by Egyptian authorities for the July 27, 2003, mass killing known as the podium (*manasa*) massacre during the sit-ins of Rabaa Square in Cairo.

Salah Salah Bardawil, Hamas's Palestinian spokesperson, read parts of sixteen documents that purportedly implicated the Palestinian Authority in plans to detonate car and truck bombs made by Al Qassam Brigades (the military wing of Hamas) in Egypt. According to Bardawil, a security committee and a media committee had been formed by the Palestinian Authority to implement these plans and exploit the results. The documents even contained articles, ready for publication and attributed to Al Jazeera, about cars that were booby-trapped by Hamas in Egypt. Some of these fictitious articles, claimed Bardawil, "allege that [there was] joint planning and sabotage between Hamas Salafists and the Muslim Brotherhood." Bardawil also read from a circular of the Palestinian ambassador in Cairo in which instructions were given to participate in the "revolution" of June 30, 2013, against Morsi. The Fatah movement claimed, on Al Jazeera, that all of these documents were fabricated.

At the beginning of the Arab Spring, Al Jazeera had revealed documents implicating the Palestinian Authority in the targeted killings of Hamas activists through collaboration with Israel. Now Hamas revealed documents that purportedly uncovered efforts by the Palestinian Authority to manipulate events in Egypt to weaken Hamas's international standing. Al Jazeera commentators speculated about the Palestinian Embassy's "role in the coordination of fabricated news against Hamas."

Al Jazeera's extensive coverage of Rabaa al-Adawiyya Square, as an alternative to unfolding events in the more famous Tahrir Square, emerged in part for the sake of convenience but it also served as a tacit critique of the anti-Morsi media. Al Jazeera Mubasher's live reports from Tahrir Square came under challenging conditions and involved a combination of secrecy and risk that might be more commonly associated with a covert military action. In Rabaa, on the other hand, Al Jazeera was free to fix multiple cameras on the center stage and provided constant, uninterrupted coverage for more than forty days. Rabaa Crossing, as the anti-Morsi journalists condescendingly called it, became a "miracle" through the lens of Al Jazeera cameras. It became the engine of news in Egypt, marginalizing Tahrir Square as the square of "secularists," the square of "traitors," and a rallying point for those who "don't care about elections." Tahrir was, in other words, the square of the "ancient regime," the *fulul*, the *baltajiyya*. The voices of Tahrir were funded by outside forces intent on undermining Egypt's path toward what Al Jazeera referred to as "greatness and leadership among world nations."

Within just a few weeks of Morsi's ouster, Al Jazeera managed to turn the tables in favor of the Muslim Brothers, and competing Egyptian and Arab media were forced to react to its coverage of the reactionary demonstrations. Using both traditional and new media, Al Jazeera created a rich environment for its reporting in Egypt. Through text message alerts, breaking newsfeeds, and live video coverage from up to six different locations simultaneously, the network pumped out a steady stream of fresh reporting to an audience thirsty for any new information. Where the stream of new reporting slowed, a cast of pundits, special guests, and reporters stood ready with fresh opinions and analysis to sustain audience interest until the next major event.

Al Jazeera, in turning the tables against the dominant Egyptian media backing General el-Sisi, positioned itself to provide the sort of dynamically antiestablishment news coverage at which it excels. In this, Al Jazeera's first objective was to demonstrate the uniformity of the arguments, images, and "lies" presented by Egyptian media outlets. These similarities in coverage were surely evidence that military intelligence and the new leadership were the source of a majority of news stories circulating through Egypt. This tactic had already proved successful in Tunisia against Ben Ali and earlier in Egypt against Mubarak. El-Sisi's lively persona and energetic speaking style gave Al Jazeera plenty of material to work with. The network created a montage of ads and short clips from footage of the general, aimed at turning viewers against him.

With seemingly little effort, the network instigated a media frenzy against General el-Sisi. The general himself gave Al Jazeera one of the more effective weapons it would use to beat him when he shut down Al Jazeera and other religiously affiliated channels just hours after his speech on July 3. As many of its journalists were arrested, the network was again cast in the defiant, underdog image that had served it so well in Afghanistan, the Iraq War, the Hezbollah–Israel war, and the Gaza conflict.

Al Jazeera went to work converting its library of images, speeches, and video clips of el-Sisi into fuel for media explosives. Unflattering montages and clips of the general ran endlessly on Al Jazeera. Assurances about the network's secure satellite locations and dedication to providing uninterrupted coverage served as constant reminders that Al Jazeera had been temporarily forced off the air. Those interruptions, according to Al Jazeera, were manifestations of the return to "old habits of blatant censorship" from the Mubarak regime.

Hassan Nafaa, a professor at the University of Cairo, told Al Jazeera that most Egyptian newspapers were filled with fabricated news and that video accounts of events were often no more credible than print. "There are newspapers that are filled with lies, absolute lies," said Nafaa. "Some of this news interests me personally, since I can retrace or detect its origin. People think that a news report that is one hundred percent based on images reports the truth, because images can't lie, but we later discover photo shopping" (*Talk of the Revolution*, July 19, 2013).

Recent "manipulations" broadcast on YouTube, added Naffa, required vigilance. Al Jazeera added that the campaigns of *shaytana* (demonization) tended to follow the prevailing culture of Egyptian societies, which favored absolute truths over relative ones. This "systematic planning" to demonize the Muslim Brotherhood and Islamic channels was a consistent theme on Al Jazeera broadcasts.

According to Al Jazeera, the *shaytana* campaign started around the time of the January 25 revolution and reached a peak just before President Morsi's removal from power. In this narrative Al Jazeera singled out the persecution of the editor in chief of the newspaper *Shuruq*, Imad Al Din Hussein. Al Jazeera also acknowledged that both liberal and religious media outlets had committed follies with disastrous outcomes. Al Jazeera described a warlike situation in Egypt's media landscape, with the Muslim Brothers under siege by negative coverage. Al Jazeera's multiple interviews with the Coptic human rights star and activist lawyer, Niveen Malik, served as evidence that the hostility was apparent to non–Muslim Brothers. Malik accused the Egyptian media of "systematic demonization of the Muslim Brotherhood." On a YouTube video, Malik said that Egyptians who would get outraged about the lynching of a Shia person would not complain about the lynching of a Muslim Brother (Al Jazeera, July 20, 2013).

From the time that el-Sisi demanded that President Morsi reach an agreement with the protesters, Al Jazeera framed the unfolding situation as a "possible coup d'état" in the making. Ahmed Mansour writes a daily column for Al Jazeera in *Ashuruq*. On June 25, 2013 (the day of the emir of Qatar's abdication) Mansour wrote an article complaining that the creation of false rumors in Egypt had become a profession. This, he worried, was cause for concern over the state of Egyptian society and its institutions. As one example, he wrote of a meeting between General el-Sisi, the minister of defense, and President Morsi that Egyptian media had described as a semi–coup d'état. While much of the column focused on spurious rumors about Egypt, Mansour, a fervent supporter and member the Muslim Brotherhood, described talk of a coup as the lone nugget of truth in a river of misinformation. By this time, talk of a military coup in Egypt was common in Al Jazeera's daily news coverage. The pro–Egyptian government *News Daily* published a study from the Egyptian Strategic Center of Studies that suggested Al Jazeera promoted the idea of a military coup by implying that there was a public consensus that a military takeover was taking place (Youm 7).

Just minutes before the military declaration that officially ousted Morsi from power, supporters of Morsi on Al Jazeera discussed the possibility of a military coup versus the legitimate election of a ruler. Immediately after the declaration by General Abdel Fattah el-Sisi, Al Jazeera announced that the pro–Muslim Brotherhood channel Egypt 25 had been shut down along with other religious channels. Al Jazeera showed a YouTube video of Morsi giving a long speech in which he refused to employ any military intervention in a democratic process. After General el-Sisi's speech, there were comments on Al Jazeera from Muslim Brotherhood supporters along with commentators who saw the alliance of Al Azhar, the Coptic pope, and the military as a new religious-military dictatorship that had been planned in order to hijack the revolution. Commentators who favored the coup were also given airtime to voice their opinions: they pointed out that Morsi had made many mistakes, alienating Egypt from the Shia and its alliance with Gaza and damaging Egypt's international reputation. They also spoke about what they called *inflat i'lamy*, a kind of media chaos with "wild" or sensational outlets in the Morsi era. According to the anti-Morsi commentators on Al Jazeera, the media chaos was characterized by a triumphant type of hate speech, which included calls not to share meals with Christians and speeches that encouraged violence. Less than four hours after General el-Sisi's speech, Al Jazeera announced the arrests of twenty-seven employees of its Egyptian Al Jazeera Mubasher channel. Al Jazeera also aired the audio portion of footage showing military security forces entering their Cairo studio and expelling the Al Jazeera team and guests during a live broadcast.

The next morning, Al Jazeera announced that Saudi Arabia was the first country to congratulate the Egyptian military, followed shortly by the United Arab Emirates. Hours later, the emir of Qatar also wished Egypt luck. Al Jazeera's Ali Gamdan reported from Cairo that following General el-Sisi's speech announcing the ouster of President Morsi, the world had witnessed another attack by security forces on a satellite channel in order to silence its voice and shut down its broadcasts. The backlash, of course, was led by Al Jazeera: "During a live broadcast in Cairo, the security forces entered the studios, forcing them to stop the coverage. Our colleagues and guests were stunned. Al Jazeera was hosting commentators and guests of varying political plumage."

Al Jazeera also displayed footage of the early demonstrations. Someone from the main studio in Doha called the Cairo studio, asking, "What went wrong? Can you hear me? Can you hear me!?" The voices of the security officers were harsh and insistent: "Please, let's go, please, let's go," they said over and over. "Other TV stations like Egypt 25, which represents the Muslim Brotherhood, as well as Al Rahma Al Shabab were also shut down and their employees were arrested following the speech of General el-Sisi," Gamden explained. "The measures were to be temporary, they were told. Many international organizations also opposed these arrests" (Al Jazeera July 5, 2013).

"We object to any intervention to shut down media outlets or to arrest journalists, whatever the political situation is. Shutting down Al Jazeera is unacceptable," Al Jazeera quoted human rights advocates as saying. Footage of soldiers enforcing checkpoints from throughout Cairo was aired. "The military said that they will issue a charter for the media that guarantees professional norms," the broadcast continued. In order to communicate its skepticism, Al Jazeera then aired pictures borrowed from another channel that showed journalists being arrested and put into a small car.

While supporters for both Morsi and el-Sisi struggled to present themselves as defenders of democracy, Al Jazeera framed Morsi's removal from power as war on political Islam. The backlash against the Muslim Brothers, Al Jazeera anchors and pundits warned, could have severe consequences around the world, with a possible return en masse of jihadi Islam. Giving the conflict between the Muslim Brotherhood and General el-Sisi a global dimension, Al Jazeera discussed extensively the audio message of Al Qaeda leader Ayman al-Zawahiri, describing the coup as a US plot against Egypt.

A War of Frames and a War of Numbers

News from Egypt and Syria dominated Al Jazeera's programing from June to September 2013. The cultural, chronological, and geographic proximity of the political upheavals invariably linked the two chaotic situations. Both countries were seen to be at the heart of the problems of the Arab world, just as they were in 1967 during the Arab–Israeli conflict. As tensions rose during the closing weeks of Morsi's regime, the violence in nearby Syria was on the minds of both pro- and anti-Morsi factions. On July 3, 2013, Amar Adeeb, a well-known Egyptian television host, called on *Cairo Today* for the ousting of President Morsi; he asserted that the president was a fraud imposing on the Egyptian people the idea of a religiously divided nation. Adeeb said that he preferred "the Syrian solution that is a bloodbath" or fifty months of blood over fifty years of the Muslim Brotherhood in power. "I am going to be a martyr," Adeeb said, paraphrasing Morsi. "This is what Morsi wants. You have to choose between me or blood. Go back to your tribe [Muslim Brotherhood]."

Al Jazeera's star preacher, Yusuf al-Qaradawi placed himself at the center of both of these conflicts, making a series of forceful statements in favor of the rebels in Syria and against the military takeover in Egypt. Pro–Muslim Brotherhood pundits called al-Qaradawi the "Sheikh of the Arab Spring" and *alim raban* (a godly scholar). Many prayed for God to "bless" him and "protect" him from the jealous and envious. In the closing weeks of Morsi's time in power, al-Qaradawi posted calls on his website for a dialogue between the growing opposition and Morsi and deemed any action to oust Morsi as *haram* (illicit).

During appearances on Al Jazeera, al-Qaradawi bemoaned the division in the Egyptian streets as *mehna* (an ordeal) and *bala* (a test). He was astonished that people had been patient for thirty years during the reign of Mubarak and yet very impatient with Morsi. Al-Qaradawi warned that when Morsi left, he would be replaced by someone even worse. On *Islam Online* al-Qaradawi was described as *tajir din* (a religious traitor), and on one Egyptian television station he was called the "Sheikh of Blood."

On Al Jazeera, al-Qaradawi asked Egyptians to follow and obey President Morsi and contended that if Morsi made mistakes, he should be accountable and the people should ask him to revise his missteps. He also criticized the *baltajiyya*, which he perceived as polluting the revolution. But al-Qaradawi's support for Morsi cost him and Al Jazeera the support of many Egyptian television commentators and newspaper writers. At the same time, events unfolding outside of Egypt further polarized perceptions of the preacher.

As mentioned in chapter 2, just four days after the abdication of the emir of Qatar, rumors circulated in the Arab press about al-Qaradawi, who had purportedly been ousted and stripped of his Qatari citizenship. Al-Qaradawi's website denied these reports, dismissing them as lies and rumors. A picture of al-Qaradawi standing between the new emir and the old emir adorned his site as evidence of his continued ties to the Qatari leadership.

Mona Chadli, host of the popular Egyptian TV *10 PM Show* (*al-Ashira masa'n*), said of Qaradawi, "Egyptians—even those who disagree with him—have respect for him because of his long career of study. It is true that many of his fatwas angered Egyptians at times, but he continues to be a landmark." But Chadli took issue with al-Qaradawi's urging "all the Muslims in the world to support their brothers in Syria." Chadli complained that al-Qaradawi's calls to action in Syria applied only to Sunni fighters. She argued that the term "Syrians" had replaced al-Qaradawi's preferred "brothers in Arabness" in his comments regarding the conflict. "He likes to say, 'Support the Sunni against the Shia in Syria,'" she said.

"He asked everybody who has the ability to fight [to do so] and everybody who has a sword to use it, and whoever has a cannon or [other] weapons to use them against [the Shia]. They should go to Syria to fight," Chadli said of al-Qaradawi's statements. "Why didn't he ask the Qatari people to fight in Syria if he is so proud of the Qatari leadership and his citizenship and his passport?" Chadli charged that al-Qaradawi's hope was for the Sunni of Egypt, Iraq, Sudan, and other countries to fight the Shia of Lebanon and the Shia of Syria. The *Daily Telegraph* echoed Chadli's criticism, writing that Muslim Brotherhood clerics who called for Sunni jihad in Syria "risk further inflaming sectarian tensions across the Middle East" (*10 PM Show*, June 2, 2013).

The first episode of *Sharia and Life* after the Egyptian military coup was hosted by Yusuf al-Qaradawi and was devoted to answering email questions from viewers centered almost exclusively on Egypt and Syria. Al-Qaradawi took the opportunity to praise the first-ever unified official start to the month of Ramadan in the Arab world, which he considered a sign of progress in Islamic countries. (Traditionally, each country waited to observe the beginning of the crescent moon within the borders of its own country.) "It is the first time that all Arab countries have observed the start of Ramadan at the same time," he told his audience, "accepting the appearance of the moon in Saudi Arabia as the official beginning for all twenty-two Arab countries." Al-Qaradawi prayed for the protestors of Rabaa al-Adawiyya, advising them to be patient.

Wasfi Abu Zeid of the International Union of Muslim Scholars asked al-Qaradawi if critical circumstances in Cairo had caused his hasty return to Qatar. "I didn't run away," al-Qaradawi responded. "Wherever I go, I am with Egypt, defending it in whatever circumstance. I'm with justice and the Egyptian people. I was invited to attend the *iftar* [the evening fast-breaking meal] of the emir of Qatar, which is a recurring opportunity each year. I didn't want to miss it, especially after the rumors by the media suggesting that I do not fear God and don't do any investigative reporting. Rumors suggested that I was expelled from Qatar" (Qaradawi.net, August 5, 2013).

Al-Qaradawi described his relationship with the men, women, and children of Qatar as excellent. He had become, he said, literally, legally, and metaphorically one of the people of Qatar. In the same breath, he stressed that there were no boundaries between Arab countries. "All Arab countries are the same," he explained. "Even if I carry Qatari citizenship, I'm still Egyptian" (Al Jazeera April 9, 2012).

In response to a question about the Egyptian media, he spoke of a culture of hatred and hooliganism, dominated by *baltajiyya* (thugs of the regime) bent on inciting violence against certain peoples like the Palestinians, the Syrians, and the Turks. He reiterated that President Morsi had supported the Syrian people, stoking the rage of Iran and Hezbollah. He referred to Hezbollah as *hizb a-shaytan* (the party of the devil) and alleged that it had supported the Syrian regime in order to escalate hatred against Syrians everywhere. He described support for the Syrian people as the "duty of all Muslims" (Al Jazeera, July 6, 2013).

Al-Qaradawi denounced the military coup against Morsi, whom he described as a "legitimate president who was elected by fair ballot." He went on to imply that the military's seizure of power was part of a larger hidden agenda. Morsi's June 3 ouster, he said, "had been planned for a long time" (Al Jazeera, July 21, 2013).

Given the chance to question General el-Sisi live on Al Jazeera, al-Qaradawi chastised the general, asking, "Who made you commander in chief? You were, before, just an officer. You have sworn obedience to President Morsi. Who gives you the right to overthrow the president?" Al-Qaradawi said the ouster of an elected president was expressly forbidden in Islam. He quoted from the Quran, "Aslam ala man itaba'a al huda" (Peace upon those who follow guidance) (Al Jazeera July 25, 2013).

Following these verbal attacks on el-Sisi, al-Qaradawi became a major target of criticism in the Egyptian media (Al Jazeera, September 22, 2013). "Al-Qaradawi, this ambiguous personality," is how one commenter described him. "His religious opinions follow a political roadmap called the Muslim Brothers," charged another (Amr Adeeb, *Cairo and Its People* [*Al Aahira wa Nass*], May 12, 2014).

Many of these television channels invited other religious leaders to counter al-Qaradawi's fatwas. Dr. Ahmed Karima of Al Azhar University appeared on Egyptian television to counter the Al Jazeera personality's pro–Muslim Brother statements. Karima attacked al-Qaradawi's arguments as poor constructions built on false premises. Karima described the International Union of Muslim Scholars, over which al-Qaradawi presides, as a charity organization created to replace the only legitimate league of Muslim scholars, of which Al Azhar University is a part. He charged that, as a son of Al Azhar, al-Qaradawi had benefited from the backing of the scholars (*ulama*) of Al Azhar when a "Wahhabi war" was waged against him. Karima then proceeded to examine Egypt's *ahl al hal wa aqd* (those who are qualified to rule), a group whose four major authorities consist of Al Azhar and the religious elite; the military; the police; and the legal system.

As for the ouster of Morsi, Karima was effusive. "Thank God, Egypt is back to its Egyptness and civility," he cheered. "*Wasatiyya* [the middle path] of Egypt is well respected everywhere." For eight years, said Karima, the Muslim Brothers had "killed innocence" and attempted to impose their own constitution, which he called the book of their "ideologue," Sayyid Qutb. The Brothers, he claimed, saw the whole of Egyptian society as riddled with apostasy and *yahilyya* (atheism).

Morsi's legitimacy was weak, Karima asserted, because he had used religion to manipulate voters during Egyptian elections. According to Karima, the Muslim Brothers had told many voters, "If you vote for Morsi you will go to paradise; if not you will go to hell." "Many ordinary citizens voted for Morsi because of this rhetoric," Karima claimed, because they were convinced that doing so was their "duty as good Muslims." This, Karima said, constituted a wholesale disempowerment of the Egyptian people. He referred to the Muslim Brothers as "sheikhs of *yahl*" (ignorance). To Karima's mind, the Brotherhood had bestowed on itself a false mandate to rule in the name of the Quran. Morsi's removal, he said, was *halal* (lawful) since the Muslim Brothers represented the *fitna* (unrest). To drive home his point, Karima invoked a saying of the Prophet, "The people know better their own situation" (Al Arabiya, December 3, 2013).

Muhammad Hassanein Heikal, the legendary Egyptian journalist, was extremely critical of the pro-Morsi and Muslim Brotherhood slant presented by Al Jazeera Mubasher. He questioned whether the emirs of Qatar would support Al Jazeera Mubasher's style of coverage in their own country. It was an even bigger mistake, according to Heikal, to launch the network in Egypt, where it became a "source of propaganda" for the Muslim Brotherhood (CBS Egypt, March 11, 2013).

Al Jazeera Mubasher's coverage alternated between interviews and news spots from around Egypt featuring a breaking-news ticker and a text message feed, where the sentiment was predominantly pro-Morsi. Meanwhile, Al Jazeera Arabic broadcast live feeds from various squares across Egypt, sometimes on split screens showing two, three, four, or even as many as six different events at once. However, the central screen was always set on Rabaa al-Adawiyya Square. The footage was part of a cocktail of news, interviews, collages of bloody footage, and unflattering sound bites from General el-Sisi, contrasted with Morsi's words of praise for him and the army.

Video footage of General el-Sisi swearing allegiance to President Morsi was played repeatedly on Al Jazeera. One montage, aired daily on Al Jazeera during this time, showed Morsi saying, "Our army is our capital," followed by General el-Sisi assuring viewers, "The army of Egypt is a lion and the lion doesn't eat his children." One Al Jazeera pundit seized on the irony of the statement, noting that under some circumstances the lion does kill its cubs.

Perfecting Al Jazeera's Repertoire of Media Frames

Al Jazeera's Ahmed Mansour was notably absent from coverage of the unraveling news in Egypt during this period. His Cairo-based talk show, *Without Borders*, did not air for months. However, his program *Witness of One's Time* (*Shahid ala al asr*) was broadcast and advertised regularly. The episodes featured commentary and interviews with politicians and leaders of the midcentury Algerian war of liberation against the French. Most likely the episodes had been taped months prior, since Mansour was in Egypt participating in Muslim Brotherhood rallies and gatherings, which were posted to YouTube. In these videos, Mansour speaks to the crowds about shifting from a strategy based on support for Morsi to one based on support for the ideals of January 25, 2011. In this way, the Muslim Brotherhood would claim the founding moment of Egyptian democracy for itself. Mansour's audiences heeded much of what he said. His speeches became the focus of Al Jazeera reports and were reprinted as columns in *Ashuruq* and other newspaper outlets that were affiliated with the Muslim Brothers. On July 10, 2013, Ahmed Mansour's daily column in *Ashuruq* was entitled "Witnesses of a Slaughter."

Having covered wars in Afghanistan and Iraq, Mansour knew that in the aftermath of a tragedy, firsthand information comes from witnesses and doctors. The minute he learned of a historic slaughter during the dawn prayer in Rabaa al-Adawiyya, Mansour rushed to the field hospital there. The next day, Mansour's column described the scene he had found. Everyone in the field hospital, he wrote, was in shock. The doctors' white uniforms were covered in blood. At a press conference held by the physicians' union soon after the massacre, Mansour wrote of the conspicuous absence of local and satellite media, although a few Western journalists were on the scene. Mansour concluded that a cover-up was under way.

A field hospital doctor, Hisham Ibrahim, accused the Egyptian media of treason for their failure to report on the massacre. Citing as his source Dr. Jamal Abdelsalam Amin, the secretary general of the physicians' union, Mansour reported that the number of "martyrs" had been fifty the previous evening, followed by seventy-six that morning. The number of injured, he said, was more than a thousand. He also reported further details that had been provided by Dr. Mohamed Zanayti, the director of the field hospital.

"The slaughter happened during the second *sujud* (prostration) of the dawn," wrote Mansour. This accusation would paint the attackers as violating Islamic law. As evidence that the attacks had come during the *sujud*, Zanayti told Mansour, "The believers arrived at the hospital without shoes; [they] had been recovered by rescuers while facing Mecca and their clothes showed that they were from all classes of society. And most of them were youngsters." In the aftermath of the attack, Zanayti said that the field hospital's rudimentary facilities had served 450 people per hour, including 150 who had been injured by *rasas hayy* (live bullets). "It was a fountain of blood," he said, adding that the facility should be cited in

Guinness World Records for its efforts. A person identified in Mansour's column as "the bomb witness" said, "They fired during the second *raka'a* [bowing low with forehead touching the ground], first with tear gas, and when we were in the state of *sujud*, they fired at us with live bullets."

On July 11, 2013, Mansour wrote in *Ashuruq* that the concern for Egyptians was not the ousting of Morsi, but rather the stolen revolution of January 25, 2011. The revolution that rallied all the people of Egypt had effectively eradicated fear and taught Egyptians to defend their rights. A crowning achievement of that movement, Mansour wrote, had been the first-ever election of an Egyptian president by means of the ballot, the doing away of thieves and corruption, and the passage through parliamentary vote of an Egyptian constitution. But the coup of July 3, 2013, brought back the fear of the Mubarak regime. "It killed the legitimacy of January 25th," he wrote, "and replaced it with a coup that was made according to a movie plot." According to Mansour, the 22 million people who took to the streets on June 30 had been played by the remnants of the old regime. Mansour described a group of aristocratic women he met in Rabaa al-Adawiyya. They had come, they said, to defend their vote in the first free balloting in Egypt's history. "Egypt became ours on January 25th 2011," they told him, adding that those who died in the squares had not all been Muslim Brothers.

In its coverage of demonstrations in Egypt and Tunisia, Al Jazeera succeeded in creating a revolutionary atmosphere. In Tunisia, the president was more impressed by Al Jazeera's coverage than by updates from his own military. Media experts claim that Al Jazeera reported exaggerated numbers of demonstrators through its media outlets in both Tunisia and Egypt. During the Libyan revolution, the network sometimes claimed imaginary victories for the revolutionaries, placing itself at "the heart of the events" that it had helped to create.

Al Jazeera reporter Majid Abdel Hadi described Morsi's political trajectory as a journey from prison to presidency, then right back to prison under accusations that he had made a joke of the Egyptian justice system during his time in power. Now, said the reporter, he shares a prison with his former nemesis, deposed president Hosni Mubarak. Al Jazeera spoke of its objectivity and dedication to precision as it delivered unfolding news from Egypt.

Dr. Mamoun Fandy, president of the London Global Strategy Institute, raised another critical issue in a September 23, 2013, column in *Asharq al-Awsat* about Al Jazeera. Fandy, an Egyptian-born American scholar, contends that calls to jihad for Egyptian democracy on the satellite stations (including Al Jazeera) put the sovereignty of the state at risk. The state, argues Fandy, has no sovereignty when muftis in one country can unilaterally spur military engagement in a war against a foreign government—in this case Syria. Hezbollah, in Lebanon, and Hamas, in Gaza, are prime examples of political parties whose actions undermine the sovereignty of the state. Calls for jihad by non-state actors like the *ulama* of the *umma* (scholars of the Muslim nation), muftis and religious leaders, like al-Qaradawi, take the decision to go to war out of the hands of the state, says Fandy. This type of situation, by definition, undermines the foundation of democratic nations. If decisions of peace and war are no longer viewed as the sole domain of the sovereign state, this spells the end of the nation-state and opens the gates to a new transnational form of policy. As an illustration of the very serious nature of these concerns, Fandy offered the example of Osama Bin Laden's 1996 declaration of war against the United States as a misappropriation of Afghan state sovereignty. Other journalists and op-ed writers in the Arab world made similar points.

Anthropologist David Kertzer argues, "The contrast between the symbolic and the real is that the real, in fact, involves the manipulation of symbols as much as the symbolic, and the symbolic is not without its material consequences" (1996,154). This idea was vividly illustrated during the events of the summer of 2013 in Egypt. On July 23, Al Jazeera aired a news report about the bias of the Egyptian media against the Muslim Brotherhood, read by Fatima Triki. The report opens with dancing and singing by Ilham Chahine, a famous actress who had been vindicated in court after being accused by the Muslim Brotherhood of prostitution and lowering the moral standards of Egypt. Her audience follows her, singing and dancing in a karaoke-like setting with her lyrics projected on a large screen. Three lines in Chahine's song are emphasized for dramatic effect:

> Leave without being ousted, and don't come back and get mad.
> The one who enters our house will be lost, and the one who leaves our
>   house is yet to be born.
> This world [was] given to thieves and leaves the poor without money.

"These 'hours of *suhkria and tagrid*' [merrymaking and singing] are unprecedented in the history of Egypt according to Egyptian and Arab experts," Triki says of the scene. "The so-called guardians of freedom are making fun of the ousted president."

The newscast examined a collage of segments from popular Egyptian television, aired by an Egyptian news station. Clips of ultraliberal pundits, centrist journalists, and comedians were placed alongside each other, with no acknowledgment of the differences in accepted conventions and style that exist between the genres. Clips of postrevolution statements by comedian Bassem Youssef (a kind of Jon Stewart of Egypt), Amr Adeeb (more akin to Rush Limbaugh), his wife, Lamis (a liberal), and many others were played against seemingly contradictory statements from before the revolution. The subjects of the piece were portrayed as sycophants, eagerly hustling their way up the new power structure.

Another clip followed of Ilham Chahine and another woman telling a bearded representative of the Muslim Brothers and Salafis to shut up. Ilham used the Arabic word *us*, which, in that context, can be translated equally well in a number of ways. What is not readily apparent from the clip, though, is that it is taken from a comedy bit comparable to something that might be seen on *Saturday Night Live* or on a Conan O'Brian show in the United States. The result, according to Al Jazeera, left viewers with a false impression of popular attitudes toward the Muslim Brotherhood.

Amid the cacophony surrounding the decisions made by the new interim government just hours after President Morsi's arrest by the military, Al Jazeera focused on non–Muslim Brotherhood voices. For example, Al Jazeera interviewed members of the April 6 movement about its opposition to the draconian measures employed by police investigating members of the media. Targets of these investigations included Al Jazeera team members like the director of Al Jazeera, Adbelfatah Fayed. The new regime in Egypt hyped up the dander of terrorism to shut down Al Jazeera.

During these chaotic times, some on the religious right also attempted to clean house. The Salafi Anur party excommunicated Amr Khaled, a television preacher fond of European clothing and known to advocate mixed-gender gatherings. Anur representatives stated that Khaled "doesn't understand Sharia."

Fridays of Rejection, Rage, *Zahf*, and Breaking the Coup

The competitive tradition of giving names to Friday protests only intensified following the ouster of President Morsi. The coverage of all of these Fridays on the news was dominated by images of blood, coffins, and funerals. Al Jazeera dubbed the gathering of pro-Morsi protesters the following week the "Friday of Rejection" of the military coup. Footage showed demonstrators vowing, "We will show them rage!" Articles about the Friday of Rejection also ran on Al Jazeera's website. A Friday counterprotest was organized by the backers of the coup, which they called the "Friday of Independence."

Al Jazeera correspondent Abdallah Shami covered the massive support for Morsi in the city of Nasser. Shami spoke of the possibility that demonstrations might move toward the headquarters of the military after the Friday sermon. He also mentioned rumors about demonstrators demanding the return of legitimacy and refusing any premature elections.

From Tahrir Square, a correspondent told of the worsening situation for Al Jazeera employees, who received continuous threats from *baltajiya*. Their equipment, he said, had been confiscated and reporters could not do their work properly, despite their engagement with both sides of the conflict. Safety conditions in the square, he said, were entirely contingent on the protester's ability to police themselves. "The security is in the hands of people's committees [organizations within the protest groups]," he said. "There was a rumor that pro-Morsi protesters would walk to Tahrir Square, but those rumors were denied."

He then described a complex series of mobilizations and countermobilizations by different groups and organizations like the June 30 front, which had collected millions of signatures to bring down President Morsi, and the pro–Morsi Movement of Salvation. Organizers of Friday of Independence protests, meanwhile, demanded the institution of a minimum wage and improvements to basic living standards (Al Jazeera, July 7, 2013).

On the first Friday of Rage, President Morsi was deposed. An Al Jazeera news report showed a coffin hoisted on the shoulders of protestors in a large, shouting crowd moving like a wave into Al Azhar Mosque. "This is Al Azhar Mosque during an overwhelming Friday of Rage," explained the voice of Al Jazeera reporter Tamir al-Mishal. The open coffin was lowered to offer the camera a view of a body wrapped in green cloth. "We will take revenge with our blood!" people shouted.

"This is the funeral of three men [killed] during the protest against the assault of the presidential palace from the Muslim Brothers," al-Mishal continued. The camera zoomed in on somebody wearing a Palestinian shawl around his head and holding his hands in a prayer position. "The funeral is being conducted in the presence of the *murshid* (general guide) of the Muslim Brotherhood, Mohammed Badie," said al-Mishal. "In the mosque, the *murshid* and the *ikhwan* (Muslim Brothers) avoid talking about politics, but their faces express the pain caused by the political situation that is now gripping Egypt and bringing it into a dark tunnel."

The three coffins were placed on the floor of the mosque, flanked by the Egyptian flag. The bodies were wrapped with green fabric on which the name of Allah was written. "God help us! These *baltajiyya* are against freedom of speech. I express my opinion, they kill us with bullets, and this is not [even] Gaza," cried a veiled woman in black, surrounded by her children. "This is not Gaza where Palestinians were killed by Jews. The ones who killed them were Muslims like us." A large banner, emblazoned with the image of a slain protester and the words "Martyr of Egypt and the Muslim Brotherhood," hung above the crowd. "Freedom! We will continue our work," people shouted as the camera zoomed in on an open coffin.

Al-Mishal went on, "The marchers during the funeral were calling for the return of President Morsi and repeating what he said during his last speech, that this was all a *muamara* (conspiracy) against him and against Egypt." Agitated youngsters wearing T-shirts and Palestinian shawls shouted, "Between us and them there is blood." The crowd repeated the words.

"In Tahrir Square, and close to the perimeter of the palace of Itihadya, there are strong voices against the president and his constitutional declaration," said al-Mishal. Most of the people wore Western clothes, with some of the women wearing headscarves. "I gave my voice to [Morsi], he had to be *amin* [honest]; he is neither *amin* nor follows *din* [religion]," a woman in a headscarf told Al Jazeera cameras. The camera zoomed in on a barbed-wire area with soldiers carrying weapons and then to the flag of the Dustour (Constitution) party.

"The street has the last word," al-Mishal concluded. "The squares and the streets of Egypt are polarized and nervous." The camera cut to al-Mishal, standing with people behind a prisonlike gate. "As long as the politicians can't find a way to end the crisis, the protests will continue" (Al Jazeera, July 7, 2013).

By this time the banners displayed by the protesters and shown on Al Jazeera had become more professional-looking and aesthetically sophisticated than those displayed during the initial period of the Arab Spring. This shows that revolutionary practice was being perfected in terms of organization and display of symbols.

Following the coup, Mohammed al-Beltagi, a star of the Muslim Brotherhood and oratorical master, became a staple of Al Jazeera Mubasher. Al-Beltagi kept busy stirring up the crowds from onstage; he also appeared on every news outlet in need of an interview. He would lose his daughter of just seventeen during the raid on Rabaa.

"You are witnesses before God," al-Beltagi told pro-Morsi demonstrators in Rabaa, "because you have been here for more than twenty days—leaving your families, your activities, your work, your money. I am glad there are still people in the world who put their interest in the *umma*, the interest of humanity before their personal interests. You are creating a miracle. In January 2011 we were thankful to God to be on the squares in the winter without the extreme heat of the summer, and we resisted for eighteen days. And this is the miracle of all miracles. In the middle of the summer, during Ramadan, nothing stopped you from your resistance—not sleeping in the streets or fasting, or hunger, or thirst, or excessive force, or even the [extreme] heat. People asked, 'Are you human beings? What is their interest, what are they gaining from hunger and thirst in this heat?' . . . This is a noble attitude, this is a patriotic attitude" (Al Jazeera Mubasher, August 10, 2013).

On the stage of Rabaa, symbolic funerals took place, and songs that don't translate well to any European language, culturally or linguistically, were sung.

The rather perplexing, "Oh Son, Don't Burn My Liver" was one of them. "We have only the Moshaf [the Quran]," al-Beltagi said from the stage of Rabaa. "This is our presence against the coup; we want the return of legitimacy in spite of the media's stigmatization of our cause. . . . The stage [here in Rabaa] is on its thirtieth day and is still filled with the same level of rage" (Al Jazeera, August 11, 2013).

A militant interviewed by Al Jazeera warned the military rule not to spill blood in the name of national security. "Blood is sacred," he said, and "will be a curse now and later. The crisis will not be resolved with blood. Looking at blood brings blood and moves people, even those as hard as stone" (Al Jazeera, August 12, 2013).

Live Bullets of Truth

During the rapid and dramatic events in Rabaa Square, Al Jazeera produced fast-paced, riveting reporting focused more, at times, on emotional impact than on narrative. The following summary is of one such newscast, where we are introduced to three heroic photographers, whose stories are delivered at such a fast pace that each seems almost cut off by the story that follows.

The newscast begins with the story of the photographer Ahmed Shalafi. On August 14, 2013, the day of the raid on Rabaa Square, Shalafi was critically injured while reporting on-site for Al Jazeera. He tells us that the bloodbath in Nasser City and Rabaa will never leave his memory. In the midst of the chaos and confusion, as he attempted to take photographs, both his camera and his head had been shot through with bullets . We are given barely a moment to process the tragedy of Shalafi's story before we are introduced to Aiman Shad and Ahmed Asim.

Unlike Shalafi, Aiman Shad is not a professional photographer. He is, we are told, a citizen-reporter. He decided to cover the demonstrations and sit-ins spreading across Egypt following a wave of security operations that targeted civic protests over the "military roadmap." As a young photographer comes into focus in the crowd, though, we find that it is not Shad but his friend, Ahmed Asim.

"This is [Asim's] camera after a soldier shot him with a large number of *cartouches* [bullets/rounds]; it was abnormal," says Shad. "They attacked us with trucks and with gas bombs. This camera belongs to Ahmed Asim." Footage of soldiers shooting at civilians airs during Shad's voiceover. Two young men are killed on-screen as the crowd stampedes away from the soldiers. "A young photographer brought to light the moments [he] wanted to document during the slaughter of the republican guard in Nasser City." The scene cuts to a man with a camera on his desk; he says, "They gave me a camera with blood on it. I looked at the camera, and then I knew it was the camera of Ahmed" (Al Jazeera August 10, 2013).

The Al Jazeera report leaves the viewer to puzzle over whether the bloody camera on the desk is actually Asim's. It is unclear who, exactly, Aiman and Ahmed are. In a flash, the audience feels the emotional toll of three young men whose lives were disrupted by their desire to document the history unfolding in their country.

After the news report, viewers were bought back to the studio, where the topic of media freedom became the focus of the discussion. Questions of why and how journalists were being silenced brought back bleak memories of life under Mubarak. Al Jazeera's Mohamed Hassan claimed that all newspapers were under military control. Television and radio coverage, he said, also followed specific rules in accordance with the angle of the putschists.

According to Al Jazeera, the danger for journalists in Egypt was only increasing. Journalistic efforts to expose the truth were too often met with *rasas hayy* (live bullets), making it nearly impossible to be a journalist in Egypt. "The first bullet that a sniper shot penetrated the heart of the young photographer-witness in order to hide the truth! The photographer-witness chose the dangerous road to uncover the truth with his photographs: these are bullets of truth," said the anchor of *Harvest of the Day* while reporting the main evening news. (Al Jazeera, August 13, 2013).

This focus on the dangers Egyptian journalists faced served to reinforce the image of Al Jazeera's journalists as courageous servants of truth. The network excels at creating martyr narratives around its journalists and photographers. This is a pattern that goes back to the Iraq War. Its reporting of the killings of reporter Tarek Ayoub and of Qatari cameraman Ali Hassan al-Jaber by Qaddafi forces are more recent examples. Al Jazeera builds its frames on the themes of blood, martyrdom, and truth. The network promotes, in daily ads and clips, the memories of fallen journalists as the basis for this three-part foundation.

One Al Jazeera ad spotlighting its coverage of extreme poverty declared, "We shed light on people on the margin; we bring special news reports; photographers died to bring us the truth," behind an emotional montage with one man shouting, "Even apostates or Israelis wouldn't do this" (Al Jazeera, August 14, 2013).

In another ad, soliciting viewer suggestions and videos, a disclaimer reads, "Al Jazeera will not accept racist comments," beneath a montage of unidentified people saying things like "Three bullets entered my daughter" and "God is my only help." Al Jazeera's logo then appears, with the subtext "Egypt between two roads." Fahmi Huwaidy, a prominent Egyptian columnist and frequent guest of Yusuf al-Qaradawi on *Sharia and Life*, asks, "The army or the people? Who protects the democratic change?" (Al Jazeera, August 15, 2013).

Two days after the raid on Rabaa, August 16, came the summer of 2013's second Friday of Rage. Al Jazeera focused its coverage on Saudi Arabia's and Jordan's support for the raid on the sit-ins. The oil-producing nations of the Persian Gulf have outsized sway in the Arab world and set the dominant tone in its media outlets. Within this power dynamic, Saudi Arabia and the Emirates tend to align on one side with Qatar on the other.

Al Jazeera gave ample airtime to Qatar's minister of foreign affairs, who emphasized his country's interest in the unfolding events, saying, "Egypt is the spine of the Arab world and what happens in Egypt has a direct effect in Syria" (Al Jazeera August 7, 2013).

Following the raids, Al Jazeera relied heavily on footage gathered from the Internet that "incriminated" the Egyptian army in Rabaa. Al Jazeera anchor Salam Khadr, reported, "The mosque of Rabaa has burned after [becoming] a true slaughterhouse. The fires burned down everything. This Black Wednesday, as it is called, was full of fire and bullets. But a mosque burning down is not the only thing that happened, not the only transgression. Security forces swarmed over the area and started to shoot protesters who were trying to help the wounded. The bullets hit everything that moved." The screen showed the charred walls of the Rabaa mosque and the bodies inside. More footage was shown, including that of a strong-looking man in a pink shirt carrying a wounded person on his shoulders. After a few steps, he was shot. Wounded, on the ground, he struggled to determine whether the person he had been carrying was still alive.

"Here we have pictures taken by Internet activists in which two men of the security forces are hitting and trampling a bearded man on the ground," the anchor said. "The number of people killed and wounded was not known until now." The shocking footage showed a policeman holding a young man by his neck and another plainclothes policeman hitting him in the chest with his boot—a kind of running karate-style kick. "Many of the captured people are journalists and we don't know their fate," the commentator explained over footage. "Close to Nahda, security forces [were] shooting pro-Morsi protesters," he added, explaining that the police were not alone in attacking protesters. They were accompanied by *baltajiyya* (thugs) and other "civilians with rifles." The anchor continued his frightening summary. "In Suez, the police fired without reason on the protesters. Internet activists show here a policeman putting civilians clothes on over his military uniform [to disguise himself]!" (Al Jazeera, August 16, 2013).

A report by Basim Ghadr included a montage of disturbing pictures from the Internet and video footage showing smoke coming from a mosque. "In the Al Imam Mosque, at least two hundred and fifty bodies, cadavers, were piled up. People brought them from the streets and the field hospitals that had been raided and burned down," Ghadr said. Footage showed bodies wrapped in white fabric, some displaying names written in black marker, though many bodies had not yet been identified. The floor of the mosque was scattered with identification cards.

The "martyrs" of the Al Imam Mosque were difficult to identify because they had all been burned and so had not yet been returned to their families. To Al Jazeera's reporters, the brutality of the killings had a single explanation, an utter lack of respect for human dignity. "The dead could not be buried because permission hadn't been given from the authorities," said Ghadr. "The authorities would deliver the bodies [only] when the families signed a document saying that they had died of natural causes and not from bullets" (Al Jazeera, August 17, 2013).

In the wake of the event, trucks with white-uniformed police waited next to rows of coffins covered with Egyptian flags. A gathering of the police with the minister of interior followed, and at the police-occupied mosque the funerals for the police officers who had died during the disruption of the sit-ins were conducted.

Al Jazeera aired another story on the same news bulletin that accused the regime of not fulfilling a promise to give the protestors secure passage out of the squares. Footage showed the police using bullets and tear gas against those who chose to abandon the sit-ins and leave the squares. Another news report on the same day explained how the authorities "legitimize violence against the sit-ins in the squares" (Al Jazeera August 17, 2013). Al Jazeera news reports accused Egyptian television of labeling "Muslim Brothers as *baltajiyya*" in big red dots on the screen, of being responsible for the chaos and the killing. Al Jazeera interviewed Egyptian experts who examined images from Egyptian television, concluding that the *baltajiyya* were working for the Egyptian security forces and were not members of the Muslim Brotherhood. "The story of the other side [the Muslim Brothers] was totally absent from all Egyptian televisions," the Al Jazeera report concluded. "Water cannons were not used in the squares [to break up] the sit-ins but heavy tear gas was used, cartridges and bullets shot. Snipers were [positioned] everywhere on the terraces to shoot demonstrators. In most countries of the world, for example in Turkey, the number of deaths [during a quelled protes] would be very small. After twelve days of sit-ins to block the demolition of one park in Istanbul, only a few people were killed. But the sit-ins in Nahda and Rabaa are embarrassing to the Egyptian government. And the violence used to break them up is even more embarrassing. This enlarges the circle of violence and the grim situation in Egypt. Is this high price really worth it to end the sit-ins?" (Al Jazeera, August 17, 2013).

Another Al Jazeera report exposed the moral bankruptcy of the Egyptian media "hiding behind the stories of the military." Al Jazeera criticized the lack of investigative journalism when Egyptian media reported that bodies had been hidden under the stage at Rabaa so that their deaths could be blamed on the regime. Al Jazeera investigated the area behind and under the stage to prove the Muslim Brotherhood's innocence. One of the most striking news reports showed footage of young and old men walking, while hoisting white flags, toward military tanks, which opened fire on them. Accompanying footage of peaceful sit-ins, a voiceover repeated the government's claim that the Muslim Brothers posed a danger to the survival of the Egyptian state (Al Jazeera August 17, 2013).

The Deadly Battle of Spin

On August 17, 2013, Egypt Mubasher reported from inside the Al Fatah Mosque that people were holding Qurans and trying to prevent security forces from entering. A journalist protester, a veiled woman by the name of Hibah, reported by phone and webcam to Al Jazeera. "We are praying and God gave us patience," she said. "We want to stop oppression and to help the oppressed. The problem is not Morsi; the problem is a humiliated people." A long interview about the situation in the mosque, the fear, the children, the women, and the disinformation about the true situation in the mosque proceeded. The anchor directed Hibah toward a man in civilian clothing trying to get into the mosque. She walked through the area, which was filled with men only, toward the civilian to ask what he had to say. He was looking for weapons, he said, and when he had been assured there were no weapons, he wanted to get into the sit-in safely. A man, a protester, spoke to Al Jazeera about the dangers of leaving the mosque, since security forces with thirteen trucks were waiting to arrest the protesters. The interviewer saw smoke and wondered, "What if it was tear gas?" At the end of the report, Hibah explained that the smoke actually came from a fire extinguisher used to protect women from the *baltajiya*.

Mohammed Jawadi, a heart surgeon, poet, and writer close to the Muslim Brothers and also a former classmate of Morsi at Zagazig University, is a regular guest of Al Jazeera. He commented daily on the events following the Morsi's ouster and especially after the press conference of Mostafa Hegazi, the president's spokesperson. "The history of people is not the history of presidents," Jawadi explained. "The revolution has been suppressed, but it will be victorious because it has values and the spokesman is just a strategies and media man. [He is] just embellishing the picture of Egypt of the coup. These are fascist forces. The speech of el-Sisi on July 3, 2013, announced that we are entering a period beyond fascism. He speaks like a patriarch and gives people absolution. He came with tanks and blood."

The anchor asked if the curfew in Cairo would help the regime. Jawadi assured viewers that a curfew anywhere would spur other public outbursts in unexpected places. He mentioned three factors driving the unrest. First, he said, the protestors knew there is no unbiased media in Egypt. Second, in Egypt there was a blending of patriotism and religion. Third, people considered the authorities untrustworthy and without values. "Even British colonists had more values than [their] rulers," he said.

The voice of Prime Minister Hazem al-Beblawi discussing the possibility of suspending the Muslim Brotherhood's license to operate as a political party accompanied split-screen footage from Alexandria, Helwan, and Minya. Al-Beblawi, Jawadi said, must suffer from amnesia. The Muslim Brotherhood, he explained, was not a political party, although it was instrumental in the creation of the Development and Freedom Party. The proposition, he said, revealed a lack of political awareness by the prime minister, whom he portrayed as old and out of touch with reality. Religious ties to politics, he added, remained strong throughout the secular governments of Europe. In Germany, for example, the Christian Democrats had been the ruling party since 2005. Switzerland, a bastion of secular governance, flew the cross on its national flag. Even in the Netherlands, former struggles between Catholics and Protestants informed the culture and legal code. Meanwhile, Jawadi contended, Egypt's five biggest political parties had religious ties. It would be crazy to attempt to ban them from participation in Egyptian politics. The prime minister's statements, he said, were rooted in the one-party political structure of the preceding century (Al Jazeera, August 20, 2013).

Al Jazeera focused its coverage on the *baltajiyyas'* attacks against Morsi. On its website, Al Jazeera posted links to Amnesty International and the Egyptian Karama (Dignity) Organization, which excoriated Egypt's human rights record. An Al Jazeera interview with Egyptian politician Ayman Nur helped to connect the dots. "I smell the scent of Mubarak," said Nur. "The old regime didn't go through cleansing" (Al Jazeera, August 20, 2013).

Al Jazeera's reporting of the revolution in Egypt brought together all the material necessary for the construction of the sort of media frames that were, at this point, familiar to the network's viewers: (1) Islamophobia is not just a Western phenomenon, but an Arab one as well, characterized by the stigmatization of the Muslim Brotherhood and the repression of its supporters. (2) A distinction can be made between "bad" Gulf countries (Saudi Arabia and UAE) that support authoritarianism and "good" Gulf countries (Qatar) that support the Arab people in their quest for democracy. (3) The old regime with its human rights violations has been restored in Egypt.

Violence and Stereotypes

The stigmatization of the Muslim Brotherhood and the liberal use of strong words like "terrorism" by the new military government were popular topics on Al Jazeera broadcasts. According to Wail Kandil, a guest of Mahmoud Murad, the host of *What's Behind the News* (*Ma wara' al khabar*), the military was attempting to institute a new value system, defining what is good and what is evil, what is terrorism and what is activism. The term "terrorism," the military said, was indicative of the total collapse of any bridge between the parties. As the military manipulated the conversation to consolidate political gains, it argued, Muslim Brothers were being punished collectively for the mistakes of a small group among them. Pro-el-Sisi guests were permitted to offer their take on the situation. In defense of the marginalization of the Muslim Brothers, one pro-el-Sisi pundit invoked the words of the UK prime minister, David Cameron, saying, "Don't ask me about human rights when national security is threatened."

"How could you say that thirteen million people who voted for Morsi are terrorists?" an Al Jazeera interviewer asked a pro-el-Sisi guest, during one of these exchanges.

"Eighty-three churches and police stations were burned down," the guest responded.

"Don't get angry. You are talking with a lot of anger," the interviewer scolded. "You are answering a question I didn't ask. What you said is your opinion and I don't want to take the responsibility for it just to please you."

Al Jazeera portrayed the Muslim Brotherhood as "the first wall that was set to protect the protesters of Tahrir Square on January 25, 2011. They were the ones who won the Battle of the Camel and set up field hospitals to help the wounded and the killed." This description ran counter to popular portrayals of the Muslim Brothers as opportunistic free-riders during the revolution.

"Egyptians know their history by heart and they know political Islam can't be taken out of the equation," said Egyptian journalist Wail Kandil. "Social peace can't return without them. After the 1973 war, this army didn't shoot a single bullet at any enemy, and now they are shooting Egyptians" (*Talk of the Revolution*, August 19, 2013).

During the Arab Spring, star Palestinian reporter Masjid Abdel Hadi gained acclaim for his poetic use of language and metaphor. References to blood were ubiquitous in his reports, with descriptions like "the very dark color of blood of the arteries.". The coffin was a common visual device in these reports, as were images and video footage of people suffering. Hadi's voiceovers were delivered in a melancholic, almost monotonous cadence. He gave a reading of the political discourse of el-Sisi on August 19, 2013. "The things that don't make God happy, we will take care of," Hadi quoted el-Sisi from a recent appearance by the leader. "Internet activists pounced on this slip of the tongue. El-Sisi, they said, had accidentally told the truth in a room full of high officers and government officials. But this was a small part of all that was said in front of his officers and intelligence and was dominated by its Egyptian dialect. 'What we said, is it going to change? *La* (no).' This is the sentence, the only sentence, that was true, in the man's forty-five-minute talk.

"*La* (no) was repeated at least twenty times in the talk. The former president, whom he refused to name, was being imprisoned and could not respond to him. Accusations of conspiracy and treason were plenty. He described himself and his colleagues as transparent and honest. 'When I tell you that we are *shurafa* [noble and honorable], do you think I don't mean it? These are not empty words.'

"The innovation in the Arab political lexicon that el-Sisi introduced was swearing in the name of God that his words were true and that he had no intention of becoming president. . . . 'They say this is military rule. I swear again this is no military rule,' he said. 'The former regime used democracy to climb to power but took the ladder up [behind it],' el-Sisi said of Morsi. 'I swear, again, that I was told that [the Brotherhood was] going to govern for five hundred years.'

"After swearing this many times, he broke his oath when he was sworn in, in front of Morsi, who chose him," As Hadi made this final statement, the camera zoomed in on Shouki Alam, the mufti of Egypt. The link between religion and politics lends additional credibility to the report (*Talk of the Revolution*, August 19, 2013).

A second report on the same day, by Hadi, focused on Shouki Alam, who had been appointed by the sheikh of Al Azhar, Ali Gomaa. "Two religious personalities were present next to el-Sisi on July 3, 2013, the sheikh of Al Azhar and the pope of the Copts in order to bless the army's coup," said Hadi. "The sheikh of Al Azhar preferred to go on retreat in order to make others take responsibility for any bloodshed. He also asked the Muslim Brothers in a letter to find a solution to the crisis, but the Muslim Brothers refused [to cooperate with him] because he was a part of the coup. He said he knew about the coup only through the media and he refused to be part of the political conflict. Two days before, he wrote a letter saying that legitimacy can't be brought back with bloodshed. Many churches were burned by unknown people amid the days of total chaos."

In the chaos following the coup, many Christian churches were burned. In a Coptic television interview posted on the website Christian.Dogma.com and rebroadcast by Al Jazeera, Father Fadi Ayoub Youssef told an interviewer that the interim government had provided no security for his church in Al Minya.

A clip of el-Sisi followed, with the general asking, "What did you do to help people?"

The mufti of Egypt then appeared on-screen saying, "Taking up arms, demonstrations, [and] sit-ins are *haram* [illicit]."

"Maybe his last religious discourse is to ask the citizens to stay away from violence in order to help the people in power," Hadi's voice suggested over footage of the mufti. "He asks, in the name of religion, to oust others from religion" (*Talk of the Revolution*, August 19, 2013).

In a third report from Hashish Jaber, a star Turkish soccer player, Emre Belözoğlu, was shown making a *raka'a* (low bow) and waving four fingers after scoring a goal, a sign of support for the Rabaa Square protesters. Footage of the Turkish city of Borsa followed, showing Prime Minister Tayyip Erdogan giving the same hand signal before a large crowd, which responded in kind; some also held up Qurans.

"This was a sign of solidarity with the Rabaa sit-in," explained Jaber. "This new sign is also known to all those who resisted the army coup in Egypt and outside of Egypt. [An icon of]the four fingers, with a yellow background, is very popular on the Internet, Facebook, and Twitter. The army could never erase Rabaa, even if it were burned to the ground" (*Talk of the Revolution*, August 19, 2013).

Later in the newscast, Majid Abdel Hadi targeted Mohamed el-Baradei, the interim government's former minister of foreign affairs, with a collage of Egyptian media clips that were critical of him. El-Baradei had received strong criticism, especially after the visit of Catherine Ashton of the European Union. El-Baradei also helped found the Ahel Sulta (People of Power) and Ahel Thawrah (People of the Revolution) movements that portrayed Al Jazeera journalists as traitors to the Egyptian media.

The Egyptian media, Hadi said, were a propaganda force undermined by their own mistakes. On-screen, an Egyptian anchor was shown holding a script provided by Hassan Hamid, the spokesperson of the grassroots movement Tamarod (Rebellion). Hadi warned of the new racism emerging in Egypt against Palestinians and foreigners since the coup. Egyptian television personalities were shown accusing Morsi of being of Palestinian origin. The new Egypt was portrayed as becoming like Israel, closing doors and building walls rather than bridges. Under military rule, he said, Muslim Brothers were not seen as true Egyptians. They were accused of collaboration with Turkey and perhaps Iran.

Resistance to Al Jazeera's Message

On August 22, 2013, the main news bulletin featured three remote interviews about the situation in Egypt. The result was a major fiasco, as each successive guest gave well-known anchor Jamil Azerin responses that appeared to diverge starkly from his expectations. It was a virtual rerun of the control room documentary, from the early days of Al Jazeera, when the editor in chief had fumed behind the scenes after a producer invited the wrong experts. The resulting YouTube clip was viewed nearly 2 million times and translates as follows:

AZERIN: We have with us Dr. Hassan Naffa. Dr. Hassan Naffa is with us from Cairo. What is your read on what is going on in Egypt now? There are still many demonstrations everywhere in spite of the repression.

NAFFA: When you watch Al Jazeera, you believe that the whole of Egypt is boiling. People think that Egypt is full of demonstrations and that everywhere there are problems. This image is not true at all.

AZERIN: How do you explain this, doctor? We didn't fabricate this footage and this reality. This is what we see in reality. We didn't create it.

NAFFA: Yes, you didn't create it. There are eighty million people in Egypt and there are only a few demonstrations in three districts, and there are twenty-four Egyptian soldiers who died in Sinai, but you don't talk about that. And also [soldiers died] in Arish. I don't see any trace of that in your coverage. You focus only on these scenes of killings, on some of the people who went to demonstrate. This is a part of Egypt; this is not a picture of the whole of Egypt. And it is the responsibility of Al Jazeera to show the full picture. You asked me about my impression and I am telling you. What I see on Al Jazeera is not the truth about Egypt. . . . Is this [journalistic] professionalism? I don't think so.

AZERIN: Dr. Hassan, I don't think that you were watching our news bulletin. And now from Cairo we have the journalist Souleiman Juda. Could you give us your impressions of the developments in Egypt?

JUDA: *Usted* [sir or professor] Jamil, are you talking about the demonstrations? In the north of Sinai and Helwan? Are you talking about two of the twenty-seven districts of Egypt? There are twenty-five districts in Egypt that don't have any demonstrations. There are two districts with demonstrations. My voice joins the voice of Dr. Hassan . . . and this is also what I said when I was your guest in Doha, that I think there is a lack of objectivity. I think we need to be honest and objective with your viewers.

AZERIN: Mr. Juda, stay with us; there is now somebody else from Cairo joining us. Aiman Assayad, the former adviser of the ousted president Morsi. Mr. Aiman, first of all, you and the Muslim Brothers government are the subject of accusations . . .

ASSAYAD [INTERJECTING]: What do you mean "with you"; who are you? What are you talking about?

AZERIN: I mean the administration of Mr. Morsi.

ASSAYAD: Then you have to ask Morsi himself. [It is] his group, not mine; I have nothing to do with him.

AZERIN: You were his adviser.

ASSAYAD: Yes, I was his adviser. But I had objections about his style of running the country, which brought us to this point, and I resigned in November

2012. This news didn't reach Al Jazeera, I guess. (*Talk of the Revolution*, August 22, 2013)

Conclusion

During the month of Ramadan in 2013, two public squares seemed to regulate the rhythm of life in Cairo. Those opposing the Muslim Brothers gathered in Tahrir Square, where the Tamarod movement called for the collective *iftar* (breaking the fast during Ramadan) with music, drama, comedy, and dancing organized by many of the very artists who had opposed the nomination of Alaa Abdel Aziz, Morsi's minister of culture and the director of the Egyptian opera.

Rabba Square, in contrast, was the square of the Muslim Brothers, where the daily events consisted of Quran recitations and marathon speeches. Rural Egyptians, who arrived on buses from many parts of the country, used the square as a school, a community kitchen, a market, a mosque, and the site of any number of other functions. Egyptian media mocked the use of the word "square" by Al Jazeera. The only real square, Egyptian media figures like Amr Adeeb and Bassem Youssef argued, was Tahrir Square.

Still, Rabaa al-Adawiyya took on a symbolic connotation throughout the Arab world. Celebrities like the legendary singer Um Kalthoum enshrined the square in a popular mythos in their songs and movies. As mentioned earlier, the name Rabaa comes from that of an eighth-century Sufi saint named Rabia. The fourth girl born to a dirt-poor family, she became a dancer to support her family before repenting and leading a life devoted to God. The Muslim Brothers compared Egypt to Rabia, in that it was an inherently pious but lost country in need of repentance. The media's take on Rabaa Square was heavily polarized, with the majority of Egyptian media aligning against the Muslim Brothers, with the exception of a few religious TV stations that also found themselves subject to censorship.

Meanwhile, few could have expected the sudden change in the popular perception of Al Jazeera from that of a hero of the Arab Spring to a victim of the interim government's media crackdown. If Al Jazeera had earned the hatred of the Arab world's old regimes, its position was relatively unchanged with regard to the establishment that emerged after the Arab Spring. The Tunisian Ennahda party served as a notable exception to this dynamic. But even in Tunisia, the secular non-Ennahda citizenship asked serious questions about the objectivity of Al Jazeera's coverage of the ruling party. Other Egyptian newspapers initiated a serious frontal attack on Al Jazeera.

The unprecedented structural trauma in Egypt's contemporary history has opened a seemingly unbridgeable gulf between secularists and political Islam. To paraphrase Arkoun, fear and mistrust have created a new layer of mythical history that pushes a prospective humanist project in Arab societies out of reach (2008, 33). Arkoun retraces the history of the antihumanist forces to the 1960s and the 1970s, when Islam came to be considered the only source of personal and political salvation. The Muslim Brotherhood emerged after the death of Nasser in 1970. It advocated the importance of Islam as a source of answers to the most complex religious and scientific questions at a time when Arab "secular" governance had failed to bring prosperity and social justice to the Arab world. Arkoun believes that Islam became a *mot-sac*, or container concept (literally "word bag"). The word "Allah," he says, appears 1,697 times in the Quran, while the word "Islam" appears only 6 times. This contrast, he argues, has been reversed in the modern vernacular, with the word "Islam" overtaking the mighty "Allah" in terms of cultural importance. This fixation on Islam (embodied in the Arab world by *ulamas* in service of the state) as the judge of the illicit and licit, the beautiful and the ugly, and the true and the false serves as an effacement of God, says Arkoun, and eliminates the possibility of a separation between the spiritual and the temporal worlds. Arkoun makes a plea to the Arab world to move beyond this historical impasse, asking, "How long could anyone resist the violence of the enraged crowds and the many wars conducted under the banner of the party of God, the holy war, justice and development, the Liberation Front, the Axis of Good and Evil, democracy and human rights, unlimited freedom, national construction, intolerable terrorism, the tyranny of oppression, anarchy, division?"

Strauss, Bourdieu, Arkoun, and Kertzer's symbols help us grasp the world around us, and creating names and titles matters greatly in media and politics. Since "symbols play a crucial role in relating one group to another," they "impel people to action" (Kertzer 1996, 6). Al Jazeera possessed a unique set of resources to provide coverage of the dramatic events in Rabaa and Al Nahada and Al Fath Mosques. Al Jazeera utilized a degree of access that no other media outlet could match to report from the heart of the Muslim Brothers' sit-ins. It was an opportunity that gave Al Jazeera a chance to bask in the limelight of a captive Arab audience. Morsi's ouster allowed the network to reprise its familiar role as an antiestablishment media voice, following a short-lived, and arguably ineffective, proestablishment position during its coverage of the Muslim Brothers and Ennahda governments. If its popularity is in decline, Al Jazeera remains at its most powerful when serving as a disruptive force for the Arab political order.

7

BULLETS OF TRUTH AND MEDIA MARTYRDOM

Our Tarek! Our martyr! We shall follow your lead.

—Al Jazeera (April 9, 2003)

Al Jazeera, *Inshallah*, has the bullets of the truth.

—Al Jazeera (April 14, 2011)

It is with Qatari blood that Al Jazeera builds its credibility . . . exactly as it did
with Palestinian and Iraqi blood.

—Al Jazeera (March 12, 2011)

This and the remaining chapters in part II of this book follow a radically different progression of time and space than the previous chapters due to the emphasis here on the events after August 14, 2013. Transnational linkages and sustained conflicts disrupted the construction of a linear chronology. For example, while it is easy to establish a fixed timeline in Egypt after the deposing of Morsi, developments in Syria often occurred simultaneously and affected outcomes in Egypt, Libya, and Yemen. Sociologist Pierre Bourdieu and historian Roger Chartier discussed the idea of chronology as "daily sediments" of history. The events of the Arab Spring were disruptive and seemed never-ending, with the unbelievable endurance of the regime in Syria as one example. In addition, the media played a role in propagating misinformation and bias, which drastically altered how audiences processed these rapidly unfolding events. Specifically, I will examine Al Jazeera's framing techniques before and after the outbreak of the Arab Spring. It is important to understand the implications of Al Jazeera's description of its fallen journalists as martyrs and the way it legitimizes organizations by emphasizing the color of blood in its news reports.

Martyrs and Heroes of the Insurrections

The series of revolutionary events known as the Arab Spring allowed Al Jazeera to refine and expand its repertoire of frames. Since the network's launch on November 1, 1996, its storytelling conventions have evolved in such a way that its news coverage both maximizes audience engagement and advances its own worldview. Deliberate framing of news coverage, combined with developing realities on the ground, has allowed the network to create powerful new symbols that in turn will influence the tone of future reporting.

Rabaa, the Cairo square where a forty-five-day sit-in was crushed in a rampage of bloody violence, became one such symbol of resistance and defiance. Al Jazeera's coverage during this period is filled with colorful phrases like "bullets of truth and martyrdom," "dark blood," "Fridays of Rage," "million-person marches against the coup," and "Islamophobia of Arab generals." These phrases show the depth and richness of Al Jazeera's repertoire in communicating the theme of *qahr* (oppression).

Through its coverage of the Arab Spring, Al Jazeera sought to break the vicious circle of fear that had kept autocrats in power for generations. The network employed a rich Islamic lexicon, enhanced by the fatwas of its star preacher, Yusuf al-Qaradawi, to add spiritual heft to its advocacy of popular power.

This chapter takes a look at the stark transition of Al Jazeera's news coverage from nominally objective journalistic reporting to advocacy, bordering on propaganda, on behalf of the more religiously aligned antiestablishment camps, especially in Egypt. During this period Al Jazeera's reporters, who have faced many of the world's most dangerous assignments during the network's eighteen-year run, were transformed into "heroes" and "martyrs" in the cause of Arab liberation. Statements by their families, along with other reporter-witnesses, were used to bolster the almost religious reverence Al Jazeera bestowed on its reporters. This treatment went beyond the sort of tribute Western news organizations pay to journalists who dedicate their lives to their craft. Al Jazeera's elevation of its fallen reporters to a level occupied by heroes of Islamic history opened a new horizon of interaction between the profane and religious worlds that prompts important questions about the network's attitude toward its position as the oracle of the Arab world.

Al Jazeera's consistent use of religious language to describe political conflict certainly enabled the network to expand. It earned the brand and the credibility necessary to compete directly with religious media outlets across the Islamic world. Meanwhile, the use of religious terms to describe political struggles began to give Al Jazeera a more profane veneer. This dance between the sacred and profane (and the network's strategic positioning of itself on the sacred side of the embrace) grew more intimate as Al Jazeera began to associate the protests it backed with the Islamic holy day of Friday.

The naming of Fridays as days of protest became an essential component of Al Jazeera's coverage of the Arab Spring and lent a kind of rhythm to the protest culture. The existing norm of assembling every Friday for religious services made

Fridays the natural choice for days of protest. In some ways, shifting the focus of Friday gatherings from religious worship to political protest could be seen as disruptive of the power of political Islam. However, the ongoing association of political demonstrations with the day of worship imbued them with a spiritual undercurrent that might not otherwise have been present.

A Brief History of Reporting Martyrdom on Al Jazeera

To understand the importance of conventions like named Fridays, declarations of martyrdom, and the use religious imagery and terminology, one must understand the importance of framing in the presentation of news coverage. Jehane Noujaim's *Control Room*, a documentary detailing Al Jazeera and its relations with the US Central Command (CENTCOM), demonstrates that how information is presented can be just as important as what information is released. CENTCOM is represented largely by a single person, Lieutenant Josh Rushing. The film depicts a constant struggle over censorship between Rushing and Al Jazeera reporters. Throughout the film Rushing and other US representatives complain about Al Jazeera's propagandist style. Members of the Al Jazeera broadcast team level similar criticism of US news stations. Despite urging from Rushing and other CENTCOM representatives, Al Jazeera continues to broadcast graphic footage of dead and severely injured women and children. The broadcasts increase pressure on US soldiers to either leave Iraq or reduce the number of civilian casualties. In Noujaim's film, Al Jazeera wins in the end. The news network is able to push the super power.

This success had some powerful repercussions. First, it showed that if Al Jazeera could stand up to the United States, it could certainly stand up to its own regime in Qatar. More important, it showed that the United States could be the bad guy. The images shown by Al Jazeera promoted fear and disgust in the hearts of the Arab people, as well as hatred and anger. Hatred and anger, though, can lead to individual acts of violence.

In its coverage of the Iraq War, the 2006 Lebanon War, and the series of Israel–Gaza military conflicts, Al Jazeera routinely showed highly graphic pictures and video footage of people who had been wounded or killed. During the Syrian civil war and the continuous protests in Egypt after the Rabaa massacre, even more graphic pictures of bloodshed filled Al Jazeera's broadcasts. The Tunisian French journalist and scholar Abdelwahab Meddeb called the broadcast of such graphic footage in the absence of any disclaimer about its potentially inflammatory nature as "pornography of horror" (Meddeb 2009).

When Al Jazeera showed footage of captive US soldiers being paraded before members of the Iraqi regime, Donald Rumsfeld said (as reported in *Control*

Room), "We know that Al Jazeera has a pattern of playing propaganda over and over again. When a bomb goes down they grab some women and some children and pretend that the bomb hit the women and children. And it seems to me that it's up to all of us to try and tell the truth. And recognize that we are dealing with people who are willing to lie to the world in an attempt to further their case. Ultimately they are caught lying and they lose their credibility. One would think that would not take long for that to happen dealing with people like this."

Lieutenant Rushing provides his own opinion of Al Jazeera's effect on the battlefield: "I'm watching Al Jazeera and I can tell what they're showing and I can tell what they're not showing by choice. Same thing when I watch Fox on the other end of the spectrum. They play to their demographic. The part that disappoints me is that the Arab nationalists have to include the anti-Americanism" (*Control Room*).

"Objectivity is a mirage" in the news business, advises Lance Bennet in *Politics of Illusion*. Gadi Wolfsfeld states in his book *Making Sense of Media and Politics* that there exists a cultural bias which produces the framing of news reports. "The decisions made by news editors are based primarily on assumptions about what they assume their particular audience—and their potential audience—wants to hear about" (Wolfsfeld 2014, 49). Journalists and news reporters generally use framing techniques that promote a central idea, also known as ideological framing (Wolfsfeld 1997, 2014, 51). Other scholars, such as Entman, Graber, Norris, Patterson, del Carpini, and Jamieson, have developed similar arguments on framing.

Al Jazeera's coverage of the Iraq War often ran counter to Western media accounts of the war, with some in the United States going so far as to label the network a "mouthpiece for terrorists." Fox News, however, displayed the same lack of objectivity that Al Jazeera has been criticized for. Yet, due to Al Jazeera's coverage and broadcasts of Iraqi government speeches, Western officials and media often scrutinize their actions to a greater degree than they do Fox. In the years since the onset of the Iraq War, attitudes toward Al Jazeera have certainly shifted. Even the president of the United States, Barack Obama, admitted to using Al Jazeera as a source of news. New York City cable companies now provide Al Jazeera English to subscribers. The network has made remarkable strides in gaining legitimacy in the eyes of the West. International interest in the Arab Spring bolstered even further Al Jazeera's image as a respected news source.

As Fox News has clearly demonstrated, intricate framing is not so necessary on programs where colorful opinions are an accepted part of the format. Faisal al-Kasim, the host of *The Opposite Direction*, for example, compared President Barrack Obama to a "malicious fox" wearing "preacher clothes" to Cairo. "President Barack Obama . . . misled us with the sweetness of his tongue and evades us like a fox," al-Kasim told his viewers. "What did we harvest from one year of Obama's sweet talk. . . . Weren't we tricked by his color? Didn't he himself admit that he failed to make any progress with Palestinians? Didn't his speech to the Zionist lobby show staunch support for Israel? Wasn't the applause of the Zionists during his speech unrivaled? Didn't the Iraqis get more killings and bombings from Obama?" (Al Jazeera, December 6, 2009).

Al Jazeera combined this resentment toward the United States with support for the Arab uprisings to establish the historical context of the unfolding events that portrayed the Arab Spring as a signal that the global balance of power was about to shift. The network framed the Arab revolts as a new "Arab dawn" that would lead to the rise of a new Arab century and the subsequent decline of the United States, or what Al Jazeera calls "the fading of the American century."

After the fall of autocratic leaders in North Africa, Al Jazeera promoted Islamist parties in Tunisia, Morocco, and Egypt. Additionally, the network promoted Islamist commentators to expert status in the public eye by virtue of their repeated guest appearances.

The Cameraman Martyr

The killing of the Qatari cameraman Ali Hassan al-Jaber in the spring of 2011 by the Qaddafi regime was a watershed in Al Jazeera's reporting on the Arab Spring. The network abandoned its slogan "opinion and counter-opinion" and began a trend toward coverage that overtly blurred the lines between journalism and advocacy. Following al-Jaber's death, the network took on a militant tone against Qaddafi that would carry over to its coverage of antigovernment movements across the region.

The theme of martyrdom had long been common in its coverage of the wars in Afghanistan, Iraq, and Gaza. During the Arab Spring, though, Al Jazeera began to present its own correspondents as freedom fighters and martyrs in the battle against tyranny. It is not uncommon for media outlets reporting from dangerous areas to emphasize the bravery of their correspondents and the importance of their role in offering a look inside largely closed-off situations. But rather than lauding its journalists for delivering reporting on the Arab Spring, Al Jazeera began portraying them as heroes and martyrs in support of the very movement they were reporting on.

This had not been the case prior to the Arab Spring. Al Jazeera journalists were not, for example, presented as freedom fighters during the Iraq War. In 2003, the Al Jazeera correspondent Tariq Ayoub, who was killed on the roof of a Baghdad hotel during a US raid, was given the generic name of "martyr," but he was never portrayed as a fighter against the US invasion of Iraq. During the

Arab Spring, Al Jazeera not only expressed its support for Arab demonstrators in the struggle against their rulers but branded itself as an active part of that struggle.

Where the network had previously maintained some air of objectivity, during the Arab Spring Al Jazeera proudly proclaimed its involvement in a shooting war against the Arab world's established rulers. The network contrasted the *rasas al hayy* (live bullets) faced by protestors with the *rasas al haqiqa* (bullets of truth) fired in return by Al Jazeera journalists. The network also described its reports as "bullets of light" and "bullets of truthfulness in the cause of Arab citizens."

The network assured its audience that it was a stronger ally than the military forces backing the old regimes, saying during an April 14, 2011, broadcast, "[It is the] bullet of truth that will prevail." Al-Jaber's death at the hands of Qaddafi's *rasas al hayy* opened the door for Al Jazeera to mount its own offensive against the government *qahr* and stand beside those demanding freedom (*Harvest of the Day*, April 14, 2011).

Al Jazeera's broadcasts after al-Jaber's death made it clear that the network's portrayal of this battle would be that of a struggle of more than just secular proportions. The broadcast of April 12, 2011, showed the first images of the fallen cameraman's body accompanied by a soundtrack of *Ali, ya Ali*, Marcel Khalife's iconic Shia revolutionary song about the assassination of Ali, the cousin of the Prophet Muhammad. The ode to the Shia tradition's ultimate martyr played alongside images of the fallen al-Jaber forms a culturally loaded link between the two Alis. The Al Jazeera commentary erases any question about the intended link between the fallen cameraman and the Ali of the song. The former is going to paradise as a martyr, just as his namesake did (*Harvest of the Day*, April 11, 2011).

Reporter Said Boukhafa, narrating the scene, drew the age-old metaphor pitting knowledge and light against ignorance and darkness. "With bullets fired into [al-Jaber's] back, [Qaddafi's forces] responded to the camera's light by revealing their faces and their hands drenched with the blood of innocents," Boukhafa stated as images appeared on-screen of al-Jaber working behind the camera. The reporter's description of the slain cameraman, Ali, resembles that of a holy man:

> This is the man who carries the camera and a lover of light. The name [Ali] relates to a history of victories. Ali has an original aura—from his *kufiya Arabia Khalijiya* (Arab Gulf headdress) with its [black] strings, to the beautiful prayer mark on his forehead and the abundant white hair of his beard.

A close-up of al-Jaber's face appeared on-screen.

> Ali Jaber went to Libya searching for an answer to the question that Colonel Qaddafi asked [us] when he was surprised by demonstrations against his regime. [Qaddafi] asked, astonished, "Who are you?"

Footage of Qaddafi taunting the protesters interrupted the image, with the dictator assuring listeners, "We are more deserving of Libya than those crickets [the protesters]."

Boukhafa continued:

> In order to find those crickets the camera was looking everywhere, without success. [The camera of Ali Jaber] found millions of Libyans seeking bread, freedom, and human dignity in the streets of Benghazi, Bayda, Tripoli—a whole [nation] of people kept for forty years behind a *khayma* [tent].

Al Jazeera's camera zoomed in again on the coffin of al-Jaber, covered with the Qatari flag, and hundreds of people wearing white Qatari gowns. The song of Ali was again played with the refrain of the singer Marcel Khalife, "Ali, but he came back . . ."

> It is with Qatari blood that Al Jazeera builds its credibility . . . exactly as it did with Palestinian and Iraqi blood. The name of Ali Jaber is added to those of Tarek Ayoub and Atwar Bahjat [a Palestinian and an Iraqi, respectively], witness-martyrs. Noblest are they who are martyrs of the word and the photograph in the age of the Arab publics' revolutions against despotism.

On-screen an imam led a special prayer over the body of al-Jaber, and the "Song of Ali" played in the background with the refrain "We will not let go his blood from this earth." People in white Qatari gowns kissed his coffin.

> Sadness will reign in the house of Ali, or any house that knew him. Sadness will reign in all the houses of people who care about freedom in the Arab world. Everybody will understand, except for the killers, that the light is still shining from the lens of his camera and his own eyes. Light is power, and power [energy] according the law of physics doesn't vanish but is transformed from one thing to another. Let's wait and see who will [survive the other]: [al-Jaber] or his killers?

"Al Jazeera, *Inshallah*, has the bullets of truth," Boukhafa assured viewers, wrapping up the segment. "The bullet killed [Ali] from behind. We will take our pictures from the front." The newscast ended with Boukhafa anointing Ali "the first martyr of Al Jazeera in the Libyan revolution" (*Harvest of the Day*, April 11, 2011).

The day before this report on the death of al-Jaber, Al Jazeera had aired a segment in which crowds had gathered around a giant television screen with Algerian star anchorwoman Khadija Bengana larger than life. The crowds were waving flags and banners emblazoned with the name "Al Jazeera" to watch the network's broadcast (*Harvest of the Day*, April 10, 2011).

The now-famous video of Qaddafi dressed in a dark gown and headgear aired on- screen. "I'm here in Tripoli and I'm not in Venezuela," Qaddafi proclaimed beneath the shelter of an umbrella. "Don't listen to the broadcasts of those dogs [Al Jazeera]." With his own words, Al Jazeera succeeded in promoting within the dictator's own country an image of Qaddafi as a megalomaniac who viewed his own people as "subhuman."

Bengana delivered the news while standing in front of the square. "The course of events developed in the country of Omar al-Mukhtar [the hero of the Libyan revolution during the Italian occupation] so quickly that the popular intifada (uprising) led to armed confrontations with the militias of Qaddafi," she said, "and the revolutionaries now defend their dreams [of freedom] with their lives."

Again, a clip of Qaddafi aired, with the dictator saying, "You [Al Jazeera] destroy popular power and freedom in Libya. You give us a bad reputation and present a distorted view [of Libya]." Breaking into a mocking tone, the Libyan leader continued, "Thank you, our brother in Qatar. Is this what you want? Is this the water and salt [our countries] have shared? Is this the blood and brotherhood we share?" (*Harvest of the Day*, April 10, 2011).

As the segment continued, Bengana's voice accompanied footage of dead bodies and blazing fires. "In Benghazi and Ubrika, the camera of Al Jazeera recorded what it could record of fierce battles," she said. "These are pictures of the dead and wounded."

Scenes from a cramped hospital, with images of wounded Libyans soaked with blood, filled the screen. The reporter continued, "As freedom has a price we have to pay, the truth has a very high price as well. Daily dangers are shared by the Al Jazeera team and the revolutionaries of the Libyan people. Let's record in the register of the Libyan revolution the killing of our colleague Ali Jaber, the chair of Al Jazeera's camera department. He was killed by a bullet in Benghazi."

Photos of Ali adorned the screen, giving way to footage of a Libyan doctor draped in white explaining how a bullet entered Ali's head from the back and shattered the window of the car he was in. The doctor presented his condolences to Al Jazeera, Qatar, the Arab viewers, and "all the fallen martyrs in our beloved nation."

Footage of a square in Benghazi, crowded with people waving banners for Al Jazeera alongside photos of al-Jaber, followed the doctor's statement. The crowd was shouting the same words for Al Jazeera that Palestinians sing for their country against Israel: "With our soul and blood we will redeem you, Al Jazeera." Bengana assured viewers, "The course of events in Libya will not be stopped by the killing of the camera."

The camera focused on a banner reading, "The blood of Ali al-Jaber will bring the end of the despot." Bengana continued, "The practices of the Libyan regime were exposed by al-Jaber, not only to the Arab world but to the whole world. That is why he was killed. He gave his professional life for a new life, where he is transformed into a symbol and a guiding light, showing that Al Jazeera has been and is always on the side of the people who work hard for freedom. We say again, you [Ali] uncovered the truth. Your vision is new."

Footage followed of Libyans who had gone so far as to rename a school after Ali al-Jaber. A female soldier in a veil offered her condolences to Al Jazeera. "The blood of the martyrs of Qatar is mixed with the blood of the Libyan people," she shouted, adding "There is no God but God."

"We want to thank Al Jazeera, and we offer our condolences to all for the loss of the martyr [Ali]," said another woman. "We say he is our martyr, before he becomes the martyr of Qatar. . . . We are with you in heart and *zeal* (soul), and continue your coverage of the truth and our crying to the whole world."

Ali went to cover the event, said Bengana; instead "he has become the event itself."

Al Jazeera turned the killing of its cameraman to a media event, where Al Jazeera journalists and staff members, family, the emir of Qatar, and Yusuf al-Qaradawi were all featured, singing his praises as an Al Jazeera *shahid* (martyr). In Islamic countries, unlike Western nations, where the term "martyr" might be applied to anybody who dies in service of a noble cause, the designation *shahid* can be obtained only by those engaged in jihad for the *umma* and for God.

Cultivating Rage

Hassan al-Banna, the founder of the Muslim Brotherhood, in his book *Khutab al jumua* (Friday sermons), wrote that Islam chose Friday as the day to celebrate the beauty of the faith every week and to be the last day on earth (al-Banna 2005, 9–11). Al-Banna argues that the mosques on Fridays are filled with men who are clean and who sit together on the floor with no differences between them. All of them consider themselves equal and filled with love for God and each other as they turn their faces to Mecca. Al-Banna describes Friday visits to the mosque as a kind of light in the hearts of Muslims. Therefore, Muslims should hurry to attend the mosque on time for prayer and work hard during the week with an eye toward the Friday congregational sermons.

Al-Banna is no different than most Muslim clerics in speaking about the importance of Friday, but there is a difference in the designation of Friday as a day for mobilizing the masses. Al Jazeera refers to it as "Inaha al juma's al adima" (It's the mighty Friday).

Al Jazeera's coverage of the Libyan revolution was marked by symbolism and emotionally charged images and words. References to blood, sacrifice, and martyrdom were central to the network's continuous coverage. Fridays were among the strongest symbols of sacrifice and *shahada* (martyrdom) that Al Jazeera systematically used to draw attention to the protests. The *khutba* (congregational sermon) on Friday served as a prime venue for galvanizing support for the revolution. Friday became synonymous with uprising and revolution. For example, one of Al Jazeera's recurring statements is that the number of people participating in daily protests grows exponentially on Fridays. The main news bulletin, *Harvest of the Day* changes its name on Fridays to *Friday Harvest* (*Hasad al-Jumu'a*).

Friday in Syria: From Resistance to Revolution

Al Jazeera makes it clear that there is really just "one Friday under different names." As Al Jazeera reporter Majid Abdel Hadi put it, "[Friday] . . . is for *sumud* [resistance] in Syria, for *thaba't* [steadfastness] in Yemen, for *tahara* [cleansing] in Egypt and for other countries in the Mashreq and the Maghreb and places in between that are in search of freedom, which has only one color [red], even if the paths that lead to this freedom range from the less bloody to overwhelmingly dark red." He continued, "This Damascus, the capital with a name always linked to Jasmine, continues a popular mobilization that started in Dara to the south more than three weeks ago. It is expanding horizontally in geography and vertically with the will of the people in search of the answer to one question about freedom on the altar of freedom."

The reporter says that poisonous gas is being used by the authorities in Sahat al-Huriya (Freedom Square). Images of the wounded merged with Palestinian star reporter Majid Abdel Hadi's commentary assuring the demonstrators and viewers that something like "the victorious revolution in Egypt" is within reach. He added, "Today [Friday], the Arab is counting his ribs" (*Harvest of the Day*, April 4, 2011). Here "ribs" is a metaphor for the structure provided by an individual, a family or social nucleus. The Arab "counting his ribs" is trying to figure out whether his family members are still alive.

On-screen, a victim of the violence lies in an open coffin, covered in flowers except for his face. Crowds of mourners file past. Then, Hadi's voice dramatically intones, "This is the Friday of the Martyrs, where the [people] climbed over a wall of fear that took forty years to build." Hadi recites a string of superlatives about the charismatic leader Omar al-Mukhtar (1858–1931), the symbol of Libyan resistance. A picture of al-Mukhtar chained by Italian soldiers during the colonial era appears on-screen, followed by a scene of the movie *Lion of the Desert* (1981), starring Anthony Quinn as al-Mukhrar. Quinn, dressed in a traditional Libyan gown and headgear, is shown defiant in the face of execution (*Harvest of the Day*, April 4, 2011).

An interview in which Al Jazeera's star preacher issues a fatwah to kill Qaddafi follows the newscast. Yusuf al-Qaradawi appears live, sitting behind a long white table with a bluish background in the network's main studio in Doha. A split screen sporadically presents al-Qaradawi opposite his interviewers. At other times, photos of protests appear on-screen. Mohamed Krichen, the Tunisian anchor and Eman Ayad, the female Palestinian anchor, conduct the interview. Ayad, wearing a bright blue jacket with straight hair and makeup, an almost Fox News look, sits between al-Qaradawi and Krichen, dressed in a dark suit. With Ayad asking most of the questions, al-Qaradawi responds directly to the camera, never looking the anchorwoman in the eyes. This is not the result of an infatuation with the camera, as the preacher's fluid interactions with Krichen demonstrate. For Westerners, this willful absence of eye contact with a woman might appear dismissive or sexist. Pious Muslims would see this body language as an act of respect.

"Welcome, your Eminence," says Ayad after introducing al-Qaradawi. "The latest development in Libya is the use of military air strikes against unarmed citizens. These Mirage bombers are not small planes. They carry weapons—rockets—that are used against the demonstrators. What's your opinion about what is going on?"

Al Qaradawi's response is a long speech that weaves together religious, political, and philosophical themes in an argument against Qaddafi's fitness for office:

> What could we as humans say? The truth. I don't want to say anything to Qaddafi. A human being should address only *ya'kilum* [reasonable people]. Discourse is for people who understand. The ones without reason shouldn't be addressed with *khitab* [discourse].
>
> This man lost his mind a long time ago. He was described as a madman. Signs of his madness? He wanted to be a philosopher with a theory

like that of Marx or Mao Zedong. . . . We observed his behavior many times. He was becoming a laughingstock. He was *madhaka* [an object of ridicule] in every Arab summit, with his embroidered chairs and the tent that he transports to every part of the world, with all the costs that it entails. . . .

[Look at] the kind of life that he imposed on the Libyan society; there is no House of Representatives or *shura* [consultative] institutions of *shura*. He is the institution. You [Qaddafi] are not a president. You are not everything.

If you are the father of the people, where is your kindness to your people? How do you explain the father who kills his children? The commander who kills his soldiers? To kill in this way? We didn't see anybody doing this, even in Israel in Gaza. . . . You are harsher [than Israel]. You bomb your people with [war] planes. You send mercenaries to kill civilians. [These mercenaries] are paid with Libyan money. . . .

The Libyan people have been patient for forty-two years of [Libya's] decay. In the end, the people had to revolt. The problem is that Qaddafi and the ones like him don't read history, and even if they read history they wouldn't understand it. (*Harvest of the Day*, March 19, 2011)

A Friday to Free Female Prisoners

From Al Jazeera's daily coverage of the Arab uprisings, a viewer quickly gets the impression that Al Jazeera focuses more on Fridays and their meaning to the protestors than do nonreligious media outlets. Comparison of Al Jazeera's coverage of events with coverage of the same events by competing news outlets, like Al Arabiya and Nesma, confirms this. In the period from January 2010 to September 2013, there were 101 named Fridays in Syria, 35 in Egypt, 6 in Jordan, 4 in Algeria, 3 in Morocco, 2 Bahrain, 2 in Libya, 1 in Sudan, 7 in Tunisia, 2 in Yemen, and 1 in Gaza. Since the start of the Arab Spring, Arab protesters have established a tradition of organizing and naming protest marches after Friday prayers, protests that embody the protesters' dissatisfaction with and anger toward their rulers.

Al Jazeera's Friday theme developed long before the Arab uprisings, but the network has no patent on the convention of naming Fridays. Other Arab media outlets have used the Friday theme as a hook for news coverage, especially more recently, as they have begun largely following Al Jazeera's lead in giving every Friday a different name and theme in every country. But Al Jazeera has used the central theme of named Fridays to convey a mobilizing message. Just as the weekly Sabbath serves as a periodic realignment with the spiritual for believers of various faiths, the weekly return to a day of rage, or protest, or solidarity kept Al Jazeera's audience constantly returning to a mindset of revolution. At the same time, this focus on Fridays implies a sort of piety among those featured in the coverage. In the Muslim world, Fridays are a day to gather in the name of God and community. When a group assembles for a Friday protest, those same values of God and community are transposed to their cause. The news report on the Friday to Free Female Prisoners in Syria begins with women clad in black gowns and veils, walking and shouting for freedom (*Harvest of the Day*, June 6, 2011). Al Jazeera reporter Majid Abdel Hadi begins: "For [female prisoners] and for their freedom, activists have called for demonstrations of the Haraïr [Free Women Prisoners] on the path of freedom and only freedom in this land of Syria—not out of weakness but out of pain for the nation."

The scene cuts to a woman showing a handful of shell casings to other women. The camera zooms in on dead bodies. "The brother kills the brother," the reporter says of the tragic scene. "We are eyewitnesses to the killings of young people. This footage from Benyas was dated May 7 [seven days earlier] in the Syrian calendar; a photograph takes a long time to cross the Syrian information and security blockades." The camera closes in on women in white, crying and running from the sounds of gunfire. Then we see a dead woman on the ground.

"Who killed this lady?" Hadi asks. "She is one of four women who left their village of Al Mrqab to demand freedom for female prisoners. These women had no explosives or weapons." "They demanded freedom for the others," Hadi continues as a woman cries over the bodies of the dead. "But [the Syrian government] took away their right to live. A bitter reality."

The names of twenty female prisoners flash across the screen followed by another image of women crying over a dead body. The reporter ends by stating that in the latest protests, female prisoners are free even behind bars; they have broken the barrier of fear and reached a higher level of independence.

The Friday of Warning

In Yemen as well, a Friday was named for a macabre scene of government violence. A March 18, 2011, Al Jazeera broadcast provides a bloody picture of life under the rule of President Ali Saleh. As the segment opens, blood is everywhere on the street, as well as in an overcrowded, rudimentary hospital. "Just after the Friday prayer," Al Jazeera reporter Nasreddine Alawi says in a subdued tone, "on what has been called the Friday of Warning, thousands of people were gathered when dozens of snipers aimed their weapons at the chests and heads of the people in prayer. The Square of Change was transformed into the Square of Chaos. The field hospital, even with its limited resources, was able to help a large number of victims" (*Harvest of the Day*, March 18, 2011). Video of the bloody scene gives way to an on-screen tally of the victims, forty dead and two hundred wounded.

The Rhythm of Friday

An April 29, 2011, special news report draws attention to the trend of naming Fridays: "From the Friday of Dignity to the Great Friday and Friday of Rage, the days of Friday continue to come in, the only common thread being the color of dark blood," says an Al Jazeera reporter. Images of demonstrators in Syria fill the screen. The demonstrators shout, "We prefer to die rather than live in humiliation."

The reporter recalls what he refers to as "the spark of revolution that was ignited more than a month ago in the quiet city of Dara. . . . Tanks entered the city, where water and electricity are cut off," he says.

An image of a banner reading "Better death than humiliation" appears on-screen. The reporter resumes, "That is why the Friday of Rage was born—a Friday that has many meanings: For the first time, the Muslim Brotherhood has joined the demonstration. This Friday also shows the divide within the Baath party, from which more than one hundred members resigned. The army is also worried about how to deal with the demonstrators."

Soldiers who were executed for refusing to shoot demonstrators are described in the report as victims of the violence themselves: "Many problems are growing within the army because of its complex ethnic makeup," Majid Abel Hadi says as images of the soldiers' coffins are shown on-screen. According to Hadi, the Friday "warning" resulted in five hundred dead (*Harvest of the Day*, April 29, 2011).

Libyan Friday of Hope

The importance of framing is readily apparent in the choices made by news outlets in their coverage of the Libyan uprising. Al Jazeera's coverage consistently referred to those killed in the conflict as martyrs. By contrast, the Libyan state media described those aligned against the Qaddafi regime as "mercenaries, Al Qaeda, or invaders."

Framing played an important role in the initial reporting on the opposition to Qaddafi. Some outlets described the protesters as "rebels" or "freedom fighters," while others stuck to the more neutral term for their actions as "opposition." The wording reflects a systematic attempt by these media outlets to shape perceptions of factual reporting.

The heavy use of religious terminology by Al Jazeera correspondent Mahmoud Al Jazairi in an April 30 broadcast from Libya is telling in this sense. "The praise and invocation of God are back in Freedom Square in Ajdabiya," Al Jazairi begins. "Six weeks [after the city was emptied by government order], and it seems as if God created between Thursday and Saturday a great day called Friday. Thousands of people have a deep desire for prayer and have gathered to pray. They came to awaken Ajdabiya to painful memories. The prayer ends, but the stories of their wounded lives don't" (*Harvest of the Day*, April 30, 2011).

The city of Ajdabiya had been deserted for a month and a half, and that Friday was the first time that the families who had fled the city were allowed to return. The segment shows hundreds of people sitting in the open air, listening to the Friday congregational sermon. Driving home the correlation between religion and the struggle against Qaddafi, Al Jazairi interviews an imam to the accompaniment of a Quran recitation. "[More than] 260,000 people fled Ajdabiya, and the number of those who returned is small," he says. "Ajdabiya stands at the crossroads between being a ghost town and a city that wants to be reborn."

The Egyptian Fridays for Justice

Throughout the Arab Spring, Al Jazeera presented major events, occurring at different times and different places, according to the theme of successive named Fridays. In doing so, not only was the network able to creatively group various events in a single, more marketable package, but it was also able to cast itself as an active participant in the unfolding events.

An example of this can be found in an April 7, 2011, news report. The segment begins with crowds shouting, "Bring him to court!" A banner scoffs, "The gang is still governing." "From the Friday of the Revolution to the Friday of Trials and Cleansing," Dalil Omar, an Egyptian Al Jazeera reporter says, "Egyptians [demand] a just trial. The revolutionaries demand it to uproot the tree of corruption until Hosni Mubarak can be sentenced to death."

An iron cage containing an effigy of former president Mubarak sits beneath a tree with names of allegedly corrupt politicians carved on its bark. The reporter recounts the charges against the Egyptian leader: "attacking and killing the revolutionaries, stealing the money of the state, leading a corrupt political life, and committing election fraud . . . exporting natural gas to Israel." He continues, "In order to achieve what they are asking for, [the demonstrators] prayed to God to rescue their revolution. The people criticize the Shura [consultative] Council for its slow steps in bringing down the symbols of the old regime and bringing them to justice."

As Dalil Omar is wrapping up his report, the mufti of Al Jazeera, Yusuf al-Qaradawi, interrupts the programming with what is billed as breaking news from Cairo. The news presenters, Mohamed Krichen and Eman Ayad, introduce al-Qaradawi: "The great scholar and president of the International Union of Muslim Scholars is joining us live in the studio" (*Harvest of the Day*, February 2, 2011).

Conclusion

The sudden eruption of the Jasmine Revolution created a domino effect in the Arab world. It spurred revolutions that not only changed the landscape of the Arab world but also inspired antiestablishment protests, including the Occupy movements in the United States, on a global scale. The self-immolation of Mohamed Bouazizi served as the catalyst for the Arab Spring. However, the Tunisian scholar Fethi Benslama argues that it was the construction of the narrative around Mohamed Bouazizi as a martyr that gave the Arab Spring its mobilizing effect. This narrative synthesized factual and imagined elements (projections of the feelings of humiliation felt throughout the entire Arab world) into a single legend. The narrative was a powerful tool to counter the *qahr* (oppression) and the mighty power of a crushing state; a narrative for the powerless to identify with; and an act of resistance by a powerless person who refused to be humiliated and had only his body to express his resistance. Benslama argues that an imaginary dimension accompanies this image of revolt against submission (2011,12).

The revolution stemmed from a religiously forbidden act of self-immolation: in the Islamic tradition suicide is an act against the creator and the basic principles of Islam. The narrative that transformed Bouazizi's act from one of suicide to martyrdom forced imams and Islamic scholars to accept a new definition of martyrdom. It added a profane dimension to the term "martyr," which had previously been used solely in a religious context. Benslama speaks about a new sacrality emanating from Bouazizi's act. It is the religious dimension of martyrdom that legitimates this profane act. Benslama writes that a new matrix has been created outside the religious configuration for demanding rights. Benslama argues that the Bouazizi event broke through the rigid religious and identity framework of the Muslim world, creating the possibility of a new universal interpretation. But the manner in which the Arab Spring has unfolded demonstrates how the religious framework of interpretation is now in competition with this universal claim for freedom (Benslama 2011, 74).

The Al Jazeera cameraman Ali Hassan al-Jaber, killed by the bullets of Colonel Muammar el-Qaddafi's forces in the spring of 2011 became the "first martyr" of the Arab Spring. Al Jazeera strained to surround the fallen cameraman with a religious aura. The profane martyrdom of Bouazizi was replaced by religious symbols and prayers, and his death by suicide was replaced by the killing of al-Jaber as the rallying event against Arab dictators.

It appears as though Al Jazeera is actively working to replace the profane matrix of martyrdom that the Jasmine Revolution created with a religious one. Al Jazeera enabled the religious framework to catch up with the secular definition of martyrdom and human rights that, for a time, surpassed it. As Benslama argues, if the public in Tunisia and the Arab world succeeded in rejecting a religious definition of Bouazizi as a martyr because his suicide was prohibited in Islam, Al Jazeera managed to erase the secular traces of Bouazizi's martyrdom and replace them with highly religious symbolism.

The hyper-religious naming of events by Al Jazeera, with the blessing of in-house preacher Yusuf al-Qaradawi, can be seen as a competition for religious leadership in the Arab world and the *umma* between al-Qaradawi and the Saudi grand mufti, Sheikh Abdulaziz al-Sheikh—or, in a broader sense, between Qatar and Saudi Arabia. When al-Qaradawi intervenes in the news or comments during his own show, he creates a news event. The Friday protests and marches might appear to have occurred spontaneously after the Friday congregational sermon; however the consistent call for mobilization on a day framed by al-Qaradawi as a Friday of anger or rage led to the perpetuation of a systematic naming of Friday protests in Egypt, Libya, Syria, Yemen, and Bahrain, along with Sunday protests in Morocco.

In Egypt after the fall of Morsi, expectations rapidly diverged from reality as the interim leaders continually failed to respond to citizens' demands. The power relations between government and citizens have remained stagnant and have been particularly detrimental to Egypt's stability. Protesters took to the streets as news emerged that the interim council had attempted to pass legislation restricting the oversight of military affairs by the central government. Under the previous regime, the military played an influential role and enjoyed a high level of autonomy.

Mubarak's fall from power was a result of many factors, namely rampant corruption, brutal repression, and high levels of poverty. These problems have remained since Mubarak's fall and have impeded democratization efforts. With the elections of November 22 and 23, 2015, the interim leaders had to respond to the citizens' demands and provided complete transparency in all rulings. Egypt's citizens have consistently demanded the formation of a civil government rather than military rule.

The Arab Spring brought mixed results for the countries that were most affected. Tunisia's Ben Ali became a pariah after the Jasmine Revolution; only Saudi Arabia would grant him exile. The Egyptian president, Hosni Mubarak, was humiliated in prison but freed after Morsi's ouster. In Syria, Assad survived the Arab Spring. Only Qaddafi was defeated, humiliated, and killed in a grizzly manner. Al Jazeera broadcasts showed somebody holding Qaddafi's golden gun shortly after he was killed. Al Jazeera continues to run a collage of Qaddafi threatening his people, shouting *"zanga zanga"* (street by street), and of his son promising a bloodbath for the rebels. In the end, the "bullets of truth" beat out the live bullets.

The Arab Spring spawned a new era of polemics between different political groups played out both on the streets and on television. One of the most important controversies now dominating the Arab transnational space, regardless of the national setting, is the characterization of the whole of the Arab world as a clash between Islamists and secularists. Many fear the consequences of this discussion, especially in the presence of the orthodox Salafis. However, I believe that this new dynamic brought by polemics will not result in the conversion of people to Islamism, secularism, or even Salafism.

The new polemics elucidate the contours of each ideology, making the argument on each side sharper. Since the emergence of Islamism as a politically motivating force in the public space during the 1970s, it has not stopped moving toward accommodation of the modern functions and mechanisms of democracy.

Al Jazeera stands as a shining example of the Qatari investment in the knowledge economy. The network represents the spirit of Qatar as a transactional state. The growth of Qatar's international influence in a variety of fields (journalism, media, sports, fashion, think tanks, etc.) is an expression of the transactional niche Qatar has built to maintain its fragile position between two giants in the Middle East, Iran and Saudi Arabia. Each of these giants sits on huge oil resources and represents the de facto leadership of Islam's two major sects.

Qatar, with friendly ties to all parties in the Middle East, including Israel, Iran, Iraq, and previously Hezbollah and Syria, also wants to be a guiding force in Sunni Islam. Therefore, the competition with Saudi Arabia for political and religious leadership of the Arab world is approaching ugly proportions. Qatar is pushing an ideology that is a marriage between a softer version of Wahhabism and the ideology of the Muslim Brotherhood as represented by al-Qaradawi.

If the Arab revolutions destabilize the political equilibrium in North Africa and the Middle East, Qatar will rely on its oil money and Al Jazeera to bring a new regional equilibrium. Saudi Arabia is likewise heavily reliant on oil money and the strength of the Wahhabi movement to absorb the rage and despair created by high unemployment.

Qatar's transactional attitude is reflected in Al Jazeera's treatment of moderate political Islam. The network endorses a North American model of liberalism and neoliberalism for the Arab world, only Islamized and without a European-style welfare state. Qatar's transactional nature makes it a swifter player in the world of globalization, in turn neutralizing some of the inherent advantages of its powerful neighbors. The rise of Salafi movements empowered by Saudi Arabia, however, stands as a potentially limiting force on Qatar's potential.

It remains to be seen whether all actors in political Islam, including Salafis and secularists, will be able to find a place in a new democratized political configuration. The outcome will depend on the ability of players to move toward a more universal, inclusive worldview that has respect for human dignity and accepts religious pluralism but is also tolerant of nonreligious actors.

The future of Al Jazeera, meanwhile, will hang on its ability to serve as a voice of defiance and resistance in a new Arab world that is becoming more pluralistic and whose media landscape is becoming more diverse. The explosion of talk shows is ending the age of silence characterized by the old Arab regimes. But will Al Jazeera continue to be a pioneer as it was before and during the Arab Spring by promoting salient frames to the publics that increase their self-identification with the satellite channel?

The creation of Al Jazeera Mubasher in Egypt was one solution to these problems, delivered in a very chaotic and dynamic media marketplace. Since the Egyptian dialect mixed with some standard Arabic is the most popular and well-understood language in the Arab world and is dominant in Egypt, it could become the new language of Arabic television.

In addition to how the network will navigate a media landscape it helped to create, one wonders who will fill the void left by al-Qaradawi, whose program stopped airing after Mohamed Morsi was deposed. What religious issues will the network focus on in the future? Will Al Jazeera represent the voice of moderate Muslims, positioned against the Salafis of Saudi news outlets?

Al Jazeera coined the extreme *qahr* frame as the tipping point from dictatorship to democracy, offering three ways to stop it. *Qahr* can be stopped through submission, as was the case in most Arab countries before the Arab Spring; revolution, as in the case of Tunisia and Egypt; or jihad, as in the case of Syria.

While advocating action against the old regimes, Al Jazeera promotes the idea that the potential violence of political Islam will decline through participation in democracy and open debate in the public space. This will lead to a more pacific environment where violence is no longer seen as legitimate. Rached Ghannouchi, the ideological mentor of al-Qaradawi, has said that in the 1970s he believed in using violence against rulers, but now the despotism has disappeared. The impetus to use violence disappears against a democratic regime respectful of human dignity.

Al Jazeera's bullets of truth, symbolizing the blood of its journalists, "martyrs" dying for truth that is as spiritual as it is journalistic, are more than just daily news nuggets and scoops about dramatic situations in the Arab world and beyond. They are expressions of the soft anger Al Jazeera has been instrumental in cultivating throughout its existence and that only intensified during the period of the Arab Spring. This kind of controlled or soft rage has been promoted by Al Jazeera's programing and sanctioned by Yusuf al-Qaradawi. However, the Arab Spring signaled a new period where the rage is expressed in a large-scale, organized way on Fridays. Fridays became the time for the overt expression of the bullets of truth forged by the rage of Arab masses and beyond the ability of Arab governments to tame.

And with those bullets, Al Jazeera was trigger-happy in reporting "the truth." Anger, blood, and protest remained the themes of choice for Al Jazeera journalists rallying alongside the protesters. Beyond media martyrdom, anger as a thematic topic made its debut in 2001, with al-Qaradawi's first appearance on the network, and it has been a recurrent theme since 2004.

The Egyptian revolution began on Tuesday, January 25, 2011, called a day of rage. Three days later, a massive protest was held in Cairo. Al Jazeera and other media outlets bestowed on it the title "Friday of Rage." After Morsi became president, the naming of Fridays continued. Protesters against Morsi and the Muslim Brotherhood labeled one the biggest protests against him the "Second Friday of Rage."

After the ouster of President Morsi, the Muslim Brotherhood organized the Malyonyat Jumua't al Ghadab (the Million-Person March of the Friday of Rage) against General el-Sisi, followed by the Million-Person March against the Coup, the Million-Person March of the Martyrs, the Million-Person March against the Terrorist Coup, the Million-Person March of the People to Protect the Revolution, the Friday of Loyalty to the Blood of the Martyrs, the Friday Million-Person March of the Youth Foundation of the Revolution, and marches against the coup.

Friday as a theme has been a gold mine for Al Jazeera in terms of generating easy, prepackaged news. For an outlet that thrives on instant news, the existence of Friday as a ready-made news theme has been a cash cow. The Friday stories generate the interest of Arab publics while stoking political controversy. For example, in the new political configuration of Egypt, the Ministry of Religious Affairs imposed a number of bold decrees: (1) The same Friday sermon should be read in all mosques; (2) *zawaya* (brotherhoods or maraboutic spaces) should not hold a Friday congregational sermon unless the mosques are located far from their neighborhoods; (3) imams or preachers should not be members of political parties.

In sum, Friday as a day of rage, as a bullet of truth, is becoming an expression of the desire for democracy, civil rights, and freedom. All citizens, religious and secular, claim Friday as an important day for mobilization or demobilization of the masses. The process of emancipation of the Arab world must also include the emancipation of Friday for all, such that the religious connotation is just an expression of identity and not a call to establish a religious regime. Al-Qaradawi himself promoted the ideals of democracy more than any other preacher before the rise or after the fall of the Muslim Brotherhood in Egypt.

8 ISLAM NEAR AND FAR

If your anger is provoked and you don't get angry, you are a jackass. . . . We should get angry. If somebody cursed your father or your parents or your mother, you might fight him and even kill him. If somebody is insulting your religion, your faith, and your Prophet, what do you do?

—Yusuf al-Qaradawi (Al Jazeera, September 17, 2006)

We call on Muslims to get angry for God, his Prophet, and his Book.

— Yusuf al-Qaradawi (Al Jazeera, September 17, 2006)

We can get angry. Some Muslims, all they possess is anger, true anger; to protect the Messenger of Allah is required and legitimate. We have the right to defend our family and our honor; it's our right to be angry. But our anger must be calculated and we must not act recklessly.

—Yusuf al-Qaradawi (Al Jazeera, September 16, 2012)

If they don't allow us to build the [Turkish] mosque in this location [Amsterdam], Al-Jazeera will bring the news to the world.

—Ahmed Soulu, quoted in *Het Parool* (May 15, 2007)

We will devote this episode of *In Depth* to the growing phenomenon of Islamophobia in the world in general, and specifically in Europe and the United States, and its transformation to an industry supported by different institutions.

—Ali Dafiri (Al Jazeera, March 3, 2013)

Islam in the West: From Extinction to Revival

A photograph of a crescent moon atop the Eiffel Tower adorns the June 22, 2006, cover of the *Economist*, accompanied by the title "Tales from Eurabia." It was a year when cartoons insulting the Prophet Muhammad set off angry protests across Europe. The *Economist* termed the cultural border between Europe and the Middle East and the resulting contentious relationship between Europe and its Muslim population "Eurabia." "Eurabia" and other terms such as "Londistan" in the United Kingdom and "Borgorokko" in Belgium were more effective at inducing fear of Islam in Europe than describing actual conditions on the Continent. The cover story in the *Economist*'s Eurabia issue confirmed as much, stating, "For the moment at least, the prospect of Eurabia looks like scaremongering."

This fearmongering with respect to Islam in Europe and the West has two major sources: first, the growing presence of visible Muslim communities in Europe; and second, the terrorist attacks on the World Trade Center in New York in 2001, the Madrid train bombings in 2004, and the London subway bombings in 2005, perpetrated by extremists in the name of Islam. These events radically changed the way Muslims in the West are viewed to this day, feeding a cycle of fearmongering and sporadic eruptions of cultivated anger by Muslims. This Muslim backlash is often led by international Islamic leaders and satellite television broadcasts in Arabic, Turkish, and Urdu. Muslims, including non-Arab Muslims, increasingly turn to Al Jazeera as a source of empowerment in the face of this widespread fearmongering and perceived Islamophobia.

Ahmed Soulu, a Turkish representative of the Aya Sofia Mosque, the largest Turkish mosque in Amsterdam, promised Dutch politicians there would be negative media attention and negative political ramifications if the demands of the Turkish community to rebuild their mosque were not met. He cited the media frenzy over the Danish political cartoons as an example of the kind of uproar such attention might garner. Many Muslim groups and organizations in Europe feel empowered by Al Jazeera in the face of a rising Islamophobia from a powerful Far Right.

In *The House of War: Dutch Islam Observed*, I explored what I call the trifecta of coercion: coercion of Europe's Muslim migrant community from below, from within, and from above:

> Coercion from below is how one's migrant status affects common and even universal pressures—the pressure to make a living, to succeed in one's profession, to have a place in one's community, but the way that this coercion occurs among migrant imams and the influence that the imams consequently have throughout the European Muslim community is strongly significant to the issue of integration. (Cherribi 2013)

The second element of the trifecta, coercion from within, refers to the pressures experienced both by individual European Muslims and by their communities. This pressure is produced by the conflict between messages conveyed by the larger society and the Muslim religious establishment.

Coercion from above, the third element of the trifecta, is twofold. It is exerted both by official Islam, represented by embassies and government programs, and by radical unofficial Islam, represented by a message of Muslim transnationalism and anti-Western activism. Radical unofficial Islam uses official Islam—governments, civic organizations, and their programs—as vehicles for gaining access to poor, uneducated, and isolated immigrants. For radical unofficial Islam, Europe is a hunting ground and its quarry is the disenfranchised seeking empowerment. This coercion is also brought to bear against well-educated and affluent European Muslims through the Muslim migrant underclass, whose very presence at times makes the more economically advantaged or more literate feel guilt or estrangement. Within them the ancient question persists, "They are Muslims and I am Muslim, but surely we are entirely different individuals?" (Cherribi 2013, 5).

I argue that "Europe's Muslim 'problem'" is the result of the trifecta of coercion, the construction of which has been greatly aided by the media. Al Jazeera played an instrumental role in this process. It did not create the concept of Eurabia or the problems Muslims face within their communities. However, Al Jazeera interpreted the contentious events involving Islam in Europe and the West in a manner that fueled the anger of Muslims and their rejection of European civilization. Al Jazeera promotes identification with the larger Islamic *umma*, a transnational Islamized sphere that includes Muslim communities in Europe and in the West, as well as those in the Middle East, North Africa, and Asia. The notion of *umma* functions as a protective shield against expressions of racism and Islamophobia (Cherribi 2011). Islamophobia and Al Jazeera's framing of Europe and the rest of the West are both forces that alienate Muslims.

Arkoun argues that the modern history of Islam starts with 9/11, a watershed that alienated Islam completely from the West (Arkoun and Maila 2002). Nilufer Göle calls the attacks a turning point in global relations, where Islam is now perceived as a threat to civilization (Göle 2011, 81). In this environment, Al Jazeera became the most significant interpreter and voice of meaning of all subsequent events for captive publics in the Arab world and its diaspora in the West. As a dominant media player in the Arab world, it succeeded in playing the role of defender of Islam, the Arabic language, and vulnerable Muslim communities worldwide (Miles 2005). In this chapter I examine how Al Jazeera used pivotal events such as the legislation prohibiting the veil in French public schools, the Danish cartoons of the Prophet Muhammad, the statements by Pope Benedict XVI about the Prophet, the Paris riots, the ban of the *burqa* and *niqab* (full face cover), the *Innocence of the Muslims* movie controversy, among other things, to promote frames of identification with the larger *umma*.[1]

Al Jazeera enthusiastically promotes these frames. For example, it featured the Islamic veil a key element in the struggle for Islamic identity, cultivating a certain level of anger within Muslim communities in Europe and the West. Al Jazeera consistently frames anger as a normal and healthy reaction by Muslims to attacks on Islamic identity. The right to wear the veil and to command respect for the

Prophet forms the backbone of the network's tangible identification strategies. The amount of programming and number of news reports on the veil is signifi-cant. Al Jazeera typically frames the battle for the veil in heroic terms, describing the "resistance of the Muslim communities" in France to "arbitrary" rules of the "godless" French. Khadija Bengana, the premier Al Jazeera female anchor, wore the veil for the first time during an interview with the French minister of interior amidst the legislative debate in France over the veil and Turkish prime minister Recep Tayyip Erdogan's push for acceptance of the veil in public office and in state institutions after decades of a ban against the veil in Turkey. A look at the data from 1996 to 2013 clearly shows Al Jazeera's agenda of promoting the veil and a resulting backlash in the West.

A significant percentage of Al Jazeera's programs, such as *A Rendezvous with the Diaspora* (*Maw'idun fi al-mahjar*) and *Sharia and Life*, focus on the Arab and Muslim diaspora in the West, specifically in Europe. Al Jazeera's coverage of the French veil debate in the early 2000s boosted Al Jazeera's prominent position within the Arab and Muslim communities in Europe and elsewhere in the West.

Al Jazeera's reputation benefited from three types of events during this time: first, events framed as examples of Islamophobia, such as the legislation against the veil in France, the ban on minarets in Switzerland, and the ban on the *burqa* and *niqab* in the Netherlands; second, events related to Muslims as a whole, such as the cartoon controversy in the Netherlands, statements by the pope, and the movie *Innocence of the Muslims*; and third, events framed as cel-ebrating the achievements of Arabs and their communities, such as the building of mosques and the success of Muslim entrepreneurs and scholars.

These three types of events are regularly covered by Al Jazeera. All of them fall under a larger frame, *ghorba*, which is defined by the Algerian sociologist Abdelmalek Sayyad as burning nostalgia for one's country of ancestral origin. Al Jazeera became the place to cool off the burning *ghorba* of Europe's Muslim diaspora by transforming the country of origin into an integral part of the *umma* and the holy places of Islam and Islamic memory. Al Jazeera reinforced Islamic memory as a twenty-four-hour frame of reference for life by its adoption of Mecca Time.

In the following paragraphs, I will address the concepts of *hijra* (emigration) and Mecca Time, *ghorba*, and the impact of Bengana's decision to veil herself before an interview with the French minister of interior. The symbolic weight of an Algerian anchorwoman who speaks French like the French but also rep-resents a large North African community (5 million Algerians, Moroccans, and Tunisian) gave Al Jazeera an unmatched level of credibility in the battle over the veil in Europe.

Al Jazeera's Yusuf al-Qaradawi, president of the European Council of Fatwa and Research in Ireland, himself an emigrant for most of his life, also provides an important voice for the diaspora, occasionally becoming involved in heated topics like the French and British riots of 2005–2006 and 2011, promoting a stance of soft anger and calming the Arab publics. The strong perspective provided by Al Jazeera's reporters and commentators in these cases went beyond simply providing a Muslim perspective on current events in Europe. By confronting the issues from the point of view of Europe's Arab and North African immigrants, the network was testing the boundaries of European and Western hegemony over an international Muslim audience.

Ghorba, Hijra, and Mecca Time

The concept of time is an important ethnic and religious marker in communities of an ethnic diaspora (Laguerre 2004, 2011). The rhythm of prayers, religious holidays, and times of rest, such as the closing time of businesses on Fridays for Muslims, Saturday observation of the Sabbath for Jews, and Sunday church services for Christians, for example, serve as important cultural markers. Al Jazeera's introduction of Mecca Time as its operating time enhances the identification between Muslim communities in the West. As part of an informal experiment for this book, I asked twenty random mosque-goers in Amsterdam, Paris, Luxembourg, Atlanta, New York, Morocco, Kenitra, Rabat, Casablanca, and Tunis about the importance of Mecca Time. Most of them spoke about the centrality of Mecca in resolving discrepancies among Muslim countries about the time of prayer or the period of fasting during Ramadan. The issue of the official beginning of Ramadan was discussed on Al Jazeera by al-Qaradawi, who used as an example the Muslims living in Scandinavia or other locations where days are either very long or very short depending on the season, which throws off the number of hours one might be expected to fast. Most of the Muslims I spoke with said that in cases of doubt, people should follow Mecca Time. An Egyptian Dutch man told me that Hajar al-Aswad, the Black Stone of Mecca, is the center of the universe. He believes that if the Black Stone were removed, the whole world could collapse. "Wherever you are in the world, the geometry leads you to Mecca," he told me. For him, Mecca is the focal point of the world. When I asked him how he knows or where he got his information, he said that he heard about it on a television show that featured a French study on the importance of Mecca to the geographic stability of the world. He offered the massive Abraj al-Bait Tower built by the Saudis as "proof of that." Al Jazeera refers to Mecca Time as a central point around which the twenty-four-hour news operation rotates, seven days a week, exactly like the annual *hajj* where the pilgrims walk around the Black Stone seven times. Mecca is the city clock, or the "chronopolis," that determines the Muslim religious temporality for the global *umma*. By making Mecca Time the chronological metric of Al Jazeera, the network represents the central node linking all Arab publics, including those within the diaspora in the West, as satellites of the sacred city clock. The centrality of Mecca becomes even more important in the diaspora in that it reduces the impact of *ghorba*. The temporality of the Muslim diaspora is organized around Mecca Time as a religious reference, since all Muslims around the world have prayed daily, for the past fourteen centuries, toward Mecca. By adopting Mecca Time, Al Jazeera takes on the religious legitimacy represented by Islam's most holy city.

When al-Qaradawi calls via Al Jazeera for a Friday of Rage, the Friday becomes a chronological extension of the geography of Mecca, where Muslims communicate their "joys, sorrows, and intentions to Allah." Friday functions as an energizing force for the following week. It is the day when believers are infused with the energy to face the *qahr*.

Three characteristics define Friday: the congregational prayer, fellowship, and the infusion of spiritual energy for the next weekly cycle (Laguerre 2004, 57–81). Laguerre argues that Muslims of the diaspora who live in cities are haunted by a struggle to balance the cultural religious rhythm of their lives, according to Muslim temporality (hegemonic temporality), with norms of the host societies. Muslims see Western temporality as a Christian construct and believe it should be replaced by a more familiar Muslim one. Muslims of the diaspora live within their own Muslim temporality, parallel to the temporality of mainstream society. But in Muslim and Arab countries there has been a public debate since postwar independence from Western powers about using the Hijri calendar and having a day off on Friday. Maghreb countries were the last to introduce this change, although in Morocco there is a long break during the day for the Friday prayer but not a day off; Moroccans resume their work after the prayer.

Most of the Maghreb countries follow the Gregorian calendar, with some using Western names for months and others using the Arabic names of Islamic months. In the Mashreq and the Gulf, the Arab calendar is used. Another divide between the Maghreb and the rest of the Arabic world is the use of Arabic numbers in the Maghreb, as opposed to the use of Indian numerals in Arab countries. Al Jazeera, however, consistently uses Arabic numerals, breaking with the Gulf and Egyptian convention. Laguerre argues that the diaspora temporalities are an identity marker for Muslims. The same is true, he says, for many Jewish communities (Laguerre 2004).

The Battle for the Veil in Europe

France was the site of Al Jazeera's most spectacular success in advancing its image as the voice of a global *umma*. France is home to Europe's largest Muslim community, numbering more than 5 million. During the controversy surrounding what was called the "veil debate" in 2003, the network succeeded in taking center stage, especially in the eyes of Arabic-speaking viewers. The controversy came to be seen as an indicator of the difficulties the Arab diaspora faced in its attempts at integration in Europe. Al Jazeera, through its coverage of the controversy, managed to position itself as the hero and the defender of Muslim rights in Europe, especially after the Algerian anchorwoman, Khadija Bengana, chose to wear the veil. Bengana's sudden decision provided a clear message about Al Jazeera's stance on the debate. The network's extensive coverage of the veil controversy served as a bridge between intensive coverage of the war in Baghdad and enhanced coverage of Arabs and Muslims living in the West. In this sense, the network's coverage of relations between the Western and Arab worlds shifted from the war in Iraq to the war on the veil in Paris. In 2003, the *niqab* and *burqa* were not yet issues in Europe. The big issue in the European public sphere was the legislation to ban the veil in French schools. In this debate, Al Jazeera found a new cause to champion in its efforts to Islamize pan-Arabism.

As an issue, banning of the veil fits within what Robert M. Entman describes in *Projections of Power* as a "substantive frame" that "performs at least two of the following basic functions in covering political events, issues, and actors, "[Substantive frames] define problematic conditions or effects ... identify [their] causes ... endorse a remedy or improvement ... [and] convey a moral judgment" (2003, 5).

The issue of the veil in France was framed substantively by Al Jazeera as a problem not just for girls and women in French public schools but for all Muslims around the world. The moral judgment conveyed by Al Jazeera's coverage is clear. The problematic conditions are faced not only by Muslims in France, but by Muslims everywhere. And the causes are linked not only to the French interpretation of secularism but also to attitudes about the separation between church and state in Christian-majority nations, which stand in stark contrast to the traditional Islamic view of the relationship between religious and political spheres.

My corpus of data shows the variety of ways the veil appears on-screen during Al Jazeera's broadcasts. I draw on qualitative case studies of the network's most important coverage of the veil debate, the 2005 French riots and the controversial *Innocence of Muslims* movie. I also draw on discussions with scholars and observers, as well as my own interpretation of the discourse and the visuals appearing on Al Jazeera. The most common appearance of the veil on Al Jazeera is the one most often ignored by previous published studies of the channel: its presence in the advertising carried by the network. Throughout Al Jazeera's twenty-four-hour newscast, viewers are exposed to numerous ads encouraging women to buy and wear the veil. During the height of the debate over the veil in France, for example, the network ran an average of five veil ads per day. One such ad features a shoulders-up shot of a beautiful, fair-skinned woman with blue eyes and elegant makeup, wearing a tightly drawn white-and-black scarf that covers her hair and extends over her shoulders. This is not a Hermès scarf of the kind that Sophia Loren might have worn in a 1950s film. This is pure Islamic chic, modestly stylish and severe in conforming to religious rules on color and form. A wealth of psychological research demonstrates the power of visuals for human processing and retention of information (Graber 2001). Research on the impact of advertising has shown that the context in which ads are embedded, or what comes before and after an ad, is often important for retention and subsequent consumer behavior (Bronner and Neijens 2006; Moorman et al. 2005). I do not make any claims as to the effectiveness of the veil ads on Al Jazeera in terms of veil sales or increased incidence of veiling among women, nor do I the argue that there is a specific link between the choice to air veil ads and news coverage about the veil. I only wish to point out that the veil is often presented in a glamorized form throughout the day in routine advertising, even when it is not the subject of news and current affairs programs. One could draw a parallel with the Christian Broadcasting Network's ads for Christian music that fill much of the advertising space on that American channel.

With that advertising context in mind, I turn to my case studies of Al Jazeera's coverage of the veil debate in France. The issue came to the forefront of the public discourse in mid-2002 after two French students were thrown out of school for refusing to unveil themselves. The controversy led to legislation banning the veil, as well as other religious symbols, in public schools in January 2004. During that period, the debate leading up to the Iraq War in March 2003 eclipsed the veil on Al Jazeera's news agenda for an extended period. Using the Arabic Al Jazeera search engine, which enables one to search all programs and their transcripts, I searched the keyword *hijab* (the Arabic word for "veil") to identify the number of times it was the focus of a program, an episode, or a news item.

Between December 2002 and April 2005, the veil was the subject of no less than 282 episodes of current affairs programs and longer news stories aired by Al Jazeera. I read the transcripts of each of these and identified the most important examples of veil coverage from Al Jazeera's current affairs programming, based on length and audience size.

The veil was also the focus of dozens of bulletins or very short news items during the channel's daily programming not counted among the 282 substantial treatments of the veil just mentioned. I also counted no fewer than 676 instances of current affairs episodes of programs and news stories from 2005 to 2013 dealing with the veil, the *burqa*, and the *niqab*. In the following section, I begin with some highlights that exemplify the tenor of Al Jazeera's reporting on the veil before turning to examine four case studies of the network's portrayal of the veil in its current affairs programs.

Al Jazeera aimed to report on every incident concerning the veil in Europe and around the world in its headline news programs each day. Al Jazeera uses the term *hijab*, which I translate here as "veil." Al Jazeera saw the veil as an issue of great importance. The channel sought out news on the veil that other outlets often failed to highlight. The four examples of prime-time programming below illustrate how the channel planned highly visible current affairs programs on the veil, positioning itself at the center of the debate and promoting European treatment of the veil as an issue of global importance.

Al Jazeera's news reporters', anchors', and guests' prediction of a negative reaction among Muslims around the world to the French ban on the veil proved to be an understatement. By August 29, 2004, video footage of two kidnapped French journalists in Iraq reading a prepared statement from their captors had been rebroadcast by most European news channels after first appearing on Al Jazeera. The statement indicated that the journalists would be killed unless the French government ended the ban on veils in French schools within forty-eight hours.

The first example I offer of Al Jazeera's coverage of the veil debate is that of the anchorwoman Khadija Bengana's decision to wear the veil in the midst of the uproar over France's law banning the veil in schools. This change in the anchorwoman's appearance led to press coverage throughout the world, largely praising her bold decision. I draw on coverage in both the Arab and world media to discuss the impact of her decision. The weekly program *Today's Interview* provides the second example, in which a renowned French intellectual, a convert to Islam, outlines his highly critical take on the French legislation. The third is an episode of the weekly program *Sharia and Life* in which French secularism is portrayed as a sort of wedge between the country's young Muslims and their identities. As noted previously, *Sharia and Life* boasts an audience of some 10 million and is hosted by the highly respected religious scholar and imam Yusuf al-Qaradawi. The fourth case is an episode of Al Jazeera's Arabic version of *Crossfire*, in which two people debate a divisive current events issue each week, with the veil featured prominently in the program, as I will discuss. In each of these well-known current affairs programs, which are replayed at least three times a week on the twenty-four-hour news channel, the issue of the veil in France received considerable attention, with a perspective challenging the ban on the veil disproportionately represented in each case.

Veiling the Star Before the Big Interview

The website Arabian Business made Khadija Bengana number 59 on its 2012 list of the hundred most influential women in the Arab world. The blurb accompanying her name on the list focused on her decision to wear the veil, reading, "Khadija Bengana has become one of the most familiar faces on Middle East television. Her defining moment as a journalist—and as a public face of the women of Islam—came when she decided to wear her *hijab*, on air, just one day before the Eid al-Fitr holiday. Overnight her cropped, modern haircut and trendy Western-style blazers gave way to a salmon-colored [dress and] veil, sparking a mix of public emotions. Bengana worked in Algerian TV before joining Al Jazeera" (alkhabarnow.net, December 18, 2012).

Khadija Bengana is an icon for the large Algerian and Muslim community living in France. She not only comes from Algeria, where many still live with the trauma of a decolonization process that cost a million lives in the Algerian War of Independence. Bengana fled Algeria in 1994 when Islamic radicals threatened her life because she refused to wear the veil. This elegant Arabic-speaking anchorwoman, who also speaks fluent French, made a major political and cultural statement during the crucial period of the French national debate over the veil in 2003 and the subsequent passage of the legislation in 2004 by changing her look and donning a veil. Her decision attracted the attention of the world media (BBC News, November 25, 2003).

News reports from around the world on Bengana's first televised appearance as a veiled woman noted her salmon-colored dress and veil as a statement that modernity and a highly visible and distinguished career as a woman are wholly compatible with Islam. Her appearance in the veil was also described by various media outlets as a lesson to French society and the French government about the archaic nature of the legislation against the veil (akhbar.khayma.com). Arab media and religious leaders agreed that it was even more "humiliating" to the French when she wore the veil while interviewing then-French minister of foreign affairs Dominique de Villepin. Her eloquent, fluent French and her professional demeanor stood in stark contrast to popular notions about the cultural implications of the veil (Rai al-Youm, March 24, 2014).

The subjects of the interview with the minister of foreign affairs were the captive French journalists in Iraq, which by extension touched on the issue of the veil in France. The French government agreed to have the minister interviewed on Al Jazeera because officials wanted to use all available channels to communicate the government's stance to the kidnappers. However, Bengana's choice of dress turned the spotlight from the French prisoners to the French government's stance on the veil. By donning the veil, Bengana turned the issue of the veil into a personal matter. She also challenged norms governing the way successful, professional women should appear. Wearing the veil would have previously been unprecedented for anchorwomen on most Arab global channels (*Al Jazeera Magazine*, 2004). However, the timing of her change in dress, along with the implicit message it carried regarding a politically charged issue, also raised questions about the neutrality of the news anchor (Khamis 2006,56).

The move changed the unwritten rules of competition between Arabic satellite news channels such as MBC, Al Arabiya, and Al Jazeera by specifically targeting female viewers and widening the circles of identification for women in the audience who, although often unveiled, might still have a predisposition toward visual messages of religiosity (De Swaan 1997). The veil is a sign of cultural and religious belonging to the broader Islamic community (the *umma*) and a marker of civilization that Al Jazeera builds upon daily by delivering programming and messaging targeted to a wider Muslim and Arabic-speaking audience. Among non-Muslims, the veil imparts to the Muslim women who wear it a mark of distinction and otherness. The veil is also considered a form of protection against social ills. It is thought to bolster respect and trustworthiness and to provide a "crown" of distinction and aura of religiosity.

In an opinion article for the London-based Arab newspaper *Al Hayat* (June 26, 2003) entitled "Veil of the Head or of the Brain?" the well-known Arab poet Adonis, then living in France, wrote of Bengana's appearance, "The most important question in the Arab-Islamic media outlets was, 'is Al Jazeera going to keep her on board?'" The answer was yes. She remains veiled and visible on Al Jazeera today. Her popularity has increased because of what is seen as a bold action on her part. However, there has never been much public discussion over whether the network might have asked her to wear the veil. She is on record as saying it was an entirely personal decision. She has said that she wore the veil because she wanted to "defeat the devil" (BBC News, November 25, 2003).

The impact of Al Jazeera's programming on the veil can be found in both newsrooms and in public opinion. The prevalence of the veil on Arab news channels is growing. Since 1970, Egyptian TV has forbidden anchorwomen from wearing the veil, except on religious programs. In 2002, five Egyptian female TV journalists decided to wear the veil. The growing popularity of the veil among female journalists has made it difficult for Egyptian TV to find qualified, unveiled presenters. Moreover, 95 percent of Arabic-language schools of journalism now embrace the veil. Al Jazeera's example, in 2004, placed even more pressure on national broadcasters throughout the Arab and Islamic world to allow female newscasters to wear the veil (al-qaradawi.net).

The paradoxical embrace of the veil by the elegant Algerian anchorwoman who had once fled violent extremists in her homeland in 1994 rather than wear it provided a new narrative about the meaning of the veil. A July 25, 2005, story on Al Jazeera's Arab-language website reported that more female news presenters on various channels had begun adopting the veil themselves, making the veil the norm rather than the exception on Arabic news outlets. The story features photographs of anchorwomen from other Arab channels and offers praise for Bengana, whom the story credits for having started this trend (Almashaheer.com).

The French Exception

The show *Today's Interview* took a more direct, if less dramatic look at the debate over the veil, with a well-known French scholar depicting the controversy as driven by the convergence of anxieties peculiar to French culture and misconceptions about the links between Islam and terrorism. The show covers political, cultural, and religious issues and features a different interviewer for every broadcast. The presenters are both men and women (sometimes veiled and sometimes not). The show is not generally religious in nature, but it is not uncommon for guests to be very religious or to discuss the day's topics in religious terms.

A French expert on Islamic movements and political Islam, François Burgat, was the guest on *Today's Interview* on December 12, 2003. Burgat speaks Arabic fluently and is one of the most widely known converts to Islam in France. He was an outspoken critic of the French legislation, arguing that the veil is more a French obsession than a European one because of what he calls the "French exception." He explains that the French fear competition between Islamic culture and the existing French culture. He argues that this fear has led to a kind of criminalization of Islam in France.

In this appearance on *Today's Interview*, Burgat disentangled the relationship between religious fundamentalism and violence, stating that there is no agreed-upon scientific evidence to support this supposed link. Islamists, argued Burgat, had won elections in Turkey with no incidence of violence. He referred to Saudi Arabia as another country where fundamentalism is often falsely equated with violence. People who accuse the country of propping up international terrorism, he said, fail to acknowledge that the Saudis have been unable to control terrorist activity even within their own boarders after falling victim to numerous attacks.

The Global Mufti and the Veil

A common format on Arab television is a forum of one or more imams discussing questions regarding the Quran's answer to modern questions, or *Sharia* law. Al Jazeera's foremost such program, *Sharia and Life*, hosted by Yusuf al-Qaradawi, devoted an entire one-hour episode to the prohibition of the veil in France. By focusing on this uniquely Muslim topic, al-Qaradawi added legitimacy to Al Jazeera's programming and enhanced the network's international reputation as a good Muslim channel. Al-Qaradawi's reputation extends beyond the geographical borders of the Arab world. The then-mayor of London Ken Livingston, asked the French prime minister to reconsider the restriction on religious rights after the mayor had met personally with al-Qaradawi during his controversial visit to London in July 2004 (BBC News, July 7, 2004). In India, a Sikh religious leader with a strong respect for al-Qaradawi's views was reported by the French press as showing solidarity with France's veiled Muslims in September 2004, asking the French minister of foreign affairs, "If I take my turban off, will I not look like a hippie?"

On the program and through his website al-Qaradawi launched an Islamic crusade against the French ban on the veil. He also wrote an angry public letter to French president Jacques Chirac in which he openly criticized Al Azhar University's highest religious authority for endorsing a non-Islamic act. He was referring to the French minister of interior's visit to Cairo on December 30, 2003, where he met with the sheikh of Al Azhar to obtain his support for legislation banning the veil in French schools. The sheikh's endorsement of the French legislation sparked widespread anger among his religious colleagues, as well as the mufti of Egypt and numerous international Islamic organizations.

Spirited Debate

The Opposite Direction is a popular and controversial Arabic-language current affairs program. The host is a British university-educated journalist, Faisal al-Qassem, who has presented more than 220 programs since 1996. Among similar programs on other Arab channels, this program is the most popular. It is also intensely provocative, with al-Qassem and his guests discussing current events in an abrasive, sometimes rude manner. Common topics include tensions between the West and Arabs and Muslims, attitudes toward Arabs and Muslim migrants in Europe, conflicts and crises of democracy in Arab countries, and the future of pan-Arabism. The show consists of two guests (almost always two men) with diametrically opposed views debating the topic of the day, with al-Qassem acting as a moderator. Al-Qassem tries to make the case for each of the views at the start of the program, but once the discussion begins he routinely takes sides without admitting or recognizing that he is doing so. Very often, guests on the program wind up shouting at each other, their behavior devolving into what could fairly be described as temper tantrums. This is a relatively new phenomenon in the Arab TV landscape. Viewers are also invited to call in with questions. Al-Qassem often pushes his own point of view with suggestive or leading questions. For example, he once asked his guests, "Why doesn't the US want to make a distinction between jihad and terrorism?"

The use of the term "jihad" as a struggle for freedom is common in al-Qassem's commentary. He is also critical of the Gulf states for supporting "US imperialism." This flamboyant style and harsh criticism have attracted viewers to the program and sent its ratings upward. There have been multiple instances where a guest has become so angry that he walked off the set and left the studio. Some Arab countries have even withdrawn their ambassadors from Qatar's capital, Doha, in response to inflammatory episodes of the program.

On April 6, 2004, the renowned scholar of Islam Mohammed Arkoun, who served as a member of the French State's Committee on the Veil and who supported the conclusion of the committee in support of a ban on the veil in public schools, agreed to appear on the program to debate Ibrahim Khouli, a professor of Islam at Al Azhar University in Cairo, on the understanding that the show's host would not speak against Arkoun on air. Although the program started well, al-Qassem eventually began to interrupt Arkoun, stifling his attempts to support his argument and giving Khouli the opportunity to advance a one-sided argument that Islam and a secular state are incompatible.

Even for renowned scholars like Mohammed Arkoun, the format of the show makes it difficult to engage in any sort of public discourse that might diverge from the religiously infused rhetoric of the mediator. Many Islamic preachers see the separation between church and state as a product of Christianity. The power of the religious discourse on television is the fact that it can speak to a wide variety of publics with buzzwords and common religious symbols and imagery that have been inculcated in the audience for centuries.

Veiled Polarization

Hallin and Mancini's (2004, 67) typology of media systems concentrates on European and North American examples and the interaction of media systems with the political systems in these countries. There is the Mediterranean, or "polarized pluralist," model characterized by both strong state intervention and "savage deregulation"; the North European, or "democratic corporatist," model with a strong public broadcasting focus; and the North Atlantic, or "liberal," model in Britain, the United States, Canada, and Ireland with a market-dominated media system. Al Jazeera would fit easily into the North Atlantic, or liberal, model and would be comparable to CNN or other US networks if not for the hefty amount of religious broadcasting on the Arab channel. But given the constant religious messages by al-Qaradawi and others in the network's current affairs programming, even if one ignores the advertising of the veil throughout the day and the constant drumbeat of off-the-beaten-path stories about the veil in Al Jazeera's daily news program, one has to come to a different conclusion.

The image of itself that Al Jazeera tries to inculcate in the public mind—that of a network offering "the opinion and the other opinion"—is really an optical illusion that masks its religious grip in an increasingly fragmented Arab media field. Al Jazeera is not a liberal or neutral channel; rather it is a religious channel that occasionally provides airtime for a liberal or neutral perspective. The pluralist programming facade of Al Jazeera hides the active dissemination of a mono-denominational religious message. In other words, the straight news coverage givesa pluralist perspective, but the underlying religious message overtly advanced in the current affairs programs undercuts this semblance of balance.

Marc Lynch, in his book *Voices of the New Arab Public: Iraq, Al-Jazeera, and Middle East Politics Today*, discusses the wide variety of publics that Al Jazeera serves, including an "Islamist" public. He describes Al Jazeera as the Arab Fox News (2006, 47). Lynch rejects "reckless allegations about Al Jazeera's being some kind of 'Jihad TV' or an 'on-line *medrassa*,' the new Arab public sphere, given its ever-greater centrality to Arab life, actually under-represents Islamism" (2006, 83).

I agree with Lynch that Al Jazeera is more conservative than liberal and "consumed by questions of authenticity and identity" (Lynch 2006, 19). But I venture one step further to argue that the authenticity and identity provided by the channel's Islamic agenda is a resuscitation of the pan-Arabism that was declared dead for all intents and purposes after the successive failures of Nasser's Egypt. Using issues like that of the veil in France, Al Jazeera is working to build a global Muslim identity, to mobilize shared public opinion on this and other issues, and to construct an imagined *umma*, a transnational Muslim community.

The patriotic and energetic formats of Al Jazeera's programming may resemble those of Fox News, and the coverage is, like Fox's, laden with opinion, but the similarities end there. Unlike Al Jazeera's, Fox News's anchorwomen do not display their religious beliefs by wearing a cross or a veil, and the leading Fox News current affairs program does not feature a religious leader like al-Qaradawi who offers his interpretations of religious laws.

Al-Qaradawi spoke in this capacity following the 2004 Asian tsunami. Speaking as the head of the European Council for Fatwa and Research located in Ireland, al-Qaradawi delivered a sermon blaming immorality and a thriving sex trade in the region for bringing on the disaster, saying, "These [places] are notorious because of this type of modern tourism, which has become known as 'sex tourism. . . .' Don't they deserve punishment from Allah?"

The sermon was carried by Qatar TV and posted to al-Qaradawi's website (Al Jazeera, December 23, 2002). Lynch, Al Jazeera, and others tend to describe al-Qaradawi as a moderate, but this example paints him as the Jerry Falwell of the Arab world. The disconnect is especially important in this case, as the government of Qatar, treating al-Qaradawi as a moderate mainstream leader, relies on his religious edicts as the basis for its policy decisions or as ex post facto justifications for actions it has already taken. In this sense, it can sometimes be difficult to discern who is following whom.

The literature on media–government relations points out the problems of a relationship like that between al-Qaradawi and the Qatari government, especially in times of war and crisis, when the news is often international and event-driven. The term "indexing" refers to the shaping of the media index by the political elite that is subservient to government (Entman 2003, 5), suggesting that the news in a society could not be expected to provide an impartial account of war when journalists take their cues from national political elites who are likely to be on the same side of an issue, at least at the start of a war or crisis. And throughout such a crisis, news that relies on official sources is presented within the "contours of the [national] debate" (Livingston and Bennett 2003, 366). Indexing news to official input does not rule out reporter involvement in framing the story. Entman suggests that even though the White House dominates US news, it does not control the framing of the story. According to Entman, framing the news involves selecting "some aspects of a perceived reality, to highlight connections among them, and thereby to make a particular interpretation and evaluation more salient than others" (2003, 5).

The metaphorical model of the "cascade" that Entman formulates in his book *Projections of Power* (2003) to explain the shaping of frames projected into news about foreign crises, public opinion, and elite thinking is applicable to the analysis of a global media outlet such as Al Jazeera. Entman's model is confined to the United States and focuses on the power of the White House and government officials, as well as elite spokespersons, to influence the frames around issues in the news that influence public opinion. The feedback loops in Entman's model show the interactive and interdependent nature of the struggle over the framing of issues.

Bullets of Kindness: Response to French and British Riots

Aside from the veil and other religious issues, how does Al Jazeera cover news related to Arab and Muslim communities? How would one characterize Al Jazeera's coverage of the riots in France that began in October 2005? On the basis of a content analysis of its daily news programs as well as other popular current affairs programs, I contrast Al Jazeera's reporting with selected French and British networks' coverage of the same events. In doing so, I explore whether, and how, an Islamic perspective is evident in Al Jazeera's coverage of the riots in France. I also discuss the framing of this topic in connection with Al Jazeera's earlier coverage of the veil.

For Muslim viewers of Al Jazeera, especially those outside France who would have had no other source of local French news, the ban on the veil in French schools served as yet another example of a Western power imposing its will on a peaceful Muslim community. Al Jazeera's news and current affairs programs suggested that, by "invading" the Muslim community in France with legislation banning the use of religious symbols in schools, the French provoked a response from the entire international Muslim community. In the words of one Al Jazeera news analyst, "If you touch one finger, the whole body will react as one" (Indymedia, 2005).

Al Jazeera connected the story of the riots in France and the issue of the veil to the larger transnational Muslim community around the world. The network ran daily coverage of the Paris riots and made them a focal point of its prime-time evening news shows. One special report was titled "The Deeper Reasons Behind the Violence in Paris" (Al Jazeera, November 7, 2005). On programs like this, experts presented various explanations for the acts of violence and riots transpiring in France. Some blamed the widespread marginalization and poverty of Arab and Muslim migrant youth. Others blamed decades of failed attempts by the French government to integrate migrants of Arab and Islamic origins. The experts stressed the depth and complexity of the problems.

One man interviewed for the piece decried the treatment of the immigrant population by French police. "We left Morocco in order to work for my children," he said. "Even the Moroccan police [with their reputation for brutality and corruption] don't treat us the way the police here are treating us, nor do the Algerian or Tunisian police treat us this way."

Al Jazeera's coverage stressed the Arab and Islamic origins of the protesters. In reality, though, the rioters were representative of the suburban migrant population in France. Many were sub-Saharan Africans (many of whom are not Muslim) and Berber migrants from the Maghreb, who do not consider themselves Arab.

Al Jazeera's coverage of France's immigrant population rarely acknowledged this distinctions between the migrant populations, instead describing them as "Arab and Muslim" or of "Arabic and Islamic origins," with the "and" reinforcing a recurring Al Jazeera portrayal of Arab culture as inextricably tied to Islam and vice versa. This is a clearly identifiable, though subtly executed feature of Al Jazeera's riot coverage. Through this frame, the network effectively Islamized a social conflict that probably had more to do with ethnic and economic divisions than religious affiliation. Al Jazeera's choice of expert commentators reinforced this theme, as the network consistently turned to religious leaders, imams, and religious community members to provide the point of view of the immigrant community in Paris.

When reporting on the acceptance of Islam in Europe, Al Jazeera offers a far more favorable view of the British than the French. The secular star Sami Haddad presented a live episode of his program *More than One Opinion* in which he linked the French treatment of Muslim youth to the "savage" model of French colonialism in Algeria, quoting from the *Independent* (Al Jazeera, December 14, 2005), "The emergency law that has been given a new life in France was used [during the Algerian War]. It is a message that is characterized by screaming savagery. It means that France wants to deal with the immigrant youth in the same way it dealt with their grandparents more than a half century ago during the Algerian War." Haddad also accused the minister of the interior at the time, Nicholas Sarkozy, of manipulating the crisis to serve his presidential ambitions. This followed an introduction that had raised the question of whether the political success of the Far Right leader Jean-Marie Le Pen was a sign that France stood on the brink of a civil war.

Haddad went so far as to suggest that the conflict might prompt a mercy killing of the French model of secular integration that began in its colonies and has since been applied to immigrants within its borders. "Is this crisis a bullet of kindness to the body of France's forced integration model and an allegory of the French revolution's failure?" Haddad asked.

Meanwhile, the British newspaper the *Independent* argued that "freedom in France means prohibition of the headscarf for Muslim school girls, that equality means multiplication of unemployment of the French of Muslim or African origin in addition to discrimination in the public job sector. The slogan of fraternity means the failure of the policy of integration. Does this policy lead to burying the tradition, religious and cultural roots of the second and third generation of the children of Arab and Muslim migrants?"

Joining Haddad in the London studio were Dr. Mohamed Bechari of the General Federation of Muslims of France and the secretary general of the European Islamic Conference; Azam Tamimi, director of the Institute of Islamic Thought; and French senator Jacque Myard.

"You called this rioting," Haddad interrupted as Bechari attempted to comment on the unrest. "But some, . . . maybe the French press, want to see an emulation of the Palestinian Intifada and so called it Intifada." Just minutes after the episode began, Sami Haddad had posed the leading question, "Don't you think that all responsibility for alienating these citizens and the Muslim associations lies with the French government? They don't know whether they belong here or there."

"I don't think that there is a contradiction between belonging to the French citizenry and belonging to the Islamic faith," Bechari responded. "This is not a religious problem."

"There were some violent incidents in the UK in the eighties: Liverpool, Brixton, south of London, Bradford, and some weeks ago in Birmingham." Haddad continued, turning to Azam Tamimi, "All these [incidents] had to do with marginalization and poverty et cetera, but there were no cars set on fire as was the case in France. Do you think that the British model works better for the grandchildren, second and third generations of migrants than the situation now in Paris when it comes to the treatment of citizens of foreign roots?"

"In the name of God the merciful. Surely the Muslim is much more respected in Britain than in France. No doubt about it," Tamimi said. "Sir, France doesn't respect Islam or the Muslims when she conditions integration upon the removal of the headscarf from the head of the woman. . . . This is a fundamental right."

The discussion then turned to the fatwas of religious leaders, including Yusuf al-Qaradawi. In the face of Bechari's refusal to Islamize the riots and the violence, as many fatwas did, the secular Sami Haddad went out of his way to defend al-Qaradawi, saying, "Oh, sir, the elevated preacher Dr. al-Qaradawi issued a fatwa to help calm the hearts of these people."

Haddad went on to ask, "You know there are between sixteen and eighteen million Muslims in Europe. Do you think this phenomenon, this French disease will be contagious to all of Europe?"

Bechari's critical response, that the riots could spread to Belgium, the Netherlands, and Germany, seems now like a self-fulfilling prophecy. Small-scale riots would soon break out in Belgium, the Netherlands, and even peaceful Sweden; the consequences, however, were minimal.

Promoting Soft Anger and Calming the Arab Publics

Al Jazeera's religious voice, embodied by Yusuf al-Qaradawi, is a fundamental element in the construction of the network's dominant narrative (Cherribi 2006). Broadcasts of the mufti's weekly television program, alongside posts to his website, together form a rich source of information about Al Jazeera's message of an

Islamized pan-Arabism. Just days after the riots began, al-Qaradawi appeared on the main evening news calling for calm and openly opposing all expressions of violence. He eloquently described the hardships endured by France's marginalized immigrants, from government policies limiting their access to health care and employment to rampant discrimination and racism. He urged the French government to open a dialogue with its immigrant population, particularly second-generation Muslims and Arabs. Al-Qaradawi expressed his opposition to the violence and destruction taking place in African and Muslim enclaves of French suburbs and cities, saying, "We regret very much the escalation of violence to the level of burning cars and public property and the harming of public goods, including those of the French state. I hope that these sacred days after Ramadan will bring peace and friendship, and we wish you well [Muslims in France] for the holidays." "As Arabs and Muslims, we wish France and its friendly people peace and security, especially considering that French positions on Arab and Islamic causes are more just and free than [those of] the American hegemony," al-Qaradawi added, calling on political and religious leaders in France to work together (Al Jazeera, November 17, 2005).

Amidst this call for restraint, though, al-Qaradawi also singled out the French president, blaming Jacques Chirac's actions for perpetuating the hostile atmosphere on Paris' streets: "What I did not expect was that President Chirac would intervene himself in this struggle and make this decision," he said. "I thought President Chirac was the only one who could solve the problem and work on a kind of understanding by asking Muslim men and women and Muslim leaders if the veil was a religious obligation, because we cannot forbid a Muslim woman from fulfilling her duties toward Allah. This is something that logic will not allow. We were surprised by President Chirac's decision, based on [the recommendation of] a committee that he himself nominated and, that, with all regrets, contains people who have no link to Islam, do not understand or know Islam, do not distinguish between the licit and illicit and are not engaged with Islam" (Al Jazeera, November 17, 2005).

It is important to note the role of Faisal al-Qassem, the presenter of the most popular political discussion program, *The Opposite Direction*, in Al Jazeera's coverage of the riots. The riots were the topic of discussion during the weekly program's November 8, 2005 broadcast. Al-Qassem was joined by two Arab guests of opposing views and two French citizens, who also represented opposite sides of the debate. Al-Qassem's on-screen demeanor is a more aggressive, Arab version of the hosting style of BBC's *Newsnight*'s Jeremy Paxman or Fox News's Robert Beckel. In keeping with the show's usual format, al-Qassem began the November 4 broadcast by presenting a series of compelling questions with the show's dramatic opening music in the background.

"We ask three questions," al-Qassem begins. "Are the riots that France is witnessing organized or spontaneous? Why has Paris failed to contain the crisis and does this have something to do with personal political calculations? And has the integration policy that Paris has followed for years failed? The death of two African teenagers by electric shock after running in fear from a police raid led to the igniting of flames in the suburbs of Paris for eight consecutive nights. This crisis reaches beyond the everyday lives of people in the cities and the suburbs and has placed France's model of integration in the balance. But the minister of interior, who aspires to become the next president of the French Republic in the coming election, sees the 'rabble' that has committed these acts of violence and says law and order must be restored the hard way. But eight nights of fire showed that the crisis is deeper."

A clip from a news report by French Al Jazeera correspondent Abdelkader Damich links the crisis to the broader history of immigration in France, reminding viewers of Chirac's own Algerian immigrant origins. Damich describes life in the immigrant suburbs where "the flames of despair were nestled for a long time in the ghettos." Damich goes on to describe life for residents of the ghettos:

> The children of the migrants are theoretically French citizens, as the laws of the Republic tell us. It's easy to distinguish them by their habits, behavior, and their religious rituals. It's easy to recognize them because they are generally without jobs, and frequent or inhabit poor neighborhoods. Their days start with coffee and bread, and family fights, and fruitless trips in search of work. If we take a moment to reflect on the available examples, we will understand their destiny and their identity. Are they French or not French? . . . Will the wall of social and ethnic apartheid be removed from the continent of the Berlin Wall? Or has the old continent lost, in France, the kindness of civilization?

The presenter immediately turns to Abderrahmane Dahmane, a high-ranking member of the governing party in France for a response. Dahmane, an ethnic Moroccan who speaks Moroccan Arabic, talks exclusively in French throughout the program, with Al Jazeera providing a voiceover by an Iraqi-accented translator. For North African viewers in France, the accent serves as a reminder of Iraq and the Palestinian Second Intifada, which Al Jazeera often links together. Dahmane denounces all acts of violence by the rioters as unjustifiable, siding with the French government and playing into Al Jazeera's portrayal of him as a traitor to the Arab people.

Al-Qassem responds by painting Dahmane as an apologist for the French establishment. "Why are you a greater royalist than the king?" he asks—an expression that might be analogous to calling someone "more Catholic than the pope." Al-Qassem tells the rest of the panelists that Dahmane "has forgotten the dramatic situation and the problems of the people living in the degrading human conditions of the ghettos, and he instead speaks about Muslim terrorists. Is this a matter of Muslim terrorism or a matter of a racist state that treats the poor in a way that is not different from the apartheid regime in South Africa?"

Haytham Manaa, a Middle Eastern immigrant to France and representative of the Arab League of Human Rights, responds by describing the immigrant experience in France as "a situation of total desperation." Dahmane counters by saying there are twelve thousand doctors and many university professors from North Africa and other Arab countries working happily in France. He does not deny the existence of discrimination or even outright racism in the job market and in society, but he also avoids endorsing his fellow guests' depiction of the situation where immigrants live as a colonized people within France. Instead, he stresses that political engagement, rather than rioting, is the only way to solve these problems.

Manaa fires back, "Breaking things is the only option left for these young men, who are marginalized and pushed out of the whole system, from the media, from work. Fifty percent of young [immigrant] men who have a doctorate or high school diploma are out of work because of their features. . . . These young men have only one way to express their capacities, culture and identity, and that is destruction. Nothing is left to them. This policy needs to change; otherwise they will keep coming back to this style [of protest]. They have no means other than the stones of the Palestinians armed for Intifada, because they have no legitimate means of participation."

"I don't believe in violence," responds Dahmane. "My Islamic culture, my Moroccan culture make me a wise man who knows how to defend himself in a civilized way. I don't call on young people to go rioting in the streets. I want them to organize themselves in a political way. Today we are presenting the worst image of our society."

Al Jazeera's main evening news approached the story of the riots in France in the same way it had the story of the veil in France, relying heavily on the expertise of Yusuf al-Qaradawi, featuring the imam on regular appearances as a guest commentator, in addition to the multiple reruns of his weekly show, *Sharia and Life*, aired throughout the week. His message was clear: the French government must engage French Muslims in a dialogue to examine possible solutions to the problems experienced by the community. Al Qaradawi also asked the Muslims in France to help the French government and local authorities restore order. During this period, al-Qaradawi took on the role of peacemaker, remaining above the fray in the often ugly interchange between those sympathetic to the rioters and those sympathetic to the government.

Al Jazeera's reporting on both the veil and the riots in France can be seen as part of a broader attempt at creating an ideological regime based on religious identification. The network's reading of the events in France was instrumental in driving forward an Islamized pan-Arabic discourse over the events for a number of reasons:

1. Al Jazeera's base in the Middle East and consequent proximity to Palestine (including Gaza) and, even more important, to Iraq, which, together with Syria, was seen as one of the last strongholds of Arab nationalism in the region at the start of the millennium.
2. The network's success in linking issues like the riots to the marginalization of North African migrants.
3. The framing of the discord as representative of an overall failure of the French model of "forced" integration and myths about the values of the French revolution: liberty, equality, and fraternity.
4. The linking of the French measures to contain the riots to French colonial actions against Algerians.
5. The argument that any acceptable solution to the problems of migrants in France must be based on the recognition of their Arab Islamic identity.

Can Al Jazeera Criticize Al Jazeera?

Pierre Bourdieu's title posing the question *Can TV Criticize TV?* (see Schneidermann 1996) seems particularly appropriate in reference to Al Jazeera. The network has devoted a number of programs to examining its own contributions to the world of media and journalism. For instance, it spotlighted a 2006 study by Hugh Miles, who went to Egypt, Palestine, the United States, Switzerland, and France to study how Arab publics watch Al Jazeera. He was very positive about Al Jazeera, which he saw as a form of media resistance to the Western model. Al Jazeera clearly constructs itself not only as an Arab media outlet but also as an Arab bulwark against the hegemony of the United States and Western media.

Al Jazeera portrayed the Paris riots as a direct extension of French secularism's incompatibility with the religious and cultural diversity of Arab and Muslim guest workers from former colonies, as well as their children and grandchildren. By drawing parallels between the riots and the Palestinian Intifada, the network painted the suburbs of Paris as a mirror image of the West Bank and Gaza. During the riots, al-Qaradawi appeared on the main evening news to give a fatwa on the riots, further Islamizing the conflict in the eyes of viewers and providing religious leaders and religious organizations an opportunity to enter the national debate and claim the role of broker in the hypersecular atmosphere of French politics. The weight of al-Qaradawi's words in this capacity is evidenced by the visit of French dignitaries to Qatar to meet with the mufti personally.

Copenhagen in the Year of the Cartoon Prophet

Over the past two decades, Al Jazeera has positioned itself as the Arab world's preeminent voice in major controversies between the Arab Islamic world and the West. For three months, after the infamous cartoons of the Prophet concealing a bomb beneath a turban were published in the Danish newspaper *Jyllands-Posten*, there were no massive protests on the Arab street or in Denmark. It was not until Al Jazeera ignited a media frenzy over the cartoons that the issue became an object of discord throughout the Arab world, sparking international boycotts of Danish products. Once Al Jazeera and Saudi Arabia's Al Arabiya began reporting on the cartoons, they become a focal point of meetings of the Arab League and the Conference of the Islamic States.

On September 30, 2005, *Jyllands-Posten* published twelve cartoons depicting the Prophet Muhammad. One of the depictions shows the Prophet wearing a turban, which appears to conceal a bomb. Another one shows the Prophet wielding a sword. The cartoons did not go without negative feedback in Denmark. The *Jyllands-Posten* received some angry letters. A number of Muslim diplomats voiced complaints about the comments, and five thousand people demonstrated in Denmark's capital toward the end of October. However, there were no significant international incidents. Over the following six months, though, the efforts of individuals like the Palestinian imam Abu Laban, who had studied in Egypt, worked in the Persian Gulf as engineer, and moved to Denmark with his family in the mid-1980s, succeeded in bringing the cartoons to the attention of the international Arab media and political elite. Along with the help of the Arab blogosphere, Laban succeeded in linking the Palestinian–Israeli conflict to a larger problem between Islam and the West. Al Jazeera and Al Arabiya were instrumental in providing reporting and programming that supported this link.

The Vatican's Jihad Revisited

Pope Benedict XVI's comments on Islamic history followed a similar media arc. Al Jazeera's reporting on the pope's words allowed for only one interpretation: the pope had shown a pronounced disrespect for Arabs, Muslims, and Arab Islamic civilizations. The story was framed as part of a larger "American-Christian-Zionist conspiracy" against Islam and the Arab world. Al Arabiya's reporting on the pope's comments was markedly less inflammatory than Al Jazeera's.

On September 12, 2006, Pope Benedict XVI delivered a speech entitled "Faith, Reason and the University: Memories and Reflections at the University of Regensburg, Germany." The pope questioned the concept of Jihad, or holy war, and quoted a fourteenth-century Byzantine emperor who said, "Show me just what Muhammad brought that was new and there you will find things only evil and inhuman, such as his command to spread by the sword the faith he preached" (BBC News, September 15, 2006).

Over the following days, the pope was painted as an "Islamophobe" by many who called in to the Al Jazeera and Al Arabiya shows, as well as by those who contributed to the discussion boards on their respective websites. In his Friday sermon from the Omar Bin al-Khattab Mosque in Doha, Yusuf al-Qaradawi called for the passage of "laws that protect the holy sites and the Prophets"

"The governments of the Arab and Islamic states and peoples should apply pressure on international bodies to enact these laws," urged the mufti, "to obtain an apology from these newspapers, and even to allow Muslims the opportunity to publish articles in the offending newspapers for an entire month to defend our Prophet, peace be upon him. . . . . It is the duty of the nations in this regard to boycott all goods from those who dared to insult the Prophet of God, peace be upon him, because money from the sale of these goods goes to them. The obligation, the duty is to boycott them politically by withdrawing their ambassadors to Denmark and closing their embassies at home." He stressed "the imposition of duty on every Muslim everywhere." Al-Qaradawi called on the Arab governments "to stand with people in the same trench . . . expressing Muslim unity and cohesion in the face of our enemies and prove to them that they must respond when they offend the Prophet and our dignity" (qaradawi.com).

Al-Qaradawi links the diaspora to the concept of *hijra*, which historically refers to the migration of Muhammad, during his flight from Mecca to Medina. He left his tribe and his social network as a heretic and a fugitive. However, Muhammad converted a majority of Medina's population to Islam. This moment is often seen as the beginning of Islamic history, but it has also been mythologized as a very powerful part of the Muslim imagination. Al-Qaradawi asks his followers in the Arab world to live like the companions of Muhammad in Medina. In other words, al-Qaradawi is telling his viewers to blindly follow him, as did Muhammad's followers in Medina. The *hijra* shows the distance between the representations that make up the imagery of the publics and the social realities interpreted by these representations (cf. Arkoun 1984; Lewis 1994; Rubin 1995).

This is not an entirely new concept. Historically, various interpretations of the *hijra*, lacking any reflexive or critical context, have provided demagogic preachers the necessary source material to legitimate almost any action.

Al Jazeera's TV preachers consistently engage in this sort of practice. They echo the words of contemporary militants, notably the word *jahiliyya*, which is condemned by the Quran. *Jahiliyya* is often used to label Western societies anti-Islamic. Islam, according to these TV imams, is synonymous with liberty and good in the past and for the future. There is no real liberty or real doctrine outside the realm of Islam, they claim. Their views of society are based on interpretations that have been propagated through the writings of orthodox militants and contemporary Muslim preachers hoping to instill public fervor in their audience.

It is important to note that the religious messaging on Arab satellite stations only increases calls for ever more elaborate rituals while steadily adding to the number of activities considered *haram* (forbidden). These forbidden things, based on *hadiths* (life lessons attributed to the Prophet) or Quranic verses serve to found and legitimate the operation of *ta h lil*, which is the action of rendering something religiously acceptable, and the *ta h rim*, which is the action of rendering something religiously forbidden. Transgressions against these rules can lead to *takfir* (excommunication). Even if al-Qaradawi has no real authority to prohibit Muslims from practicing Islam or to excommunicate them, by using these instruments of *ta h lil* and *ta h rim* al-Qaradawi adds to his symbolic power. The popularity of these interpretations, of course, may ultimately determine whether the imam has a dominant or weak position among his public.

Innocence of the Muslims

"How can this happen in a country we helped, in a city we helped save from destruction? Hillary Clinton could have said these words," mused Al Gharibi, the anchor of *Behind the News* (Al Jazeera, September 18, 2012), regarding the "American shock" following the terrorist attack on the US embassy in Benghazi, which took the life of the US ambassador, Christopher Stevens, and three other Americans. The attack dominated both North American and international news cycles. The attack occurred on the anniversary of the 9/11 World Trade Center attacks, just weeks before the US presidential election. It came amidst growing Muslim anger over a controversial movie, *Innocence of the Muslims* produced in the United States. "This is the anger of the street. This anger is being exploited by some elements that may have a private agenda," declared a guest on the show.

Friday, September 14, 2012, was a day of anxiety in the West. Embassies in Cairo, Sana'a, Khartoum, Tripoli, Kabul, and Islamabad were all on high alert, with the number of those demonstrating against *Innocence of the Muslims* in each of these capitals in the hundreds. Still, this was not as pronounced as the backlash had been against the 2006 Danish cartoons.

Al Jazeera's September 18, 2012, news report on the movie shows US officers in uniform putting into a police car a man whose face is covered with cloth and who is wearing baseball cap. A voiceover explains, "Nicola or what we saw of him [the man with the cloth on his face] . . . has been mentioned in relation to the anti-Prophet movie. This is his photograph, taken some days ago, showing him getting into a police car surrounded by journalists. If he listened to the news, he would know what kind of fire he has ignited in the world. Nicola Nasli was detained for interrogation by the police after being accused of bank fraud. But the freedom of speech he claims for himself didn't compel him to uncover his face, and he couldn't face the public given the things he has done."

Nasli is shown with fingers pointing at him from all directions. One photo shows Lady Justice pointing out the accused. A banner at the bottom of the screen reads, "Seven Copts abroad were accused of collaboration with the anti-Prophet movie." The Egyptian prosecutor has asked Interpol to arrest the "seven Copts" as well as Florida preacher Terry Jones, who had recently announced his intention to hold a mass Quran burning, viewers are told. "The crisis is burning every day," the voiceover intones over images of Jones's Florida church. "Google and YouTube didn't remove the movie from their search engines, as Muslims had requested."

Black-and-green flags reading, "There is no God but God and Muhammad is his messenger" fill the upper half of the screen. The scene cuts to footage of Indonesian women with white scarves gathering in front of a building as the reporter continues telling the audience that Egyptian associations have filed a lawsuit against Google for not complying with its own rules of service. "Google itself offered its apologies for an overly glamorized picture of the wife of the US president, Michelle Obama. Meanwhile, in France there is further commotion around an attempt to publish cartoons deriding the Prophet in a magazine, just hours after a French court ruled against the publication of photos of Kate Middleton and her husband, the Prince of Wales [Middleton had been unwittingly photographed topless while on vacation in France]. Is this a double standard in interpreting what provokes the anger of the public?"

On September 20, 2012, the publication of new cartoons depicting the Prophet in the French magazine *Charlie Hebdo* were the second topic covered by the evening news. "The minister of foreign affairs of France closed all its embassies in the Islamic world on Friday fearing protests against the anti-Prophet cartoons," said news anchor Abd Samad Nasser. "There will be protests on Saturday next to the Great Mosque of Paris."

The anchor offered harsh criticism of the French free speech law that allowed the cartoons to be published in the first place. It is important to note that Al Jazeera translated the word "cartoon" into the Arabic for image or picture. The confusion for the Arab viewer is important because the choice of wording eliminated an important distinction between the anti-Prophet drawings and the photographs of the Duchess of Cambridge that had been published in *Closer*, a French gossip magazine. A French attorney joined the program and explained that the French justice system could not shut down the magazine over the anti-Islamic cartoons. He explained that the cartoons fell under France's broad protection of freedom of expression.

"What happened to this freedom when the French justice did not allow the publication of the half-naked pictures of members of the [British] royal family?" asked the anchor. "The same justice is absent when it comes to Islam. Can we talk about a double standard here even when the two events are different?"

The attorney tried to explain the difference between a criminal case and the civil suit brought against *Closer*. Despite the attorney's efforts, the anchor succeeded in portraying the two events as two sides of the same coin.

Al Jazeera's reporting on *Innocence of Muslims* took a starkly different tone following the attack on the US Embassy in Benghazi. The network first described the producer of the film as an Israeli American working in real estate and living in California. It took Al Jazeera, as well as most other media outlets, two days to correct the mistake, reporting that he was actually an American Egyptian Coptic Christian. After the embassy attacks, the network downplayed the link it had helped to draw between the movie and the United States.

One commentator on Al Jazeera's Washington, DC–based show, *From Washington*, described the creator of the movie "hardly American." The show's host, Aberrahim Foukara, said that all the media outlets had been fooled by the rumor, leading to more chaos. A lot of people, he said, "could have paid the price" for the lax verification efforts by the media. "Certainly, that the US ambassador and his team in Libya were attacked with fire raises a very important question. How is it possible that the US Embassy was attacked on 9/11, 2012. Does it mean that somebody was waiting for a reason to harm the US?"

Al Jazeera's anchors also pointed the finger at radical elements close to Al Qaeda. Al Jazeera, like many Western media outlets, blamed the movie for inciting Islamophobia and hatred that could lead to more violence in the Muslim world. Parallels were immediately drawn between the movie and the Danish cartoons published in 2005. Despite Al Jazeera's role in stirring up anger over the cartoons years before, it drew a clear distinction between the cartoons and the film. As portrayed by Al Jazeera, the cartoons were a "secular event" but the intent of the film was to trigger religious hatred and racism and Islamophobia. Al

Jazeera commentators also noted how the film plays to the radical Salafi agenda. The cartoons were not intended to be blasphemous but to break a taboo against freedom of expression, whereas the film was rude, depicting the Prophet as a fool, a womanizer, and a fraud (France Culture, February 14, 2013). The network focused on Hillary Clinton's condemnation of the movie by calling it "disgusting"; also, the secretary general of the UN, Ban Ki-moon, condemned it as a hate film, and Pope Benedict XVI arrived that afternoon in Beirut with a message of peace to mitigate the confrontation between religions.

Al Jazeera also focused on the challenge that outrage over the video posed to Egypt's new head of state, Mohamed Morsi. The new president would need to demonstrate an ability to contain radicals and maintain security, or risk losing credibility with North American and European creditors. The network portrayed Morsi's reaction as solid and pragmatic, keeping a newly tranquil Egypt out of the fray. Morsi urged demonstrators to remain in Tahrir Square and to remain calm.

With the attacks occurring just weeks before the US elections, Al Jazeera interviewed radicals, fundamentalists, and evangelicals who expressed their hope that Romney would win. The Republican challenger was portrayed by the network as "a crusader," whose presence in the White House would push forward the jihadist agenda of a global war between Islam and the West.

Al Ghadab: Testing the Boundaries of the West

Most of Al Jazeera's slogans and program titles connote a platform for the vulnerable. Labels such as "those who need a podium," "the voice of the voiceless," and so on not only create a frame to guide perceptions of the network, but also contribute to a larger super-frame of *ghorba*, "the unbearable rift between a human being and a native place, between the self and its true home" (Said 1994), or "ethnospace" (Appadurai 1991), geographic displacement and its negative effects (el-Khachab 2010); this is a burning nostalgia or "yearning desire" felt by people in exile. This concept of exile applies to the Arab diaspora suffering from *qahr* of displacement and Islamophobia, but also to those living in Arab countries who suffer from *qahr* of injustice and arbitrary physical violence. *Al ghorba* is even the title of an Al Jazeera television show. The program is presented as a place for the *umma* to transcend all forms of *qahr*, including injustice and marginalization. Through this frame, Al Jazeera presents itself as the hub of a burning nostalgic virtual reality where all the parts of the *umma* unite to bear witness to and rectify their shared suffering through Friday demonstrations and mobilizations against the veil legislation in France, the Danish cartoons of the Prophet, Islamophobia in Egypt, the *hijra* (emigration) in the West, and authoritarian regimes throughout the Arab world. In this view, Al Jazeera is the salvation for the *exilio/insilio*, the internal exiles living under Arab dictatorship and the literal exiles of the diaspora in the West. Al Jazeera, running literally on Mecca Time, tries to be the epicenter of the Arab-Islamic world. Since everything revolves around Mecca as the center of the universe, where nostalgia or *ghorba* but also a yearning to be the founding moment of Islam, Al Jazeera becomes the virtual Mecca.

If al-Qaradawi was instrumental in galvanizing support for the boycott of Danish products and mounting a day of rage against the pope, he was even more successful in issuing a fatwa to calm mollify the Arab publics who were outraged by *Innocence of the Muslims.*

To put the controversy over the *Innocence of the Muslims* in perspective, it is important to understand certain realities of the geopolitical situation in the Gulf region. Since 1979 Iran and Saudi Arabia have been engaged in a contest over the leadership of political Islam. In this environment, every incident and event affecting the international Islamic community becomes an ideological battleground between these two countries.

The rise of Salafism has now complicated the situation for the countries of the Arab Spring, mainly Tunisia and Egypt. Secular movements there have criticized the practice by Islamists such the Muslim Brothers and members of the Ennahda party of deploying military might to protect Western interests, especially US embassies, from militant Salafists while doing comparatively little to protect the secular Muslims from the same Salafi radicals. In addition to the major divisions between Shias and Sunnis, there are equally important divisions within Muslim societies between moderate and radical Muslims of all sects. While, given the chance, the moderates tend to invest in democracy, most Salafis refuse to play the game of popular rule.

Obama's tepid embrace of the Muslim Brotherhood during his appearance in Cairo following Morsi's election actually put in place a powerful wedge between the ascendant Islamist power and the Salafi fringe. Salafis view complete separation of the Muslim world from the West as the only viable way to build Islamic governance in the region.

On a side note, it is worth pointing out that the Islamists of the Maghreb were not voted into power as part of a groundswell of support for theocracy, but rather benefited from the political opportunities created by secular movements. John Esposito asks a fundamental question that often seems lost in Western and Arab media reporting: "Who speaks on behalf of one billion Muslims?" The answer is certainly not the Salafis, who led the demonstrations against the *Innocence of Muslims.*

Al-Qaradawi's fatwa on Al Jazeera calmed a restless public. The mufti warned about protesters who might use the opportunity to stigmatize Islam. He advised that the protests be peaceful and "civilized." He severely condemned the attacks on the US Embassy in Benghazi, saying that Muslims should be hospitable to all their guests. This was a change in tone from al-Qaradawi's previous fatwas, which stressed mobilization and "controlled rage."

Because he is the president of the European Council for Fatwa and Research in Ireland, al-Qaradawi's fatwas regarding Muslims in the West carry special importance. As noted in my previous work, *In the House of War*, Muslim diaspora in the West, labeled *hijra*, have long been targeted by their countries of origin such as Turkey, Algeria, Morocco, Tunisia, and Pakistan, as tools for controlling political opposition and dissent at home, as well as a source of income for the state through the flow of remittances, money transfers sent by immigrants and their children. These governments tightly control the appointment of imams and the management of mosques in Western Islamic communities (Cherribi 2010). The diaspora Muslims have additionally been targeted by a variety of organizations (secular and religious, national and transnational) that want to reinforce the culture of their mother countries via media, religious, cultural, and educational activities such as lessons in Arabic, Turkish, or Urdu. Al Jazeera Arabic has the same goal of domesticating the diaspora by catering to the *ghorba* (burning nostalgia) with religious connotations.

Al Jazeera Arabic was born at a time when the Arabic-speaking diaspora was entrenched in a number of identity crises related to the rise of a new generation of Muslim Europeans and an accompanying rise of anti-immigrant and anti-Muslim parties in Europe. From its infancy, Al Jazeera catered to an emerging market of vulnerable Muslim communities, fashioning itself as a champion of their cause in the fight against racism and discrimination. However, Al Jazeera has always treated the Muslim citizens of Europe as an extension of the Middle East, while less accessible Muslims in the US market were considered out of reach. Al Jazeera has worked to extend its reach in recent years among non-Arabic-speaking audiences through its English-language website. The Al Jazeera English website does not (at the time of this writing) provide an index of the kind given on the Arabic site, and the English content often does not reflect what is found in the Arabic version. For example, the July 25, 2005, story on the French veil debate from the Arabic website is nowhere to be found on the English site. The two websites cater to very different audiences.

This is even more true of Al Jazeera's efforts to open the US market through its Al Jazeera America cable channel. The channel relies on a US-centered programming model rather than the international/Arab-focused product that is the topic of this book. After a little over a year on air, the channel has only around 13,000 viewers (*NRC Handelsblad*, November 20, 2013). However, this could be the beginning of a major expansion. Al Jazeera's programming model has potential for growth nearly everywhere and in every sizable language market. The network's focus on ordinary people, pension for bombastic reporting, and deft ability to deliver programing that tells a cohesive story across multiple programs could make it a tough competitor for US media outlets that face problems with declining viewership and audience fatigue (*Newsweek*, May 23, 2013).

9 THE EMANCIPATION OF POLITICAL ISLAM?

Ghannouchi: The Muslim world today needs an intellectual revolution . . . in order to be innovative and productive . . .

Arkoun: and be a contributor!

Ghannouchi: to be able to contribute to contemporary civilization.

—Rached Ghannouchi and Mohammed Arkoun (Al Jazeera, June 17, 2002)[1]

We didn't understand the value of freedom either in our Sharia or in our societies.

—Sheikh Abdel Fattah Moro (Al Jazeera, May 2, 2014)

On a beautiful summer day in early June 2013—just days before the eruption of protests in Istanbul's Taksim Square and the crumbling of the first Islamist parties to participate in the Egyptian political process—the Tunisian capital of Tunis had embellished its main streets in anticipation of a visit from Turkish prime minister Tayyip Erdogan. I was walking along one of the city's posh arterial streets, Avenue Habib Bourguiba. The street was adorned with hundreds of small red flags, each with a white crescent and star. From afar, you could hardly distinguish between the Turkish and Tunisian flags, since they look almost identical. Erdogan, who was and remains an active supporter of democratic political Islam during the Arab Spring, was greeted in a festive atmosphere by the Tunisian government and supporters of the Ennahda party, whose leader, Rached Ghannouchi, drew inspiration from the Turkish Justice and Development (AKP) party.

Erdogan's visit came at a significant time, against the backdrop of massive protests in Egypt against the Muslim Brotherhood and its party, the Freedom and Development (FDP) party. Tunisia was looking more and more like the only remaining hope for political Islam in the region. Turkey and Qatar focused their efforts on preventing an Islamist failure in Tunisia. The two nations had invested tremendous effort in supporting the development of Islamist parties in the Arab world.

Istanbul and Doha are the destinations par excellence for parties with an Islamic orientation. After the deposing of President

Morsi, Muslim Brotherhood strategists met in Istanbul in July 2013 to decide how the party would move forward. Qatar's capital, Doha, has been described as the capital of political Islam. Qatar has also been labeled the "sponsor" and the "impresario" of the Muslim Brotherhood (Kepel 2013, 290–298). Many summits on political Islam and the challenge of governance have been organized by exiled Islamists living in Qatar and attended by advocates of political Islam from around the world, such as Hassan al-Turabi (Sudan), Abassi Madani (Algeria), and Rached Ghannouchi (Tunisia). Qatar is home to the Doha Center for Arab Strategic Studies, a think tank and main organizer of the summit of political Islam, where leaders of Islamist parties throughout the Arab world meet.

Doha, site of Al Jazeera's headquarters, has achieved the status of a world-class power broker based on a "subtle" media power backed by oil money. Qatar derives its symbolic power primarily from the global reach and influence built by Al Jazeera since the network's creation in 1996. Doha also enjoys a reputation as a city of global diplomacy and entrepreneurship and as home to a bustling media empire. The so-called Doha Rounds of World Trade Organization negotiations are just one recent event spotlighting the growing global reputation of the city named by its emir the "sacred city of the vulnerable."

This unmatched regional influence has allowed Al Jazeera to shape Arab perceptions of the brand of political Islam to which the Qatari government has long been sympathetic. Al Jazeera's coverage of rising Islamist political parties also helped to smooth the rough edges of political Islam by holding a mirror up to them, giving decision makers the opportunity to abandon or adapt untenable positions.

The rise of Al Jazeera's transnational activism on behalf of disgruntled Arab publics using cutting-edge technologies and a rich multimedia platform led to three major transformations in the Arab world: first, the "Al Jazeera effect," which helped thwart twentieth-century government censorship tactics during the first revolutions in the twenty-first-century Arab world; second, the popular embrace of notions of pan-Arab unity, "freedom," and democracy, a kind of revolution against submission to autocracy; and third, the growth of organic political Islamic movements that can be described as revolutionary in the historically contentious relationship between Islamism and democracy. These three revolutions changed the dynamics of power in the Arab world.

The Palestinian Wadah Khanfar served as director general of Al Jazeera from 2003 to 2011. During an interview in Davos, Switzerland, during the World Economic Forum, Khanfar spoke proudly of Al Jazeera's role in paving the way for Arab awakenings from Oman to Morocco. He argued that the Muslim Brothers and political Islam will become more pragmatic in an era of newfound legitimacy than will secularist groups (Wadah Khanfar, *Guardian*, May 20, 2012).

On the Avenue Habib Bourguiba, the main artery of the Tunisian revolution, I stopped at the Dar Al Kitab bookstore. Many books about Qatar in French and Arabic were on display. I spoke with one employee about some of the books on Qatar. He ended up talking for almost an hour and a half about Qatar and Al Jazeera and how Qatar is perceived by Tunisians. He felt that Qatar promoted the agenda of the Ennahda party, and that's why it became more controversial in Tunisia after the revolution among the youth and non-supporters of political Islam. The same thing happened in Egypt when Al Jazeera promoted the Muslim Brotherhood agenda. However, Al Jazeera remains a staunch supporter of democratic political Islam, which sees the emancipation of its ideology as the only way for it to gain greater acceptance. If people want to proclaim their "Muslimness," it doesn't necessarily mean that they want Islam to hold too much sway over their lives!

The Al Jazeera Effect as Revolution

The Al Jazeera effect can be summarized as the dominant position Al Jazeera acquired at the inception of the transnational Arab media landscape. It succeeded in shaping the field from its infancy, imbuing it with new conventions and discursive and visual frames that would be adopted by any new media outlets subsequently entering the field. Al Jazeera enjoyed this advantage by virtue of its role as a founder of this new media field, which transcends the local political and media fields of individual Arab countries. People without satellite dishes used an improvised antenna made from a couscous pan in order to access the crisp visual content and discourse that served as a refreshing departure from the censored journalism provided by local broadcasters. From the start, Al Jazeera took the side of the Arab publics against their governments, enraging the entire political establishment in the Arab world. This Al Jazeera effect went beyond the media field, extending deeply into the politics of the Arab world, essentially subjugating both local political and journalistic discourse. The effect even branched into the religious, economic, and intellectual fields, further broadening the network's influence. The network's diverse and competent staff succeeded in promoting a kind of pseudo-neutrality to increase its dissemination of the "illusion of truth." In other words, the network succeeded in creating content that was persuasive without appearing argumentative. The network has become the fulcrum of a new political economy of visual and discursive goods and values in the Arab marketplace. The rapid proliferation and intense competition of Arabic satellite television with a rich online presence has grown to include more than a thousand satellite channels, many privately owned and many funded by Arab, Western, and non-Western states, competing for the hearts and minds of Arabs and Muslims living throughout the world. Satellite TV did not create the explosive chain of Arab revolutions but contributed diligently to the creation of the necessary conditions for change (Belkziz 2012, 270). An unprecedented media revolution accompanied the Arab Spring. The volume of live footage and constant coverage of the revolutions served to empower Arab publics. The competition for information during the Arab Spring has been intensified with the growth of cyber activism groups, both religious and secular.

The creation of Al Jazeera itself was a revolution in the Arab world that drove the political, religious, and cultural configuration of Arab regimes to change (el-Nawawy and Iskandar 2003, 31). BBC Arabic had 14 million listeners in 1994. With the financial support of Saudi Arabia, the BBC and the Saudis wanted to launch the most influential media outlet in the Arab world. However, because of the network's critical perspective on domestic issues in Saudi Arabia, the project ended (Abderrahim Foukara, Emory University, February 17, 2012). Qatar, which is roughly equal in population to Amsterdam, took over the project (el-Nawawy 2001, 32). Kraidy (2000) speaks about an asymmetrical interdependence between the network and its Qatari backers, since the effect of Al Jazeera is many times larger than its geographic size. In early 2000, 70 percent of Arab satellite TV viewers watched Al Jazeera (el-Nawawy 2001, 33). After 9/11, subscriptions increased 300 percent. Al Jazeera's niche in the market was perfect. Five years after the inception of Al Jazeera it employed 350 journalists across fifty countries. As a country that participated in the first Gulf War, Qatar succeeded in situating itself in the middle of the region's most contentious factions, Americans and Israelis on one side, Iraqis, Palestinians, and Syrians on the other side. Perhaps this offers some insight into the willingness of the Qatari-built news network to situate itself in the midst of conflict and controversy.

Al Jazeera brought an end to "mind numbing-years of drab propaganda, endless soap series, and outdated cabaret acts" (el-Nawawy 2001, 43). It also widened the circles of identification among Arabs. The host of *The Opposite Direction* was the son of a poor peasant family with eleven children (el-Nawawy 2001, 116). Al Jazeera's symbolic power grew stronger over the years as it put more distance between itself and its competition. Arab pundits, journalists, and commentators on Al Jazeera stress the power and the cutting-edge nature of its reporting. It was not only the expertise and mastery of the journalistic métier, but the affinity for regional fieldwork of its Arab and Muslim reporters and their possession of the cultural and linguistic capital necessary to work effectively in that field that allowed Al Jazeera to deliver powerful reporting on the second Iraq War. Western journalists needed translators and had different problems adjusting to Iraqi society when they were imbedded in military units or stayed within the Green Zone. Al Jazeera was seen as dominating the competition in Iraq, reporting on the real-life daily experience of poor Iraqis. Al Jazeera reporters argued that the contradictions of the Western media were obvious because they were obliged to acknowledge the genuine work Al Jazeera was doing in its reporting on topics like the killing of civilians and the capture of marines. President George W. Bush and British prime minister Tony Blair criticized Al Jazeera for showing POWs. It works in favor of Al Jazeera when Western powers and Arab states attack the network.

Al Jazeera has built up for itself a capital of symbolic power that thrives on the slogan "the opinion and the other opinion" and provides an Arab perspective that is wide open to Islamic input. By symbolic power I mean "the capacity to intervene in the course of events, to influence the actions of others and indeed to create events, by means of the production and transmission of symbolic forms" (Thompson 1995, 17).

Among the most important elements in Al Jazeera's construction of Arab Islamic identity frames are the power images linked to a story or a person. These images have almost the same magic as the powerful iconic image of, say, the tearing down of the Saddam Hussein statue in Firdous Square in Baghdad. For example, on April 8, 2003, Tariq Ayoub, an Al Jazeera correspondent, was killed in a US air strike at the Al Jazeera office in Baghdad. His companion, the cameraman Zuheir Al Iraqi, "was hit in the neck by shrapnel in the blast, which the network charged was a deliberate strike." And on March 18, 2004, the Iraqi cameraman Ali Abd Al Aziz and the Iraqi correspondent Ali Al Khatib of Al Arabiya, another Arab-language channel, were killed. During the Arab Spring, a Qatari camera operator was killed by Libyan bullets. The reporting of these deaths bolstered the frame of the journalist-martyr. In addition, images of murdered journalists, women, and children as well as tanks and armed vehicles on the streets continue to dominate the screen. Al Jazeera developed the frame of bullets of truth against the arbitrary violence of *qahr*.

Al Jazeera's portrayal of Taysir Allouni, its internationally recognized reporter in Afghanistan, as a personification of victimhood is another example of the network's practice of using its journalists as powerful symbols. European media, such as France 1, used to start their news broadcasts by counting the number of days since a French Journalist had gone missing in Iraq, Lebanon, and sub-Saharan Africa. Al Jazeera adopted a similar practice but on a more dramatic scale. The network's focus was on injustice, though, recounting Allouni's jailing in a European prison rather than capture by terrorists or kidnappers. This symbolizes a trend in the Arab media in which many newspapers have their own martyr or symbol of intellectual or social resistance to tyranny. Not only on the website of Al Jazeera but also on many of its TV programs and in advertising segments can we find the slogan "from within the field to behind bars." This refers to correspondent Allouni's moving from the field of journalistic duty to incarceration. Allouni has become more than a symbol. He is part of the politics of icon-making in the field of Arab journalism. Allouni brought the first interview of Osama Bin Laden to the world. He was also the only journalist to report directly on the Taliban from Afghanistan in October 2001. He is behind bars in Spain because of accusations that he had links to Al Qaeda and Taliban leaders. When Al Jazeera's office in Kabul, Afghanistan's capital, was bombed, Allouni, who is a Spanish citizen of Syrian origin, left and went to Baghdad during the second week of the US invasion, in March 2003. In Baghdad, too, he escaped US bombs, but his colleagues were not so fortunate. When the United States announced an official end to the Iraq War, Allouni returned to Spain, where he was arrested and imprisoned in September 2003. According to reports by Al Jazeera, the jailing of Allouni triggered waves of outrage in the Arab world. Allouni is considered an icon of the struggle against persecution and attacks on freedom of the press. Al Jazeera describes his imprisonment as punishment for the channel's "objective" reporting. Al Jazeera displays his photo proudly in advertisements, television banners, and on the Web, calling attention to the fact that he is behind bars because he was doing his job and bringing news to the world from the field in the Taliban's Afghanistan.

A Revolution Against Submission

Al Jazeera's contributions to the cause of freedom, resistance, and democracy are part of its corporate image. What distinguishes Al Jazeera in the field of Arab media is its tireless efforts to take the side of the oppressed and vulnerable Arab people. Al Jazeera encouraged resistance by being the first network to promote the naming the of Fridays as days of protest in order to counter all forms of *qahr*, global and local. Al Jazeera gave visibility to resistance and opened the local field of contestation to a pan-Arab one. Its practice of airing confrontations between its guests with opposing views made the network a kind of parliament of the Arabs in the absence of a political agora. Paraphrasing Abram de Swaan, Al Jazeera exorcised the political agoraphobia from the Arab publics Satellite TV contributed to an unstoppable collective action. The footage that was shown via satellite brought an end to the possibility of compromise with the authoritarian regimes in that Al Jazeera fueled the people's anger against these regimes (Belkeziz 2012, 271). Al Jazeera and Al Arabiya are considered two important instruments of mobilization. Al Jazeera and Al Jazeera Mubasher had an intensive presence in Tunisia, Libya, Yemen, and Syria. The same was true of its competitor Al Arabiya (Belkeziz 2012, 279). The interdependence of cyber activism and Al Jazeera was critical for continuing the revolutionary momentum during the Arab Spring. This relationship has three characteristics: first, the use of Internet footage on television; second, the use of the Internet to present breaking news, as in the case of Tunisia; third, the use of the Internet to disseminate ready footage for broadcasting by protesters, as was the case in Yemen (Belkeziz 2012, 292).

It was also crucial that, to paraphrase Bourdieu, Al Jazeera had a greater impact on the media elite than on the Arab publics themselves, since the media created through the logic of competition a belief in their own truth. In other words, the narrative of each media outlet during the Arab Spring was seen as truth by the channel as a whole. When you watch Al Arabiya's and Al Jazeera's coverage of Egypt or Tunisia, you have the impression that you are watching two different worlds. In covering the events of the Arab Spring, Al Jazeera and Al Arabiya, supported by Saudi Arabia, had distinctive styles. Al Jazeera broadcast political press releases from the Syrian opposition and from Hamas. Al Arabiya's slogan for its coverage of Syria was "Syria the revolution" (Belkeziz 2012, 281). The Iranian network Al Alam became the official voice of the Bahraini uprising.

Satellite TV also contributed to the liberation of language. There is a complementary relationship between public mobilization and the old and new media mobilization. Mobile devices were an extension of the media outlets in remote places where journalists could not reach them. Satellite TV, or "the media of the citizen," contributed to the transformation of national uprisings into transnational Arab uprisings (Belkeziz 2012, 283). Al Jazeera and Al Arabiya have become for the Arab media landscape what the US military presence is in the Gulf, the ability to act on the spot (Belkeziz 2012, 289). In hindsight, by closing Al Jazeera's Cairo bureau, the Egyptian regime of Hosni Mubarak showed that it had failed to learn from the Tunisian example. At the same time, the regime closed the door on any chance of telling its own story on Al Jazeera. In other words, Mubarak could have attempted the judo technique of wrestling Al Jazeera to the floor using its own force against it, rather than meeting it with direct force. The battle between the old regime and the official media against the new forces of globalization, satellite TV, and cyber activism serves as a microcosm of the entire Arab Spring. The triumph of the camera and the digital image led to the defeat of the old rulers. Al Jazeera was instrumental in helping political Islam win the elections in Tunisia and Egypt. The network created a reality that impacted what Belkleziz calls "the social universe" (2012, 300). Bourdieu argues that the media show things by hiding other things and, in turn, they hide things by showing other things. The Islamizing of the cultural and political components of pan-Arabism is the essence of this show-and-hide game that Al Jazeera plays.

Revolution within Political Islam

How did Al Jazeera contribute to the domestication of political Islam? It did so, first, by constantly confronting the views of secularists and Islamists in its programs about governance. Second, by acting as the Mecca of political Islam, Al Jazeera gained enormous symbolic power among Islamists and the larger public since Islam is the popular culture of the Arab world. Al Jazeera is headquartered in a "Wahhabi-lite" country, Qatar, and, through the sermons and fatwas of al-Qaradawi, advocates a Wahhabism infused with the Muslim Brotherhood's long-lived and rich tradition. Al Jazeera's religious program *Sharia and Life* hosted by al-Qaradawi, and the many religious experts from around the world who appear on the show, help paint Al Jazeera as a global Islamic network. Al-Qaradawi promotes reconciliation between civil society's values and Islamic values. However, he gave some very controversial fatwas during the Arab Spring (see chapter 5). Al-Qaradawi also has a heavy presence online in the form of online fatwas. Al Qaradawi has led IOL (Islam online), an interactive online platform, since 1999, in addition to contributing to Twitter, video sites, and micro blogs.

Al Jazeera's inclusive approach to all aspects of political Islam, from radical to moderate to conservative, has resulted in five major achievements: (1) promoting political Islam as a mainstream political philosophy instead of reducing it to a narrow jihadist ideology; (2) gaining the trust of all major political Islamist actors, who see Al Jazeera as an important ally; (3) overrepresenting opposition leaders in Arab countries, especially advocates of political Islam, on many of Al Jazeera's talk shows; (4) shifting the political focus onto the controversies between political Islam and secularism and between Sunnis and Shias. These five achievements led to the domestication of political Islam, and later to its relative emancipation. *Sharia and Life* does not feature only al-Qaradawi. From time to time the call-in program hosts other scholars, religious leaders, and Muslim activists, and there are guests from around the world, from Chicago to Miami to London and Jakarta, Malaysia, and many African countries, including Nigeria and Senegal. Below is a diagram showing the representation of al-Qaradawi's network of religious scholar associates who are highly influential in their own countries.

Sharia and Life gave Al Jazeera a powerful network of Islamic scholars whose heavy symbolic weight embellished its image in the Muslim World. Rached Ghannouchi, Mohamed Amara, Ahmed Raisouni, and Mohamed Ahmari are just a few individuals of high intellectual caliber who support the network.

Five months before the Arab Spring, the leader of the Tunisian Ennahda party wrote on aljazeera.net (August 12, 2010) that it is outrageous to ask if it is possible to be British and Muslim at the same time. Ghannouchi argues that the labels "Muslim" and "British" belong in two separate categories, the first having to do with faith and religion, the second with political and cultural identities. The two labels are not comparable, according to Ghannouchi, and since millions of Muslims are already British and pray in more than a thousand mosques in Britain, there is no need to ask intellectuals and pundits to answer the question. Muslims are already part of the British society; they have their own schools and organizations, and they participate in various aspects of British life, including governance, as citizens. Their influence has increased since the first Muslim was elected in 1997 in the British Parliament. In 2005 there were four Muslim members and in 2010 there were nine. More recently, in May 2016, London elected its first Muslim mayor. Muslims participate in all political parties except for those on the far right. This is the reality of Islam in Britain, argues Ghannouchi. Ghannouchi doesn't understand why radical parties within or outside Islam were prompted to ask these questions. Islam is plural and doesn't have one church that represents it. For Muslims and non-Muslims, radicals and militants represent a small minority that has a bigger voice than its numerical size would suggest. These are the elements that confuse religion and citizenship. Ghannouchi believes that this question is nonsense, since Islam is a universal religion and not linked to a specific territory. Ghannouchi cites the *Encyclopaedia Britannica*'s entry describing citizenship and nationality as synonymous. Radicals try to shroud the link between religion and citizenship in ambiguity, citing Turkey's inability to gain membership in the EU as evidence that Europe as a whole is closed off to non-Christians. Some Islamic thinkers, like Sayyid Qutb, who wrote the best-selling book *Milestones* (1964), wrongly mistakenly thought that the nationality of Muslims was their faith. However, civil society in Muslim-majority countries has enlarged the idea of citizenship. In Ibn Hisham's biography of the Prophet, Jewish tribes, the Ansar immigrants, and the new believers constituted a nation of politics and not a nation of faith. In spite of his support for al-Qaradawi, Ghannouchi holds a critical attitude toward exclusive attitudes among Muslims and has developed a more inclusive attitude toward non-Muslims and secularists.

Ghannouchi argues that the Jews of Medina were part of the Islamic *umma* according to the constitution of Medina. He elucidates the conflation of belonging to a state or nation with adhering to a doctrine or religion, which he says leads to a type of exclusion from the right of citizenship. This confusion is fueled by radical Muslims, Jews and Christians, and ultra-secularists, argues Ghannouchi. He explains that the difficulty of digesting and accepting the idea of a "British Muslim" is based on an exclusive interpretation of democracy in advanced societies and a failure to understand the principles of Islam as a religion and a way of life, "a religion based on the belief in the absolute oneness of God as the creator of heaven and earth." Ghannouchi believes that Islam has a universal message and liberates everybody, as the Quran states, "O people . . . O children of Adam" rather than "O Muslims." Islam is born liberated and serves as a liberating force in order to create a model state for a plural society with different religions and ethnicities. Jews were part of the first Islamic nation. Islam suffered greatly at the hands of tribal narrow-mindedness and from the experiences of previous empires, where theocracy ruled. Throughout history Islamic societies were diverse communities opposed to religious oppression and ethnic cleansing. The world's oldest churches and synagogues sit within the House of Islam. Ghannouchi argues that Jews were persecuted only after Islam receded from Europe, and not under it. Ghannouchi also argues that Muslims live on five continents and are adopting the global sovereignty of the state. In addition, as a result of Islamic culture, democratic transformations, and the global spread of ideas and information, the concept of citizenship is growing in the Muslim world, with political doctrine evolving and becoming more open, with guarantees of freedom of faith and participation in public affairs increasingly joining the conversation.

Ghannouchi argues that the expansion of Dar Al Islam (the House of Islam) globally has a pacifying effect and reduces the fear of Islam. He adds that the concept of citizenship guarantees freedom of religion. Ghannouchi calls on Muslims to be proud of their British citizenship, in spite of the colonial past of British Muslims. Ghannouchi is critical of European politicians who still hold a colonial mentality and commit injustices against Muslims. He sees Palestine, Kashmir, Iraq, and Afghanistan as wounds that should not be reopened by politicians. Ghannouchi prefers the moderate British secularism to the secular orthodoxy of France, which seems to betray a national grudge against religion. He also sings the praises of tolerance in Britain, where police uniforms are tailored for Muslim policewomen so that they conform to Muslim standards of dress. He believes that the British society is perhaps the most open and tolerant society in the world.

He praises Prince Charles, who made a plea during his well-known lecture at Oxford in 2010, for the return of the spiritual values that have been lost in European societies. Ghannouchi argues that there are many radical young Muslims living in Britain, but their radicalism is based on Islamic texts that are responses to anti-Islamic policies in religiously intolerant countries. He calls on British elites to be aware of this and to stop blaming Islam for the actions of radicals, since Islam is compatible with democracy. He asks the Muslim elite, especially imams of mosques and writers, to advocate the values of citizenship in Islamic culture in order to end opposition between the sphere of citizenship and the sphere of religion. There is no citizenship that assumes the exclusion of religion, and there is nothing in religion that precludes citizenship. During the French colonial period, the French wanted the Islamic identity to be diffused, and the reaction of Muslim scholars was to excommunicate people who had French citizenship. This fatwa was withdrawn when French colonialism came to an end.

On another note, when al-Qaradawi was attacked by other preachers, Ghannouchi stood up to defend him. But he stayed faithful to his principles of tolerance and the rejection of *takfir* (excommunication of Muslims), which became a popular instrument for undermining opponents of political Islam. Ghannouchi's defense of al-Qaradawi can be summarized as follows (Al Jazeera, September 18, 2008):

1. It is not acceptable under any circumstances to attack al-Qaradawi.
2. Al-Qaradawi's concerns are balanced and reasonable.
3. It is the right of al-Qaradawi, as the president of the Sunni world, to voice his concerns.
4. Al-Qaradawi represented the concerns of the whole Sunni world against certain Shia practices.
5. It is the right of all Muslims to maintain the unity of Islam.
6. Any doctrinal trespassing within the Muslim world should be stopped.
7. Muslims should outlaw the *takfir*, or excommunication.
8. The problem of our Shia brothers is they exaggerate and wish to place their spiritual leaders on the same level as the prophets. Nobody opposes the victory of Hezbollah over Israel, but there is no need to link defeat of Israel to Sunni tradition.

According to Ghannouchi, al-Qaradawi plays the role of an external engine that supports Islamic parties from the Al Jazeera pulpit in Doha. Al-Qaradawi was instrumental in preaching support for the political agenda of the Muslim brotherhood and Ennahda in Egypt and Tunisia. He defended the process of shaping and crafting the controversial constitutional declaration of the deposed President Morsi. On *Sharia and Life* a caller argued that Israel's strength lies in its religious parties, which are similar to the parties of the Arab world. During the Ennahda party congress in May 2016, Ghannouchi surprised the Tunisians by calling on them to embrace democracy and to reject political Islam in order to be inclusive of all citizens (Al Jazeera, May 21, 2016).

Television, Revolutions, Islam, and Democracy

The Arab publics have not been the same since the revolutions (Pew Forum on Research and Public Life 2011a, b; Tilhami 2013; Zayani 2012). The grip of Arab states on a mediocre media landscape was broken, and the Arab publics were given the chance to breathe, feel, and behave with more freedom. There was an epistemological break with the long history of monopolized newsgathering going back to the birth of national radio and television in Arab countries since the 1960s. The rise of satellite television brought a revolution of ideas about the self-definition and self-determination of Arab individuals and groups. Sociologist Mohammed Boudoudou, of the University of Mohamed V in Rabat, says, "Al Jazeera is introducing a sense of democracy and self-reflection. All the taboos imposed by the Arab government were broken. And Al Jazeera paid the price for it. Journalists were killed."[2] The April 2007 Casablanca and Algiers bombings, orchestrated by groups that claimed to be related to Al Qaeda in the Maghreb, were covered for hours on Al Jazeera by reporters on location long before the Moroccan or Algerian news services announced the tragedy. Before Al Jazeera, the international *umma* was generated through sermons and religious edicts, except during the Nasser period, with its radio voice of the Arabs. It is now generated by Al Jazeera and other Arab satellite channels through real reporting and competitive news agendas. Al Arabiya, for example, stresses the self-confidence of Arabs. This blossoming freedom of the satellite media in the Arab world is not unlimited and must be understood in context: Al Jazeera and Al Arabiya are still operating in undemocratic Arab countries. This means that both channels must try to please the rulers who subsidize them if they wish to survive.

Paraphrasing the French democratic scholar Pierre Rosanvallon (2012–2013), contemporary citizens experience a double bind since they want more protection from the state while enjoying more freedom. This double bind is a worldwide trend, which can be illustrated by the fact that citizens refuse to accept authoritarianism. However, they want more authority in schools and on the streets. Citizens' need for freedom and security shape the public discourse of democracy. The consequence, according to Rosanvallon, is the narrowing of the margins where politicians and the political process can maneuver. In the Arab world, this situation is no different than in the rest of the world when it comes to sharing the values of both freedom and security. The Muslim Brotherhood and Ennahda parties in Egypt and Tunisia are experiencing the same pressures that Rosanvallon is talking about. Millions of protestors still regularly go to the streets to show their dissatisfaction over their lack of freedom and security.

That the idea of redistribution of wealth was not part of the Egyptian and the Tunisian revolutions is not surprising. In both the French and the American Revolution, the problem of distribution was ignored (Rosanvallon 2012–2013). Redistribution, however, became an increasingly significant issue in European and American societies. Rosanvallon makes a distinction between equality as a measure and equality as a relation. Equality as a measure became very important during the Second World War in Europe but less so in the United States. This is the recognition of the equality of individuals in order to explain equality of status. On the other hand, says Rosanvallon, there has been a narrowing of concern for economic inequality. The principles of recognition and redistribution seem to be mere diversions. The notion of equality of conditions is now different than that of equality of status because redistribution has become a contested principle of equality. Thus there is a difference between equality of status and economic equality. In Tocqueville's vision of the march toward equality, the development of equality is a providential development: "Il est universel et durable. Il échappe chaque jour à la puissance humaine." He talks about *révolution irrésistible*, which has almost a religious character linked to the providential dimension, adds Rosanvallon (2012–2013).

How is a nation of equality created? Rosanvallon argues that this was a major challenge between 1849 and 1914, which elicited two types of response: one based on an extreme and negative construction of the nation and the other as a redefinition of the nation in terms of its cohesion and distinguishing characteristics, a nation based on redistribution. Rosanvallon writes that the revolution of redistribution will define the nation and its conceptualization of equality (2011). In Egypt and Tunisia, questions of equality were masked by the false debate over gender and Islamic aspects of democratic governance.

It took Europeans and Americans two major intellectual revolutions in the public sphere to finally address the issues of redistribution. The first stemmed from the work done in the social sciences after 1870 and 1880 that gradually informed a new conception of society, especially among new liberals in England like Tom Green, Adolph Wagner in Germany, and Alphred Fouillée in France, who spoke of a sociological ideology that apprehends society as an organism and modifies forever the idea of independence, the idea of solidarity, and the social debt. The second intellectual revolution was the reconceptualization of society according to a subjective mode (Rosanvallon 2012– 2013). Rosanvallon argues that major transformations of European and American societies at the end of the nineteenth century were linked to the fear of revolution. That was clear in Germany, for example, with the social policy of Bismarck, who wanted to avoid class warfare that could be fueled by the rise of socialist ideas in Europe. The same happened in France with the rise of socialists in 1903 and 1918. The takeaway from European and American histories is that it is important to address issues of redistribution and the idea of the welfare state, no matter how limited are the financial resources are of the state in the new Arab democracies. Arab countries have to follow their own path, but issues of redistribution cannot be limited to *zakat* (Islamic charity). *Zakat* as conceived in religious terms has be modernized to become the basis for a welfare state. Churches in Europe have not had a monopoly on charity since the advent of the modern state. Indeed, there were many intellectual, political, religious, and social coalescence in Europe that led to the rise of the welfare state. Rosanvallon argues that between the two world wars, during the 1930s, there was a revolution of industrial societies that constituted a break with the past. That was a historic moment of redistribution. In the new Arab democracies, a break with the past seems remote because the "religious past" is reactualized daily in the practice of political Islam.

Even in Europe and the United States there is an ongoing crisis of the welfare state. According to Rosanvallon, three aspects of this crisis have led to a divorce between equality and freedom: the emergence of a new mode of production, the advent of the society of defiance, and new requirements for the equality of conditions (Rosanvallon, 2012–2013). In Arab societies, the ideas of democracy and equality of conditions were objects of intellectual discussion, but the gap between the intellectual elite and the majority of illiterate people is still unbridgeable. A long history of practice of democracy is also missing. The Muslim Brotherhood hopes to reverse this trend by campaigning with a simple, almost populist message that frames the illiterate as resembling the Prophet. The supreme guide of the Muslim Brotherhood makes the televised plea: "We are the party of the ordinary people, not the party of the people who are doctors and in liberal occupations, but the majority of the people who don't have access to schools."

Rosanvallon explains that the emergence of new modes of production engendered a new mode of particular interest to modern capitalism that has been developed since the industrial revolution. Rosanvallon argues that capitalism reduces the plurality and complexity of society to a unique dimension, the value of things, which is the production of a society of generality. Society started to reshape social classes according to the new mode of production. The development of technology led to a more service-oriented society than to the production of goods. The new mode of production is characterized by the rise of services.

Rosanvallon argues that the Arab revolutions led to a break with old modes of production and reshaped the idea of responsibility and innovation, introducing an individualization of perceptions (Rosanvallon 2012–2013). During the Arab Spring, the "individualization of perceptions" was engendered by new technologies and the globalization of human rights repertoires by the growing number of NGOs (Boli and Thomas 1999). The individualization of perception, or explosion of subjectivity in cyber space, meant that collective action needed a public vehicle in order to be expressed. The vehicle for collective action and social change found its political framework in the reinvention of Friday by religious and secular groups alike as a day for voicing democratic claims, a day for renewing defiance against the established order and its elite. In that sense, Arab societies since the Arab Spring can be called "Friday societies," which means that ideas of responsibility, rights, and duties are defined and redefined on Fridays (although in Morocco people protest mainly on Sundays). The form of democracy that arose after the revolutions led by political Islam did not include the notion of a welfare state. Even Al Jazeera does not address the question of welfare in the Arab world.

Salafi and Democratic Values

When al-Qaradawi, for reasons of health or travel, could not appear on *Sharia and Life*, another member of his vast network of muftis and Islamic scholars would replace him. On December 8, 2011, *Sharia and Life* examined the prospects for Islamic political action after the Arab revolutions. The program discussed fears about the rise to power of political Islam, the political future of the Salafi movement, and the "truth" of the conflict between Islamists and secularists. It also discussed the ability of Islamists to run a government from the perspective of economics and finance. According to the presenter, Osman Osman, revolutionary mobilizations in Arab societies like Tunisia, Egypt, Yemen, Libya, and Syria gave rise to political debate between intellectual groups, militants, and Islamic activists. Whether the Islamic movements were ready to govern Arab societies and replace old regimes in a rigorous way from a political and economic standpoint was now contentious. Now that despotism had ended, Islamic parties had gained from the former conditions of oppression and marginalization to prosper and become sizable movements.

Mohamed Hamid Ahmari, director of the forum of Arab and International Relations in Qatar, was the guest on that day. He explained the rise of Islamist parties as the future of Arab countries, because Islam is a "fundamental" source of pride, identity, and self-respect for all Arab and Islamic countries. In that sense, Islam is a source of freedom and liberation against *qahr* and despotism. Islam is the main toolkit, according to Ahmari, for resistance. Ahmari believes that democracy means change, and as long as Muslim parties and governments continue to find new solutions and are ready for change, people will not grow tired of them. He spoke about a cab driver in Turkey who was a secularist but liked Prime Minister Erdogan's government because it brought prosperity to Turkey. Osman Osman asked Ahmari, "Do Islamic parties have a political, economic and social program for reform in order to counter this phobia and fear of Islam?"

Ahmari answered that there is propaganda in the West against Islamists but also propaganda disseminated by homegrown secularists. Ahmari argued that the propaganda advanced by Western media was a kind of continuous warning against the "scary, intimidating Islamists." The fact that the Salafi party in Egypt got almost 30 percent of the vote was not surprising, he argued, since Egyptian prisons in the 1970s of the past century were full of Salafi students from Egyptian universities. The Salafis were the majority during the imprisonment of the Muslim Brothers. Muslim Brothers and Salafis in parts of the country, especially in Alexandria, were allies. There is a Salafi base in Egypt. There was no real communication between the Muslim Brothers and the Salafis in Egypt about the differences between Islamist parties. Ahmari argues that there are only small groups within the Salafi movement that have a violent jihadi orientation; most abide by and strive to return to the way things were during the time of the Prophet. Ahmari says:

> A relevant question on the issue of democracy is whether we can consider political Islam parties, such as the Muslim Brotherhood and the Salafis, as one block. I argue that the Islamic movements are clearly different from one another. Most Salafis are against democracy in its Western form. How do we explain their emergence as a political party on the Egyptian ballot? Salafis will become a normal political party by taking the step of participation in democratic elections. In fact, this participation is tacit acceptance of democracy.

In contrast, Ahmari describes the extreme secularism of Turkey as *ghorba*, a kind of estrangement and alienation of Arabic principles. This estrangement never happened in Arab countries like Egypt, while orthodox secularism, as in France, Tunisia, and Turkey, has proved problematic. People in Turkey and Tunisia, after a long struggle, have succeeded in regaining Islamic values. The test for Islamic parties is the way they will deal with tourism from the West and non-Muslim minorities.

In one of his appearances on *Sharia and Life* in the early 2000s, Ghannouchi explains that the political life of the past was based on a single person, the dictator, and when the dictator left, the people discovered freedom and normal life. People are free to have their own ideas. Ghannouchi says that, in 2005, representatives of the October 18 movement had already signed documents to codify the relationship between religion and state, and equality between the sexes: "In short, about the kind of government we want. We want a democratic state that recognizes the Arab Islamic character of the country . . . and that is actually what the Ennahda party wants. We have a government of national unity, a coalition. We do not want to go back to the times of bitter experiences with the single party. We do not want to go from the RCD to Ennahda, we want a plural democracy. . . . We work with two secularist, modernist parties, and we want a coalition between a moderate secularism, a moderate Islam, and a moderate Islamic movement. This is the natural situation, since extremism is not good for our societies. We are societies of moderation and dialogue, and our partners share with us this ability."

Osman Osman asks about the difference between Islamists and secularists. Ghannouchi doesn't answer but argues that he wants to build one nation, a nation that confronts the problems of unemployment and injustice. Good solutions and rational solutions are needed, and it is imperative to bring to an end the legacy of dictatorship and oppression of the past: "We need a transitional justice."

He calls for a national dialogue. Ghannouchi believes that he has a political manifesto and that he would never enforce via the police a dress code or adherence to a list of acceptable foods or beverages, or even beliefs. The goal of the state is to serve the citizens within a legal framework that respects the rights and freedoms of all and to ensure that civil society discusses and does what it wants. "We inherited a regime where women were not allowed to wear the *hijab*; we will not impose *hijab* on Tunisian women. They are free to choose their own way of life." Muslim people, he said, have the right to choose and nothing will be imposed by force.

Al Jazeera also interviewed Isam al-Aryan, the leader of the Salafi party in Egypt. He expressed his astonishment at the "hostile" attitude of the West and the Western media to the democratic victories of Islamic parties. He said that the West should understand that all Egyptian citizens have the right and duty to act as partners in political, cultural, and social life. The most important thing, he said, is strong economic development for the country and wealth and equity for everybody. He said that political Islam offers the best chance for economic development in the Arab and Islamic world. Osman Osman asked if Islamists might use democracy to secure a position of power but then exercise the sort of despotism of the old regime.

"We were and we still are not asking for absolute power," al-Aryan answered. "If we are in a position of power, we will take the responsibility with our partners in our nation. Egypt lives in a time when Allah wants to grant freedom and democracy and leave despotism behind. Islamist parties and movements share the responsibility to exercise political practice in dialogue and competition" (Al Jazeera, December 8, 2011).

Mohamed Nour, a spokesperson for the Salafi party, was asked on another occasion how his party would deal with tourism, entertainment, alcohol, women, and government. "First, we respect the ballot. Second, we do not have any thorny questions and our orientation is not far from the general Islamic orientation, which is to guarantee the rights and the freedoms of people and to work in the interest of the people." He argued that the "scary" picture of the Salafis as negatively affecting the economy in general and tourism in particular is wrong. "Take, for example, the number of tourists who visit the pyramids, three million every year," he said. "The number of people who visit the Eiffel Tower is twelve million a year. There wasn't a real tourist industry in Egypt [before the Arab Spring]. [The old regime] preferred to talk about [economic] concepts [that led to] immoral behavior and market them to us as tourism. Tourism is a bigger concept; it is part of the whole economy. We have a complete vision of the economy that we want to present to the Egyptian nation. We want to build a good nation and good people. We want to build a true modern, contemporary society."

Asked by Osman Osman how he would put this vision into practice, Nour responded, "We have a project that some specialists are working on. We do not pretend that we have a perfect vision, but we are going to learn and go forward. Thank God the people put their confidence in us; we value their trust and will proceed with the help of God" (Al Jazeera, July 2, 2012).

The Salafi message is starting to dominate Gulf-funded Arab satellite television. The amount of time devoted to television programs in Arabic varies from 1,460 hours in Saudi Arabia to 1,008 hours in Jordan, 248 hours in Morocco, and 180 hours in Sudan. The number of hours devoted to such programs in other countries like Tunisia is unknown (Belkeziz 2012, 19).

Khamis Khayati, the *enfant terrible* of Tunisia, argues that secularists believe the extremist Salafi message infiltrates Arab homes in order to present an alternative to the political discourse of the country. In essence, it refuses to recognize differences between religion, citizenship, and democracy. The millions of illiterate people in the Arab world, 45 percent of whom are women, are easily swayed by religious television channels. The Salafi approach to society as constant and unchangeable is strongly represented in this programing. Salafi messages touch on excommunication, migration, renaissance, governess, and jihad, among other topics. Salafis are looking to return to a lost paradise and the creation of the ideal Islamic state. They open the door for arguments that deprive people of their freedom in the name of religion. This notion of self-censorship in the name of religion is dangerous. During Ramadan, the marketing of food and audiovisual products is important for Arab viewers, who on average spend a minimum of two hours and fifteen minutes a day watching television. Tunisian TV shows three hundred minutes a week of commercials, mainly for food, beverages, and cell phones (Khayati 2006, 36).

The Arab revolutions are transforming the public space with new terminology, introducing new concepts and ideas such as *thawra* (revolution), *nidal* (struggle), and *asha'b yurid esqat anidham* (the people want to topple the regime). The Arab Spring opened the realm of the unimagined and the unthinkable in terms of radical transformations in political Islam, including the Salafi movement. Arab societies have shown that democratic change is possible in spite of their tribal and ethnic divisions and the rise of political Islam. Al Jazeera and its pundits were instrumental in this radical transformation, presenting political propaganda as objective analysis in covering the events of the Arab Spring events (al-Kadhimi 2012, 10–11). The Arab revolutions were not based on a philosophy of change, but rather succeeded because of their advocacy of human rights and equity and an awareness of the extent of injustice inflicted on Arab societies. The Arab revolutions occurred in an interesting political setting where the majority of Islamists still rejected Western-style democracy, with its religious and ethnic pluralism.

The mass mobilization benefited from social media, new ways of mobilization, and satellite television networks such as Al Jazeera. However, it is clear that without the spark of the Tunisian revolution, the Arab Spring would not have been possible (al-Kadhimi,2012, 19).

The Muslim Brothers in Egypt, the AKP in Turkey, the PJD in Morocco, the Ennahda in Tunisia, and the El Wasat in Egypt were always very clear in their acceptance of the ideals of democracy (al-Kadhimi, 2012, 27). Hizb ut-Tahrir was the first party to reject the democratic model of the West and to propose a new system that would lead to a caliphate (al-Kadhimi, 2012, 27–29). Salafis in general reject democracy, for the five following reasons: First, they perceive democracy to be a Western product that is alien to Islamic culture; second, they believe that the source of governance must be Sharia, rather than the people, as in democratic systems; third, they believe that *ahal hall wa al'aqd* (those who are qualified to select or depose the ruler), not a parliament, must be in charge; fourth, they believe the Shura system, rather than the people, must be the basis for choosing the government, since Shura is not binding but informative; fifth, they believe that the people must obey the ruler, whereas in a democracy the ruler can be impeached or disobeyed.

The Arab Spring was a serious litmus test for political Islam parties, including the PJD in Morocco, which had serious discussions about participating in the February 20 movement. The secretary general, Abdelilah Benkirane (now the prime minister), refused to participate in the protests, which led to backlash within the party. Some of the party militants preferred silence over vocally refusing to participate in the February 20 movement protests. The political Islam movements seemed to have difficulties during the ground zero period after the fall of the regime. This stemmed from an inability by Islamist parties to transition from *fiqh darura* (a discourse about patience) and *ibtila* (life's challenge) to a more political discourse that seizes the moment of transition in society. Instead, during the Arab Spring, this moment was characterized by fear of transition and of political Islam (al-Kadhimi, 2012, 41–44). The army and the secularists have fueled this fear for at least the past two decades. Islamist parties should move from an internal political culture that is generally opaque and top-down to one of greater transparency and democratic practices within the party.

Some Far Right parties in the Netherlands, like the Partij voor de Vrijheid (PVV), have no mechanism of transparency, and people are appointed by the leader to different positions. These parties function like the Salafis. Every decision is accepted by acclamation. In the Maghreb, Islamists and secularists, especially in Morocco and Tunisia, developed a template for dialogue and cooperation. But that is not yet the case in the Mashreq. The Mashreq still holds discussions between conservatives and reformists. It is important to make a clear distinction between *da'wa* (proselytizing) and politics. The Ennahda party succeeded in developing a successful model that distinguishes between missionary work and political practice. Many movements in the Mashreq didn't succeed in separating *da'wa* and politics (al-Kadhimi, 2012, 45). However, with the intensification of political debates on television, a distinction between discourse and a call to prayer or a call to resolve pressing political, economic, and social issues is becoming more visible. In my view, this signifies a growing separation in the practice of political Islamic parties between *da'wa* and politics that is of the same magnitude as the separation between state and church in the West. It is the separation of preacher and politician. It is a way to prevent politics and religion from interfering in one another's affairs. This separation is not always feasible, but there is an observable trend. In my case, living in the Bible Belt of the United States helps me to understand the configuration of political Islam much more than I did when I was living in the most "liberal city of the world," Amsterdam.

Three years after the Arab Spring, political Islam parties are starting to critically evaluate their experience in power, especially after the disastrous experience of the Muslim Brotherhood in Egypt. Ennahda in Tunisia and PJD in Morocco know that self-evaluation and self-critique are part of maturity. Since political Islam has always been in the opposition, it has no previous experience in the day-to-day management of political issues. These parties are therefore in the process of developing politics of practice. Political Islam will be the dominant political force in the future of Arab societies; therefore, it is in a position to take on the role of guarantor of democracy and justice.

Olivier Roy (2012) argues that political Islam parties are becoming just as conservative a force as the conservative parties in Europe. But what about the Salafis? They were affected more than any other political force by the Arab Spring, since they were dealing with society and politics not through participation but through the fatwas of preachers. The period of Bouazizi put an end to the traumatizing period of Bin Laden. Jihadi Salafis broke from the ideology of obedience to the ruler, *al khuruj al musalah*. Calls for change in the Arab world moved from an emphasis on premeditated violence à la Bin Laden to pacifism and sacrifice à la Bouazizi (al-Kadhimi 2012–2013, 49–50). Al-Kadhimi distinguishes three Salafi groups: supporters of violent change à la Bin Laden; advocates of selective violence in the House of War (the West) and not against people in the House of Islam; and those who reject violence categorically based on respect for convention and *maslaha shar'ya* (legal public interest), in which jihad is allowed only when the legal ruler calls for it (al-Kadhimi 2012–2013, 51).

After the self-immolation of the Tunisian fruit vendor Bouazizi, a period of ambivalence reigned among Salafi groups of all plumage, from loyalists to the ruler to rebels against him. Al-Kadhimi identifies five groups of Salafis, who differ in their reactions to the Arab Spring: first, those who describe the Arab Spring as *fitna* (*strife*); second, those who think rulers in those countries are *qafr* (apostate) and that *khuruj* (ousting) these rulers is legal; third, those who describe the Arab Spring as *nazilah* (new) and therefore have placed a moratorium on interpretation; fourth, those who eventually supported the protests; and fifth, those who supported the protests from the start (al-Kadhimi 2012–2013, 53).

The fringe of jihadi Salafis who don't support the pacific transition to democracy and are active in Libya, Syria, and sub-Saharan Africa see the Arab Spring as an opportunity to fight the *qufar* (both Arabs and non-Arabs) and the oppressors using the *taqfi* (excommunication) to legitimize violence.

Al-Qaradawi and Human Rights

Al Jazeera's attempts to tame political Islam were aided by al-Qaradawi, who gave the network the highest legitimacy in defining the movement. Nobody at Al Jazeera has disagreed openly with al-Qaradawi or questioned his fatwas. In other words, a counter-frame to al-Qaradawi's theological claims and fatwas remains conspicuously absent on Al Jazeera. These theological claims have civil and political consequences, including violence and death, as when the killing of a political leader like Qaddafi is ordered or suicide bombing in certain conditions of *qahr* is censured. The compatibility of such claims with the human rights standards established by successive declarations and agreements since 1759 has never posed a problem for Al Jazeera and its leadership. The alternative Islamic Declaration of Islamic Rights lacks universality. Al-Qaradawi himself said on the BBC that he speaks his mind and is not afraid of speaking the truth to the emir of Qatar about his dislike of the US and Israeli presence in Qatar.

Mohammed Arkoun laments the absence of an independent high court of justice at the global level that would make all countries compliant with the human rights laws and would transcend the taboos and idiosyncrasies of local cultures. A global court tests the compatibility of all statements based on religions and ideologies with human rights. Certain verses of the Quran used by al-Qaradawi and other muftis to craft a fatwa, such as *surat 9, at-tawba* (The Repentance), should be used in the twenty-first century (Arkoun 1989, 94). Since the Quran speaks without ambiguity about absolute criteria that guarantee the salvation of humans, *surat* 9 is very explicit about the believers who accept these criteria and those who reject them, referring to them as apostates. Arkoun puts this *surat* in historical perspective in order to take these criteria out of time and be compliant with human rights standards. Arkoun examines *surat* 9, which concerns jihad. It speaks about poor people opposing rich people, about the provision of alms and charity for the poor, about the people who supported the migration of the Prophet to Medina, and about the rich who found excuses not to participate in "the jihad." Arkoun says that the proclamation of human rights in France was born under nearly the same conditions. In both cases, *surat* 9 speaks about the universal man and about people who are socially and ideologically defined. It sets for concrete rules for a society divided between infidels and believers in the Quran. The Quranic discourse, says Arkoun, has shown its efficacy in encouraging the emergence of free people who are responsible for their lives and families, but not as citizens of a civic society that is governed by elected representatives, as in the case of the French Revolution.

What can Islam say about the revolutionary phenomenon during the Arab Spring and its democratic potential after dictatorship? According to Arkoun, revolutions emerge in a specific historical context that limits their transcendental reach. That is why Muslims have to read *surat* 9 concerning jihad in its historical context when the Prophet had to survive by fighting his opponents militarily, politically, and religiously. Arkoun elaborates on this by saying that all religions and secular revolutions have to be recognized and surpassed. Their positive goal is often appropriated by muftis or religious or state bureaucrats in order to reestablish new hierarchies and inequalities. Arkoun warns us that this comparison between revolutions and religions will be judged as unacceptable by theologians and revolutionaries. The priest of secularism and the priest of religion will not pursue a new compromise in order to redefine the concept of religion in light of revolution. Arkoun asks many questions about revolutions and religions. What philosophical criteria does the secular revolution substitute, from the revelation to the triumph of a new political, social order? Arkoun argues that revolution engages people in the worship of God through respect for his rights that were guaranteed by the internalization of religious discourse. Theological discourse transforms the revealed discourse into a dogmatic closure where only believers plainly enjoy the rights recognized by revelation, which leads to the reinvention of social hierarchies, political, economic, and cultural inequalities that revelation meant to abolish. Arkoun believes that if we read *surat* 9 as theoretical and judicial, we fall into the trap of dogmatic closure, but if we read it in the larger framework of the general economy of the Quranic discourse, it becomes more open to the people's spiritual dimension.

Arkoun believes that secular revolutions since 1789 should be studied for their capacity to give meaning and symbolism to human existence, but also for the way these revolutions broke down hierarchies and inequalities with the help of new agents of secularization, controlling dogmatic closure and refusing to limit interpretation. Revolutions, according to Arkoun, uncover the hidden function of the sacred as articulated by religions. The constant passage to transcendence opens, according to Arkoun, infinite ways to alter the meanings that lead to the reification of doctrinal systems, political orders, and juridical codes. Arkoun finds that only a scientific and intellectual modernity linked to an open secularism can lead to the unveiling of the hidden stakes in the discursive practices of human societies.

The French revolution of 1789–1792 demonstrated how the discursive activity of social actors helped the creation of a free and liberated context from the hold of traditional religions. Arkoun explains how the Republic in France was "re-securitized" through the reconstruction of a national secular imagery. He explains how the nationalism of the nineteenth century and its expansion in the twentieth century led to the institution of a secular sacred (Arkoun 1989, 93–99). Al-Qaradawi, according to Arkoun's view, misses the philosophical and historical perspective in making his fatwas. Arkoun argues that al-Qaradawi's fatwas serve Al Jazeera's large audiences instead of anchoring them in universal principles that can neutralize the exclusion mechanisms between and within religions.

Can Political Islam Evolve and Produce Democracy?

Can the current crisis of democracy in the Arab world lead to a transformation of political Islam? Can it lead to new democratic values where democratic political Islam is fully included?

Actually there is a correlation between the crisis of democracy in the West and the rise of political Islam in the West. Marcel Gauchet (2015) gives two explanations for the renewed interest in religion in the public space:

1. The vitality of religion comes from within European societies, rather than being imposed on them.
2. Muslim migrants and transnational pressures are not the only sources of religious vitality in Western society, though they remain a powerful trigger for a revealing phenomenon.

It is interesting that many scholars fail to mention the impact of satellite television and religious channels that exist all over the world: for example, American televangelical broadcasts in many European languages and Shia and Sunni attempts on Islamic TV to galvanize the Muslim diaspora. Looking at the historic identity of Arab societies, we see a process of transformation from introvert to extrovert movements in the democratic arena after the Arab Spring. Gauchet sees the presence of the religious phenomenon on the democratic scene as paradoxical. Three elements can explain this paradox:

1. Reasons related to the metamorphosis of historic identity within society.
2. Reasons that have to do with the transformation of democracy.
3. Reasons related to the evolution of culture and individuals. (1985, 64)

Gauchet speaks about the emancipation of religion after the long quarrel between the church and democracy. This resurgence of religion will lead to the end of the religion of politics. The religion of politics is the cult of collective liberty in the sense that freedom will win, leaving the religion of politics to its own triumph. Thus democracy is not a finality, but a framework where different options are possible.

Tocqueville argued that religion is one of the foundations of political life in the United States. Rousseau spoke about civil religion; Al Burger and Casanova spoke about public religion. Rousseau said that democracy and Christianity are incompatible. We say the same thing now about Islam and democracy because Islamists did not take part in the Enlightenment. Rousseau explains that religion obstructs secularism; that is, democracy goes beyond the laws of divinity. In France, democracy pertains to equality and a deep-seated feeling of entitlement by the government; in the United States it pertains to liberty and individual freedom (Gauchet 1985, 80).

Will religion be the ideological replacement for democracy (Gauchet 1985, 81)? Mohammed Arkoun is amazed to see how Islam is now framed outside its historical and social contexts. It becomes bigger than the words of Allah, the Quran, and all its constituent elements. In French, "islam" with a lowercase *i* refers to religion and "Islam" with a capital *I* refers to civilization. In other languages this distinction between lowercase and capital forms does not exist. However, Islam is coming to be seen as a monolithic entity that is opposed to democracy. Arkoun blames Muslims and non-Muslims for contributing to this reification of Islam in the Arab and Muslim world, equating it with everything that is the opposite of the West (modernity secularism, liberalism, etc.). Many Muslim scholars believe that Islam and its connections with modernity and progress shouldn't be debated in the narrow framework of secularism (al-Jabri 1994). Al Jazeera plays an important role in polarizing the "impasse" of secularism in the Islamic context. It gives plenty of airtime to the controversies between secularists and Islamists. Sometimes it creates them deliberately, as it did on the show hosted by Faisal al-Kasim, *The Opposite Direction*, when the notorious Moroccan Salafi Mohamed Fizazi debated a guest with secularist views. Al-Kasim ignited a major controversy by saying about the radical Salafi Fizazi that "he is *almani* [a secularist]" and saying to the guest, "You are secularist." Fizazi unleashed a torrent of criticism and disapproval that reached an absurd level of hostility. Fizazi excommunicated the guest on the television program. The same Fizazi, a couple of years later, became more inclusive and hosted the king of Morocco in his mosque in Tangiers. As long as discussion remains centered on Islam and secularism, it will be difficult to move ahead. To break this impasse the focus should be on liberty and freedom of expression and the right to otherness.

In sum, the Arab Spring and Al Jazeera helped to move political Islam movements, including the Salafi movement, closer to a consensus on democratic values. There has been a 360-degree change. Al-Qaradawi delivered sermons and fatwas that promoted democracy as a system. And the naming of Friday protests went through a democratization process that also became a tool for asserting democratic values. All of this happened on Al Jazeera, in secularized Mecca Time, where events were framed mainly in religious terms so that these religious connotations were neutralized by their daily secular use and interpretation by pundits. Even the word "martyr," as Benslama argues, took on a secular meaning.

POSTSCRIPT
OUT OF ORDER

ARAB MEDIA AND DEMOCRACY IN DISTRESS*

What discourages Algerians is the Arab Spring.

—Ali Dilem (Algerian cartoonist, Chouf Chouf, May 28, 2014)[1]

Meanwhile, the body of the man who started a revolution now lies in a
simple grave outside Sidi Bouzid, surrounded by olive trees, cactuses, and
blossoming almond trees.

—Yasmine Ryan (Al Jazeera, January 20, 2011)[2]

Paxman: It is the case, is it not, that Qatar has been playing a role in present
events in Egypt, that it is at odds with the military government there, and that
Al Jazeera is largely run by the government of Qatar. Is that not correct?
Negm: I am not the spokesman for the government of Qatar, and Al Jazeera is
not run by the government of Qatar. Actually BBC is like Al Jazeera. BBC World
Service is funded by the foreign ministry and has its own charter.

—*BBC Newsnight* host Jeremy Paxman interviewing the Al Jazeera
English news director Salah Negm (February 6, 2014)

It is hard to avoid the conclusion, based on images and reports of any
reputable international news outlet, that the revolutions sparked by
the Arab Spring have devolved into a morass of human rights violations, refugee crises, and daily violence administered by warlords and
strongmen. This is the result of two seismic changes taking place in
the Arab world. The first is the accelerated decomposition of the
nation-state system installed by the West following the collapse of the
Ottoman Empire. This is characterized by efforts to draw new national
boundaries based on conflicting nationalistic, ethnic, and religious
affiliations. The second is the recomposition of a "proto-state," as
the Islamic State has emerged as a new power in the region, claiming
territories in Iraq, Syria, and Lybia where traditional state power has
receded (Gilles Kepel, France Culture, May 11, 2014; Olivier Roy, *Le
Monde*, November 30, 2015). These processes of decomposition and
recomposition bode poorly for the stability of the region, as partition

becomes an increasingly likely scenario in Syria, Iraq, and Yemen. Neighboring powers, particularly Iran, Turkey, Saudi Arabia, and Israel, meanwhile, will look to expand their influence, taking on a more active role in the region in an attempt to mitigate the risk posed by regional instability.

Most of the Arab world is in deep crisis. Foundational institutions like the nation-state and the Arab League, as well as the idea of Arab citizenship in a unified Arab space, have grown brittle in the face of conflicts that are symptomatic of both regional problems and the idiosyncratic dysfunction of individual states (Adonis 2013; Kepel 2014). Both the ideologies of "Arab unity" and "Islamic solidarity" are increasingly seen as myths that nobody believes in anymore. Both successes and failures of the Arab Spring are in large part a function of the interchange between politics and media. In a region marked by disorder, they are both out of order. The triumph of chaos and violence has enhanced perverse forms of repression and identification with radical Islam (Kepel 2014). Traditional solidarity networks are under attack. This pressure on the old solidarity structures is driving a fragmentation of Arab society. A number of turning points helped to steer the Arab world from the crossroads of the Jasmine Revolution toward the current atmosphere of chaos.

The self-immolation of the Tunisian fruit vendor Bouazizi ignited a flame of hope and revolutionary spirit that overtook the Arab world. Al Jazeera grabbed hold of this flame, as an Olympic torch runner might, and carried it to every corner of the Arab world, promoting Fridays as days not just of worship but of rage against autocratic rulers. However, the post–Arab Spring world and the associated growing pains of the democratic process have been characterized by a radicalization of media and politics.

The process of media framing and a series of crucial tipping points were deciding factors in the outcomes of the Arab Spring revolutions. Political and religious tensions, new class dynamics, and unprecedented online political activism backed by Arab satellite media were all significant factors in the antiestablishment movements that have gripped the Arab world since 2010 and continue at the time of this writing. In a period characterized demographically by a quickly growing young population, often called a "youth bulge," those disenfranchised by the political process triggered the Arab Spring. The movement throughout the Arab world was instigated principally by this highly digitized youth population and amplified by an overwhelming anger built up over the course of decades against restrictive social structures. Amidst the spree of revolutions against authoritarianism came the first real test of the viability of democratic Islamism. Al Jazeera was instrumental in making political Islam visible as a sociological reality. In Tunisia, Al Jazeera, which was banned under Ben Ali, covered the return of the Tunisian Islamist leader in exile, Rached Ghannouchi, who was welcomed in a celebration that included the same songs that were sung by the supporters of the Prophet Muhammad after he immigrated to Medina. Al Jazeera also covered the return of its star preacher, Yusuf al-Qaradawi, to an immensely crowded Tahrir Square. The event transformed the symbolic epicenter of the revolution into a large mosque with a *mihrab* (pulpit) in the middle.

Frames are an important part of the mental maps that help us to understand the world around us. Without being aware of these frames and the ideological biases behind them, we will not be able to understand how processes of exclusion are produced and reproduced. Understanding frames is essential if we wish to liberate ourselves from the undercurrents of bias that insidiously influence our daily interactions. The research that forms the basis of this book has contributed to our understanding of different frames used by Al Jazeera. However, ongoing research is needed to reveal the porosity of society to different ideologies and framing strategies so that we may seek remedies that go beyond mere containment.

Opportunities for Further Research

The author's dataset has yielded important information about the transformational interchange between Al Jazeera and the Arab Spring revolutions. Perhaps more important are the questions arising from the analysis of this information. To name a few: What has become of the democratic aspirations for freedom, democracy, and dignity that once buoyed the hopeful air of the Arab Spring? What has become of the once influential voices of democratic political Islam? How will the ideologies of pan-Arabism and Islamic solidarity inform the reconfiguration of authority and power in the post–Arab Spring Middle East, if at all?

Each of these questions represents an opportunity for future research that applies a comparative perspective and analytical tools to social media and the growing number of major international media outlets operating in Iran, Turkey, Israel, Lebanon, the Gulf states, and North Africa. This future research should entail an exploration of new theories to examine evolving roles and alliances in the Gulf region through media frames—including social media strategies of extremist and jihadist organizations—from a comparative perspective. Contrasting the ways different media outlets frame the Saudi coalition against the Houtis in Yemenis one example of a potentially fruitful research approach.

Other potential topics for new research include ISIS's framing of Arab regimes through the group's online magazine *Dabiq*; the framing of Qatar's involvement in the coalition against the Islamic State, given the country's support for groups like the Muslim Brotherhood that are considered radical by neighboring regimes; the role of media in the construction of the Shia–Sunni divide; the role of Gulf states, specifically Oman, in brokering the P5+1 nuclear deal with Iran (France Culture, September 7, 2015); framing of the Muslim Brotherhood as dangerous and radical in the political discourse of Gulf countries, excluding Qatar; framing of radicalized Salafism by Arabic-Iranian media outlets like Al Alam; Egyptian media framing of Islamist groups as a threat to stability throughout the Middle East; financing and recruiting efforts by jihadi networks; and the impact of fundamentalist preachers distributing sermons via the Internet.

In the future I plan to use Roberto Franzosi's approach to textual analysis focused on narrative lines combined with the theoretical perspective and the concepts of genesis and structure used by Bourdieu in his book *The Rules of Art* (1996). I intend to code for actor and actions, in time and space, in a way that can be analyzed using network models: actors related to other actors via different types of actions and GIS (geographic information system) maps of where interactions take place. Furthermore, the release of new software with an NLP (natural language processing) component will allow me to look for word co-occurrences within a window size and within the same sentence. I can then ask such questions such as "Which other words is ISIS ("Islamic State," for example) commonly associated with?" by examining words placed between one and three spaces before and after the word.

The Syrian refugee crisis also represents, unfortunately, a new human disaster. The struggle by European leaders to respond to the wave of Syrians seeking refuge in Europe spotlights the close proximity of Europe to the Middle East. Despite the fact that the two regions are often portrayed as worlds apart, the Middle East is the backyard of a divided Europe. It is, therefore, not surprising to see the smoke-and-dust clouds of war in Syria drift westward toward Budapest, Berlin, Paris, and London. A research project could be undertaken to contrast portrayals of the refugee crisis by media outlets in each of the countries directly involved. Such a study could, and should, be extended to political speeches and debates in European legislative bodies. Different analytical tools should be used to study the narrative frames and, as Franzosi put it, to "transform words to numbers" in order to examine different trends.

Rabaa: A Fatal Tipping Point

It is impossible to examine the Arab Spring without looking at the impact of Al Jazeera's coverage of the historic uprisings. I focused mainly on Tunisia, Egypt, Gaza, and the Arab diaspora in the West, with a less extensive discussion of other ongoing regional conflicts such as the dramatic situations in Syria, Bahrain, Yemen, and Libya. Touching on these areas fulfills the criteria of theoretical sampling—that is, the "selection of natural cases that include the necessary conditions for application of theoretical assumptions, which in turn steer research and are used to interpret findings" (Wilson and Taub 2006, 5). I believe that Albert Hirschman's theory, voice, and loyalty are suitable for gauging the participation of Arab populations in their newly found "democratic" configuration (Wilson and Taub 2006, 5–7). Dissatisfaction with change leads to an exit, which is a form of escape, and the use of voice should be seen as an expression of the will to change. For example, the marathon sit-ins of Rabaa Square in Egypt were framed by Al Jazeera as loyalty to the ideals of the Muslim Brotherhood. The two other options (voice and exit) were not possible, since the pro-Muslim protesters were afraid they would be killed or arrested if they left their public sanctuary in Rabaa. The forty-five days of sit-ins at Rabaa Square were framed by Al Jazeera as the highest form of expressing voice in a "militarized conflict." To be more accurate, the possibility of voicing descent was possible only when the protesters, empowered by Al Jazeera and other TV stations, made their voices heard by rest of the world. Al Jazeera brought their voice to live television.

The new rulers of Egypt represented a "return of fear" that was widespread during the Mubarak regime, but those reflexes of fear were abandoned and people approached tanks, hoisting white flags when they were shot at. Their heroic expression of voice can't be described with words. Media and political actors who oppose the Islamist parties painted a grim scenario of further deterioration of economy and society under Islamists. The fear of Islamists can be compared to that of new immigrants or outsiders when they try to settle in established neighborhoods. Norbert Elias argues that the outsiders are seen as inferior, raising fears about safety and cleanliness. The book by Wilson and Taub, *There Goes the Neighborhood*, is helpful for developing an understanding of the transition that occurs after intense social eruptions. In Egypt and Tunisia, Islamists in much the same way as the nineteenth-century African Americans who left the American south for Chicago. The widespread fear in Egypt turned from the repression of Mubarak toward the economic and social implications of Islamist rule. The racial context of Wilson and Taub is very informative, even if we are dealing with two totally different social and political contexts. Young people, intellectuals, the middle class, and elites under the old regime saw themselves as victims of a revolution that was supposed to bring democracy and economic progress, not Islamism and new restrictions. In Tunisia and Egypt, the old media elite, who had worked for the old regimes, became the new opposition media, and Al Jazeera lost its critical outsider edge after Islamists came to power.

The brutal and bloody dispersal of the sit-ins of Rabaa was a turning point in Al Jazeera's coverage. The network's tone became more radical, mirroring the way some Egyptian media outlets grew enthusiastically anti–Muslim Brotherhood and anti–Al Jazeera. Pro– and Anti–Muslim Brotherhood outlets produced a discourse that erected boundaries between social groups, praising groups whose values mirrored their own dismissing opposing groups whose values they considered inferior.

Following the fall of Morsi, Yusuf al-Qaradawi experienced a marked decline in visibility, but his influence remains strong. Broadcasts of *Sharia and Life* have not aired since July 25, 2013, and al-Qaradawi was conspicuously absent from the public eye for a prolonged period that same year. But amidst rumors of his having been banned from Egypt for preaching al- Qaradawi appeared on Al Jazeera just days before the presidential elections in Egypt, calling for a boycott of the contest between General el-Sisi and the only challenger, Hamdeen Sabahi. The call for a boycott was discussed at length in Egyptian media. Al-Qaradawi became, like Al Jazeera, a source of polarization in an Egypt that, according to the official Egyptian media, strongly supports the presidency of el-Sisi.

During the Egyptian elections after the ouster of Morsi, Al Jazeera and Egyptian media outlets focused on the low turnout during the presidential race. On one hand, Al Jazeera criticized el-Sisi's attempt to "seek legitimacy" through what it described as an "undemocratic process." Egyptians did not bother to vote, network voices argued, because the result was widely known before the ballots were cast. The official Egyptian media, on the other hand, criticized the Egyptians for staying home instead of voting. Al Jazeera used a collage of clips from different TV shows to critique el-Sisi and the Egyptian media for using the Egyptian people as a target of ridicule. Al Jazeera's coverage of the ascendant el-Sisi has a déjà vu quality, reminiscent of the network's coverage of the exiled Tunisian dictator, Ben Ali. The low turnout in Egypt led to the addition of a third day of balloting. Al Jazeera again offered harsh criticism of the Egyptian government's move to change the rules in the middle of an election.

There are, of course, many possible scenarios that can explain the low turnout. Egyptians may have been suffering from election fatigue or voting fatigue. The lack of choice of candidates may have caused voters to stay home. The Egyptian people may have simply been tired and out of patience with the violence and the problems surrounding implementation of democratic rule. Meanwhile, various social movements and the Muslim Brotherhood called for a boycott of the election. There is no available data regarding the influence of al-Qaradawi's call for a boycott or of Al Jazeera's negative portrayal of el-Sisi.

There are specific aspects of el-Sisi's campaign that may have discouraged voters from turning out. The general didn't lead a ground campaign, and he had no real political platform beyond some promises of large-scale infrastructure projects and social housing. There were no plans to modernize the economy and society, such as investment in Egypt's youth. Additionally, el-Sisi could not speak openly about issues that had the potential to upset the paradoxical coalition between the two groups that constituted his strongest base of support, the Salafist al-Nour party and the Copts (Sophie Pommier, France Culture, May 29, 2014).

An Al Jazeera news bulletin described el-Sisi's victory, saying, "Invalid ballots caused the defeat of the presidential candidate, Sabahi." The bulletin reported sarcastically that el-Sisi received 90 percent of the votes, describing Sabahi, the only other candidate, as finishing in third place. Anchors and commentators for the network argued that the army had always been in charge, both before and after the Arab Spring. Fearmongering over the Muslim Brotherhood, they argued, had been a convenient way to marginalize youth protests that had briefly interrupted military rule. Plans for the return of the army, according to the Al Jazeera account, were studied carefully before the electoral victory of the Muslim Brotherhood in 2012. The ban on the Muslim Brotherhood following Morsi's ouster was a convenient means for the army to control the opposition. This, according to the Al Jazeera narrative, is how the Egyptian revolution of January 25, 2011, was co-opted by the very powers it was meant to topple.

Regardless of whether one subscribes to this version of events, the oft glossed over detail at the heart of the back and forth between Morsi and el-Sisi is that the most populous nation in the Arab world faces a distinct lack of sovereignty. Egypt cannot survive without money from the Gulf states, whether from Qatar during Morsi's rule or Saudi Arabia under el-Sisi. The involvement of Gulf countries imposes a political agenda on Egypt, affecting its policy choices regarding Iran, the Syrian civil war, and support of the Salafis over the Muslim Brotherhood, to name just a few. The influence of the Gulf monarchies on the internal affairs of Egypt can't be underestimated. Without help from the Gulf, Egypt would have gone bankrupt. Both the Egyptian official media and Al Jazeera routinely oversimplify the complexity of the Egyptian situation as a conflict between secularism and political Islam. The reality is that the new government is using fear of political Islam as an excuse to gain support, undermining the chances of any real democratic reform, secular or otherwise.

The Arab Spring as a state of revolution, as a mode of action, as a *mot d'ordre*, as a metaphor, as a symbol, and as a strategy of mobilization is intertwined discursively with Al Jazeera (Hassaneen Heikal, CBC Egypt, December 13, 2012). The discourse of Al Jazeera on the Arab Spring represents the revolutionary state of mind on the Arab street. Discussions by other media outlets of the Arab Spring, without exception, cite Al Jazeera's role, as the object either of praise or of blame. Al Jazeera and Qatar are seen as the other face of the Arab Spring. Al Jazeera forms the ideological space of the exile, the Mecca of the vulnerable, the location where the voiceless can find their voice against the authoritarian Arab establishment. Al Jazeera is also *ghorba*, the burning nostalgia that serves as a refuge for those wishing to escape terror and violence from Morocco to Palestine. Al Jazeera promotes freedom and democracy underpinned by political Islam. This vision is fused with a pan-Arab philosophy and an eclectic memory, based on a shared regional history. By reinterpreting major historic events in the Arab world, Al Jazeera has provided a hopeful alternative narrative to the Western depiction of perpetual violence and dysfunction. Al-Qaradawi plays the important role of idealistic missionary for this narrative. In spite of the suspension of his program, *Sharia and Life*, after the fall of the Morsi regime, al-Qaradawi remains a durable voice in the telling of the history of the Arab Spring.

As Philip Seib states, Al Jazeera has been a victim of its own success in some ways. In the years after the Arab Spring, Al Jazeera has been more controversial than ever before. The network has been blamed for the expansion of chaos in the Arab world, the spread of "Sunni rage," the rise of ISIS in Iraq, and the widespread violence perpetrated by the recruits of different jihad groups in Syria.

The magical aura of Al Jazeera seems to have evaporated with its negative drumbeat against post-Morsi Egypt. The outsized focus on attacking el-Sisi's credibility has diminished the network's own credibility. Al Jazeera, which touted its support of Arab publics and Arab citizens, is now strongly associated with the Muslim Brotherhood in its battle between the Egyptian media and other Arab outlets. The stigma of supporting one specific strain of political Islam has weakened Al Jazeera's image as "the voice of Arab publics," as it was broadly seen to be before and during the early months of the Arab Spring. The opponents of Al Jazeera have succeeded in portraying the network as synonymous with a hegemonic, imperial media force. It has also been associated with the increasing confusion in the Arab world, particularly in Egypt, Iraq, Libya, and Syria. In this sense, the network's efforts to bill itself as a driver of change rather than simply as a documentarian seems to have backfired.

Al Jazeera and Its Double

Al Jazeera has been instrumental in forcing political Islam to adjust to democratic values through the creation of a transnational public space for discussion and debate. The experience of political Islam in power has led to an adjustment in thinking about democracy in society. In Tunisia, the Ennahda party helped protect democratic reforms, relinquishing control of the government despite its strong support from Al Jazeera. The Muslim Brotherhood, despite the full support of Al Jazeera and Qatar, was unable to hold power long enough to see a single democratic transition of power. The battle between Al Jazeera Arabic and Egyptian authorities is ongoing, amplified by the network's fight to free its journalists imprisoned in Egypt.

This state of exile from democracy where Arab publics are currently bogged down is, as Edward Said would call it, "one of the saddest fates." Just as CNN was the theater for the first Gulf War on television, Al Jazeera brought the unfolding Arab Spring to a global audience, especially with regard to the revolutions in Tunisia, Egypt, Yemen, Libya, and Syria. The network also reported on the dislocation of populations under autocratic regimes. Therefore, Al Jazeera became a voice of dissonance and rebellion. The network brought the bitterness, anger, and rage of revolution to life for large audiences.

The experience of many Al Jazeera journalists, including al-Qaradawi, living in exile in Doha, Qatar, gives both the network and the nation a strong connection with the exile and nostalgia experienced by displaced people throughout the region. Al-Qaradawi, for example, remains an Azharite, turning his pulpit into a place where all the scholars of Al Azhar can listen to him or compete with him. The disruptive effect of Al Jazeera is amplified by the diversity and experience of these exiled Syrian, Moroccan, Algerian, Egyptian, Lebanese, and Eritrean journalists.

Even if Al Jazeera is seeing its dominance over the Arab media landscape slip after the Arab Spring, it will remain an important part of the Arab media configuration. Its image as victim or underdog will continue to endear it to audiences who identify with its pervasive frame of *qahr*. Oppressive regimes, like that of Egypt, are only helping to advance the agenda of the network by imprisoning its journalists and attempting to stamp out its ability to report.

Al Jazeera's injection of its own interpretation of Islam and democracy into the conflict serves as a force for Islamizing or re-Islamizing Arab publics from below. This bottom-up ideological delivery mimics the symbolic emergence of the sparkling pearl from the depths below, in contrast to the top-down institution of Saudi Wahhabism or the secular authoritarianism in the Mediterranean.

Qatar and its alter ego, Al Jazeera, have attained a great deal of status in the context of the transactional state. This progress is, in part, a byproduct of Al Jazeera's mission to eclipse competing media outlets by sitting constantly at the center of controversy. The symbolic world of Al Jazeera operates on Mecca Time and revolves around Doha, the Mecca of the vulnerable, setting Al Jazeera and Qatar up as a direct cultural competitor with Saudi Arabia, the center of the Islamic world. In this contest, the balance of ideological power among Sunni Muslims and the Arab world is essentially up for grabs.

Meanwhile, during the writing of just this postscript, a number of disturbing events have developed that further threaten to destabilize the region. The "third war on Gaza" and the rapid rise of ISIS in the frontier of Iraq and Syria are the two most severe examples. The consequences of the international campaign to weaken ISIS caused extremists to counteract the narrative of their decline.

In hindsight, Europe seemed to be the collateral damage of this strategy—for example, with the millions of refugees from Syria trying to cross into Europe and increased attacks on soft targets in Europe.

In response to these attacks, al Jazeera employed framing tactics that had the unintended consequence of appearing to legitimize violence. This promotion of verbal "violence" became evident in France alone after the terrorist attacks against *Charlie Hebdo*, the Bataclan shootings in 2015, the Hypercacher (kosher) supermarket attack in 2015, the vehicular massacre in Nice in 2016, and the beheading of an eighty-four-year old priest in Rouen, also in 2016. Al Jazeera distanced itself from the attacks, but its initial response shed light on the impetus behind them. What effect does word choice have on the promotion of extremism? Does labeling terrorism as "so-called terrorism" make it a more sympathetic cause? Further scholarship should be devoted to exploring these links.

With the outbreak of a new war between Israel and Gaza, Al Jazeera framed the conflict with images of blood and accounts of "the heroic" resistance of Gaza. The network placed the blame for the bloodshed squarely on Arab regimes, most specifically Egypt. The network accused Egypt of conspiring with Israel to "strangle" and "break" Hamas. Gaza will continue to be an important focus for Al Jazeera. It serves as a reliable way to boost viewership. It also serves as a convenient weapon against Arab regimes that defend their national interests at the expense of pan-Arab unity. Pan-Arabism is still a source of mobilization for many Arab publics and remains a potentially strong vehicle for the spread political Islam.

Meanwhile Syria and Iraq are quickly following the path of Yemen and Libya, bordering on failed state status, with the surprising rise of the Islamic State in Iraq (Dawlat al-Khilafa). Like most international media outlets, Al Jazeera reported on the conquest of Mosul by the proclaimed caliph, "Abu Bakr al-Baghdadi," and the destruction of religious and cultural sites on the orders of the radical leader. ISIS news has become a dominant regional force as the group's reach has expanded in both Iraq and Syria, growing closer to the Saudi border. The danger posed by ISIS to the Gulf countries puts more pressure on Qatar to strengthen ties with its neighbors. Qatar, suddenly, has multiplied its diplomatic channels with Saudi Arabia, UAE, and Egypt. Al Jazeera scrapped a news segment on Saudi Arabia and shut down its Al Jazeera affiliate in Egypt, Al Jazeera Mubasher Egypt (*New York Times*, December 22, 2014). The media freedom flag that Qatar once waved appears to have become collateral damage of attempts to forge a united front against what is seen as the common threat of ISIS. Qatar has a lot to lose when principles become a commodity or a bargaining chip. The emir can't afford, for example, to send al-Qaradawi back to Egypt, as the numerous media outlets have claimed. To do so would represent a surrender of its mission of disseminating an ideology of Wahhabism infused with Islamist-democratic ideology.

There has been enormous pressure on Qatar to cut ties with al-Qaradawi from the UAE, which issued an international arrest warrant for the mufti and called on Interpol to carry it out. The UAE has also banned the International Union of Islamic Scholars, headed by al-Qaradawi (Ashraq Al Awsat, December 25, 2014).

In Tunisia, the most successful Arab Spring country, the self-immolation of another fruit vendor calls into question how much progress has been made. Hamed Abdellaoui, a twenty-one-year-old vendor of figs of Barbary, a popular summer fruit in the streets of Maghreb countries, found himself in a situation similar to that of Mohamed Bouazizi in 2010. Abdellaoui burned himself in protest against police *qahr* (oppression) (*La Presse*, July 7, 2014). A police officer had confiscated Abdellaoui's scale and demanded bribes from him. An editorial on the incident in the Tunisian newspaper, *La Presse*, asked, "What really happened?" three years after the revolution. It seems an almost cyclical symptom of oppression and pushback in the Arab world. But there is reason for optimism, at least in Tunisia. There, years of oppression and frustration pushed Islamists and secularists in Tunisia to work together in order to form a functional government. Fire can cause destruction, but it can be a source of cleansing, bringing the hope of a new, prosperous Tunisia. While problems remain, the nation experienced its first democratic transition of power since the implementation of military rule. Whether Tunisia can continue on its current track, and whether its neighbors will follow its example, remain to be seen.

As anger and rage are becoming widespread in various forms (sectarian, religious, ethnic, and political) because of dysfunctional political systems, the emancipation of political Islam in its institutionalized form (political parties) will not be sufficient to establish democracies. But the spread of chaos and the threat of extreme radical groups, as in Iraq, Syria, Yemen, and Libya, should serve to encourage a renewed process of democratization that will include the alternately emancipated and marginalized political Islamic parties alongside secular groups, in order to stop the cycle of political despair and de-civilization that currently engulfs the Arab world. Only a civilizational awareness will end this downward spiral. In the words of the novelist Driss Chraibi: "Civilization, ma mère, or la mère du printemps" (Civilization, my mother, or mother of spring).[3]

NOTES

PREFACE

1. All transliteration in this book follows the *Encyclopedia Islamica* system for Arabic letters. Requisite spelling, consonants, short and long vowels, and diphthongs are used; diacritical marks for the consonants *z* and *t* and the short vowels *ā, ū, ī*, however, are not.
   http://referenceworks.brillonline.com/entries/encyclopaedia-islamica/
   system-of-transliteration-of-arabic-and-persian-characters-transliteration.
   The names of individuals conform to those used by the persons or networks themselves, when possible. Otherwise, the preferred spelling of the *New York Times* is used.
2. On February 12, 2013, Abubakr Jamai spoke to my students via Skype at Emory University.
3. On February 12, 2013, Abubakr Jamai spoke to my students via Skype at Emory University.
4. *Hendi* is the Tunisian name for prickly pears; *molinos de viento* in the section title refers to Don Quixote de la Mancha's attack on the windmills.

CHAPTER 1

1. Approximately fifteen books offer a similar analysis of the Arab Spring. Of the six published since 2010, none focuses exclusively on Al Jazeera Arabic over an extended period of time or includes a systematic and in-depth examination of its most popular and provocative programs.
   Barkho (2010) provides an excellent analysis by contrasting coverage of the Middle East by Al Jazeera and Western media. However, whereas Barkho limits his study to the Middle East, *Fridays of Rage* expands upon his research design to include Al

Jazeera's coverage of events across the globe as well as the network's efforts to connect with international Arab and Islamic communities.

Lahlali (2011) examines the Arab media landscape in its entirety. While Lahlali describes the major players and trends that shape this landscape, the specialized survey of Al Jazeera in *Fridays of Rage* allows for a more detailed analysis of their media framing, ideological motives, and reporting techniques.

Mellor, Ayish, Dajani, and Rinnawi (2011) focus on developing Arab media industries. Since their book was published, it provides a wealth of knowledge about the early stages of the Arab Spring. *Fridays of Rage* traces this theoretical framework through the present day and accounts for the media's role in manifesting these concepts.

Miladi (2011) looks at Al Jazeera's role in Tunisia and across multiple Arab revolutions. *Fridays of Rage* provides a less focused look at the network, examining Al Jazeera's origins, evolution, and efforts to expand its audience across the globe.

Samuel-Azran (2010) contrasts war coverage by Al Jazeera and US news media. His analysis offers tremendous insight into the ideological factors that determine how journalism is executed in the United States and Middle East. *Fridays of Rage* expands upon Azran's analysis of Al Jazeera by examining how the network frames conflicts.

Mahjoob and Murphy (2011) contextualize the current alignment of the Arab media in light of recent social and political upheavals. *Fridays of Rage* advances this discussion by deconstructing Al Jazeera's role in affecting social and political outcomes.

Approximately fifteen books offer a similar analysis of the Arab Spring. Of the six published since 2010, none focuses exclusively on Al Jazeera Arabic over an extended period of time or includes a systematic and in-depth examination of its most popular and provocative programs.

Barkho (2010) provides an excellent analysis by contrasting coverage of the Middle East by Al Jazeera and Western media. However, whereas Barkho limits his study to the Middle East, *Fridays of Rage* expands upon his research design to include Al Jazeera's coverage of events across the globe as well as the network's efforts to connect with international Arab and Islamic communities.

Lahlali (2011) examines the Arab media landscape in its entirety. While Lahlali describes the major players and trends that shape this landscape, the specialized survey of Al Jazeera in *Fridays of Rage* allows for a more detailed analysis of their media framing, ideological motives, and reporting techniques.

Mellor, Ayish, Dajani, and Rinnawi (2011) focus on developing Arab media industries. Since their book was published, it provides a wealth of knowledge about the early stages of the Arab Spring. *Fridays of Rage* traces this theoretical framework through the present day and accounts for the media's role in manifesting these concepts.

Miladi (2011) looks at Al Jazeera's role in Tunisia and across multiple Arab revolutions. *Fridays of Rage* provides a less focused look at the network, examining Al Jazeera's origins, evolution, and efforts to expand its audience across the globe.

Samuel-Azran (2010) contrasts war coverage by Al Jazeera and US news media. His analysis offers tremendous insight into the ideological factors that determine how journalism is executed in the United States and Middle East. *Fridays of Rage* expands upon Azran's analysis of Al Jazeera by examining how the network frames conflicts.

Mahjoob and Murphy (2011) contextualize the current alignment of the Arab media in light of recent social and political upheavals. *Fridays of Rage* advances this discussion by deconstructing Al Jazeera's role in affecting social and political outcomes.

2. "Youth bulge" refers to the large percentage of young adults in a country's population. During the Arab Spring, Arab countries had the highest young adult population in their entire history.

3. The inspiration for the title of this section came from an article by Loïc Wacquant and Ivan Deyanov (2002) entitled "Taking Bourdieu into the Field."

CHAPTER 2

1. http://www.aljazeera.net/programs/pages/0dd9734c-373e-4864-95fe-1f7bb14b65c6. Accessed August 5, 2014.

2. Kaaba is the black stone in the middle of the great mosque of Mecca that defines the *qibla* (the direction in which Muslims should face when they pray).

3. The titles of these books are *Les pays du Golfe de la perle à l'économie de la connaissance: Les nouvelles terres du liberalism*, by Caroline Piquet; *L'énigme du Qatar*, by Nabil Ennasri; *Qatar les Nouveaux Maitres du jeu: Paris Demoplis*, by Olivier Da Lage, Mohammed el-Oifi, Renaud Lecadre, Willy Le Devin, Michel Ruimy, and Jean-Pierre Séréni; *Qatar: Les secrets du coffre-fort*, by Christian Chesnot and Georges Malbrunot; *Qatar, Une Education City*, by Mehdi Lazar; and *Le PSG, Le Qatar et l'argent*, by Arnaud Hermant and Gilles Verdez.

4. This argument was also made by speakers at a Doha conference titled "Fifteen Years of Al Jazeera," who singled out the network as putting Qatar ahead, diplomatically, of other small, wealthy Gulf countries. http://studies.aljazeera.net/events/2011/12/2011126103137766181.htm. Accessed August 14, 2014.

CHAPTER 3

1. The photo of President Ben Ali visiting Bouazizi in the hospital before he died is telling. The medical staff members stand with their arms crossed in front of them, while the president and his entourage stand with their hands clasped, almost apologetically, in front of them. http://www.bbc.co.uk/news/world-africa-12120228.

2. This underground network developed organically, rather than as a planned system of antigovernment communication.

3. This was a common feature of reporting during this period. Both local and foreign reporters relied on pseudonyms to avoid retribution from the Ben Ali regime.

CHAPTER 4

1. http://aljazeera.net/programs/pages/8f0fae6b-22d5-4cda-bc5f-64c679ef12c2. Accessed July 12, 2014.
2. These include UN Resolution 242 on November 22, 1967; the Camp David Accord in 1978 (Carter, Sadat, and Begin); the Madrid Conference of 1981; the Oslo Agreement in 1993 (Rabin, Arafat, and Clinton)' the Camp David summit in 2000 (Clinton, Arafat, and Uhud Barak); Taba in 2001; the Saudi Peace Plan in 2002; the Roadmap of 2003 with the Quartet (the United States, the European Union, Russia, and the United Nations); the Geneva Accord in 2003; and Annapolis in 2007 (Bush, Uhud, Olmert, and Mahmoud Abbas).

CHAPTER 5

1. "Spring Revolutions and the Media Spotlight Gap," transcript. http://aljazeera. net/home/print/0353e88a-286d-4266-82c6-6094179ea26d/a2295fdc-bcc4-4749- a459-06f2e3f4a173. Accessed July 7, 2012.
2. This is a subtle reference to a Muslim Brotherhood slogan.
3. Pro–President Mubarak mercenaries raided Tahrir Square on camels and horses.
4. The dates, titles, and topics of these episodes (the final four episodes of Heikal's show to air on Al Jazeera) are as follows: October 29, 2011: on the Egyptian files (episode 3); October 28, 2011: the state of political deadlock (episode 2); October 27, 2011: the international climate and the balance of forces and interests (episode 1); January 20, 2012: the Arab situation after Tunisia (episode 4).

CHAPTER 6

1. Alaa Sadek on his Twitter account @alasadek, July 18, 2013 (see also http://www. twsela.com/?p=8586 and http://www.el-balad.com/558915. Accessed May 4, 2014.

CHAPTER 8

1. Timeline of the Paris riots: http://www.aljazeera.net/NR/exeres/806FCCCE- 2A85-4B49-BBB0-6A65C6F8FC04.htm. Accessed June 6, 2014.
   Analysis of events in France until 2006 is based on the data collected for my article "From Baghdad to Paris: Al-Jazeera and the Veil" (Cherribi).

CHAPTER 9

1. http://www.aljazeera.net/home/print/0353e88a-286d-4266-82c6- 6094179ea26d/97a5fb34-69c0-4ecd-a6cf-9c9dad8c3eab. Accessed July 25, 2011.
2. I spoke via Skype to Professor Mohammed Boudoudou, University of Mohammed V in Rabat, Morocco, May 8, 2007.

POSTSCRIPT

* The inspiration for the title of the postscript came from the book of Thomas Patterson, *Out of Order*. New York: Vintage, 1994.

1. http://www.chouf-chouf.com/actualites/dilem-sur-canal-ce-qui-decourage-les-algeriens-cest-le-printemps-arabe/. Accessed August 5, 2016.

2. http://www.aljazeera.com/indepth/features/2011/01/201111684242518839.html. Accessed August 5, 2016.

3. Oum Rabi', the name of a river in Morocco meaning "Mother Spring," is also the title of a novel written by Driss Chraibi in 1982. His other novel, *La Civilisation, ma mère!*, was written in 1972.

REFERENCES

Abdelmoula, Ezzeddine. 2015. *Al Jazeera and Democratization: The Rise of the Arab Public Sphere*. London: Routledge.

Abu Zeid, Wasfi Ashur. 2011. *Al Qaradawi: Al Imam a'thai'r*. Sultan Publications.

Adonis, Al-Kitâb Le Livre II. 2013. *Hier le lieu aujourd'hui*. Paris: Seuil.

Appadurai, Arjun. 1991. "Global Ethnoscapes: Notes and Queries for a Transnational Anthropology." In *Recapturing Anthropology*. Santa Fe, NM: School of American Research.

Arkoun, Mohammed. 1984. *Essais sur la pensées Islamique*. Paris: Maisonneuve & Larose.

Arkoun, Mohammed. 1989. *Ouvertures sur l'islam*. Paris: Jacques Grancher.

Arkoun, Mohammed. 2008. *Humanisme Islam: Combat et propositions*. Rabat: Marsem.

Arkoun, Mohammed, and Joseph Maila. 2003. *De Manhattan à Bagdad: Au-delà du bien et du mal*. Paris. Desclée de Brouwer.

Aron, Raymond. 1970. *Marxismes imaginaires: D'une sainte famille à l'autre*. Paris: Gallimard.

Ash, Timothy Garton. 2013. "Endless Harvest of Misery Heralds New World Disorder." *The Age* (Melbourne), April 27.

al-Banna, Hassan. n.d. *Khutab al jumu'a. Al Qahira*? Cairo.

Barkho, Leon. 2010. *News from the BBC, CNN, and Al-Jazeera: How the Three Broadcasters Cover the Middle East*. New York: Hampton Press.

Belkeziz, Abdelillah, et al. 2012. *Taghyeer fi al-alam al-Arabi: Ayu hasiala*. Al markaz al Arabi. Beirut: Markaz dirasat al-wahda.

Bennett, W. Lance. 2011. *News: The Politics of Illusion*. Chicago: University of Chicago Press.

Benslama, Fethi. 2011. Soudain la Révolution! De la Tunisie au monde arabe—La signification d'un soulèvement. Paris: Éditions Denoël.

Benson, Rodney. 2006. "News Media as a "Journalistic Field": What Bourdieu Adds to New Institutionalism, and Vice Versa." Political Communication, 187–202.

Boli, John, and George Thomas, eds. 1999. Constructing World Culture: International Nongovernmental Organizations since 1875. Stanford, CA: Stanford University Press.

Bonsey, Noah, and Jeb Koogler. 2010. "Does the Path to Middle East Peace Stop in Doha? Al Jazeera's Influence on the Israeli–Palestinian Conflict." *Columbia Journalism Review*, February 16, 2010. www.cjr.org.

Bourdieu, Pierre, ed. 1965. *Un art moyen: Essais sur les usages sociaux de la photographie.* Paris: Minuit.

Bourdieu, Pierre. 1977. *Outline of a Theory of Practice.* Cambridge: Cambridge University Press.

Bourdieu, Pierre. 1979. *La distinction: Critique sociale du jugement.* Paris: Minuit.

Bourdieu, Pierre. 1984. *Distinction: A Social Critique of the Judgment of Taste.* Cambridge, MA: Harvard University Press.

Bourdieu, Pierre. 1991. *Language and Symbolic Power.* Cambridge: Polity Press.

Bourdieu, Pierre. 1996. *The Rules of Art: Genesis and Structure of the Literary Field.* Translated by Susan Emanuel. Cambridge: Polity Press.

Bourdieu, Pierre. 1998. *On Television and Journalism.* London: Pluto Press.

Bourdieu, Pierre. 2013. *Manet: Une révolution symbolique.* Paris: Seuil.

Bourdieu, Pierre, and Robert Chartier. 2010. *Le sociologue et l'historien.* Marseille: Agone, Raisons d'agir, and INA Éditions.

Braizat, Fares, and David Berger. 2012. "The Impact of Arab Satellite Channels on Public Opinion." In *The New Arab Media: Technology, Image and Perception*, edited by Mahjoob Zweiri and Emma C. Murphy, 123–138. Ithaca, NY: Ithaca Press.

Braudel, Fernand. 1995. *The Mediterranean and the Mediterranean World in the Age of Philip II*, vol. 1. Berkeley: University of California Press.

Bridges, Scott. 2014. *18 days: Al Jazeera English and the Egyptian Revolution.* Editia.

Bronner, A. E., and P. Neijens. 2006. "Audience Experiences of Media Context and Embedded Advertising: A Comparison of Eight Media." *International Journal of Market Research* 48, 81–100.

Butsch, Richard, and Sonia Livingstone. 2013. *Meanings of Audiences: Comparative Discourses.* New York: Routledge.

Chamkhi, Sonia. 1972. *Cinéma Tunisien Nouveau: Parcours autres.* Tunis: Sud Éditions.

Cherribi, Sam. 2006. "From Baghdad to Paris: Al-Jazeera and the Veil." *Harvard International Journal of Press/Politics* 11, 121–138.

Cherribi, Sam. 2008. "U.S. Public Diplomacy in the Arab World: Responses to Al-Jazeera's Interview with Karen Hughes." *American Behavioral Scientist* 52(5), 755–771.

Cherribi, Sam. 2010. *In the House of War: Dutch Islam Observed.* New York: Oxford University Press.

Cherribi, Sam. 2011. "Islamophobia in Germany, Austria and Holland." In *Islamophobia: The Challenge of Pluralism in the 21st Century*, edited by John L. Esposito and Ibrahim Kalin, 47–62. Oxford: Oxford University Press.

Cherribi, Sam. 2012. "Arabic Al-Jazeera: Transnational Identity and Influence." In *The Sage Handbook of Political Communication*, edited by Semetko Holli and Maragret Scamell. Thousand Oaks, CA: Sage.

Chesnot, Christian, and Georges Malbrunot. 2013. *Qatar: Les secrets du coffre-fort*. Paris: Michel Lafon.

Chraïbi, Driss. 1972. *La Civilisation, ma mère!* Paris: Gallimard.

Chraïbi, Driss. 1982. *La Mère du printemps*. Paris: Seuil.

Chua, Amy. 2003. *World on Fire: How Exporting Free Market Democracy Breeds Ethnic Hatred and Global Instability*. New York: Doubleday.

Cipriani, Roberto. 2013. "The Many Faces of Social Time: A Sociological Approach." *Time and Society* 22(1), 5–30.

Da Lage, Olivier, Mohammed el-Oifi, Renaud Lecadre, Willy Le Devin, Jean Michel Ruimy, and Pierre Séréni. 2013. *Qatar les nouveaux maitres du jeu*. Paris: Éditions Demopolis.

Darwish, Ali. 2010. *Social Semiotics of Arabic Satellite Television: Beyond the Glamour*. Writescope Publishers.

Ennasri, Nabil. 2013. *L'énigme du Qatar*. Paris: Armand Colin.

Entman, Robert M. 2003. Projections of Power: Framing News, Public Opinion, and U.S. Foreign Policy. Chicago: University of Chicago Press.

Entman, Robert M., and Andrew Rojecki. 2000. *The Black Image in the White Mind: Media and Race in America*. Chicago: University of Chicago Press.

Erdbrink, Thomas. 2011. "Al-Jazeera TV Network Draws Criticism, Praise for Coverage of Arab Revolutions." *Washington Post*, May 14.

Fandy, Mamoun. 2007. *An Uncivil War of Words: Media and Politics in the Arab World*. Westport, CT: Praeger Security International.

Filiu, Jean-Pierre. 2012. *Histoire de Gaza*. Paris: Éditions Fayard.

Franzosi, Roberto. 1995. *The Puzzle of Strikes: Class and State Strategies in Postwar Italy*. Cambridge: Cambridge University Press.

Franzosi, Roberto. 2004. *From Words to Numbers: Narrative, Data, and Social Science*. Cambridge: Cambridge University Press.

Friedman, Thomas L. 2013. "From Beirut to Washington." *New York Times*, October 18. http://www.nytimes.com/2013/10/20/opinion/sunday/from-beirut-to-washington.html?hp&_r=0. Accessed August 27, 2014.

Fromherz, Allen J. 2012. *Qatar: A Modern History*. Washington, DC: Georgetown University Press.

Garcin, Thierry. 2014. "Palestine: Rapprochement ou réconciliation entre l'Autorité palestinienne et le Hamas?" France Culture, Enjeux Internationaux, May 20.http://www.franceculture.fr/player/reecouter?play=4841812. Accessed May 20, 2014.

Gauchet. Marcel, 1985. *Le désenchantement du monde. Une histoire politique de la religion*. Paris: Gallimard.

Gauchet. Marcel. 2015. « Le fondamentalisme islamique est le signe paradoxal de la sortie du religieux » in Le Monde, September 21, 2015.

Girardet, Raoul. 1995. *Nationalismes et nation*. Complexe, Collection Questions au XXe siècle. Brussels.

Göle, Nilüfer. 2011. *Islam in Europe: The Lure of Fundamentalism and the Allure of Cosmopolitanism*. Princeton, NJ: Markus Wiener.

Goudsblom, Johan. 1995. "Summary of 'The Worm and the Clock': On the Genesis of a Global Time Regime." *Amsterdams Sociologisch Tijdschrift* 22(1), 142–161.

Graber, Doris A. 2001. *Processing Politics: Learning from Television in the Internet Age*. Chicago: University of Chicago Press.

Graber, Doris A. 2002. *The Power of Communication: Managing Information in Public Organizations*. Washington, DC: CQ Press.

Graber, Doris A. 2010. *Media Power in Politics*, 6th ed. Washington, DC: CQ Press.

Graber, Doris A. 2011. *On Media: Making Sense of Politics*. Boulder, CO: Paradigm.

Graber, Doris A., Denis McQuail, and Pippa Norris, eds. 2008. *The Politics of News/The News of Politics*. Washington, DC: CQ Press.

Hafez, Kai, ed. 2008. *Arab Media: Power and Weakness*. London: Continuum.

Hallin, Daniel C., and Paolo Mancini. 2004. *Comparing Media Systems: Three Models of Media and Politics*. New York: Cambridge University Press.

Hammad, Suhaila Zainal Abidin. 2011. *The Invisible Hands Behind the Al Qaeda Tapes*. Beirut: Al Rayan Publications (in Arabic).

Hanafi, Sari. 2012. "The Arab Revolutions: The Emergence of a New Political Subjectivity." *Contemporary Arab Affairs* 5(2), 198–213.

Haniyeh, Ismail, et al. 2010. "Al-Qaradawi's Efforts in the Service of Islam and Support the Palestinian Cause." Arab Media Center, Cairo, under the auspices of the Ministry of Awqaf and Religious Affairs, Gaza, Palestine.

Al Hroub, Khaled, ed. 2006. *Arab Media in the Information Age*. Abu Dhabi: Emirates Center for Strategic Studies and Research.

Ibrahim, Saad Eddin, 2013. Al ikwan al muslimun namudajan. in mustaqbalu al-islam asiyassi fi-al alm alarabi. Beirut: Dar alwahda.

al-Jabri, Mohamed Abed. 1994. *Dimuqratiya wa-huquq al insan*. Beirut: Al-Wahda.

Jallad, Farah Fakhri. 2011. "A Content Analysis of How Al Jazeera English and Arabic Channels Framed the War on Gaza." Unpublished PhD diss., Arkansas State University.

Juma, Mohamed. 2006–2007. "Hamas wa sulta." In *Qira'at Naqdiyya fi Tajrubat Hamas wa Hukumatiha, 2006–2007* [Critical assessments of the experience of Hamas and its government, 2006–2007], edited by Mohsen Saleh et al., 74–92. Beirut: Markaz Al Zaytuna Centre for Studies and Consultations.

el-Kaderi, Issa Nahawand. 2008. *Kira'a fi thakafat al-fadaiyat al-arabiya: al-wukuf ala tukhum al-tafkik* [Insight into the Arab satellite channels culture: On the edge of dismantling]. Beirut: Centre for Arab Unity Studies.

al-Kadhimi, Nawaf. 2012. *Islamists and the Spring of Revolutions: The Practice, the Triggers, Ideas*. Cairo: Altanwir.

Kassab, Akram. 2007. *Al Manhaj Ada'awi inda Al Qaradawi: Mawahibuhu, wa adawatuhu, wa wassailuhu wa aslibuhu wa simatuhu*. Cairo: Wahba Press.

Kepel, Gilles. 2013a. *Passion Arabe*. Collection Témoins. Paris: Gallimard.

Kepel, Gilles. 2013b. "Leçon inaugurale: Après les révolutions arabes, guerres ou paix?" *Les Rencontres de Pétrarque*, France Culture, July 22.

Kertzer, David I. 1996. *Politics and Symbols: The Italian Communist Party and the Fall of Communism*. New Haven, CT: Yale University Press.

el-Khachab, Walid. 2010. "Sufis on Exile and *Ghorba*: Conceptualizing Displacement and Modern Subjectivity." *Comparative Studies of South Asia, Africa and the Middle East* 30(1), 58–68.

Khemais, Khayati. 2006. *Tasrib al-raml: al-khitab al-salafi fi al-fada'iyat al-'Arabiyah* [Filtering sand: The Salafi discourse on Arab satellite television].Tunis: Dār Saḥar lil-Nashr.

Kingsley, Patrick . 2011. "Julian Assange Tells Students That the Web Is the Greatest Spying Machine Ever." *Guardian*, March 15. http://www.guardian.co.uk/media/2011/mar/15/web-spying-machine-julian-assange. Accessed July 2, 2012.

Kraidy, Marwan M. 2008. "Al Jazeera and Al Jazeera English: A Comparative Institutional Analysis." Annenberg School of Communication. (Posted at ScholarlyCommons, http://repository.upenn.edu/cgi/viewcontent.cgi?article=1282&context=asc_papers). Accessed July 2, 2016.

Kraidy, Marwan M., and Joe F. Khalil. 2009.*Arab Television Industries*.London: Palgrave Macmillan.

Kurzman, Charles, ed. *Liberal Islam: A Sourcebook*. New York: Oxford University Press.

Laguerre, Michel S. 2004. *Urban Multiculturalism and Globalization in New York City: An Analysis of Diasporic Temporalities*. London: Palgrave MacMillan.

Laguerre, Michel S. 2011. *Network Governance of Global Religions*. London: Routledge.

Lamloum, Olfa. 2004. *Al-Jazira: Miroir rebelle et ambigu du monde arabe*. Collection Sur le vif. Paris: La Découverte.

Lawson, Tony, and Joan Garrod, eds. 2001.*Dictionary of Sociology*.New York: Routledge.

Lazar, Mehdi. 2014. *Le Qatar aujourd'hui*. Paris: Michalon Éditions.

Lewis, Bernard. 1993. *Islam and the West*. New York: Oxford University Press.

Lewis, Bernard, and Dominique Schnapper, eds. 1994. *Social Change in Western Europe: Muslims in Europe*. London: Pinter.

Livingston, Steven, and W. Lance Bennett. 2003. "Gatekeeping, Indexing and Live-Event News: Is Technology Altering the Construction of News?" *Political Communication* 20(4), 363–380.

Lynch, Marc. 2006. *Voices of the New Arab Public: Iraq, Al-Jazeera, and Middle East Politics Today*. New York: Columbia University Press.

Mearsheimer, John J., and Stephen M. Walt. 2008. *The Israel Lobby and U.S. Foreign Policy*. New York: Farrar, Straus & Giroux.

Meddeb, Abdelwahab. 2009. "Pornographie de l'horreur." *Le Monde*, January 12, 2009. http://www.lemonde.fr/idees/article/2009/01/12/pornographie-de-l-horreur-par-abdelwahab-meddeb_1140741_3232.html. Accessed July 5, 2014.

Meddeb, Abdelwahab. 2011. *Printemps de Tunis: La métamorphose de l'histoire.* Paris: Édition Albin Michel.

Mellor, Noha, Khalil Rinnawi, Nabil Dajani, and Muhammad I. Ayish. 2011. *Arab Media: Globalization and Emerging Media Industries.* Cambridge: Polity Press.

Miladi, Noureddine. 2011. "Tunisia: A Media Led Revolution? Are We Witnessing the Birth of the Second Republic Fueled by Social Media?" January 17. http://www.aljazeera.com/indepth/opinion/2011/01/2011116142317498666.html. Accessed March 10, 2011.

Miladi, Noureddine. 2016. *Al-Jazeera and the Arab Revolution: Public Opinion, Diplomacy and Political Change.* London: Intellect.

Miles, Hugh. 2005. *Al-Jazeera: How Arab TV News Challenges America.* New York: Grove Press.

Miles, Hugh. 2006. *Al-Jazeera: The Inside Story of the Arab News Channel That Is Challenging the West.* New York: Grove Press.

Moorman, M., P. C. Neijens, and E. G. Smit. 2005. "The Effects of Program Responses on the Processing of Commercials Placed at Various Positions in the Program and the Block." *Journal of Advertising Research* 45(1).

Mouline, Nabil. 2011. *Les clercs de l'islam: Autorité religieuse et pouvoir politique en Arabie Saoudite, XVIIIe–XXIe siècle.* Paris: Proche orient.

Mouline, Nabil. 2015. *Les grandes dates de l'histoire de l'Islam.* Paris: France Culture and Institut du Monde Arabe.

el-Mustapha, Lahlali. 2011. *Contemporary Arab Broadcast Media.* Edinburgh: Edinburgh University Press.

Nahawand Issa Al Qadiri. 2008. *Qira'a fi thaqafat al fada'iyyat at al rabiyya: Al wuquf ala tukhum atafkik* [Reading the culture of Arab satellites: A deconstructive analysis]. Beirut: Markaz Dirasst al Wahda al Arabiyya.

el-Nawawy, Mohammed, and Adel Iskandar. 2003. *Al-Jazeera: The Story of the Network That Is Rattling Governments and Redefining Modern Journalism.* New York: Westview Press.

Norris, Pippa. 2011. *Democratic Deficit: Critical Citizens Revisited.* Cambridge: Cambridge University Press.

Nordland, Rod. 2013. "Saudi Arabia Promises to Aid Egypt's Regime." *New York Times*, August 19.

Noueihed, Lin, and Alex Warren. 2012. *The Battle for the Arab Spring: Revolution, Counter-Revolution and the Making of a New Era.* New Haven, CT: Yale University Press.

el-Oifi, Mohammed. 2004. "L'effet Al-Jazira." *Politique étrangère* 69(3).

el-Oifi, Mohammed. 2011. "Que faire d'Al-Jazira? Le monde diplomatique." September. https://www.monde-diplomatique.fr/2011/09/EL_OIFI/20968. Accessed August 11, 2016.

el-Oifi, Mohammed. 2013. "Al-Jazeera: Les ressorts incertains de l'influence média-tique." CERISCOPE Puissance.

Patterson, Thomas. 1994. *Out of Order*. New York: Vintage.

Pew Forum on Research and Public Life. 2011a. "Religion in the News: Islam Was No. 1 Topic in 2010." http://pewforum.org/Politics-and-Elections/Religion-in-the-News-Islam-Was-No-1-Topic-in-2010.aspx. Accessed February 24, 2011.

Pew Forum on Research and Public Life. 2011b. "Muslim–Western Tensions Persist." http://pewresearch.org/pubs/2066/muslims-westerners-christians-jews-islamic-extremism-september-11. Accessed July 21, 2011.

Pew Research Center. 2011c. "The Future of the Global Muslim Population." http://pewresearch.org/pubs/1872/muslim-population-projections-worldwide-fast-growth. Accessed January 27, 2011.

Pew Research Center. 2011d. "Arab Spring Fails to Improve U.S. Image." http://www.pew-global.org/2011/05/17/arab-spring-fails-to-improve-us-image/. Accessed May 17, 2011.

Powers, Shawn, and William Youmans. 2012 "A New Purpose for International Broadcasting: Subsidizing Deliberative Technologies in Non-transitioning States." *Journal of Public Deliberation* 8(1). http://www.publicdeliberation.net/jpd/vol8/iss1/art13. Accessed June 14, 2013.

Rinnawi, Khalil. 2006. *Instant Nationalism: McArabism, Al-Jazeera, and Transnational Media in the Arab World*. Lanham, MD: University Press of America.

Rosanvallon, Pierre. 2011. *La société des égaux*. Paris: Seuil.

Rosanvallon, Pierre. 2012–2013. Course, Collège de France. http://www.college-de-france.fr/site/pierre-rosanvallon/#course. Accessed August 20, 2013.

Roy, Olivier. 2012. "The Transformation of the Arab World." *Journal of Democracy* 23(3), 5–18.

Rubin, Uri. 1995. *The Eye of the Beholder: The Life of Muhammad as Viewed by the Early Muslims (A Textual Analysis)*. Princeton, NJ: Darwin Press.

Said, Edward. 1994. *Orientalism*. New York: Vintage Books.

Said, Edward and Gauri Viswanathan, eds. 2001. *Power, Politics and Culture: Interviews with Edward Said*. New York, Pantheon Books.

Sakr, Naomi. 2007. *Arab Television Today*. London: I. B. Tauris.

Samuel-Azran, Tal. 2010. *Al-Jazeera and US War Coverage*. New York: Peter Lang International Academic.

Schneidermann, Daniel. 1996. "La télévision peut-elle critiquer la télévision? Réponse à Pierre Bourdieu." *Le Monde Diplomatique*, May.

Seib, Philip. 2008. *The Al Jazeera Effect: How the New Global Media Are Reshaping World Politics*." Washington, DC: Potomac Books.

Seib, Philip, ed. 2012. *Al Jazeera English: Global News in a Changing World*. New York: Palgrave Macmillan.

Seib, Philip. 2013. Preface to *Egyptian Revolution 2.0: Political Blogging, Civic Engagement, and Citizen Journalism*, edited by M. el-Nawawyand S. Khamis, vi–vii. New York: Palgrave Macmillan.

Shadid, Anthony. 2011. "Qatar Wields an Outsize Influence in Arab Politics." *New York Times*, November 14.

Shteiwi, Musa. 2006. "Contribution of Arab Media to Creating Social Change and Developing Civil Society in the Arab World." In *Arab Media in the Information Age*, edited by Khaled Al Hroub, 121–138. Abu Dhabi: Emirates Center for Strategic Studies and Research.

Skovgaard-Petersen, Jakob, and Bettina Graf. 2009. *The Global Mufti: The Phenomenon of Yusuf al-Qaradawi*. New York: Columbia University Press.

Stora, Benjamin. 2011. Le "89" arabe: Réflexions sur les révolutions en cours. Dialogue with Edwy Plenel. Paris: Édition Stock.

Swaan, Abram De. 1997. "Widening Circles of Disidentification: On the Psycho- and Sociogenesis of the Hatred of Distant Strangers—Reflections on Rwanda." Theory, Culture & Society 14(2), 105–122.

Talon, Claire-Gabrielle. 2011. *Al Jazeera: Liberté d'expression dans une pétromonarchie*. Paris: Presses Universitaires de France.

Thompson, John B. 1995. *The Media and Modernity: A Social Theory of the Media*. Cambridge: Polity Press.

Tilhami, Shibley. 2014. "The World Through Arab Eyes: Arab Public Opinion and the Reshaping of the Middle East." *Foreign Affairs*, October 21, 2013. Online, May 30, 2014. http://www.foreignaffairs.com/articles/140137/shibley-telhami/the-world-through-arab-eyes-arab-public-opinion-and-the-reshapin. Accessed July 9, 2014.

Tilly, Charles. 2007. *Democracy*. Cambridge: Cambridge University Press.

Tilly, Charles, and Lesley J. Wood. 2012. *Social Movements, 1768–2012*, 3d ed. Boulder, CO: Paradigm.

Voas, David. 2009. "The Rise and Fall of Fuzzy Fidelity in Europe." *European Sociological Review* 25(2), 155–168.

Wacquant, Loïc, and Ivan Deyanov. 2002. "Taking Bourdieu into the Field." *Berkeley Journal of Sociology* 46, 180–186.

Weber, Max. 1949. *The Methodology of Social Sciences*. Translated and edited by Edward A. Shils and Henry A. Finch. New York, The Free Press.

Wickham, Carrie. 2013. *The Muslim Brotherhood: Evolution of an Islamist Movement*. Princeton, NJ: Princeton University Press.

Wilson, William Julius, and Richard Taub. 2006. *There Goes the Neighborhood: Racial, Ethnic, and Class Tensions in Four Chicago Neighborhoods and Their Meaning for America*. New York: Vintage Books.

Wolfsfeld, Gadi. 1997. *Media and Political Conflict: News from the Middle East*. Cambridge: Cambridge University Press.

Wolfsfeld, Gadi. 2014. *Making Sense of Media and Politics: Five Principles in Political Communication*. New York: Taylor & Francis

Zaidi, M. 2003. *Al-Jazeera*. Beirut: Dar al-Talia.

Zayani, Mohamed. 2005. *The Al-Jazeera Phenomenon: Critical Perspectives on New Arab Media*. Boulder, CO: Paradigm.

Zayani, Mohamed. 2015. *Networked Publics and Digital Contention*. Oxford Studies in Digital Politics Series. New York: Oxford University Press.

Zayani, Mohamed, and Sofiane Sahraoui. 2007. *The Culture of Al Jazeera: Inside an Arab Media Giant*. Jefferson, NC: McFarland.

Zweiri, Mahjoob, and Emma C. Murphy. 2011. *The New Arab Media: Technology, Image and Perception*. London: Ithaca Press.

INDEX

ablution, 138

acceleration of Arab history, 99

activism, xiii, 75, 76, 79, 80, 94, 103, 118,
185, 213, 244, 246, 248–249, 269
cyber, 103, 246, 248–249

affiliation, 18, 20, 66, 119, 142, 228, 268

Afghanistan, 5, 48–49, 62, 70–71, 81, 111,
122, 166, 173, 195, 247–248, 252

akhwana, 151

Al Arabiya, 59, 61–62, 110–111, 172, 202,
221, 234–235, 247–249, 254, 288

al Azhar, 21, 37, 118, 135–137, 144–145,
149–151, 167, 171, 177, 186,
223–224, 276

Algeria, xiii, xiv, xv, xxi, xxii, 26–27, 29,
36–37, 59, 76, 81, 92, 99, 101, 146,
173, 198, 202, 214, 217, 220, 222,
227–228, 231, 233, 241, 244, 254,
268, 276

al ghorba, 239

alim, 61, 169

Al Jazeera, xi, xiii, xiv, xvi, xviii, xx, xxi,
25, 27, 28, 29, 30, 31, 32, 33, 34, 35,
36, 37, 38, 39, 40, 41, 42, 43, 44, 45,
46, 47, 48, 51, 54, 55, 56, 59
Akthar min ra'y, 21, 35–36
Al Ittijah al Muakis, 35–36
Al muharibun al qudama, 21

Bila Hudud, 21, 36

domestication of political Islam, 42, 250

effect, 5, 9, 43, 152, 244, 245

emersion, 141

English, 9, 66, 67, 111, 113, 161, 194,
241, 268, 286, 288, 289, 291

Fi'l umq, 21

From Washington, 21, 238

Hadith al thawra, 21, 36

Liqa'al-yawm, 21

Liqa' Khas, 21, 35, 36

Mamnu'un, 21

Mubasher, 20, 37, 41, 157, 159, 161,
165, 167, 172, 178, 183, 209, 248

Nuqta sakhina, 21

Opposite Direction, 19, 20, 21, 28, 30,
31, 34, 38, 61, 68, 76, 81, 194, 223,
230, 246

outsized focus, 275

Pioneers, 21

Prison Literature, 21

Shahidun ala 'asr, 21

Sharia wa al-hayat, 21

Tarikhuna wa archifuhum, 21

Al Jazeera's injection of its own
interpretation of Islam, 276

Al Manar, 52

Al Mayadeen, 52, 72

Al Qaeda, 5, 8, 13, 37, 57–59, 168, 204,
238, 248, 254, 288
Al Qaradawi, Yusuf, xvi, xx, 13, 18, 19, 20,
24, 27, 32, 36, 37, 38, 39, 40, 49, 50,
52, 54, 59, 60, 61, 94, 103, 117, 125,
126, 129, 132, 133, 135, 136, 137, 138,
141, 142, 143, 144, 145, 146, 147,
148, 149, 150, 151, 152, 169, 170, 171,
175, 180, 192, 199, 201, 206, 207,
208, 209, 210, 211, 215, 216, 219, 222,
223, 225, 226, 229, 230, 232, 234,
235, 236, 240, 241, 250, 251, 253,
257, 263, 265, 267, 270, 273, 275,
276, 277, 278, 285, 288, 289, 292
Al-Quds, 17, 113
al udda tua'd, 128
ambiguity, 9, 10, 38, 251, 263
amin, xv, 48, 173, 178
Amman, 51, 68, 145
anachronism, 15–17
anarchy, 190
anchor, 11, 18, 20, 27, 28, 37, 55, 61, 66,
68, 86, 88, 92, 94, 125, 131, 135,
168, 180, 181, 183, 187, 201, 214, 219,
221, 236, 237, 238, 274
anchorwoman, 133, 157, 198, 201, 214,
217, 219, 220, 222
anti-establishment frames, 91
Antigone, 102
apparatus, 12, 57, 73, 116, 159
state, 57, 159
Arabic-language news, 19, 43
Arab-Israeli conflict, 23, 68, 143, 168
Arab Spring, xii, xiii, xiv, xvi, xvii, xxi, 3–7,
10, 12–15, 18, 23, 24, 28, 29, 30, 31,
33, 37, 39, 40, 41, 43, 45, 59, 61, 65,
71, 72, 74, 75, 77, 78, 81, 88, 89, 91,
93, 102, 104, 105, 106, 110, 113, 120,
121, 122, 123, 125, 126, 131, 138, 141,
151, 152, 161, 164, 169, 178, 185, 189,
191, 192, 194, 195, 196, 202, 205,
206, 207, 208, 209, 210, 240, 243,
246, 247, 248, 249, 250, 256, 259,
260, 261, 262, 263, 264, 265, 267,
268, 269, 270, 271, 274, 275, 276,
278, 279, 280, 281, 290, 291
Arkoun, Mohammed, xv, xix, xx, 11, 101,
144, 158, 190, 213, 224, 235, 243,
263, 264, 265, 266, 285
army, 26, 38, 86, 114, 124, 132–134,
136–137, 139–140, 159, 161, 164,
172, 180–181, 185–187, 204,
261, 274
ashuruq, 166, 173, 174
assassination, 69, 71, 110, 116, 144, 196
athawra, xi, xii, xiii
autonomy, 13, 36, 207

backdoor, 108
backlash, 20, 168, 212, 214, 237, 261
Baghdad, 13, 51, 117, 195, 217, 247–248,
277, 282, 286
Bahrain, 3, 18, 21, 37, 39, 51, 146, 152,
202, 207, 249, 276
ballot, 150, 171, 174, 258–259, 273–274
baltajiyya, 131–132, 161, 163, 165, 169,
171, 177, 181–182, 184
banlieues, 62
batil, 149
BBC, 3, 6, 39, 47, 61, 67, 68, 73, 74, 77,
84, 85, 110, 220–221, 223, 230, 235,
246, 263, 268, 281, 285
Benghazi, 61, 141, 197, 199, 236, 238, 241
US Embassy in, 236, 238, 241
blessing, 115, 120, 162, 207
blind, xv, 6, 64, 134–135, 235
blogger, xix, xxi, 12, 76, 77, 78, 79,
81, 94, 98
blogging, 78, 291
blood, xviii, 14, 41, 45, 47, 54, 71, 72, 82,
88, 95, 96, 112, 120, 123, 161, 163,
169, 172, 173, 176, 177, 178, 179,
180, 183, 185, 191, 192, 196, 197,
198, 199, 200, 203, 204, 209, 210,
272, 277
bath, 169, 179, 208

bloodshed, 72, 186, 193, 277

bloodthirsty, 116

Bourdieu, Pierre, xix, xxii, 4, 5, 7, 10, 11, 12, 13, 14, 15, 16, 17, 18, 19, 22, 57, 125, 152, 159, 190, 191, 233, 249, 271, 281, 285, 286, 291, 292

bullet, 21, 32, 41, 55, 72, 84, 86, 90, 104, 105, 131, 134, 163, 173, 174, 177, 179, 182, 185, 187, 188, 191, 201

burqa, 213, 214, 217, 219

buzzword, 224

Cairo, 24, 40, 51, 61, 72, 94, 108, 110, 117, 122, 127–132, 136, 141, 158, 160, 164, 166–168, 170–172, 183, 188–189, 192, 194, 206, 210, 223–244, 236, 240, 249, 285, 288–289

caliphate, 117, 143, 261

camera, xiii, 5, 11, 14, 20, 66, 69, 70, 71, 73, 77, 86, 89, 93, 94, 95, 96, 97, 112, 125, 127, 128, 129, 130, 131, 150, 158, 163, 165, 177, 178, 179, 180, 186, 196, 197, 198, 199, 201, 203, 247, 249

man, 70, 71, 180, 195, 196, 199, 206, 247

capital, xi, xv, 7, 11, 20, 43, 45, 55, 73, 74, 100, 125, 127, 172, 200, 224, 234, 237, 243, 244, 246, 247, 248, 266

cultural, 11, 62, 73

economic, 11

political, 20, 159

symbolic, 43, 62, 63, 152

transgeographic, 20

cartoon, 20, 26, 31, 41, 211, 212, 213, 214, 234, 237, 238, 239, 268

Casanova, 266

centrist, 175

chain, 8, 22, 77, 82, 95, 100, 145, 201, 245

of event, 22

charity, xviii, 147, 171, 255, 263

Islamic, 255

Charlie Hebdo, 41, 237, 277

Chartier, Roger, 10, 15, 16, 17, 18, 19, 191

chih wa-rih, xvii

CIA, 109

citizen-journalist, 77–78, 86–87, 129

citizenship, 73, 169–170, 189, 251–252, 260, 269

British, 252

nothing in religion that precludes, 252

claim, 8, 19, 42, 55, 58, 60–61, 72, 74, 77, 91, 98, 105–106, 108, 117, 124, 131, 141–142, 149, 151, 160–161, 164, 172–174, 180, 183, 185, 193, 196, 198, 206, 210, 218, 234, 236–237, 245, 254, 256, 263, 268, 277

clash, 81, 85, 161, 208

clerics, 118, 142, 148–149, 170, 200

legitimacy, 149

clip, 86–87, 104, 121, 165–166, 176, 180, 186–187, 198, 218, 231, 273, 276

CNN, xxi, 3, 6, 46–50, 55, 58, 70–71, 74, 77, 225, 276, 285

coercion, 53, 212, 213

from above, 212

from below, 212

from within, 212

trifecta of, 212, 213

coffin, 176–177, 182, 185, 197, 201, 204

collective, 13, 22, 73, 78, 95, 103, 112–113, 189, 248, 256, 266

courage, 78

conflict, xiv, 19, 22, 23, 36, 37, 56, 61, 65, 66, 68, 85, 106, 111, 112, 113, 116, 120, 123, 124, 143, 146, 161, 166, 168, 169, 170, 177, 191, 192, 193, 204, 212, 223, 228, 234, 246, 257, 268, 269, 271, 272, 274, 276, 277, 280, 281, 286

Islamizing the, 234

political, 27, 30, 31, 32, 33, 37, 186, 192, 292

contrast, xiv, 7, 26, 44, 65, 75, 96, 99, 112, 121, 141, 175, 189–190, 204, 217, 220, 227, 258, 271, 276 control, 10, 12, 15, 19, 43, 52, 54, 56, 57, 64, 78, 91, 93, 106, 108, 109, 116, 117, 123, 127, 135, 143, 146, 180, 187, 193, 194, 222, 226, 241, 274, 275

controversial, 24, 41, 56, 65, 89, 107, 217, 223, 236, 245, 250, 253, 275

Copenhagen, 234

corruption, 21, 83, 99, 119, 134, 174, 205, 207, 227

courage, 3, 68, 78, 87, 92, 129, 138, 147
  collective, 78

coverage, xiii, xiv, xxii, 6–7, 15, 18–21, 23, 28–31, 36, 38–41, 47–49, 56, 59, 65–66, 71–72, 75–76, 78, 81, 84–85, 87–93, 96, 98, 101, 103–107, 110, 113, 116, 120, 123–131, 136, 138, 142, 150–152, 157–158, 164–168, 172, 174, 176, 180, 184, 188–190, 192–193, 195, 199–200, 202–204, 214, 217–219, 225, 227–228, 230, 244, 246, 249, 271–273, 279–281

crackdown, xii, 25, 85, 158, 162, 189

credibility, 14, 45, 50, 60, 62, 104, 121, 186

criminalization, 222

crowd, 13, 65, 82, 89, 95, 162–163, 177–179, 187, 199

culturalism, 73

cyberspace, 75

dabiq, 270

Damascus, 51, 110, 117, 122, 132, 145, 200

danger, 35, 70, 97, 98, 138, 148, 180, 183, 198, 277

dar al ulum, 136

Davos, 244

da'wa, 262

democracy, 3, 5, 10, 23, 28, 30, 33, 34, 41, 42, 47, 59, 63, 65, 110, 126, 134, 139, 140, 168, 173, 174, 184, 186, 190, 208, 209, 210, 223, 240, 244, 248, 251, 252, 253, 254, 256, 257, 258, 259, 260, 261, 262, 263, 265, 266, 267, 268, 270, 272, 275, 276, 287, 291, 292
  Islam is compatible with, 252

democratization, xiv, 9, 10, 64, 207, 267, 278, 285

democrats, 92, 162
  Christian, 184

demonstration, xi, xiii, 7, 10, 24, 25, 38, 41, 76, 78, 79, 80, 81, 82, 83, 84, 85, 86, 88, 89, 90, 91, 92, 93, 95, 98, 126, 130, 132, 133, 136, 141, 158, 159, 161, 162, 163, 165, 168, 174, 176, 179, 186, 188, 193, 197, 203, 204, 239, 240

dialogue, xvi, xxi, 6, 9, 66, 119, 169, 230, 232, 258, 259, 261, 292

diaspora, xiii, 5, 8, 13, 21, 23, 40, 41, 60, 93, 95, 213, 214, 215, 216, 217, 235, 239, 240, 241, 265, 271

dictatorship, 30, 59, 75, 139, 141, 143, 167, 209, 240, 258, 264

discourse, xvi, 7, 8, 12, 17, 18, 20, 61, 68, 72, 114, 134, 148, 158, 185, 186, 201, 217, 218, 224, 233, 245, 254, 261, 262, 264, 273, 274, 286, 289
  meta, 15
  political, xvi, 18, 72, 102, 185, 260, 261, 271

distance, 14, 55, 92, 124, 136, 235, 246, 277
  temporal, 15

Djerba, 97

doctrine, 16, 29, 159, 236, 251, 252

Doha, 45, 46, 51, 52, 55, 56, 58, 59, 62, 65, 122, 141, 146, 147, 148, 152, 168, 188, 201, 224, 235, 243, 244, 253, 276, 281, 286

domestication
  of domination, 4
  of political Islam, 42, 250

dominant, xv, 4, 11, 12, 13, 20, 31, 43, 44, 52, 59, 60, 106, 159, 165, 181, 209, 213, 229, 236, 245, 262, 277
pre, 28, 36, 40, 47, 64, 103, 172
drumbeat, 12, 48, 81, 225, 275

ecumenical, 17
effect, xiv, xv, xxi, 4, 5, 7, 10, 14, 16, 21, 40, 43, 44, 55, 57, 61, 69, 97, 100, 102, 103, 127, 153, 175, 181, 206, 211, 217, 239, 245, 246, 252, 276, 277, 290, 291
Al Jazeera, 5, 9, 43, 152, 194, 244, 245, 291
democratizing, 6, 7, 11
sudden domino, 4
Egypt, xii, xiii, xiv, xvi, xvii, xviii, xxi, xxii, 3, 7, 13, 19, 24, 25, 26, 28, 29, 37, 39, 40, 41, 44, 50, 59, 60, 61, 69, 71, 72, 73, 76, 81, 88, 90, 91, 100, 104, 107, 110, 113, 117, 118, 119, 120, 121, 122, 123, 124, 125, 126, 127, 128, 131, 132, 133, 134, 135, 137, 138, 139, 140, 141, 142, 143, 144, 145, 146, 147, 148, 149, 150, 152, 157, 158, 159, 164, 165, 166, 167, 168, 169, 170, 171, 172, 173, 174, 175, 176, 177, 178, 179, 180, 181, 182, 183, 184, 186, 187, 188, 189, 191, 192, 193, 195, 200, 202, 207, 209, 210, 223, 225, 233, 234, 239, 240, 243, 245, 249, 253, 254, 255, 257, 258, 259, 261, 262, 268, 271, 272, 273, 274, 275, 276, 277, 290
Egyptian, xi, xiv, xv, xviii, xix, xxi, 7, 20, 24, 25, 36, 37, 40, 41, 44, 64, 71, 72, 73, 87, 89, 104, 110, 111, 115, 118, 121, 122, 124, 125, 126, 127, 128, 129, 130, 131, 132, 133, 134, 135, 136, 137, 139, 141, 142, 143, 147, 148, 149, 150, 151, 152, 153, 157, 158, 159, 160, 161, 162, 163, 164, 165, 166, 167, 168, 169, 170, 171, 172, 173, 174, 175, 177, 178, 180, 181, 182, 183, 184, 185, 187, 188, 189, 205, 207, 209, 210, 215, 216, 221, 237, 238, 243, 249, 254, 257, 258, 259, 271, 272, 273, 274, 275, 276, 282, 286, 291
Eid Al Fitr, 220
El Général, 103
Elias, Norbert, 15, 52, 55, 56, 272
emancipation, xix, 41, 59, 210, 243, 245, 250, 266, 278
emblematic, 60, 141, 151
empowerment, xiv, 212, 213
enemies, 13, 65, 116, 133, 162, 235
Ennahda, 3, 17, 20, 59, 95, 98, 189, 190, 240, 243, 245, 250, 253, 254, 258, 261, 262, 275
Entman, Robert, xx, 11, 14, 21, 138, 194, 217, 226, 287
ephemeral, 87
ethnocentrism, 16, 17
Eurabia, 211, 212, 213
events, xii, xiii, xxi, 6, 7, 10, 14, 15, 16, 17, 19, 21, 22, 32, 39, 40, 43, 47, 62, 66, 68, 69, 70, 72, 74, 76, 77, 81, 83, 84, 85, 86, 87, 91, 93, 94, 96, 98, 99, 100, 103, 104, 105, 107, 114, 120, 121, 122, 126, 127, 128, 131, 132, 138, 142, 152, 153, 157, 158, 159, 160, 161, 164, 166, 169, 172, 174, 175, 179, 181, 183, 189, 190, 191, 195, 198, 199, 202, 205, 207, 212, 213, 214, 215, 217, 219, 223, 227, 233, 238, 247, 249, 260, 267, 268, 274, 275, 276, 280, 281, 282
superficial events, 22

Facebook, 10, 76, 79, 80, 81, 83, 103, 132, 147, 163, 187
Fatah, 106, 110, 113, 114, 116, 118, 119, 121, 160, 164, 176, 183

fatigue, 122, 161, 242
  election, 273
  voting, 273
fatwa(s), 19, 40, 59, 60, 125, 126, 132,
    136, 137, 138, 141, 145, 149, 150, 151,
    169, 171, 192, 201, 215, 226, 229,
    234, 240, 241, 250, 252, 262, 263,
    265, 267
feeds
  live, 172
fiasco, 187
field, xx, 6, 7, 10, 11, 12, 13, 18, 56, 57,
    60, 62, 152, 162, 173, 181, 185, 204,
    208, 245, 246, 247, 248, 281, 285,
    286, 292
  autonomous, 11
  media, 5, 6, 10, 11, 73, 74, 152,
    225, 245
  political, 10, 151, 158
fiqh, 148, 150
  a-thawra, 148
  darura, 261
  new, 148
first-mover advantage, 5
fitna, 135, 136, 148, 172, 263
  na'ima, 149
flag, 95, 96, 122, 163, 177, 178, 182, 13,
    184, 197, 198, 237, 243, 272, 277
focus, 14, 15, 17, 18, 21, 22, 28, 30, 32, 33,
    36, 39, 52, 56, 62, 65, 75, 91, 95, 96,
    105, 125, 130, 142, 144, 164, 173,
    179, 180, 188, 193, 203, 209, 214,
    218, 219, 225, 242, 247, 250, 266,
    275, 277, 280
  locus, 18
footage, 13, 14, 20, 37, 75, 83, 85, 86, 89,
    90, 92, 93, 94, 95, 97, 101, 132, 163,
    165, 167, 168, 172, 176, 179, 181,
    182, 183, 184, 185, 186, 187, 188,
    193, 197, 198, 199, 203, 219, 237,
    246, 248, 249

force, xiv, xv, xvi, xvii, xviii, 3, 4, 5, 6, 7, 8,
    11, 16, 20, 22, 25, 37, 40, 41, 45, 52,
    57, 58, 59, 60, 65, 69, 73, 74, 75, 76,
    77, 78, 79, 82, 83, 84, 85, 88, 89, 90,
    91, 96, 98, 100, 106, 107, 118, 122,
    127, 128, 132, 133, 134, 139, 140,
    142, 148, 151, 152, 158, 160, 161,
    163, 165, 166, 167, 178, 180, 181,
    182, 183, 187, 190, 196, 206, 208,
    209, 213, 214, 216, 228, 233, 249,
    252, 259, 262, 275, 276, 277, 282
  destabilizing, 6
  disruptive, 190
  transformative, 5
frames
  alternative, 13
  dominant, 11, 12, 20
  identification, 13, 17, 20, 40
  pervasive, 276
  ready-made, 14
  repertoire of, 12, 41, 191
France, xvi, xxii, 11, 17, 20, 41, 48, 49, 57,
    62, 63, 92, 94, 99, 108, 109, 121,
    122, 157, 214, 217, 218, 219, 220, 221,
    222, 223, 225, 227, 228, 229, 230,
    231, 232, 233, 237, 238, 239, 247,
    252, 255, 258, 264, 265, 266, 268,
    271, 274, 277, 282, 287, 289, 290,
    291, 292
freedom, xiv, xv, xviii, 5, 7, 13, 18, 63, 65,
    67, 68, 73, 74, 77, 78, 88, 90, 93, 95,
    96, 97, 116, 121, 133, 135, 137, 152,
    153, 175, 177, 180, 184, 190, 195,
    196, 197, 198, 199, 200, 203, 204,
    205, 206, 210, 224, 228, 237, 238,
    239, 243, 244, 248, 252, 253, 254,
    256, 257, 258, 259, 260, 266, 270,
    275, 277
free market ideology, 60
free-rider, 185
Friday

to free female prisoners, 202, 203
of Hope, 204
rhythm of, 204
of warning, 203
Fridays
for justice, 205
of Rage, xxiii, 5, 41, 89, 131, 192, 279,
280, 281
fulul, 148, 161, 165
fundamentalism, 23, 119, 222, 288
funeral, 84, 92, 162, 176, 177, 178, 182

Gaza, 12, 21, 26, 28, 32, 33, 36, 37, 40, 51,
59, 70, 79, 104, 105, 106, 107, 109,
110, 111, 112, 113, 114, 115, 116, 117,
118, 119, 120, 122, 123, 124, 164,
166, 167, 174, 177, 193, 195, 202,
233, 271, 276, 277, 287, 288
General Guide, 150, 159, 177
Ghadab, 25, 126, 210, 239
Ghannouchi, 95, 96, 98, 209, 243, 244,
250, 251, 252, 253, 258, 269
defense of al-Qaradawi, 253
ghorba, 214, 215, 216, 239, 240, 241, 258,
274, 289
goods
cultural, 15, 18, 66
Gulf
funded, 260

habitus, 4, 12, 13, 73, 128
hadith, xix, 21, 36, 144, 146, 148, 236
hajj, xix, 7, 55, 77, 78, 86, 89, 147, 216
halal, 132, 133, 134, 137, 172
Hamas, 5, 21, 40, 59, 69, 104, 105, 106,
107, 109, 110, 111, 112, 113, 114, 115,
116, 119, 120, 121, 122, 123, 124,
164, 174, 249, 277, 287, 288
haram, 119, 133, 137, 146, 169, 186, 236
haramiyya, 147
Harb al Jamal, 129

harraga, xiii
headgear, 28, 37, 137, 150, 198, 201
headscarf, 96, 103, 178, 228, 229
heroism, 69, 125, 126, 131, 132, 151
Hezbollah, 36, 37, 122, 166, 171, 174,
208, 253
aligned, 52
hijab, 218, 219, 220, 259
hijra, 17, 142, 214, 215, 235, 236, 239, 241
history, 15, 17, 18, 21, 22, 26, 31, 40, 47,
60, 66, 68, 69, 78, 94, 101, 105, 116,
117, 120, 122, 133, 134, 135, 140,
145, 150, 152, 160, 161, 174, 175,
180, 183, 185, 189, 191, 192, 193,
196, 202, 213, 231, 234, 235, 252,
253, 256, 275, 281, 287
acceleration of Arab, 99
hizb a-shaytan, 171
homeland, 39, 50, 115, 222
hukm al askar, 126, 133
humiliate, 100, 183, 206, 207, 208

identification, 4, 13, 17, 20, 40, 63, 74,
100, 113, 181, 209, 213, 214, 215, 221,
233, 246, 269, 292
identity, xvi, 8, 16, 36, 40, 47, 48, 55, 68,
80, 91, 103, 115, 124, 157, 206, 210,
213, 216, 225, 231, 232, 233, 241,
247, 252, 257, 265, 287
iftar, 170, 189
ighatha, 114
illusion, xv, 14, 18, 19, 194, 225, 245, 285
imagery, 40, 41, 61, 77, 112, 132, 193, 224,
235, 265
imagination, 12, 18, 102, 235
imam, 49, 60, 132, 137, 142, 144, 149,
150, 163, 181, 182, 197, 205, 206,
210, 212, 219, 223, 228, 232, 234,
236, 241, 252
immigrants, xiii, 213, 215, 228, 230, 232,
241, 251, 272

interdependence, 32, 248
asymmetrical, 246
Intifada, 26, 69, 70, 71, 85, 113, 119, 120, 133, 135, 198, 229, 231, 232, 233
Iran, 11, 29, 36, 44, 52, 59, 118, 122, 171, 187, 208, 240, 269, 270, 271, 274
Iraq, xiv, xv, 5, 8, 26, 36, 37, 47, 48, 49, 52, 62, 70, 71, 81, 122, 161, 166, 170, 173, 193, 194, 195, 208, 217, 219, 220, 225, 231, 233, 246, 247, 252, 268, 269, 275, 276, 277, 278, 289
War, 37, 161, 166, 180, 193, 194, 195, 218, 246, 248
irhal, 126
ISIS, 3, 13, 58, 271, 275, 276, 277
Islam, xv, xvi, xix, xxii, 9, 20, 23, 31, 32, 33, 34, 41, 47, 48, 50, 54, 56, 60, 65, 93, 96, 115, 118, 132, 135, 142, 144, 145, 146, 149, 168, 169, 171, 190, 199, 206, 207, 208, 211, 212, 213, 214, 216, 219, 220, 222, 224, 228, 229, 230, 234, 235, 236, 238, 239, 240, 243, 245, 250, 251, 252, 253, 257, 258, 262, 264, 266, 269, 276, 286, 288, 289, 290, 291
political, xii, xiii, xiv, xv, xvi, xvii, xxii, 3, 16, 17, 25, 28, 30, 41, 42, 44, 45, 58, 59, 62, 65, 74, 97, 98, 103, 105, 106, 120, 121, 145, 153, 168, 185, 189, 193, 208, 209, 222, 240, 243, 244, 245, 249, 250, 253, 256, 257, 258, 259, 260, 261, 262, 263, 265, 267, 269, 270, 274, 275, 277, 278
Islamic
banking, 28, 31, 32, 33, 34, 146
movements used the Muslim Brotherhood, 140
Salvation Front, 59, 146
states, 234, 235
virtue, xiii
Islamism, 9, 47, 113, 121, 208, 225, 244, 269, 272

Islamophobia, 41, 184, 192, 211, 212, 213, 214, 238, 239, 286
Israel, xiii, xxi, 5, 11, 23, 26, 29, 32, 35, 37, 44, 50, 59, 66, 68, 69, 70, 71, 88, 97, 98, 104, 105, 106, 107, 108, 109, 110, 111, 112, 113, 114, 116, 117, 118, 119, 120, 121, 122, 123, 124, 139, 143, 164, 166, 168, 180, 187, 193, 195, 199, 202, 205, 208, 234, 238, 246, 253, 263, 269, 270, 277, 286, 289
Istanbul, xix, 182, 243, 244
istimarar, 135
itinerant, 144

jahiliyyah, 236
jamahirina al mu'mina, 135
jamra, 92
Jarha Gaza, 114
Jews, 116, 177, 215, 251, 252
jihad, 8, 115, 119, 133, 146, 148, 168, 170, 174, 175, 199, 209, 224, 225, 234, 235, 260, 262, 263, 264, 275
jihadist, 10, 239, 250, 270
Jordan, xiii, xiv, xix, xx, 16, 26, 37, 59, 68, 70, 108, 118, 180, 202, 260
justification, 25, 142, 226

Karama, 184
Kasserine, 78
Khaleej, xiii, xiv, xv, xviii, 27, 32
Khaljana, 17, 23, 24, 40
Kharijites, 148
khuruj, 262, 263
killing, 23, 58, 84, 85, 90, 106, 109, 119, 137, 163, 164, 180, 182, 188, 195, 198, 199, 203, 205, 207, 228, 247, 263
Kurdistan, 36
Kutab, 143

Lebanon, xiv, xv, 27, 29, 71, 118, 122, 130, 146, 170, 174, 193, 247, 270

legitimacy, xvi, 56, 59, 93, 111, 121, 122, 136, 139, 149, 163, 172, 174, 176, 179, 186, 194, 216, 223, 263, 273
newfound, 244
legitimate, 13, 65, 125, 137, 160, 163, 167, 171, 206, 209, 211, 232, 236
legitimacy, xvi, 56, 59, 93, 11, 121, 122, 136, 139, 149, 163, 172, 174, 176, 179, 179, 187, 195, 216, 223, 245, 263, 273
lens
Islamizing, 88, 96
Libya, xii, xvii, 3, 19, 26, 29, 37, 59, 61, 69, 72, 90, 120, 125, 191, 197, 198, 199, 201, 202, 205, 207, 238, 248, 257, 263, 271, 275, 276, 277, 278
limelight, 160, 190
lyrics, 103, 175

Maghreb, xiii, xiv, xv, xviii, xix, xxi, 17, 21, 23, 27, 28, 32, 35, 36, 38, 40, 42, 60, 97, 200, 216, 227, 240, 254, 261, 278
manifesto, 259
Maqhur, 81
martyr, 5, 65, 81, 82, 84, 95, 98, 100, 102, 119, 126, 132, 133, 134, 136, 137, 162, 163, 164, 169, 173, 177, 180, 182, 191, 192, 195, 196, 197, 198, 199, 201, 204, 206, 207, 209, 210, 247, 267
martyrdom, 40, 41, 102, 112, 120, 180, 191, 192, 193, 195, 200, 206, 207, 210
Mashreq, xiii, xiv, xv, xviii, 27, 28, 32, 35, 38, 40, 97, 200, 216, 261, 262
masira, 136
masirat
shabia, 136
McArabism, 9, 291
Mecca, 17, 45, 51, 52, 54, 55, 65, 96, 117, 142, 147, 173, 200, 215, 216, 235, 240, 250, 274, 281

Royal Clock Tower, 53, 54
Time, 45, 52, 54, 55, 56, 65, 74, 214, 215, 216, 240, 267, 276
of the vulnerable, 52, 55, 274
mechanism
of delivery, 18
media
Arab satellite, 5, 8, 269
domestic, 9
field, 5, 6, 10, 11, 73, 74, 152, 225, 245
melancholic, 185
memory, xi, xix, 22, 95, 102, 106, 158, 179, 214, 275
messaging, 14, 221
religious, 236
million-person
marches, 24, 25, 192
milyoniya, 25
modernization, 4, 10
Morocco, xi, xii, xiii, xiv, xvi, xvii, xix, xx, 3, 16, 25, 26, 55, 59, 76, 81, 100, 143, 147, 195, 202, 207, 215, 216, 227, 241, 244, 256, 260, 261, 262, 266, 275, 282, 283
Mosque, xv, 26, 32, 32, 35, 44, 62, 96, 117, 138, 147, 148, 150, 158, 160, 162, 163, 177, 181, 182, 183, 189, 190, 200, 210, 212, 214, 215, 235, 236, 238, 241, 251, 252, 266, 270, 281
Muslim, xvi, xix, 5, 10, 20, 23, 28, 39, 40, 41, 48, 49, 50, 52, 54, 55, 57, 60, 61, 65, 96, 97, 115, 117, 118, 120, 135, 136, 138, 142, 143, 145, 147, 149, 162, 169, 171, 172, 175, 177, 200, 201, 203, 206, 209, 211, 212, 213, 214, 215, 216, 217, 219, 220, 221, 223, 225, 227, 228, 229, 230, 231, 232, 233, 234, 235, 236, 237, 238, 240, 241, 243, 245, 246, 250, 251, 252, 253, 257, 258, 259, 264, 265, 266, 272, 276, 281, 289, 291

Muslim (*Cont.*)
  Brotherhood, xvi, xvii, 3, 21, 25, 28,
    31, 38, 41, 59, 115, 119, 121, 122, 123,
    125, 128, 140, 141, 142, 143, 144,
    145, 149, 150, 151, 152, 157, 159,
    160, 161, 164, 166, 167, 168, 169,
    170, 172, 173, 175, 176, 177, 178,
    182, 184, 185, 190, 199, 204, 208,
    210, 240, 243, 244, 245, 250, 253,
    254, 256, 258, 262, 270, 272, 273,
    274, 275, 282, 292
  Brothers, 25, 28, 38, 39, 115, 118, 119,
    140, 144, 146, 147, 152, 161, 162,
    165, 166, 168, 171, 172, 173, 174,
    176, 177, 182, 183, 185, 186, 187, 188,
    189, 190, 240, 244, 257, 261

Nahda, 158, 181, 182
najassa, 126, 136, 138
nakba, 121
naming, 24, 25, 158, 160, 192, 202, 204,
    207, 210, 248, 267
  hyper-religious, 207
nation-state, 6, 12, 16, 175, 268, 269
neo-pan-Arabism, 23
neutrality, 56, 68, 142, 221
  pseudo, 245
newscast, 56, 89, 93, 175, 179, 180, 187,
    198, 201, 218
newsfeed, 165
nihaya, 135
niqab, 163, 213, 214, 217, 219
notoriety, 8, 13, 48, 58, 61, 74

obedience, 149, 171, 262
objectivity, 14, 48, 61, 71, 74, 92, 125,
    142, 174, 188, 189, 194, 196
Oman, 244, 271
on-screen, 55, 88, 92, 163, 179, 186, 187,
    196, 197, 198, 201, 204, 217, 230
Ottoman, 47, 117, 142, 143, 268
outsiders, 138, 272
  neutral, 57

Pakistan, 16, 44, 55, 81, 241
Palestinian, xiv, xxi, 35, 40, 50, 66, 68, 69,
    70, 71, 79, 88, 104, 105, 106, 107,
    108, 109, 110, 111, 112, 113, 114, 115,
    116, 118, 119, 120, 121, 122, 123, 135,
    150, 164, 171, 177, 178, 185, 187, 191,
    195, 197, 199, 200, 201, 229, 231,
    232, 233, 234, 244, 246, 286, 288
  Liberation Organization, 106
pan-Arabism, xii, 7, 9, 16, 17, 23, 24, 45,
    47, 50, 60, 61, 65, 113, 121, 143, 223,
    225, 249, 270, 277
  Islamized, 9, 16, 24, 61, 230
  rebirth of, 56
pasha, 147
patriotic, 49, 61, 178, 225
pearl, 45, 46, 276
photographer, 72, 131, 179, 180
photography, 14
platform, 6, 8, 10, 13, 41, 45, 59, 65, 67,
    114, 116, 122, 125, 147, 239, 244,
    250, 273
PLO, 106, 109, 118, 119, 121, 122
polarization, 64, 85, 273
  veiled, 224
political, xii, xv, xvi, xvii, xviii, xx, xxi, 3, 4,
    5, 6, 7, 8, 9, 10, 11, 12, 15, 16, 17, 18, 20,
    23, 24, 27, 30, 31, 32, 33, 35, 37, 38, 39,
    40, 41, 43, 45, 47, 53, 56, 59, 60, 61,
    63, 64, 67, 71, 72, 75, 78, 81, 84, 85,
    86, 88, 89, 97, 98, 102, 105, 106, 110,
    112, 115, 121, 122, 125, 134, 135, 141,
    142, 143, 144, 145, 148, 149, 150, 151,
    152, 153, 157, 158, 159, 160, 162, 163,
    168, 171, 174, 177, 184, 185, 186, 190,
    192, 193, 201, 205, 208, 209, 210, 212,
    217, 220, 222, 224, 226, 228, 230, 231,
    232, 234, 240, 241, 243, 244, 245,
    246, 248, 249, 250, 251, 252, 253, 254,
    255, 256, 257, 258, 259, 260, 261, 262,
    263, 264, 266, 269, 271, 272, 273,
    274, 278, 280, 281, 282, 285, 287, 288,
    289, 290, 291, 292

Islam, xii, xiii, xiv, xv, xvi, xvii, 3, 16, 25, 28, 30, 41, 42, 44, 45, 58, 59, 62, 65, 74, 97, 98, 103, 105, 106, 120, 121, 145, 153, 168, 185, 189, 193, 208, 209, 222, 240, 243, 244, 245, 249, 250, 253, 256, 257, 258, 259, 260, 261, 262, 263, 265, 267, 269, 270, 274, 275, 277, 278

Islam will become more pragmatic, 244

politicization, 151

politics, xiii, 9, 19, 37, 47, 63, 64, 109, 115, 143, 147, 148, 149, 159, 177, 184, 186, 190, 194, 225, 234, 245, 248, 251, 262, 269, 285, 286, 287, 288, 289, 291, 292, 293

religion of, 266

pope, 20, 26, 31, 41, 167, 186, 213, 214, 232, 234, 235, 239, 240

positions, xvii, 11, 15, 17, 18, 57, 114, 137, 230, 244, 261, 290

practice, 11, 19, 54, 66, 82, 144, 149, 178, 199, 236, 240, 247, 248, 253, 256, 259, 260, 261, 262, 265, 286, 288

pragmatic, 142, 239, 244

predisposition, 12, 221

mental, xvi

prime-time show, 219, 227

principle, 12, 17, 49, 50, 60, 65, 68, 74, 206, 251, 253, 254, 258, 265, 277, 292

force in Egypt, 140

Prophet, xv, 17, 20, 47, 52, 74, 96, 133, 136, 142, 145, 172, 211, 213, 214, 234, 235, 236, 237, 238, 239, 251, 253, 256, 258, 263, 264

Muhammad, 17, 93, 117, 145, 196, 211, 213, 234, 270

protest, xi, xvi, xxi, 3, 5, 6, 7, 19, 25, 26, 37, 40, 71, 75, 76, 77, 78, 79, 80, 81, 82, 83, 84, 85, 86, 87, 88, 89, 90, 91, 92, 97, 99, 100, 101, 104, 110, 119, 125, 127, 132, 133, 136, 141, 142,

159, 160, 162, 177, 178, 179, 192, 193, 200, 201, 202, 203, 206, 207, 210, 211, 232, 234, 237, 241, 243, 248, 256, 261, 263, 274, 278

Friday, 24, 26, 176, 203, 207, 267

religious, 26

proxy, 138

publics, xiv, 12, 13, 22, 209, 213, 224, 225, 235, 293

Arab, xiv, 4, 5, 6, 7, 12, 22, 41, 55, 56, 95, 105, 113, 120, 123, 159, 160, 197, 210, 215, 216, 229, 233, 240, 244, 245, 246, 248, 249, 253, 257, 275, 276, 277

pulpit, xvi, 132, 135, 144, 253, 270, 276

pundit, xvi, 5, 8, 11, 15, 100, 157, 160, 161, 164, 165, 168, 169, 172, 175, 185, 246, 251, 260, 267

puzzle, 180, 287

Qahr, 30, 41, 81, 82, 86, 93, 98, 99, 100, 101, 102, 192, 196, 206, 209, 216, 239, 247, 248, 257, 263, 278

pervasive frame of, 276

Qatar, xiii, 6, 10, 11, 37, 38, 39, 41, 43, 44, 45, 46, 47, 48, 55, 56, 57, 59, 62, 63, 64, 65, 66, 67, 68, 69, 73, 74, 105, 110, 114, 122, 123, 124, 128, 142, 145, 146, 147, 166, 167, 169, 170, 172, 181, 184, 193, 198, 199, 207, 208, 209, 224, 226, 234, 243, 244, 245, 246, 250, 257, 263, 268, 270, 271, 274, 275, 276, 277, 278, 281, 287, 289, 292

qibla, 54, 281

qualitative, 10, 21, 121, 217

quantitative, 10, 21, 121

qufar, 263

Quran, xiii, xix, 7, 49, 96, 133, 135, 138, 143, 144, 145, 147, 171, 172, 179, 183, 187, 189, 190, 205, 223, 236, 237, 251, 263, 264, 266

Qureish, 117

Rabaa, xxi, 20, 25, 157, 158, 159, 160, 161, 162, 164, 165, 170, 173, 174, 178, 179, 180, 181, 182, 187, 189, 190, 192, 193, 271, 272
  sit ins, 160
Rabaa al-Adawiyya Square, 157, 158, 160, 164, 172
Rabat, xi, xv, xx, 51, 215, 254, 282, 285
radical, xxii, 3, 5, 6, 9, 16, 17, 57, 74, 87, 93, 116, 119, 152, 191, 212, 213, 220, 238, 239, 240, 250, 251, 252, 260, 266, 269, 270, 271, 272, 277, 278
radicalization, 6, 10, 269
rage, xxiii, 5, 17, 24, 25, 41, 45, 46, 72, 79, 81, 85, 87, 88, 89, 92, 100, 101, 117, 120, 128, 130, 131, 132, 139, 159, 163, 171, 176, 177, 179, 180, 192, 204, 207, 208, 210, 216, 240, 269, 276, 278, 279, 280, 281
  controlled, 241
  cultivating, 199
  day of, 26, 113, 117, 126, 131, 132, 203, 210
  level of, 179
  Sunni, 275
  whirlpool of, 84, 88
Ramadan, 19, 25, 38, 55, 144, 146, 160, 162, 170, 178, 189, 215, 230, 260
rasas
  al haqiqa, 196
  al-hayy, 84, 90, 173, 180, 196
Rayyan, Jamal, 68
rebirth
  of pan-Arabism, 56
redistribution, 254, 255, 256
Regensburg, 41, 235
regime, xi, xiii, xxi, 3, 6, 13, 24, 25, 37, 40, 45, 52, 53, 54, 56, 65, 72, 73, 75, 76, 77, 78, 79, 80, 81, 83, 84, 87, 88, 91, 94, 95, 98, 102, 115, 121, 122, 125, 126, 127, 128, 129, 130, 132, 133, 134, 136, 138, 139, 150, 151, 161, 165, 166, 168, 171, 174, 182, 183,

186, 191, 193, 195, 197, 199, 204, 207, 209, 210, 233, 239, 248, 249, 257, 259, 260, 261, 270, 272, 275, 276, 281, 288, 290
  apartheid, 232
  Arab, xii, xvi, 4, 59, 61, 124, 209, 246, 270, 277
  old, xvii, 131, 148, 161, 174, 184, 189, 196, 205, 209, 249, 272
religiosity, xvi, 132, 140, 151, 221
religious, xiii, xix, 4, 5, 7, 8, 10, 11, 13, 17, 18, 19, 24, 25, 26, 35, 36, 40, 41, 43, 48, 49, 50, 52, 53, 55, 56, 59, 60, 61, 62, 66, 72, 74, 80, 96, 97, 102, 103, 106, 115, 125, 126, 128, 132, 135, 136, 137, 140, 141, 142, 143, 144, 145, 146, 147, 148, 149, 151, 158, 159, 161, 162, 166, 167, 169, 171, 175, 176, 184, 186, 189, 190, 192, 193, 201, 205, 206, 207, 208, 209, 210, 212, 215, 216, 217, 218, 219, 220, 221, 222, 223, 224, 225, 226, 227, 228, 229, 230, 231, 233, 234, 236, 238, 241, 245, 246, 250, 252, 253, 254, 255, 256, 260, 264, 265, 267, 268, 269, 277, 278, 288
reporter-witness, 192
reporting, xxi, 5, 11, 13, 14, 15, 20, 23, 40, 47, 48, 49, 57, 61, 62, 66, 67, 69, 70, 71, 72, 73, 74, 75, 77, 78, 81, 84, 85, 86, 87, 91, 92, 93, 96, 97, 98, 99, 105, 106, 110, 111, 112, 125, 126, 128, 130, 149, 151, 165, 170, 179, 180, 184, 192, 193, 195, 204, 210, 219, 227, 228, 233, 234, 235, 238, 240, 242, 246, 247, 248, 254, 280, 281
  timid, 84
resistance, xiv, 12, 15, 28, 39, 59, 75, 85, 105, 107, 113, 114, 115, 118, 119, 120, 122, 123, 124, 126, 149, 158, 159, 160, 164, 178, 187, 192, 200, 201, 206, 209, 214, 233, 247, 248, 257, 277
  feminization of, 159

revisited
  Jihad, 234
revolution
  counter, 290
  is a form of ablution, 138
  Jasmine, xiv, xv, 40, 75, 76, 78, 79, 91,
    93, 98, 99, 101, 104, 206, 207, 269
  Orange, 96
  of the Roses, 96
rhetoric, 7, 14, 66, 125, 151, 172, 224
rhythm, 52, 55, 152, 189, 192, 215, 216
  of Friday, 204
riders
  free, 185
right
  Far, 212, 228, 251
rioter, 227, 231, 232
rioting, 22, 229, 232
riots, 15, 20, 22, 23, 41, 50, 81, 162, 213,
    215, 217, 227, 228, 230, 231, 233, 234
rituals
  Islamic, 28, 32, 33, 162
roadmap, 39, 123, 161, 171, 179, 282
Rosanvallon, Pierre, 254, 255, 256, 291
rujula, 101
Russia, 11, 282

Salafi, xv, 61, 148, 152, 176, 208, 209, 239,
    240, 257, 258, 259, 260, 261, 262,
    263, 266, 267, 274, 289
Salafism, 208, 240, 271
Salafist, 164, 240, 274
satellite television, xiii, 7, 10, 45, 46, 55,
    62, 72, 76, 212, 245, 254, 260, 261,
    265, 287, 289
Saudi Arabia, xiii, 11, 13, 16, 36, 37, 38,
    39, 44, 45, 54, 55, 59, 60, 64, 100,
    119, 122, 123, 143, 146, 147, 157, 167,
    170, 180, 181, 184, 207, 208, 209,
    222, 234, 240, 246, 249, 260, 269,
    274, 276, 277, 290
scenario, 139, 140, 269, 272, 273
  future, 139

scrutiny, xix, 14, 17, 18, 64, 66, 88, 161
secular, xii, xv, 5, 8, 25, 26, 40, 47, 50, 59,
    60, 61, 88, 96, 97, 106, 118, 120, 123,
    132, 141, 143, 148, 184, 189, 190,
    196, 207, 210, 224, 228, 229, 238,
    240, 241, 246, 252, 256, 264, 265,
    267, 274, 276, 278
secularism, 49, 128, 208, 217, 219, 233,
    250, 252, 258, 264, 266, 274
  moderate, 258
secularist, 5, 165, 189, 208, 209, 244, 250,
    251, 257, 258, 260, 261, 266, 278
self
  immolation, xiv, 4, 39, 76, 82, 87,
    92, 100, 101, 102, 103, 206, 262,
    269, 278
sermon, xviii, 126, 135, 142, 145, 147, 148,
    149, 176, 199, 200, 205, 207, 210,
    226, 235, 250, 254, 267, 271
shah, 94, 118
shahada, 103, 163, 200
shahid, 82, 100, 102, 126, 173, 199
Sharia and Life, 13, 19, 20, 21, 27, 28, 31,
    33, 49, 51, 54, 59, 60, 73, 117, 141,
    146, 147, 170, 180, 214, 219, 223,
    232, 250, 253, 257, 258, 273, 275
shaytan, 163, 171
shaytana, 163, 166
sheikh, 24, 39, 45, 49, 58, 59, 63, 67, 69,
    104, 105, 106, 114, 118, 119, 135, 137,
    141, 144, 149, 150, 169, 172, 186,
    207, 223, 243
Shia, 36, 44, 166, 167, 170, 196, 240, 250,
    253, 265, 270
Sidi Bouzid, 75, 76, 78, 81, 82, 83, 84, 85,
    86, 87, 88, 90, 91, 92, 95, 268
Sinai, 118, 164, 188
sit-ins, xvi, 10, 19, 25, 81, 83, 84, 95, 157,
    158, 160, 161, 162, 164, 179, 181,
    182, 183, 186, 190, 272
slaughterhouse, 181
sniper, 180, 182, 203
spirituality, 144

Square
  Rabaa, 157, 158, 159, 160, 161, 162, 164, 179, 187, 189, 272
  Tahrir, 40, 73, 90, 104, 127, 128, 129, 130, 131, 136, 137, 140, 141, 142, 147, 149, 151, 158, 160, 161, 164, 165, 177, 178, 185, 189, 239, 270, 282
state
  apparatus, 57, 159
  domination, 10
  the idea of the welfare, 255
  transactional, 45, 56, 208, 276
subordination, 9
suhkria, 175
sujud, 173, 174
sumud, 114, 200
Sunni, 21, 36, 44, 57, 59, 60, 123, 138, 144, 149, 170, 208, 240, 250, 253, 265, 270, 275, 276
Swaan, Abram de, 15, 221, 248, 292
symbol
  of otherness, 48
symbolic
  violence, 15
synagogue, 97, 252
Syria, xiv, xv, xvi, xvii, xviii, 3, 19, 25, 26, 28, 29, 36, 37, 39, 50, 68, 70, 100, 117, 120, 121, 122, 125, 132, 152, 168, 169, 170, 171, 174, 181, 191, 193, 200, 202, 203, 204, 207, 208, 209, 233, 246, 248, 249, 257, 263, 268, 271, 275, 276, 277, 278

tafjir, 108
Tahrir Square, 40, 73, 90, 104, 127, 128, 129, 130, 131, 136, 137, 140, 141, 142, 147, 149, 151, 158, 160, 161, 164, 165, 177, 178, 185, 189, 239, 270, 282
Tamarod, xvi, 187, 189
tear gas, 83, 129, 174, 182, 183
Teheran, 51, 118
televangelical, 265

terrorism, xi, xvi, 22, 41, 58, 70, 119, 161, 176, 184, 185, 190, 222, 224, 232, 277
thawra, xi, xii, 21, 36, 148, 187, 26
Tocqueville, Alexis de, xi
Tora Bora, 71
trajectory, 12, 16, 50, 144, 174
transactional
  state, 45, 56, 208, 276
trifecta of coercion, 212, 213
truth, 245
Tunisia, xi, xiii, xiv, xv, xvi, xix, xxi, 3, 6, 7, 12, 25, 26, 29, 37, 39, 40, 59, 61, 69, 72, 75, 76, 77, 78, 79, 80, 81, 83, 84, 86, 87, 88, 90, 91, 92, 93, 94, 95, 96, 97, 98, 99, 100, 102, 103, 104, 117, 120, 121, 123, 126, 131, 132, 134, 140, 141, 152, 164, 165, 174, 189, 195, 202, 207, 209, 240, 241, 243, 244, 245, 248, 249, 253, 254, 255, 257, 258, 260, 261, 262, 269, 271, 272, 275, 276, 278, 280, 282, 290
Turkey, xxi, 11, 36, 114, 122, 123, 182, 187, 214, 222, 241, 243, 251, 257, 258, 261, 269, 270

UAE, xiii, 38, 184, 277, 278
UK, 52, 185, 229
ulama, 36, 135, 136, 148, 171, 175, 190
umma, 20, 48, 52, 59, 60, 63, 66, 113, 135, 149, 150, 160, 175, 178, 199, 207, 213, 214, 216, 217, 221, 225, 239, 251
  international, 254
Uruba, xii, 135
US diplomatic cables, 110

Vatican, 21, 111, 234
veil, xiii, xv, 20, 27, 28, 37, 41, 48, 49, 94, 96, 103, 152, 163, 199, 203, 213, 214, 217, 218, 219, 220, 221, 222, 223, 224, 225, 227, 230, 232, 233, 239, 241, 282, 286
vernacular, 190

Wacquant, Loic, 74, 281, 292
Wahhabi, 16, 57, 59, 171, 208, 250
Wahhabism, 17, 45, 57, 64, 142, 208, 250, 276, 277
war (Iraq), 37, 161, 166, 180, 193, 194, 195, 218, 246, 248
wasatiyya, 171
worship, 193, 264, 269

Yemen, 3, 26, 37, 39, 51, 71, 72, 100, 191, 200, 202, 203, 207, 248, 249, 257, 269, 271, 276, 277, 278
youth bulge, xiv, xvi, 5, 269, 281
YouTube, 94, 132, 166, 167, 173, 187, 237

Zagazig University, 183
zakat, 255
zaman, zamaan, 56
Zayani, 6, 127, 253, 292, 293
zeal, 199
zulm, 126